Israelism in Modern Britain

This book unpacks the history of British-Israelism in the UK. Remarkably, this subject has had very little attention: remarkable, because at its height in the post-war era, the British-Israelist movement could claim to have tens of thousands of card-carrying adherents and counted amongst its membership admirals, peers, television personalities, MPs and members of the royal family including the King of England.

British-Israelism is the belief that the people of Britain are the descendants of the lost tribes of Israel. It originated in the writing of a Scottish historian named John Wilson, who toured the country in the mid-nineteenth century. Providing a guide to the history of British-Israelism as a movement, including the formation of the British-Israel World Federation, Covenant Publishing, and other institutions, the book explores the complex ways in which British-Israelist thought mirrored developments in ethnic British nationalism during the twentieth century.

A detailed study on the subject of British-Israelism is necessary, because British-Israelists constitute an essential element of British life during the most violent and consequential century of its history. As such, this will be a vital resource for any scholar of Minority Religions, New Religious Movements, Nationalism and British Religious History.

Aidan Cottrell-Boyce completed his PhD in Theology at the University of Cambridge, UK. He has published multiple chapters and articles in journals such as the *Journal of Religious History* and the *Journal of the Irish Society for the Academic Study of Religions*.

Routledge New Religions
Series editors: James R. Lewis and George D. Chryssides

The popularity and significance of New Religious Movements is reflected in the explosion of related articles and books now being published. This series offers an invaluable resource and lasting contribution to the field.

Israelism in Modern Britain
Aidan Cottrell-Boyce

Contemporary Spiritualities
Enchanted Worlds of Nature, Wellbeing and Mystery in Italy
Stefania Palmisano and Nicola Pannofino

Israelism in Modern Britain

Aidan Cottrell-Boyce

Routledge
Taylor & Francis Group

LONDON AND NEW YORK

First published 2021
by Routledge
2 Park Square, Milton Park, Abingdon, Oxon OX14 4RN

and by Routledge
52 Vanderbilt Avenue, New York, NY 10017

*Routledge is an imprint of the Taylor & Francis Group, an informa
business*

British Library Cataloguing-in-Publication Data
A catalogue record for this book is available from the British Library

Library of Congress Cataloging-in-Publication Data
Names: Cottrell-Boyce, Aidan, author.
Title: Israelism in modern Britain / Aidan Cottrell-Boyce.
Description: Abingdon, Oxon ; New York : Routledge, 2021. |
  Includes bibliographical references and index.
Identifiers: LCCN 2020022532 (print) | LCCN 2020022533 (ebook) |
  ISBN 9780367376673 (hardcover) | ISBN 9780429355486 (ebook)
Subjects: LCSH: Anglo-Israelism.
Classification: LCC DS131 .C68 2021 (print) | LCC DS131 (ebook) |
  DDC 303.48/24105694—dc23
LC record available at https://lccn.loc.gov/2020022532
LC ebook record available at https://lccn.loc.gov/2020022533

ISBN: 978-0-367-37667-3 (hbk)
ISBN: 978-0-429-35548-6 (ebk)

Typeset in Sabon
by Apex CoVantage, LLC

Contents

Contents

Introduction

In October 1976, the new NEC in Birmingham played host to the Ideal Home Exhibition. The event attracted 450,000 visitors over fifteen days.[1] Amongst the attractions, shoppers could experience a 'fashion parade,' a 'model radio studio,' a 'food fair,' and 'family theatre shows.'[2] At stand 2430, patrons could also find a display devoted to the promotion and sale of products supplied by the British-Israel World Federation and the Covenant Publishing house. Amongst the items promoted at the British-Israel stand were books, posters, 'heritage charts' and acetate 'slide lectures.'[3]

British-Israelism was still enjoying its moment. British-Israel organisations, clubs, meetings, newspapers, magazines and publishers were still in operation across the country and across the Commonwealth. One British-Israelist organisation alone – at its peak in the middle of the century – advertised regular meetings at over three hundred regional branches.[4] Writing in 1975, Bishop David Jenkins issued a sombre warning about the popularity of British-Israelist ideas in the shires of England:

> The size of such groups in our midst is sufficiently large to be a warning that such alienation and frustration exist and that religious quasi longings can take very curious forms when they are bound up with cultural attitudes and a concern for the wellbeing of society.[5]

Having flourished as a popular movement from the end of the nineteenth century up until the 1970s, at this point the movement fell into a seemingly irreversible decline. The decades since have seen a steady diminution of adherents. Nonetheless, and against all the odds, the movement continues to hang on with communities dispersed across Britain, Ireland, Canada, Australia, America, South Africa and even Israel.

What follows is an exploration of the history of British-Israelism in the twentieth century. In particular, this book focusses on the history of the movement in the British context. It is the story of a movement which gathered pace during the middle of the twentieth century and presented an idea, an image of Britain which – though couched in language and indeed in concepts which may appear strange – has much in common with the image of Britain that was shared by much of the population of the country during that period.

What is British-Israelism?

British-Israelism is a theory. It is not a religion or a denomination. Its adherents are not bound together by any common confessional affiliation. British-Israelists typically belong to mainstream Protestant churches. They 'do not establish churches,' they 'do not hold regular services on Sunday,' and 'members are encouraged to be good faithful members of the Church of their choice.' British-Israelists 'are not sheep stealers' and, as such, 'other Christian denominations have nothing to fear' from them.[6] They are brought into community only by their commonly held belief that the people of Britain are descended from the lost tribes of Israel.

British-Israelism first came to public attention in the nineteenth century. It originated in the writing of John Wilson: an historian and advocate of racial pseudo-science. It was popularised in the early stages of its history by a former bank clerk named Edward Hine – who would become the founder of the British Israel Identity Corporation – and a barrister named Edward Wheeler Bird. Wheeler Bird established a British-Israelist periodical – *The Banner of Israel* – which would remain the most widely circulated organ of the movement until the 1920s. Hine, Wheeler Bird and Wilson's work spawned admirers and emulators and, by the end of the century, there were already large numbers of British-Israelist clubs, classes, magazines and newsletters across the United Kingdom. It was not until 1919, however, that these disparate elements were able to organise themselves into a large and contiguous mass movement. In that year, over ninety organisations joined together in order to form the British-Israel World Federation (BIWF). The BIWF has survived to the present day, but at various points in its history it has been forced to weather schisms and defections. In the aftermath of the Second World War, a few BIWF branches, centred around the South-East, established a separate organisation, which they called the Society for the Proclamation that Britain is Israel (SPBI). The SPBI would later, itself, be rebranded as the Covenant People's Fellowship. Meanwhile, in the second half of the twentieth century, other, smaller, rival organisations emerged such as the Crown Covenanters and the Ensign Trust.

Newspapers and magazines, written and published by British-Israelists, form the basic source material of this study. The first national organ of British-Israelism was promoted by the Metropolitan Anglo-Israel Association and was called *The Banner of Israel*. Alongside *The Banner*, a number of smaller magazines were distributed by British-Israelists in the early twentieth century, including but not limited to *The British-Israel Pilot*, *The Prophetic News and Israel's Watchman* and *Protestant British-Israel Quarterly*. The BIWF – through its publishing arm, the Covenant Publishing Company – produced a number of weekly and monthly magazines, including *The National Message*, *The Covenant Voice*, *The Link*, *Wake Up* and *Crown and Commonwealth*. Other organisations published their own magazines in the twentieth century, the most notable being *Brith*, which was written and edited by members of the SPBI and latterly the Covenant People's Fellowship.

There are many worthwhile accounts of the nineteenth century origins of the British-Israel movement and of the apparent links between the rise of British-Israelism and the rise of British imperial sentiment.[7] Up to now, however, very little has been written about the history of the movement in the twentieth century, the century during which the movement grew and flourished whilst the Empire dwindled.[8] This book is an attempt to correct this omission. The following is intended to serve as an argument in favour of studying British-Israelism. It is also intended to highlight the curious disappearance of British-Israelism from the national consciousness.

British-Israelism in the public sphere

A short story entitled 'Winifred Breaks Out' appeared in *The Guardian* on 29 February 1932. It lampooned the phenomenon of British-Israelism as a familiar tendency, typical of elderly military veterans. Two friends, Miss Simpson and Miss Martin, gossip about their neighbour:

> 'Miss Oliver and Miss Gulliver are drawing conclusions,' said Miss Simpson. 'Miss Oliver said to Miss Gulliver how off it was that a man like the Colonel, who detests dogs, or did, should be joining Our Dumb Friends' League, and Miss Gulliver said yes, it was particularly odd that it happened just when Winifred was beginning to ask the Colonel for information about British Israel.'
>
> 'British Israel!' exclaimed Miss Martin. 'Why I do believe it was something British Israelitish that Winifred made me read yesterday. Yes it was!'
>
> 'If Winifred's breaking out over that,' said Miss Simpson. 'Then it must be the Colonel. He's steeped to the eyes in British Israel.'[9]

One of the reasons that the apparent disappearance of British-Israelism from public consciousness is so striking is that – until relatively recently – the topic of British-Israelism was not infrequently raised (critically and uncritically) in stories, novels and newspapers and in the Houses of Parliament. In other words, until the latter half of the twentieth century, British-Israelism still occupied space in the British popular imagination.

From the 1890s up to the 1970s, high profile companies took out advertisements in British-Israelist publications. Bovril advertised in *The Banner of Israel* during the inter-war years, whilst Cow and Gate continued to advertise in *The National Message* into the 1960s.[10] This testifies to the readership which these publications commanded but also to the belief, held by the marketing strategists at these companies, that British-Israelism was a relatively mainstream interest. Mainstream publications during the early part of the twentieth century even entertained the possibility that British-Israel theory was sufficiently conventional as to be taught as part of a rounded school curriculum. After all, the *Bexhill-on-Sea Observer* reported, in 1929, the doctrine had proven to be a source of solace for many who had endured testing times during the Great War.[11]

Popular plays and novels from the 1940s and 1950s made reference to the British-Israel movement. The third volume of Compton MacKenzie's hexalogical saga, *The Four Winds of Love*, includes several discussions of the phenomenon. When Mackenzie's semi-autobiographical protagonist John Ogilvie encounters one 'Mr Pullrose' on a train journey to London, the latter explains to him – at length – that 'the house of Israel . . . went west and were lost under a new name.' 'Do you mean to say it's never occurred to you that the new name was British?' an astonished Mr Pullrose asks Ogilvie. When, the following year, Mr Pullrose writes to Ogilvie to continue his education on matters relating to British-Israel, Ogilvie's Jewish friend Julius Stern dismisses Pullrose's letter as the work of a madman. But Ogilvie is more circumspect:

> You might have called Luther a lunatic when he started, but I don't really think you can call every Protestant a lunatic. I agree that a letter like that has all the superficial marks of being written by a lunatic, but this British-Israelite belief is widely spread. I'm credibly informed that many of our most prominent admirals and generals are British Israelites. From time to time you'll see half a page or a page in the advertisements of a newspaper with the status of *The Times* devoted to their propaganda. . . . Individuals like Pullrose may carry their belief to an extravagance of credulity but that's true of any religion . . . I could never be certified because I believed that the Ten Lost Tribes have reappeared as the British Commonwealth. Thousands of people hold that faith.[12]

For many, British Israel was nothing more than a frivolity and it was treated by some as a subject for satire. In his 1947 work *Oak Leaves and Lavender*, Sean O'Casey presented his audience with what he presumed to be a familiar trope: the aristocratic, jingoistic British-Israelist. O'Casey's Dame Hatherleigh – a 'pathetically dotty' Cornish noblewoman, living through the Battle of Britain – is well versed in British-Israelist theory.[13] As she informs her butler, Feelim:

> It is all in God's hands. All we're sure of is that England must win: British Israel can never fail. . . . Isn't it thrilling to feel that we are soul of the soul of the lost Ten Tribes of Israel and are being held firm in the hands of the Deity for a special purpose? . . . Heremon's children have a great

destiny. You've heard of Heremon? . . . The son of a Milesian father and a Tuatha de Danaan mother, the first of the line of Zarah the mother of the line of Dan . . . These are the two tribes who came over with Simeon of Wales – the ancient Kymri or Simonii, who were the remnants of the Ten Tribes, dispersed after the fall of the Assyrian Empire. Isn't it wonderful? We must dig for the Ark! The Tara that Heremon gave to his wife as a dowry and burial place – Tea Mur – the town of Teea or Tara as we call it now. . . . It is only when the Stone of Destiny is returned to the Davidic line that Great Britain and America will become one happy and united family. Mind you, its no myth Feelim.[14]

Others, however, took the threat posed by this movement quite seriously. In the 1930s, Charles Raven – Regius Professor of Divinity at Cambridge – warned that the spread of British-Israelism could undermine Britain's ability to resist the rise of fascism on the European continent.[15] The Anglican clergyman Kenneth Ross gave a series of lectures on the subject of new religious movements at the University of Durham in 1961. His lectures were collated in a volume and published by the Society for Promoting Christian Knowledge. Ross included the BIWF in his discussion. He suggested that British-Israelism had the potential to be an incendiary doctrine since it interpreted 'all that is said about covenants in the Bible in a narrow and nationalistic sense.'[16]

Part of the reason that British-Israelism remained so visible to friend, foe and satirist alike during this period was that it was often openly discussed – and promoted – by prominent public figures. Amongst the ranks of those who were drawn to the British-Israel cause in the twentieth century we find politicians, television personalities, decorated military personnel, writers and aristocrats.

British-Israelism was visible to the British public, in the first instance, in the buildings that it occupied around the country. They acquired a headquarters at 6 Buckingham Gate, less than one hundred yards from the Palace, in 1924 and remained there until 1990. Their unofficial chapel is the Orange Street Congregational Church, which is situated just behind Trafalgar Square. They acquired handsome properties in the heart of Glastonbury and at Battle in Sussex, as well as a large property in Harrow Weald which was used as a Bible College.

From the beginning of the nationally organised British-Israel movement in the aftermath of the First World War, there was always a strong connection between the movement and the military. British-Israelists tended to revere the military, and military men seem to have been attracted to the message of British-Israelism in disproportionate numbers. Even amongst ordinary soldiers there appears to have been some appeal. Kirsten Parsons wrote about her experiences running the British-Israel Canteen in Brighton during the war, claiming that the soldiers frequently requested for sermons to be delivered on the subject of British-Israel prophecy. Parsons quoted a letter written by 'one of the men':

> As our stay in Brighton is drawing to a close, I should like to say how much we have appreciated your work at the British Israel Canteen. It may be a surprise to you to know that your services and Bible talks have made a big impression on the men. In fact, they are quite ready to admit that you have made Christ and His teaching a reality.

Parsons' account of the ministry ran to three editions during the years of the Second World War.[17] More notable, though, was the role played by decorated officers in the establishment, running and sponsorship of the BIWF. During the early years of the federation, the leadership was almost exclusively recruited from the ranks of the military. Major General Charles Hadfield served as president from 1919 to 1921. Hadfield was the author of a 'rudimentary guide for students' of British-Israelism. He had also been deputy assistant to Field-Marshall Lord Roberts when Roberts was commander of forces in Ireland in the late 1890s.[18] Major James Knowles served as president from 1926 to 1940. Lieutenant Commander Donald Macmillan served as president from 1954 to 1969. In an oration to the first BIWF conference of 1 and 2 May 1919 (at which the decision to federate the various British-Israel organisations was taken), Herbert Garrison – who would be the first secretary of the BIWF – thanked those whom he considered to be the main 'architects' of the movement. Amongst those he thanked were 'Colonel A. O. Green . . . Colonel Gosset . . . Colonel Weldon . . . Colonel Arthur Prowse . . . Major de Welldon and Commander Roberts.' He also thanked the American military theorist C.A.L. Totten.[19] Totten was Professor of Military Science at Yale. He also wrote a twenty-six volume text, entitled *Our Race*, on the subject of British-Israelism.[20] He had died ten years before the foundation of the BIWF, but had proven to be influential in the dissemination of the doctrine in the United States. Herbert Garrison did not himself have a military background but, in his capacity as an administrator at the Royal Colonial Institute, he rubbed shoulders with a number of prominent military figures.[21] Indeed, he boasted that he could count amongst his patrons, 'Queen Alexandra, the King and Queen of the Belgians, Lord Kitchener, Lord Roberts, the Prime Minister and a host of other public men and women.'[22]

There was a particular interest in British-Israel theory amongst those who had served in the Middle East. In 1919, Lieutenant Colonel Harold Mavromichali Biddulph wrote to *The Banner of Israel*. He urged British-Israelist scholars to be more rigorous in their proofs. Biddulph was the eighth son of Michael Anthony Shrapnel Biddulph, who had served as Black Rod until his death in 1904. Harold Biddulph was a lieutenant colonel in the Rifle Regiment, stationed in Palestine.[23] Admiral Sir Richard Peirse was another early patron of the BIWF.[24] Peirse was the Commander in Chief of the East

India Station and would later lead the naval attack on Smyrna in the First World War. Peirse devised the strategy of deploying patrol boats to the Red Sea, Gaza and Beirut.[25] His son, also named Richard, was commander of British forces in Palestine and Transjordan from 1933 to 1936. He later wrote to General Sikorski, rejecting the latter's plan to launch an aerial bombardment of the Auschwitz concentration camp in 1941.[26] Peirse the younger also sat on the Joint Intelligence Committee during the early years of the Cold War.

In the early twentieth century, one of British-Israelism's most prominent apologists was Admiral Lord Fisher. During the First World War, Fisher served as the First Sea Lord, having held innumerable other leadership positions in the Royal Navy during the period of Britain's naval expansion. Fisher was quoted by Harold Begbie in an article in the *Daily Chronicle* on 18 December 1918 as saying that soon 'everybody will see that we are the Lost Tribes of Israel.'[27]

This connection between high-ranking military men and the British-Israel movement continued long into the twentieth century. In the late 1920s, Lieutenant Colonel T.P. Barrington lectured on British-Israel matters.[28] In his autobiography of 1939, General Sir Henry de Beauvoir De Lisle openly avowed his own British-Israelist beliefs.[29] At a meeting of the BIWF on the Shankill Road in Belfast in 1957, Lieutenant J.G. Simmons addressed the audience on the subject of 'the deepening crisis.'[30] Lieutenant-Commander Michael Hart regularly contributed to the *National Message* throughout the 1960s and 1970s.[31] In 1977, Squadron Leader Lesley Pine was appointed editor of the *National Message*.[32] Perhaps the most ardent – and high-profile – British-Israelist who was drawn from the ranks of the military during this period was General Sir Walter Walker. Walker's high-profile career in the military included appointments as Chief of Northern Command and NATO's Commander in Chief of Allied Forces in Europe. As a British-Israelist, Walker regularly contributed to BIWF publications.[33]

It was not only military figures that appeared to be drawn, in disproportionate numbers, to the British-Israel message. In particular during the early decades of the twentieth century, a large number of aristocrats – and even royalty – took up positions of patronage and of influence within the movement. Amongst these, the most determined was Princess Alice, the Duchess of Athlone. Princess Alice was the last surviving grandchild of Queen Victoria. She was born in Windsor Castle in 1883, she lived for most of her life in Kensington Palace, and she was buried in 1981 from St George's Chapel in Windsor. For much of her life, the Duchess was the chief patron of the British-Israel movement. She opened the inaugural congress of the BIWF in 1919 and she continued to attend the annual congresses for several decades.[34] Princess Alice – like many of her generation – was an avid letter writer, and she conducted correspondences with several prime ministers.[35] She was Chancellor of the University of the West Indies from 1948 to 1971.[36]

Other prominent female members of the aristocracy who joined the BIWF during this period included the Marchioness Dowager of Headfort and Lady Folkestone, the Countess Dowager of Radnor. The latter was a founding patron of the BIWF.[37] Lady Folkestone had a period of convalescence in 1876 during which she was introduced to the literature of the British-Israel movement and was ultimately converted – along with her husband the Earl – to the cause. In 1924, the Marchioness inaugurated the 'Order of the House of Israel' (OHI) and established herself as leader of the Grand Chapter.[38] She explained the aims of the order in a volume of her memoirs, published in 1927:

> The OHI was instituted with a view to enlarging the work of the existing British Israel World Federation by means of small meetings for the study of the subject . . . not only in the big towns, but also in villages and private houses.[39]

The Earl of Radnor was not the only member of the aristocracy who lent his patronage to the movement. The Duke of Buccleugh, the Earl of Meath, and the Earl of Dysart all supported the BIWF at its inception.[40] The former, whose name was Walter Montagu Douglas Scott, was a member of the royal family, owing to the marriage of his sister to Prince Henry. He was also a Unionist MP during the inter-war period. The Earl of Meath, meanwhile, was a general in the First World War and was also the son-in-law of Viscount Adare (the founder of the Irish Reform Association). This association between the aristocracy and the BIWF lasted late into the twentieth century. In 1961 Lord Brabazon spoke of his adherence to British-Israelist doctrine during a debate in the House of Lords. Brabazon was a Conservative politician who had served in Churchill's cabinet during the war. He had – in the years preceding 1939 – convened with the British Union of Fascists to organise opposition to Britain's entering the war.[41] Speaking in a debate on the issue of Christian unity, he confessed:

> I belong to the Church of England, and I am a British Israelite. I was brought up with the sole idea relative to Roman Catholicism that their chief desire was to revive the Fires of Smithfield. I have got over that.[42]

To this day, the ties that bind the BIWF with the British aristocracy remain unbroken. Up to the present day, Lady Sara Allenby, Viscountess of Meggido, serves as a trustee of the BIWF.[43]

There have long been rumours that the crowned heads of Britain were secret supporters of the British-Israel cause. The royal tradition of circumcising newborn princes appears to have bolstered this claim.[44] At least one aspect of this theory was proven beyond doubt in 1996 when a series of letters, written in 1922 by the then Prince Albert (who would be King George VI), were made public. In the letters, the future king openly expresses his commitment to the basic tenets of British-Israelist thought, writing:

> I am sure that this British Israelite business is true. I have read a lot about it lately and everything no matter how large or small points to our being 'the Chosen Race.'[45]

The attachment of some elements of the aristocracy and the royal family to British-Israelism is mirrored in the affection felt by many British-Israelists for the British aristocracy and the royal family. This tendency is embodied in the figure of Lesley Pine. A prominent British-Israelist of the mid-twentieth century, Pine also served as a curator of the history of the British nobility in his long-standing role as the editor of Burke's Peerage. British-Israelist royalism is grounded in part in an historical claim about the genealogical origins of the Royal Family. For most British-Israelists claim that the Royal Family are not descended from the tribe of Ephraim (like other British people) but are in fact of the line of David, the tribe of Judah. Furthermore, British-Israelists claim that the stone of Scone, used in the coronation of British monarchs, is the stone upon which Jacob rested his head, according to Genesis 28.[46]

During the early twentieth century, several prominent politicians also lent their support to the British-Israel cause. Lord Gisborough was a veteran of the Boer War who served as a Member of Parliament for Liverpool Abercromby and later sat in the House of Lords as a Conservative from 1895 until his death in 1938.[47] He served as the second president of the North of England Anglo-Israel Council, until his death, and also served as president of the BIWF for a period in the 1920s. As recently as the 1970s, prominent Members of Parliament expressed public support for the British-Israel movement. In 1976, Teddy Taylor MP addressed the BIWF Autumn Conference at Glasgow Central Hall. Taylor was a prominent member of the right-wing Monday Club who, in 1980, called for Nelson Mandela to be shot.[48] He represented the Cathcart constituency for the Conservative Party from 1964 to 1979 and the Southend East constituency from 1980 to 2005. Taylor 'warmed the hearts' of his audience in Glasgow, updating them on the wellbeing of the 'BI folk in the border country of Rhodesia.'[49] Taylor again addressed the Glasgow branch of the BIWF on 6 May 1978. On this occasion he spoke on the topic: 'The Law: can Britain break it and survive.'[50]

The influence of British-Israelism in the political sphere has always been most prevalent within the Unionist community in Ireland. In 1931 the British-Israelist preacher Maxwell Carnson was joined onstage at a rally in Wellington Hall, Belfast, by William Grant MP.[51] Grant was a former shipwright and an Ulster Volunteer who would go on to be elected as a representative in North Belfast and to hold several cabinet positions in the Stormont government including as Minister of Security, Minister of Labour and Minister of

Health.[52] Several very prominent Loyalist community leaders have recently been – or are currently – aligned with the British-Israelist movement. MPs, including Robert Bradford (member for Belfast South from 1974 to 1981) and John Dunlop (member for Mid-Ulster from 1974 to 1983), attended and supported British-Israelist causes and events. They spoke at British-Israelist rallies and wrote for British-Israelist journals.[53] Other community leaders like Clifford Smyth (a pundit on BBC Northern Ireland and regular columnist in the *Belfast Telegraph*) and ministers like Alan Campbell have also been open and vocal about their British-Israelist convictions. Several leading figures in the Orange Order have openly and publicly expressed their belief in British-Israelist doctrine.[54] Perhaps the most prominent British-Israelist in public life in Ulster, however, is Nelson McCausland. McCausland held a number of ministerial positions in the Legislative Assembly at Stormont up to 2017. These included positions as Minister for Culture and Minister for Social Development. At the same time, McCausland has continued to hold senior positions in the BIWF, conducting lecture tours and speaking on the subject of British-Israelism at rallies and conventions. Beyond the meeting rooms of the various Ulster-based British-Israelist organisations, there is significant sympathy for the doctrine within the Loyalist population. In the late 1990s, Ruth Dudley Edwards identified it as 'an increasingly popular . . . view of early Irish history, dismissed by historians but treasured by many ordinary Ulster Protestants.'[55] Whilst the church he established condemned the doctrine of British-Israelism, it is certainly true that Dr Ian Paisley took an interest in the movement and its teachings. Indeed, his personal library – since bequeathed to the public – holds numerous titles relating to British-Israel message, some published as late as the 1990s.

Even outside of the UK, political figures have risen to positions of authority whilst avowing British-Israel beliefs. The most notable amongst these is William Fergusson Massey, the son of a Derry farmer, who became the Prime Minister of New Zealand in 1912 and stayed in office for thirteen years. Massey was unapologetic in his avowal of British-Israel doctrine, and his public pronouncements were invariably littered with references to the providential role afforded to Britain in these latter days.[56] In 1919 he became a patron – alongside Princess Alice, Countess of Athlone – of the newly inaugurated BIWF.[57] Edmund Drake-Brockman, meanwhile, had a distinguished military career – serving at Galipoli and ascending to the rank of Major General – before entering the Australian senate as a representative of the Nationalist party. At the same time, Drake-Brockman sat on the central committee of the Protestant British-Israel League.[58] In the 1970s, Lord James Graham (a leading figure in the Smith administration, in newly independent Rhodesia) openly expressed British-Israelist views.[59]

Whilst British-Israelists wielded some clout in the corridors of political and military power, they also could be found helping to shape the cultural landscape of the UK during the twentieth century. The popular British opera singer Margery Booth lived an extraordinary life, achieving fame and acclaim at home before moving to Germany during the 1930s. She took leading roles in operas performed at Bayreuth and at Covent Garden during this period. She later moved to America, where she died in 1952. Throughout this time, Booth held a long association with the BIWF. She was a member of the organisation and performed as the opening act of its Annual Congress in 1950.[60]

During the same period, Patience Strong was accruing a degree of celebrity that would make her a household name in post-war Britain. Strong – whose real name was Winifred May – wrote poems of patriotic sentiment and encouragement which were published in the *Daily Mirror* during and after the war. Her poems were serialised in a number of volumes throughout the 1940s, 1950s, 1960s and 1970s. Strong was also an ardent British-Israelite. She wrote a book on the subject of British-Israel prophecy which was published by Bachman in 1986.[61] She actively supported the Avalon project, under the auspices of which the BIWF purchased property in Glastonbury in order to establish a British-Israelist retreat and educational centre. She spoke at the dedication ceremony of the Mount Avalon property on Easter Sunday 1970, along with Harold Stough and the Mayor of Glastonbury Cecil Hamilton Miller.[62] In fact, many of the poems that Strong published in the pages of the *Daily Mirror* express definitively British-Israelist sentiments. In 1940, Strong's poem 'Israel' was printed on the seventh page of the paper. The poem includes the following lines:

> The veil is lifted. Now we know our name, our task, our place. God is working out His purpose through the British race. And will set His kingdom up according to the Word. Israel must contend with Satan. Let these truths be heard and understood.[63]

Along with Patience Strong, the most committed of the celebrity British-Israelists during the second half of the twentieth century was Bob Danvers-Walker. Danvers-Walker's name is all but forgotten now, but during the 1940s, 1950s, 1960s and 1970s, his voice would have been familiar to the majority of the British public. He broadcast to British troops during the war via Radio Normandy, and after the cessation of hostilities he voiced Pathe newsreels, before moving into light entertainment during the 1960s. During the latter period, Walker hosted a range of talk shows and game shows including *Wheel of Fortune* and *Take Your Pick*. In the 1970s, Danvers-Walker began to dedicate his time and efforts to disseminating the British-Israel message. He began presenting 'lantern lectures' (lectures illustrated by projected images) on a variety of British-Israel beliefs. At the end of April 1976, he presented an illustrated lecture at Bristol Cathedral.[64] Soon, Danvers-Walker was receiving invitations to speak to various audiences. In May 1976, he was in Southborne, lecturing the students of Wentworth Milton Mount.[65] In January 1978, he spoke to '135 ladies in the Evergreen Hall at Bringend,' who 'broke into spontaneous applause as the first slide of the Royal Family appeared on the screen.' Every month he reported on his successes in the pages of the *National Message*.[66]

At the same time that Danvers-Walker was travelling the country with his lantern lectures, another television personality was becoming more and more prominent in the movement. Ross McWhirter was – at this point – a recognisable public figure. He had appeared as a guest on talk shows in the UK and in the USA, including *The Dick Cavett Show*, *The Tonight Show* and *The Mike Walker Show*. He was the co-presenter of a popular BBC series *Record Breakers*. In addition, he had stood as a parliamentary candidate for the Conservative Party in the Edmonton constituency in the 1964 general election. McWhirter's politics matched those of the British-Israel mainstream during the 1960s. He was socially conservative, hawkish on the issue of Northern Ireland and a fierce opponent of Britain's membership of the European Community. Throughout the early 1970s he addressed British-Israelist meetings and defended British-Israelist positions in speeches and in print.[67] Following McWhirter's assassination by the IRA, his eulogy in the *National Message* (written by Buxton Gresty) recalled the 'Revelation vision,' in which 'Our Lord speaks of End-of-Age martyrs who would be called upon to make the supreme sacrifice in their stand for Him.' Ross McWhirter, Gresty believed, was 'surely to be counted among these.'[68]

Even aside from these card-carrying British-Israelists, there were other prominent personalities who could be considered fellow travellers with the movement during the late twentieth century. In 1974, *The National Message* proudly announced that the keynote speaker at that year's conference would be Mary Whitehouse.[69] In the early 1970s Whitehouse was at the peak of her influence. She was granted meetings with the chairman of the BBC in her capacity as president of the National Viewers and Listeners Association. She spoke at the Royal College of Nursing and had attracted over a million signatories to her Petition for Public Decency. In September 1974, Whitehouse's speech to the BIWF conference was reported on in *The National Message*. She was pictured posing for a photograph with the leadership of the federation. Whitehouse stayed at the conference, after her speech, to watch a play, written and produced by young British-Israelists, which depicted a courtroom where a minister was being tried for preaching British-Israel doctrine.[70]

Often these figures were afforded space in the public sphere. At various times, British-Israelist organisations adopted media campaigns to promote their views. One such campaign took place in 1957, when consecutive editions of *The Times* included advertisements dedicated to answering the question: 'What is a British Israelite?'[71] But more often than not, during this period, British-Israelists were actively invited to discuss their views in local and national media fora. Between 1971 and 1976, a British-Israelist themed radio programme was broadcast on Radio Manx, twice each Monday at 10 am and 7 pm.[72] In 1973, C.S. McKelvey took part in a debate on LBC on John Forrest's *We Believe* show along with 'Dr Tatford of the Prophetic

Witness' and 'John Barker: a Jehovah's Witness.'[73] In April 1980 Winifred Dodd MBE was invited onto *Woman's House* to discuss her belief in British Israel.[74] As recently as 28 February 2000, the secretary of the British-Israel Bible Truth Fellowship (BIBTF) was interviewed by Trevor Barnes on *Sunday* on BBC Radio 4.[75]

All of this serves to demonstrate that British-Israel doctrine was not hidden from view in twentieth-century Britain. British-Israel ideas were widely discussed by its proponents and its opponents in novels, in the print media, on the radio and even in the Houses of Parliament.

Why Study British-Israelism?

It might appear that British-Israelism is a narrow and eccentric subject for a book. However, three significant factors make this a worthwhile and – I would argue – an important subject for study. The impact of British Israelism on British culture during the twentieth century has been underestimated. Tens of thousands of people in Britain – including, as we have seen, prominent and opinion-forming individuals – subscribed to this doctrine and, as such, their omission from the historical record itself demands to be addressed. Secondly, I would argue that a corrective is required to the study of British-Israelism. The movement is often associated with imperialist supremacy, in part because of the association between racialist movements and British-Israelism in the American context. I would argue that the notion of national election and the emphasis on authenticity, with which British-Israelist literature in the twentieth century is most concerned, belongs in a different category from the imperialism with which it is usually associated. Thirdly, and more broadly, I argue that the story of British-Israelism can provide us with a microcosm of the story of Britain itself during this period. This is not to say that the British-Israelists represented a cross-section of British society. This is certainly not the case. British-Israelists were almost exclusively white, almost exclusively conservative, exclusively Protestant. Herein, though, lies the value of studying the movement. British-Israelists represented a greater proportion of white, conservative Protestants in Britain than they did of the wider population. As such, the story of British-Israelism can tell us something about the mindset of white, conservative, nationalist Protestants in Britain. It can also tell us about the ways in which this constituency altered the course of Britain's cultural development during this period.

Euroscepticism and the cultural politics of Thatcherism provide us with a broader social backdrop to the prevailing themes of British-Israelist thought. Particularly in the later period of her career, Margaret Thatcher appealed to the nation to recall and regain its sense of authenticity. She spoke of the importance of policy makers having 'closeness to the people,' of the UK parliament being 'in tune with the instincts of the people,' as a result of 'the heritage that we have built up over the centuries.' This cultural and political attunement found its antithesis in the European Union, with its 'multilingual parliament' and its 'powerful bureaucracy.' Authenticity and sovereignty, it was argued, were far more precious than mere material prosperity.[76] In this conviction, Thatcher and the British-Israelists were as one.

It might appear that there is little distinction between the claim that British-Israelism is a product of British imperialism and the claim that British-Israelism is a product of British nationalism. Several studies have been produced in recent years with the intention of elucidating the relationship between British imperialism and British nationalism. Some scholars have argued that the latter is a product of the former. A notable example is Benjamin Grob-Fitzgibbon's *Continental Drift*. In this text, Grob-Fitzgibbon argues that the residual imperialist pomp of the early twentieth century allowed Britain to participate more fully in the European project, in the knowledge that her global power would prevent her from becoming submerged in a European federalist super-state. Only when the former began to disintegrate did a new form of isolationist nationalism come to the fore, with Eurosceptic conservatives extolling the self-reliance of Britain more full-throatedly. The decline of empire, therefore, heralded a new politics of fear, the fear that 'Britain was losing its place in the world,' that 'an imperial heritage [was] slipping away.' Grob-Fitzgibbon notes with surprise the apparent sense in the British academy that 'decolonisation had very little to do with British approaches to Europe,' since, according to his analysis, imperialism and Euroscepticism are profoundly, causally linked.[77] David Edgerton, meanwhile, has argued that cultural attachment to the notion of Britain as a sovereign state developed somewhat later than is often believed. As such, Edgerton unmoors British nationalism from British imperial exceptionalism. He argues that the left, as well as the right, responded to the changes in Britain's global standing in the world in the twentieth century by pursuing policies in the post-war period which were more oriented towards creating a national economy. These included a renewed emphasis on manufacturing (often believed by 'declinist' historians of the period to have been in abeyance by this point) and a welfare state with a heavy accent on national continuity (styled as a 'nationalised' health and insurance system). These policies stored up the assets that would then be liquidated in the Thatcherite revolution.[78]

The story of British-Israelism adds another colour to the picture painted by Edgerton and others. It provides an account of how a small demographic in British society negotiated the transition from imperial Britain to the nationalist Britain of the twentieth century. It also provides an account of the cultural resources which were at the disposal of these individuals which aided them in this process. Crucially, however, the same cultural resources that were used explicitly by the British-Israelists had been used by numerous previous generations of British men and women. These men and women, collectively constructed the character of the British nation. As such, British-Israelism provides us with a living exemplar, preserved in amber, of a Biblical vision of the British people, a vision that had once been ubiquitous.

This last claim requires some clarification. The nature of the relationship between religion and nationalism is a hotly debated issue in the field of nationalism studies. In the past, many scholars have proposed that religion was supplanted by nationalism in the era of modernity. Nationalism, it is argued, began to provide the social resources which religion had once provided and – as such – rendered religion redundant. Religion once encouraged endogamy, provided a source of cultural belonging, performed the function of organising society. Nationalism could now perform all of those functions. Insofar as religious themes were present in nationalist discourse, it was the result of the *use* of the former by the latter. In more recent times, this 'modernist' approach has been challenged by the 'ethnosymbolist' approach (most notably advanced by Anthony Smith) which argues that religious concepts helped to provide the foundations of nationalist thought. How exactly religious beliefs interact with nationalism is a secondary question. Is religion a necessary *part of* nationalism? Or is religious belief a precursor *to* nationalism? It is clear that many seemingly supra-national religions – such as Islam and Christianity – have become 'nationalised,' in their interaction with nationalist movements. This is self-evidently the case in contemporary Chechnya, in Buddhist Tibet, in Ireland and elsewhere, where feelings of national sentiment and nationalism are wedded to religious ritual and identity.[79] It is also, of course, found throughout the long history of post-Reformation Britain. During this period, as Linda Colley notably demonstrated, first England and then Britain developed a national identity which was defined 'in conscious opposition to' the 'real or imagined,' European other: authoritarian, bureaucratic and irredeemably Papist. Protestantism, according to Colley, was the adhesive which helped to bind together the four nations of Britain.[80]

The claim that religion and nationalism are often intertwined is still – somewhat – flat. It suggests that almost any religious belief could provide the basic tools of kinship and mythology to bolster the project of nation building. In Smith's recent work, he has noted the particular facility of Protestantism for the development of nationalist feeling. Smith identifies the 'covenantal' narratives, which Protestantism provides, as a stimulant of nationalist thought. It was after the Reformation that Britain first began to identify itself with 'islandness.'[81] In part this can be explained in political terms given that Britain's great rivals on the European continent – France and Spain – were both Catholic countries. Nevertheless, Krishan Kumar is right to caution that 'Protestantism was as international as Catholicism' and that, as such, Britain's 'isolation' was not an objective fact.[82] A second critical component of Britain's islandness was its Protestantism and the sense of a covenantal relationship between God and England and (later) God and Britain. Both Smith and Adrian Hastings attribute the prominence of covenantal thought in the nationalist milieu as the bequest of the Hebrew Bible. Protestants were more Biblicist, they argue, and as such they were more likely to be attentive to the narratives which described the travails of the biblical polity of Israel.[83] A similar claim is echoed by Donald Akenson in his exploration of the various covenantal nationalisms and loyalisms – including Israeli, Afrikaner and Ulster – which emerged in the nineteenth and twentieth centuries.[84]

It must also be noted that the soteriological claims of Reformed Protestantism shaped the way in which these groups read these texts. The claim that people who read the Bible more closely would necessarily gravitate towards those fragments which explicitly describe the nature of covenant is somewhat hasty. As Stanley Fish, Donald McKim, Kevin Killeen and others have pointed out, Protestants were no less likely than Catholics to construct an *analogia fidei*, in their reading of the Bible, constructed of elements which conformed to their pre-established worldview.[85] Particularly in the British context, Protestants were encouraged by their leaders to see humanity as starkly divided between the elect and the reprobate. Reformed Protestants often sought to separate into *classis*, conventicles and communities which were exclusively Godly. This in turn fed into an understanding of national election, the collective election of a Godly polity: primarily exemplified by the polity of Israel, latterly by the Godly armies of the English revolution and the 'cities on the hill' that were founded in the New World. More fundamentally, Reformed Protestants exhibited a fixation with the separation of the sacred and profane. The organisation of time and people, the Sabbath, the 'sorting out' of company, was at the forefront of many Godly Protestants' minds.[86] This provided Godly Protestants with a profound point of connection with the authors of the Biblical texts which were produced during the neo-Babylonian period. With the destruction of the temple, the focus of these authors turned towards personal purity and the recognition of separation as a 'productive expression of religious ideals.'[87] The recognition of this common concern leads us to a crucial claim about the focus of Reformed Protestants and Israelite religion. Brubaker – after Bourdieu – notes that religion 'provides a way . . . of construing sameness and difference, situating oneself in relation to others . . . identifying and naming fundamental social groups.'[88] We might add, with regards to both Protestant groups and Biblical Israelite religion in particular, that religion is primarily concerned *not* with the maintenance of separation but rather with the *act* of separation. For this reason, Israelite religious practice, as recounted in the scriptures, focusses on the continual and ongoing process of comparison and distinction. At times this focus requires not the maintenance of boundaries but the alteration of boundaries, the better to facilitate the process of separation. This focus is not confined to the ritual sphere but also arises in the social, political sphere. The Edomites – as Tebes has recently demonstrated – were constructed within the Israelite corpora, as a related group, the descendants of Esau, the fraternal twin of Jacob. However, the construction of Edom as a sibling group was closely intertwined with the identification of Edom as the antithesis of Israel.[89] The process of separation, rather than the fruits of this separation, are the primary focus of both Protestant and Israelite practical divinity.

Given that so many scholars, in recent times, have identified the interaction between covenantal nationalism, Protestantism and the Biblical topos of Israel, the study of the covenantal, Protestant phenomenon of British-Israelism provides an important part of this picture. British-Israelists express a form of nationalism which is deeply imbricated in Biblical language and imagery. This much has been expressed in the writings of Colin Kidd and Michael Barkun. This claim moreover, does *not* mutually exclude the claim that British-Israelism is a form of nationalism which uses religion. The latter claim is also avowed in accounts of the British-Israelist movement. I want to claim, instead, that British-Israelism is a form of nationalism which is facilitated by religion. In other words, I argue that a focus on 'sorting out' people and place, inherited primarily from the Biblical authors and secondarily from the Protestant reformers, provided the basis for British-Israelism as a mode of religion which is focussed primarily on discussing, addressing and continuously clarifying the difference between peoples. The presumption – at the heart of much analysis of the phenomenon of British-Israelism – that the category of 'British-Israel' precedes the practice of maintaining the separation of Israel, logically, is a false one. The act of separating and 'sorting out' Israel from non-Israel is the primary focus of British-Israel devotion. The identity of Israel as separate from non-Israel is malleable, and it changes in service of the process of separation. Israel is continually identified and reappraised using a variety of criteria: ethical, genealogical, territorial and historical. As such, British-Israelism can be seen as a form of 'religious nationalism,' in the sense adopted by Roger Friedland. Friedland proposes that – with acute focus on ethical conformity, endogamy, family filialty – religion can, itself, create the parameters of a national group and can itself essentialise the connection amongst genealogy, culture and ethics.[90] This is the task to which British-Israelists dedicate their efforts.

Existing scholarship

Goldwin Smith originated the oft-cited description of British-Israelism as 'jingoism with Biblical sanction,' in an 1890 editorial to the *Bystander* magazine.[91] More recently, this theme has been reiterated by contemporary scholars. Colin Kidd's seminal work, *The Forging of the Races*, also addresses the British roots of American, racial religion. For Kidd, the foundations of British-Israelist doctrine, as expressed in the work of Wilson, Hine and Wheeler Bird, lay in British imperialist ideology. Kidd presents British-Israelism as a 'religious justification for white superiority' and as a 'sanctification of the British imperialist enterprise.'[92] Smith's axiomatic description was also cited in an article written by Eric Reisenauer in 1999. Reisenauer argues that British-Israelism was far more mainstream in its influence than most scholars presume. He cites a contemporary commentator who suggested that 'if a poll could be taken amongst Anglo-Saxon Christians, the

belief in favor of Israelism would be carried by an overwhelming majority.'[93] Whilst Reisenauer steers clear of the suggestion that British-Israelism
was 'an oddball faith of a hyper-imperialist fringe' (it was too popular to be
so), he does reach the conclusion that it is difficult to distinguish between
British-Israelism and a broader form of racialism linked to the politics and
culture of imperialism.[94] Richard Pierard goes one step further, suggesting
that an eccentric exterior only thinly masks the British-Israelist commitment
to white supremacy and the destruction of other races.[95] Achsah Guibbory –
whilst not going as far as Pierard – draws a genealogical link from the
national, election narratives of Milton to the American exceptionalism of
Donald Trump's election campaign, visiting the 'Protestant, British, imperialist,' doctrines of John Wilson along the way.[96]

Each of these scholars, with varying degrees of nuance, subscribe to a
common presumption about the genesis of British-Israelist doctrine. It is a
creature – they contend – of a view of Britain which is informed by imperialism and white supremacy. The doctrines of British-Israelism provide a
'mandate,' a 'sanction,' or a 'fig leaf' for imperialist expansion, domination and destruction. In order to make this case, all three of these scholars
confine their studies of British-Israelism, in the UK context, to the period of
British imperial expansion in the long nineteenth century. This is surprising,
given that – by any reasonable measure – British-Israelism increased in reach
and influence in the period which coincided with the *decline* of the British
Empire in the twentieth century.

Only one scholar has looked in detail at the phenomenon of twentieth
century British-Israelism in its British habitat. John Wilson (no relation to
the originator of British-Israelist doctrine) wrote a number of essays in the
1960s, evaluating the health of British-Israelism in the UK.[97] He reached
some conclusions which are at odds with the claims of Barkun, Kidd, Pierard,
Guibbory and Reisenauer. Wilson suggested that the number of card-carrying
British-Israelists in the United Kingdom in 1968 probably numbered in the
thousands. Beyond this number, a much larger number subscribed to the
doctrine without taking the step of joining a British-Israelist organisation.[98]
A majority of members were not raised by British-Israelists, but adopted
the doctrine as adults.[99] Wilson wrote that 'British Israelism has, even on a
conservative estimate, flourished as a prophetic persuasion in England for
over a century.'[100] At the same time, Wilson was sceptical of the suggestion
that British-Israelism was simply 'jingoism with Biblical sanction.' 'Britain's
international circumstances,' he wrote 'are not such that recruits are likely
to be swept on a tide of emotional imperialism.' On this basis, Wilson contended that British-Israelism was 'flourishing' amongst those 'who have not
experienced a truly imperial Britain.'[101] Wilson considered British-Israelism
to be 'a distinctive response to social change . . . an attempt to revise and
perpetuate select aspects of the past . . . drawing most of its support from
the well-to-do.' 'British Israelism,' he believed, 'offers [British Israelists] a
defence and transcendental endorsement of cherished values.'[102]

Additional theoretical insights into the phenomenon of British-Israelism can be drawn from Zygmunt Bauman's understanding of 'allosemitism' and Andrew Crome's recent scholarship on the subject of Christian Zionism. Bauman's insights have helped a generation of scholars to better understand the seemingly contradictory attitudes of philo-Semitism and anti-Semitism, both exhibited in Western Christian culture. Bauman suggests that the topos of 'the Jew,' in Western culture, denotes irreducible otherness. This otherness is expressed in the culture in both positive and negative ways. For Bauman, the Jew is the object of 'radical ambivalence': both blessed and cursed, both a people and an antique relic of the Biblical past.[103]

Andrew Crome has used Bauman's term as a tool for analysing the phenomenon of Christian Zionism. Crome traces the history of British support for the political restoration of the Jews and argues, persuasively, that the exceptionalist narratives of British nationalism were not mutually exclusive with Zionist attitudes, but rather that the latter fed and sustained the former. Anti-Semitic and philo-Semitic tropes perform an identical function, Crome argues, in the task of promoting notions of national chosenness. British nationalism should *not* be considered a form of ethnic supersessionism, wherein the British people 'supplant' the Jewish people as an elect nation.[104] But nor should the providential nature of British nationalism be occluded. Rather, Crome argues, historians should recognise both the covenantal and missional elements of British nationalism. Both are intricately linked with Judeocentric eschatology. Britain, for most of the subjects of Crome's study, was a chosen nation. But its chosenness was a mirror image, rather than a replacement, of the chosen status of the Jewish people. As such, the distinctive role played by the Jewish people (as a protean group, the object of 'radical ambivalence') provides ballast to the claim that God works through nations his wonders to perform and thus that God works through Britain. Secondly, an essential part of the appointed role, given by God to Britain, is the facilitation of the redemption of the Jewish people through their protection from persecution, the maintenance of their restoration and their conversion.[105] Thus, both Jews and Christian Britons are bound together and both are bound to remain separated 'from the nations.'[106]

Crome does not believe that British-Israelism falls within the category that he has identified in his scholarship and indeed he has drawn contradistinctions between British-Israelism and conventional Christian Zionism. Crome writes that Judeocentrist eschatology 'undermined the standard supersessionist position, in which the Christian understood herself as the true or fulfilled Jew' and 'repurposed this narrative by drawing a firm boundary between God's promises for Jews and His promises for Christians.'[107] Thus, England is given a privileged providential position 'because of her eschatological destiny: to restore the Jewish people to Palestine.' For Crome, British-Israelists (specifically in this context Richard Brothers) signalled a 'return to the supersessionist position.' I argue that this distinction is a little too broad and – indeed – that Christian Zionists and British-Israelists have more in common than one might immediately imagine. British-Israelists do not posit a 'replacement' of the Jews by the Britons. Indeed, the cornerstone of their belief is a rejection of replacement theology in all of its forms. Nevertheless, Crome's contention that British-Israelism brings 'Jewishness and Englishness . . . uncomfortably together,' is certainly true. In actions and words, British-Israelists invite the comparison of Britons and Jews. As we shall see, this invitation has occasionally drawn the attention of anti-Semites who in turn have aggressively targeted British-Israelists. At the same time, British-Israelists have attempted to deepen and, in a sense, reify the distinctions between Britons and Jews and, indeed, between Israel and Jews. As such, the discomfort of the association and the requisite sorting out of the differences form the central conceptual practices of British-Israelist thought. This should, perhaps, not be surprising. As Zygmunt Bauman noted, 'the Jew' represents ambivalence in the history of Western thought, but the discomfort which accompanies ambivalence does not require the eradication of the source of ambivalence. Rather the source of ambivalence is invited into proximity. It is the 'one enemy without which order cannot live.'[108] The unclean beasts are invited onto the Ark, are protected and rescued from the deluge. 'For both Jews and Britons,' as the British-Israelist C.F. Parker wrote in 1948, 'isolation from the world around has helped to produce a unique mentality.'[109] For Jews and Britons to be (similarly) different from the world, they need to be different from one another.

Whilst many scholars have sought to present narratives of nationalist exceptionalism as an attempt to supplant the Jewish people, Crome's analysis demonstrates that many narratives of national 'chosenness' actually *rely* on the existence and perseverance of the Jewish people. The existence of the Jewish people serves as a definitive antithesis to Christianity, whilst at the same time standing as evidence of God's providential action in the world. The same, in various ways, holds true for the British-Israel movement.

Order of chapters

The proceeding two chapters provide a grounding in the intellectual and organisational history of British-Israelism. The first chapter provides a guide to the history of the British-Israel movement, through its rise in the nineteenth century up to the present day. The second chapter will address several key and complimentary themes in British-Israelist thought including the notion of national election, the genealogical understanding of race, the perennial theme of conspiratorialism in their writing and their particular form of millenarianism.

The remaining chapters will provide discussions of the way in which British-Israelists respond to a range of events in the history of twentieth-century Britain. The first of these chapters concerns the way in which British-Israelists address Jews and Judaism. In this chapter, I draw on the analysis of Crome and – more broadly – of Bauman, particularly in relation to the latter's concept of allosemitism. The second of these chapters will address changing attitudes to the Empire that emerged from the British-Israelist milieu during the twentieth century. Drawing on David Edgerton's analysis of the shift from imperialism to nationalism within the British political culture, this chapter highlights some problems with the conventional depiction of British-Israelism as 'jingoism with Biblical sanction.' The third of these chapters addresses the history of British-Israelists in Ireland and the history of British-Israelist attitudes *to* Ireland. It will describe the growing significance of Ulster in the imagination of British-Israelists as a synecdoche for the British-Israelist sense of Israel's role in the world. Fourth, we turn to the state of Israel, analysing the shifting sands of British-Israelist opinion on the validity of the Jewish state, from enthusiasm following Allenby's triumph in 1917 to supporting the enemies of the state of Israel in the Middle East during the latter decades of the twentieth century. The penultimate chapter concerns Russia and the Soviet Union. Russia plays a significant role in the apocalyptic thought of many British-Israelists. Russia was believed to be the embodiment of the prophesied tribes of Gog and Magog. Many understood the rise in power of the Soviet Union to represent an eschatologically significant factor which would lead ultimately to a Soviet Russian attempt to seize control of Zion. As these expectations were disappointed at the end of the twentieth century, British-Israelists expressed confusion and disorientation. This chapter will analyse those responses in relation to contemporary theories of cognitive dissonance arising from prophecy failure. Lastly, we turn our attention to the European Union, a perennial trope of British-Israelist literature in the past four decades. The Union itself represents more than a regional treaty organisation. For many British-Israelists, it functions as the modern incarnation of Babylon. As such, 'escaping' from the European Union – following the referendum of 2016 – represented a seismic and soteriological event for British-Israelists which dwarfed its political, social and economic significance.

Each of these chapters adds to a wider picture of the movement and the worldview of its members. Each adds a layer of complexity to the superficial account of British-Israelism as an excrescence of nineteenth-century imperialism. British-Israelists, above all, are concerned with what Anthony Smith calls authenticity. This focus on authenticity has provided them with the same tools as those used by other covenantal, nationalist movements in South Africa, Israel, Ulster, and many other countries. It has also allowed them to weather the storms with which history buffeted the concept of British exceptionalism during the twentieth century. In exploring these themes, my intention is to present British-Israelism as the extraordinary manifestation of some ordinary aspects of British culture. A theme which will emerge from each of these narratives will be the transition made by British-Israelists from an imperial to a nationalist and ultimately to an isolationist mentality. My claim, in addressing these themes, will be that the Biblical model of nationhood which British-Israelists explicitly reference in their literature is implicitly present in the broader British culture during this period.

Notes

1 *Birmingham Daily Post*, no. 36,726 (1 November 1976), 5.
2 *Birmingham Daily Post*, no. 36,533 (3 February 1976), 4.
3 *The National Message*, vol. 55, no. 1,645 (December 1976), 370.
4 *The National Message*, vol. 27, no. 1,199 (3 July 1948), 238.
5 David Jenkins, *The British: Their Identity and Their Religion* (London: SCM, 1975).
6 *The National Message*, vol. 59, no. 1,684 (March 1980), 33.
7 Colin Kidd, *The Forging of Races* (Cambridge: Cambridge University Press, 2006), 203–213; Michael Barkun, *Religion and the Racist Right* (Chapel Hill: University of North Carolina Press, 1997), 3–17; Achsah Guibbory, 'The Reformation of Hebrew Scripture: Chosen People, Chosen Nations, and Exceptionalism,' in *Reformation*, 23, no. 1 (2018): 100–119; Eric Reisenauer, '"That We May Do Israel's Work": Racial Election in British Imperial Thought,' in *Proceedings of the South Carolina Historical Association 1999* (1999): 97–112; Eric Reisenauer, ' "The Merchants of Tarshish, with All the Young Lions Thereof": The British Empire, Scripture Prophecy, and the War of Armageddon, 1914–1918,' in *Journal of the Bible and Its Reception*, 4, no. 2 (2017): 287–318.
8 Notable exceptions to this would be the work of Professor John Wilson [John Wilson, 'The Relation Between Ideology and Organization in a Small Religious Group: The British Israelites,' in *Review of Religious Research*, 10, no. 1 (1968): 51–50; John Wilson, 'British Israelism,' in *Sociological Review*, no. 16 (1968): 41–57; John Wilson, 'British Israelism: A Revitalization Movement,' in *Archives de Sociologie des Religions*, 13, no. 26 (January 1968): 73–80].
9 *The Manchester Guardian*, no. 26,670 (29 February 1932), 16.
10 *The Banner of Israel*, vol. 43, no. 2,205 (1 April 1919), 126; *The National Message*, vol. 43, no. 1,495 (June 1964), 187.
11 *Bexhill-On-Sea Observer*, no. 1,704 (16 March 1929), 12.
12 Compton MacKenzie, *The North Wind of Love* (London: Chatto and Windus, 1944), 118, 276.
13 Bernard Benstock, *Sean O'Casey* (Cranbury, NJ: Associated University Press, 1970), 67.
14 Sean O'Casey, *Oak Leaves and Lavender* (London: Palgrave Macmillan, 1946), 45–53.
15 *The Guardian*, no. 26,456 (7 September 1934), 5.
16 Kenneth Ross, *Dangerous Delusions* (Oxford: Mowbray, 1961), 48.
17 Kirsten Parsons, *Revival in a Canteen* (Hove: Hove Shirley, 1942), 1, 16.
18 Charles Hadfield, *British Israel, Fact Not Fiction* (Bishop Auckland: Covenant Publishing, 2015 [4th edition]), 1; Joseph Whitaker, *An Almanack for the Year of Our Lord 1897* (London, 1898), 190.
19 *The Banner of Israel*, vol. 43, no. 2,210 (7 May 1919), 171.
20 Charles Totten, *Our Race* (New Haven: Our Race Publishing Company, 1890–1892).
21 'Letter from Herbert Garrison to Sir Francis Dalton,' National Museums Liverpool, Maritime Archives, D/D/V/2/36.
22 *The Banner of Israel*, vol. 43, no. 2,213 (28 May 1919), 197.
23 *The Banner of Israel*, vol. 43, no. 2,221 (23 July 1919), 262.
24 *The Banner of Israel*, vol. 43, no. 2,210 (7 May 1919), 171.

25 Yigal Sheffy, *British Military Intelligence in the Palestine Campaign* (Abingdon: Routledge, 1998), 50.

26 Edward Westermann, 'The Royal Air Force and the Bombing of Auschwitz,' in David Cesarini and Sarah Kavanagh (eds.), *Holocaust: Responses to the Persecution and the Mass Murder of the Jews* (Abingdon: Routledge, 2004), 206.

27 *Daily Chronicle*, no. 17,733 (18 December 1918), 8f.

28 *Bexhill-On-Sea Observer*, no. 1,704 (16 March 1929), 12.

29 Henry de Beauvoir de Lisle, *Reminiscences of Sport and War* (London: Eyre and Spottiswoode, 1939), 226–231.

30 *Londonderry Sentinel* (23 March 1957), 2.

31 *The National Message*, vol. 54, no. 1,624 (March 1975), 73.

32 *The National Message*, vol. 56, no. 1,649 (April 1977), 145.

33 *Wake Up*, vol. 7, no. 2 (March 1988), 31.

34 Theo Aronson, *Princess Alice, Duchess of Athlone* (London: Cassel, 1981), 118; *The Banner of Israel*, vol. 43, no. 2,216 (18 June 1919), 221.

35 'Letters of HRH Princess Alice of Athlone to Anthony Eden,' Cadbury Research Library, AP30/F.

36 Aronson, *Princess Alice*, 243.

37 *The Banner of Israel*, vol. 43, no. 2,218 (2 July 1919), 229.

38 *The New British Israel Pilot*, no. 4 (1 October 1929), 51.

39 Helen, Countess Dowager of Radnor, *From a Great Grandmother's Armchair* (London: Marshall, 1927), 357.

40 *The Banner of Israel*, vol. 43, no. 2,216 (18 June 1919), 221.

41 Martin Pugh, *Hurrah for the Blackshirts: Fascists and Fascism in Britain Between the Wars* (London: Pimlico, 2006), 120.

42 Hansard, *House of Lords Debate*, vol. 231, coll. 281 (10 May 1961).

43 *British-Israel World Federation Newsletter* (January 2017), 4.

44 Robert Darby and John Cozijn, 'The British Royal Family's Circumcision Tradition: Genesis and Evolution of a Contemporary Legend,' in *Sage Open*, 3, no. 4 (October 2013): 1–10.

45 *The Independent*, no. 2,954 (6 April 1996), 6.

46 *Brith*, no. 4 (January 1946), 3–4.

47 Charles Kidd (ed.), *Debrett's Peerage and Baronetage* (London: Debrett, 2011), 627.

48 *The Economist*, vol. 340, no. 7,974 (13 July 1996), 53.

49 *The National Message*, vol. 55, no. 1,645 (December 1976), 382.

50 *The National Message*, vol. 57, no. 1,663 (June 1978), 169.

51 *Northern Whig*, no. 38,198 (4 February 1931), 1.

52 Michael Farrell, *Northern Ireland: The Orange State* (London: Pluto, 1980), 162, 342.

53 Norah Bradford, *A Sword Bathed in Heaven* (Basingstoke: Pickering, 1984), 74; *The National Message*, vol. 53, no. 1,618 (September 1974), 283; *The National Message*, vol. 57, no. 1,659 (February 1978), 40; *The Annual Report for 1982* (Woodford Green: Covenant People's Fellowship, 1982), 5.

54 Anthony Buckley, ' "We're Trying to Find Our Identity": Uses of History Among Ulster Protestants,' in Elizabeth Tonkin, Maryon McDonald and Malcolm Chapman (eds.), *History and Ethnicity* (London: Routledge, 1989), 191.

55 Ruth Dudley Edwards, *The Faithful Tribe* (London: Harper Collins, 1999), 134.

56 *The Wellington Evening Post*, vol. 99, no. 108 (7 May 1920), 7; *The Banner of Israel*, vol. 44, no. 2,287 (27 October 1920), 369.

57 *The National Message*, vol. 1, no. 5 (4 February 1922), i.

58 *Quarterly Notes of the Protestant British Israel League*, vol. 7, no. 3 (July 1917), 96.

59 *The Guardian* (24 February 1992), 35.

24 *Introduction*

60 *The National Message*, vol. 31, no. 1,299 (3 May 1952), 196.
61 Patience Strong, *Someone Had to Say It* (London: Bachman and Turner, 1986), 56.
62 *The National Message*, vol. 49, no. 1,566 (May 1970), 144.
63 *Daily Mirror*, no. 11,404 (27 June 1940), 7.
64 *The National Message*, vol. 55, no. 1,637 (April 1976), 124.
65 *The National Message*, vol. 55, no. 1,639 (June 1976), 191.
66 *The National Message*, vol. 57, no. 1,658 (January 1978), 28.
67 Ross McWhirter, *Ross Was Right: The Queen Betrayed* (Bishop Auckland: Covenant Publishing, 2014), 1; *The National Message*, vol. 53, no. 1,611 (February 1974), 38.
68 *The National Message*, vol. 55, no. 1,634 (January 1976), 16.
69 *The National Message*, vol. 53, no. 1,614 (May 1974), 156.
70 *The National Message*, vol. 53, no. 1,618 (September 1974), 284.
71 *The Times*, no. 53,933 (30 August 1957), 5.
72 *The National Message*, vol. 50, no. 1,585 (December 1971), 385; *The National Message*, vol. 56, no. 1,650 (May 1977), 154.
73 *Brith*, no. 335 (December 1973), 21.
74 *Brith*, no. 408 (May 1980), 28.
75 *Bible Truth*, no. 205 (May 2000), 10.
76 Margaret Thatcher, *The Collected Speeches of Margaret Thatcher* (London: Harper Collins, 1997), 495; Margaret Thatcher, *The Path to Power* (London: Harper Collins, 1995), 609–624; *The European* (19 May 1992), 14; *The European*, no. 106 (21–24 May), 9.
77 Benjamin Grob-Fitzgibbon, *Continental Drift* (Cambridge: Cambridge University Press, 2016), 1–10, 470.
78 David Edgerton, *The Rise and Fall of the British Nation* (London: Penguin, 2018).
79 Martin Schulze Wessel, 'Introduction,' in *Nationalisierung der Religion und Sakralisierung der Nation im Östlichen Europa* (Stuttgart: Steiner, 2006), 7–14.
80 Linda Colley, 'Britishness and Otherness: An Argument,' in *Journal of British Studies*, 31, no. 4 (1992): 316.
81 Anthony Smith, 'Nation and Covenant: The Contribution of Ancient Israel to Modern Nationalism,' in *Proceedings of the British Academy*, 151 (2007): 237.
82 Krishan Kumar, *The Idea of Englishness* (Abingdon: Routledge, 2016), 80; Krishan Kumar, 'Britain, England and Europe: Cultures in Contraflow,' in *European Journal of Social Theory*, 6, no. 1 (February 2003): 15.
83 Adrian Hastings, *The Construction of Nationhood: Ethnicity, Religion and Nationalism* (Cambridge: Cambridge University Press, 1997), 1–35.
84 Donald Akenson, *God's Peoples* (Ithaca: Cornell University Press, 1992).
85 Stanley Fish, *Self-Consuming Artifacts* (London: University of California Press, 1972), 22; Michel De Certeau, *The Practice of Everyday Life*, trans. Steven Rendall (Los Angeles: University of California Press, 1984), 175; Ian Green, *Print and Protestantism in Early Modern England* (Oxford: Oxford University Press, 2000), 130; Donald McKim, *Ramism in William Perkins Theology* (New York: Peter Lang, 1987), 51–119; Donald McKim, 'The Function of Ramism in Perkins' Theology,' in *The Sixteenth Century Journal*, 16, no. 4 (1985): 503–517; Andrew Crome, *The Restoration of the Jews: Early Modern Hermeneutics, Eschatology and National Identity in the Work of Thomas Brightman* (Dordrecht: Springer, 2014), 45–49; Kevin Killeen, *Biblical Scholarship, Science and Politics in Early Modern England* (Farnham: Ashgate, 2009), 66–67; Augustine, *On Christian Doctrine*, trans. D.W. Robertson (Indianapolis: Bobbs Merrill, 1958), 93.
86 Patrick Collinson, *The Puritan Character* (Los Angeles: University of California Press, 1989), 32.

87 Jonathan Klawans, *Purity, Sacrifice and the Temple* (Oxford: Oxford University Press, 2006), 73; Yaira Amit, *Hidden Polemics in the Biblical Narrative* (Leiden: Brill, 2000), 239.

88 Rogers Brubaker, 'Religion and Nationalism: Four Approaches,' in *Nations and Nationalism*, 18, no. 1 (2012): 4.

89 Juan Manuel Tebes, 'Memories of Humiliation, Cultures of Resentment Towards Edom and the Formation of Ancient Jewish National Identity,' in *Nations and Nationalism*, 25, no. 1 (2019): 124–145.

90 Roger Friedland, 'Money, Sex and God: The Erotic Logic of Religious Nationalism,' in *Sociological Theory*, 20, no. 3 (2002): 381–425.

91 *The Bystander*, vol. 1, no. 1 (January 1890), 134.

92 Kidd, *The Forging of Races*, 212.

93 J.B. Dimbleby, 'The Lost Ten Tribes: Where Are They?' in *Past and Future*, 4 (1 June 1898): 129.

94 Reisenauer, 'That We May Do Israel's Work,' 97–112 [104]; Reisenauer, 'The Merchants of Tarshish, with All the Young Lions Thereof,' 287–318.

95 Richard Pierard, 'The Contribution of British-Israelism to Anti-Semitism,' in Hubert G. Lock and Marcia Sachs Littell (eds.), *Holocaust and Church Struggle: Religion, Power, and the Politics of Resistance* (Lanham: University Press of America, 1996), 45–68.

96 Guibbory, 'The Reformation of Hebrew Scripture,' 100–119.

97 Wilson, 'The Relation Between Ideology and Organization in a Small Religious Group,' 51–50; Wilson, 'British Israelism,' 41–57; Wilson, 'British Israelism: A Revitalization Movement,' 73–80.

98 Wilson, 'British-Israelism: A Revitalization Movement,' 74.

99 Wilson, 'British Israelism,' 51.

100 Wilson, 'The Relation Between Ideology and Organization in a Small Religious Group,' 345.

101 Wilson, 'British Israelism,' 48, 55.

102 Wilson, 'British-Israelism: A Revitalization Movement,' 74.

103 Zygmunt Bauman, 'Allosemitism: Premodern, Modern, Postmodern,' in Bryan Cheyette and Laura Marcus (eds.), *Modernity, Culture and 'The Jew'* (Cambridge: Polity, 1998), 143–156.

104 Anthony D. Smith, *Myths and Memories of the Nation* (Oxford: Oxford University Press, 1999), 214.

105 Andrew Crome, *Christian Zionism and English National Identity* (London: Palgrave Macmillan, 2018), 11, 22, 24.

106 Leviticus 25: 44–46.

107 Crome, *Christian Zionism and English National Identity*, 195.

108 Bauman, 'Allosemitism,' 144.

109 *The National Message*, vol. 27, no. 1,186 (3 January 1948), 9.

1   What do British-Israelists believe?

British-Israelism was never a church. It is a belief held by members of mainstream Protestant churches. More accurately, perhaps, the term refers to a family of beliefs. This family of beliefs is not brought into harmony by canons or statutes or dogma, but rather by common sensibilities and tendencies shared by a majority of British-Israelists. As such, the question posed in the title of this chapter is a complex one. In the following sections, a number of different characteristics of British-Israelist belief will be addressed. These are not exhaustive, but they point to persistent themes that recur throughout the literature produced by the movement over the past century. They include British-Israelist beliefs regarding racial science, national election and the origins of the British-Israel people. Also included here are discussions of the broader tendencies, common amongst British-Israelists, towards conspiratorial thinking and apocalypticism.

Racial science

Fundamental to the British-Israelist creed is the belief in a providential understanding of race. British-Israelists believe that God works through nations, peoples and races in order to accomplish His will. The maintenance of the separation of races and nations, for British-Israelists, is therefore an ethical responsibility. British-Israelist theory is informed by two sources: the racialist pseudo-science of the late-nineteenth and early twentieth centuries and the Biblical accounts of genealogical nationhood.

Colin Kidd's recent research on the history of race and religion in Western culture provides a useful framework for this discussion. In his *The Forging of Races* – which includes a short history of the rise of British-Israelism – Kidd describes the process whereby the understandings of racial difference, that developed in the early modern era, were primarily founded on theological rather than scientific grounds. Whilst the Enlightenment saw new attempts to create taxonomies of race, these attempts should not – according to Kidd – be seen as a radical break from the past but rather as a continuation of originally theological arguments. Whilst Kidd does not argue that all aspects of racial theory find their origins in Christian doctrine, he does contend that 'traditions of scriptural interpretation . . . played an enormous role in . . . shaping the discourse of race in the early modern and modern eras.'[1] Many theories of race from this period presumed that racial differences could be traced to individual patriarchs: the sons of Noah. The descendants of Japhet, Ham and Shem were believed by many to have emerged as different races with different racial, physiological and cultural characters. They were referred to as the Japhethic, Hamitic and Semitic races.

Kidd's analysis highlights the perpetuation of racial taxonomies, in the nineteenth century, which were couched in Biblical jargon. One such amongst many examples is Alexander Crawford's *Creed of Japhet*, written in 1849. In this text, Crawford explores the relationship between the descendants of Shem, Ham and Japhet. Like many authors of this period, Crawford identified the descendants of Ham with 'negro races.' They were 'swart,' but were 'much more musical than the Arabian.'[2] These ideas regarding the Noachide origins of racial difference informed the ideology of white supremacy during the era of slavery in the United States. The Oxford-based Assyriologist Archibald Sayce, meanwhile, argued that ancient Palestine had been populated by three distinct racial groups: the Amorites, the Canaanites and, thirdly, a wave of Semitic invaders, including the Edomites, Ammonites, Moabites and Israelites. These theories on race often relied on pseudo-science. Sayce believed that skull shape was 'the most marked and permanent characteristic of race.'[3] His work was later recommended in British-Israelist magazines.[4] Others pointed to the variety of spiritualities as an indication of racial difference. Max Müller traced the origins of different ritual themes which he then linked to the supposed religious sensibilities of different groups to give a full picture of the spectrum of spirituality along racial lines. This entanglement of the ethnic and the ethical would be a perennial theme of British-Israelist writings.

Concepts of race did not refer solely to physiological characteristics. In the early modern period, right up to the nineteenth century, the concept of race incorporated elements of physiology, religion, language and ethics. This would continue to be the case in British-Israel accounts of race right up to the present day.

One iteration of these themes can be found in the writing of British-Israelism's founding thinker, John Wilson, in the middle of the nineteenth century. Wilson believed, also, in the Noachide origins of race. He believed that the descendants of Ham were 'the negro race.' They were characterised, as having 'little forethought or power of planning,' of having 'gentleness and affection' and as requiring 'to be cared for like children.' The descendants of Japhet were identified with Tartars. They 'have much breadth of face, and great width between the eyes.' They were 'restless and roving, and in many cases addicted to violence and war; impatient they are of restraint, and ambitious of a proud independence.' Meanwhile the Shemitic people '[were] generally called the Caucasian race, occupy the central position; and chiefly inhabit Southern Asia.'⁵ For Wilson, the people of Israel, descendants of Shem, could now be found in the Northern European race, where they continued to exhibit all of the racial characteristics of God's chosen people:

> They have evidently been given a principle of life – an onward tendency – which is not merely of use to themselves, but it, in general, gives an impetus to all with whom they come into contact; who must either yield themselves to its influence, or be broken down by it. Theirs is not merely a retentive capacity, but an inventive genius.⁶

Whilst Bible-based theories of race waned in significance within mainstream thought, they retained a central role in British-Israelist thought long into the twentieth century. In 1973, Noel Court wrote in the pages of *Brith* that the 'races of Africa,' had 'dark skin, woolly hair, broad noses and prognathous jaws.' Britons, meanwhile, were often regarded as 'long-headed' but in actuality were 'Mesocephalic, that is to say medium-headed.'⁷ These ethnic differences, in the traditional way, were traced to the Noachide progeny. For British-Israelists, the descendants of Shem were to be recognised as Caucasians, the Japhethites as Mongolians and the sons of Ham as 'the Negroid group.'⁸

In more recent times, British-Israelists have attempted to incorporate modern genetic science into the into their account of the racial origins of British Israel. In 2016, the BIWF announced that Martin Lightfoot would be chairing a working party, looking at evidence derived from haplogroup mapping. They believed that scrutiny of this evidence would demonstrate the historicity of an ancient Assyrian migration into Europe. The haplogroup appeared to demonstrate a lack of consistency in the genealogical record supporting the kinship of the Jewish people (associated with the J1 and J2 Y-chromosome) and Western Europeans (the R chromosome). Lightfoot explained this discrepancy with reference to the miscegenation of the Jewish people during the period between the destruction of the Northern Kingdom and the present day.

For British-Israelists, the claim that the people of Israel belonged to the Shemite-Caucasian group led them to the conclusion that the Messiah was unequivocally 'white.' This belief led to a number of conflicts between British-Israelists and more mainstream opinion during the twentieth century. On 2 January 1980, Radio 4 broadcast an edition of *Thought for the Day* featuring David Steel MP. In his broadcast, Steel referred to Jesus as being 'black.' This prompted a stern response from L.G. Pine, editor of *The National Message*. 'I find it hard to understand,' Pine wrote, 'how any educated man could have made such a false and stupid statement.' The editor of the *Today* programme responded to Pine's rebuke, stating that Steel had originally planned to use the word 'coloured' to describe Christ, but had been reminded by a producer that 'black people disliked this word.' The full correspondence was published in *The National Message* with the following epilogue:

> The statement that Our Lord was coloured is absolutely false and stupid. Anyone who knows the Near East knows that the inhabitants have never been coloured, let alone black.[9]

The character of the British race

'The population of the United Kingdom includes various racial elements which have entered from the earliest to modern times,' wrote L. Buston Gresty in 1962:

> Yet it is also true to say that throughout what we may call the established main population one particular strain predominates and its characteristics prevail over the length and breadth of these islands.[10]

The central belief, held by British-Israelists, that the British constitute a single ethnic group resulting from the convergence of members of the same race from different parts of Europe may appear counter-intuitive. But it was not solely the preserve of British-Israelists during this period. In 1931, Arthur Keith wrote to the *Daily Mail* expressing his opinion that 'the British People are the least mongrel, the most uniform, to be found in any country.'[11] Keith's writings were influential in British-Israelist circles and he was often cited in their literature during the mid-twentieth century.

Keith was an evolutionary biologist who developed an idiosyncratic account of the process of natural selection, contending that racial selection was a continuing process in the modern world and that racial antagonism performed the same function – in separating races – that oceans and mountain ranges had done in the primordial age. As such, for Keith, 'race-feeling' was an essential aspect of the 'evolutionary machinery' which 'safeguards the purity of a race.'[12] Moreover, the behaviours and instincts of different ethnic groups were evidence of a common ancestry. When pressed on the subject of apparently 'new' nationalisms – in particular Scottish nationalism – Keith claimed that 'the manifestations of a young nationality are not willful perversions of human nature, but have a deep significance.'[13] As such, it is unsurprising that Keith's writings were to prove so attractive to British-Israelists. He provided a scientific valence to the commonly held British-Israelist claim that the natural, innate characteristics of Britons were a reliable source of evidence for common genealogy.

British-Israelists believe that the origins of the British people have, over the past thousands of years, determined the nature of the British national character. Principal amongst these national characteristics is Christianity and particularly Protestantism. An affinity for Protestantism distinguished Britain-Israel from her continental neighbours. 'Roman Catholic Gentile Europe,' was 'steeped in idolatry and worships idols and wealth and power and materialism in every form.'[14]

Alongside Protestantism, British-Israelists saw missionary work as the particular vocation of the British people. The 'translation and dissemination of scripture' was a task 'entrusted to people of Celtic or Anglo Saxon origin' by the Almighty.[15] Wilfred Reynolds taught that Britain was a 'nucleus of God's earthly Kingdom into which all are called, whatever may be their race of colour.'[16] This is one aspect of British-Israel belief which is cited by British-Israelists as repudiation against the charge of racism or white supremacy. 'Very often people say that British Israel is nationalistic,' Dorothy Abraham wrote, in 1954, 'but it will be found to be internationalism of the very highest order: its one aim, as well as its destiny, is to bring all nations to Christ.'[17]

Britain's Israelitish origin was also the basis for the British sense of justice and – more specifically – the jury system. This was partly evidenced, for British-Israelists, by the naming traditions of the British legal establishment and in particular the 'strangely named Temple, like Israel's temple which administered Divine Law.' A notable distinction was made by British-Israelists between the Israel system of laws and the Roman system which they saw as dominating continental, Catholic Europe.[18]

Other, seemingly adiaphoric, elements were also summoned by British-Israelists as indications of the distinctiveness of the British character. They strenuously argued, for example, against the introduction of metrication, seeing the imperial system as characteristically British. In part, this was based on the British-Israelist belief that the inch was a divinely inspired system of measurement that could be traced back to the construction of the pyramids.[19] 'Decimalization,' the 'European system of road-signs' and even 'the adoption of the breathalyser,' were seen as totems of Babylon which should be eschewed and resisted by Israelites. In 1970, Tony Benn confessed to treasuring a British-Israelist pamphlet that he had received, entitled 'The Battle for the Inch.'[20] The things that British-Israelists believe about the racial characteristics of British people are not necessarily peculiar to the British-Israelist movement. The British-Israelist explanation for the *origins* of the British people, on the other hand, is.

A theory of origins

At a lecture on the subject of British-Israelism, held in January 1920, one of the speakers proposed a foolproof method of proving that the people of Britain were not ethnically related to the people of Germany. 'The British hat,' the speaker proclaimed, 'will not fit a German head.' At the end of the lecture, the speaker was approached by an audience member, who asked whether a British hat would fit onto a Jewish head. The perplexed speaker came away from the talk determined to seek clarification on this question from the leaders of the British-Israelist movement. His letter to *The Banner of Israel*, the following week, garnered the following response:

> The English hat is certainly much more likely to fit a Jewish head than a German one because, as a general rule, German skulls are more round-headed.[21]

The central claim of the 'identity theory' rests on the assumption that ten of the tribes of Israel were lost. British people, according to this theory, are the descendants of those lost tribes. British-Israelism is – of course – not the only tradition which claims to have found the descendants of the lost tribes of Israel. Throughout the modern era, the Mormons of North America, the Beta Israel, Rastafarians and many other groups have made claims relating to the whereabouts of the lost tribes.[22]

All lost tribes traditions are rooted in Biblical and apocryphal writings. The primary source for the myth of the lost tribes is 2 Kings 17:6. In this text, the chronicler tells how the Israelites were taken into captivity by King Shalmaneser of Assyria. A proportion of the Israelites had been taken into captivity ten years earlier by King Tilgathpilneser. The Northern Kingdom – a confederation of ten of the twelve tribes of Israel including Asher, Dan, Ephraim, Gad, Issachar, Manasseh, Naphtali, Reuben, Simeon, and Zebulun – was destroyed. The Southern Kingdom, which comprised only the land of Judah and Benjamin, along with some remnants of Levi (a tribe which had no land allotment) survived. The lost tribes are not, from this point onwards, mentioned in the Hebrew Bible, but their movements were referred to in a variety of apocryphal and Talmudic sources.[23] Successive apocalyptic movements throughout the history of Christianity looked forward to the rediscovery of the lost tribes as an indication of the imminence of the end of days. Some believed that the affinity of Northern Europeans for Christianity indicated a fulfilment of the prophecies of Isaiah 66, in which God promises to send out the 'survivors' to convert the nations including the 'islands at the end of the earth.' Elsewhere, the prophet writes of the restoration of Israel, when the children of Israel will return to the land from 'afar . . . from the north and west.'[24]

British-Israelists extrapolated – from the Biblical texts and from ancient historical accounts – a detailed history of the journey of the lost tribes to the shores of Britain. In the words of the founder of the SPBI, Charles McKelvey:

> Israel after their carrying away to Assyria was lost to the world . . . after centuries of migration across Europe the tribes came in to our island home.[25]

Most British-Israelists subscribe to the belief that, after the capture of the Northern Kingdom by the Assyrians, a majority of the population of Israel migrated gradually North, eventually fragmenting into different ethnic groups but ultimately arriving in Britain over the course of several centuries and of several invasions. Most British-Israelists also subscribe to the claim that the people of Britain form one tribe of Israel, rather than the entirety of Israel. It is widely believed that Britain represents the tribe of Ephraim. The United States, meanwhile, is often associated with the tribe of Menasseh. As such, both are considered to be descendants of Joseph. On this basis, Britain, the United States and the Commonwealth nations of Australia, New Zealand and Canada represent the 'company of nations' described by Jacob in Genesis 48.[26] All of this served to fulfil prophecy. As L. Buxton Gresty wrote in 1976:

> It was to enable her to perform her world mission that the expansion to the ends of the earth was promised to Israel, a promise which has been abundantly vindicated only in the development of Celto-Saxon peoples. Their pioneering enterprise, under Divine urge, has produced the great daughter nations in the continents across the oceans.[27]

The people of Israel were to be scattered amongst the nations just as it was prophesied in Isaiah 49 and in Micah 5 ('The remnant of Jacob will be in the midst of many peoples like dew from the Lord, like showers on the grass'). Amongst the nations it was their duty to be a light and to await the ultimate restoration of Israel.

Aside from this, many British-Israelites claim that other Ancient Near Eastern tribes followed paths similar to those taken by the citizenry of the Northern Kingdom. The inhabitants of Russia, for example, were sometimes identified with the people of Assyria, who had migrated northwards in the first centuries of the common era. This alleviated the apparent anachronism of the many Biblical, apocalyptic prophecies which referred to the enmity between God's people and Assyria.[28] At the start of the British-Israelist movement, there was considerable controversy between its adherents on the question of whether Britain alone, or other nations also, constituted Israel. John Wilson, the originator of the doctrine presumed that Britain constituted the tribe of Ephraim and – as such – would take precedence in leading the other tribes, but that other European countries could also count Israelites amongst their populations.[29] In the late nineteenth century – and particularly with growing enmity between Britain and Germany – British-Israelists moved away from the Wilson position, towards (what was known as) an anti-Teutonist understanding of the doctrine.[30]

In the twentieth century, however, and particularly after the Second World War, there was a greater readiness amongst British-Israelists to extend the olive branch to other nationalist movements in Europe who claimed Israelitish heritage. Of these movements, the most popular was the Bond Nederlands. This group combined anti-immigrant rhetoric and anti-Semitic conspiracy theorising with the claim that the Dutch people represented the tribe of Zebulun. Zebulun, in the Biblical sources, is identified as the sixth son of Jacob and Leah. His descendants are scarcely mentioned in the Biblical narrative, but one prophetic claim is made in relation to them. When Jacob recounts his vision of the future to his sons, he states that Zebulun 'will live by the seashore and become a haven for ships.'[31] The members of the Bond Nederlands organisation professed the belief that this prophecy had been fulfilled by the maritime trading success of their nation. This identification was approved by British-Israelists and was re-affirmed in the pages of the British-Israelist journal *Bible Truth*:

> Zebulun will see the light first. Those in the Netherlands who are aware that this strange parallel is a true one, will behave as the children of Zebulun. Being cleansed, they will dwell safely and they will receive the grace of seeing the return of the light.[32]

Harold Stough, the Secretary of the BIWF, travelled to the Annual Congress of the Bond Nederlands Israel in 1952. The congress was held at Amersfoort on June 7. He was welcomed by the President, Dr J.F. Steenmejer, and by Mr Binnendijk and Mrs Gips-Smid.[33] In the 1970s, an emissary from the movement came to live in England and settled in Glastonbury. This was Helene Koppejan (née van Woelderen). In the early 1970s she published a short book and made a documentary film, both entitled *Strange Parallels*, which advocated the Zebulun claim.[34]

Similar claims were made by and on behalf of other northern European nations. In 1937, a Scot named Adam Rutherford delivered the 'national message' to the people of Iceland. Rutherford was a pyramidologist who wrote a text entitled *Israel Britain*, published in 1934. In 1937 he became convinced that a remnant of the tribe of Benjamin had reached Iceland and he explored this theme in a work entitled *Iceland's Great Inheritance*.[35] The book was translated into Icelandish and adapted by Jonas Gudmundsson in 1940.[36] Rutherford's mission to Iceland was taken up, in subsequent years, by a small number of devotees, led by Gudmundsson. Gudmundsson published a magazine throughout the 1950s entitled *Dagrenning*.[37] In 1980, the claims of the Nordic Israelists of Iceland were publicised in British-Israelist journals and two Icelandic emmisaries – Vigdis Jonsdottir and Margret Eggersdottir – were invited to speak at British-Israelist meetings in the UK.[38]

In each of these instances, British-Israelists adopted the position of associating themselves with the other nations in the Israel family of nations, whilst at the same time reaffirming the distinctiveness of Britain *from* the nations. The Israel 'family of nations' were drawn together by their Israel identity, but it also provided British-Israelists with the opportunity to express the uniqueness of Britain, even within the Israel family of nations. In the same claim, British-Israelists accentuate their similarity to Iceland, Holland, America – and, as we shall see later, Judah – *and* their difference from these nations. In addition, by making claims about the distinctive character of the other Israel nations, British-Israelists reaffirmed the authenticity of national distinctions in general.

The belief that Britain was the true identity of the lost tribes goes hand-in-hand with the claim that the Jewish people have no – or have only partial – right to identify with the Biblical polity of Israel. This claim is amongst the most widely discussed tenets of British-Israelist thought. Many British-Israelists (starting with John Wilson) have stridently made the case that the Jews are *not* Israel, but at best only a part of Israel, and that in all likelihood only *part* of the Jewish people represent that *part* of Israel. British-Israelists also subscribe to the claim that the Jewish people are themselves only partially descended from the twelve tribes of Israel. The purity of Judah had been compromised, throughout history, by intermarriage and miscegenation. Jewish people, British-Israelists point out, intermarried with the Edomites, the descendants of Esau, during the period of the Hasmonean dynasty.[39] As Juan Tebes' recent scholarship has demonstrated, the descendants of Esau played an important role in the cultural imagination of ancient Israel, initially during the period of the seventh and early sixth century but continuing up to the period of Roman occupation. The Edomites were an ethnic group constructed in Israelite literature as an antithesis of Israel. The Edomites played the role of scapegoat and were characterised as 'evil,' 'violent,' and of low status. At the same time, however, Israelite literature accentuated the filial nature of the relationship between Israel and Edom, developing a mythology which associated Edomites with the lineage of Esau, the twin brother of Jacob-Israel. Because Edomites were portrayed in Israelite culture as both fraternal and evil, it was possible – as in Amos 35 – to accuse them of treachery and betrayal, rather than simply violence. As Tebes and others (including Nicholas De Lange) have noted, 'the figure of Edom,' was 'used and reused . . . in different circumstances and for different reasons,' across many periods of Jewish history. A similar claim, as we shall see, can be made about the British-Israelist treatment of the Jewish people. Tebes, furthermore, argues that the initial impetus for the construction of the Edomite other was the fear of Israelite assimilation within the Assyrian empire, an empire which rested on strong notions of unified Assyrian cultural identity and which sought the erasure of ethnic particularity. The construction and use of an antithetical other, he suggests, allowed for the protection of a Jewish 'cultural nationalism' and would continue to function as a cultural resource in this way for many centuries.

British-Israelists also embrace the Khazar hypothesis, popularised in the mid-twentieth century by Arthur Koestler. This theory suggests that the majority of Ashkenazi Jews are descendants of the Khazars as the result of the mass conversion of the Khazars to Judaism during the eighth century, rather than being descendants of Biblical Israel.[40] Khazar theory has, in recent times, been adopted by a number of white nationalist, anti-Semitic groups.

Claims regarding the minority status of the Jewish people within the body of Israel were apparently vindicated when, on 18 November 1918, the Chief Rabbi Joseph Hertz wrote to Captain Merton Smith – then an officer of the BIWF – in response to the latter's questions about the genealogy of the Jewish people. The former made the following series of pronouncements:

1   The people known at present as Jews are descendants of the tribes of Judah and Benjamin with a certain number of descendants of the tribe of Levi.
2   As far as is known, there is not any further admixture of other tribes.
3   The ten tribes have been absorbed among the nations of the world.
4   We look forward to the gathering of the tribes at some future day.[41]

This letter was greeted with glee by British-Israelists and has been regularly cited in British-Israelist literature from 1918 until today.

Claims that Britain, and *not* the Jewish people, represent the true descendants of the ancient Biblical polity of Israel may appear to be fanciful. But the scholarship of Terence Ranger and Eric Hobsbawn has shown that invented lineage plays a role in the development of many more mainstream nationalist traditions. Whereas tradition – commonly conceived – constitutes '[that which is] transmitted or handed down from the past to the present,' more often than not it appears to form a reversal of this: a bequest from the present to the past.[42] Either 'by forgery . . . or by imagination,' nationalist groups appear to have a tendency to 'invent an ancient past,' as a way of responding 'to novel situations.' Here we find the apparently perennial phenomenon of invented traditions:

> which seek to inculcate certain values and norms of behaviour by establishing a sense of continuity with the past and an obligation to maintain such continuity with the past.[43]

In his essay on 'The Highland Tradition,' Hugh Trevor-Roper outlines the semi-mythological claims made by advocates and architects of Scottish nationalism. The nineteenth century saw concerted attempts by nationalists to construct a classically Caledonian, Ur-identity dating from the pre-Roman era. Patriotic fraudsters like James Macpherson presented an ancient Scottish *ethne* with its own classical culture. His fabricated epic, the Ossian cycle, presented the Highlanders as a *Kulturvolk* with an 'ancient, original and distinctive' tradition of dress, poetry and spirituality. These ideas seeped through the culture, reaching full efflorescence in the writings of Walter Scott and in the cultural phenomenon of King George IV's visit to Scotland in 1822 (during which the monarch was portrayed by David Wilkie in full Highland garb). The Sobieski Stuarts built their various theories regarding the origins of Scottish tribal origins, tartans and customs on these pseudo-historical claims. These in turn contributed to the surge in popular, Romantic Scottish nationalism during the nineteenth century.[44]

There is no great qualitative difference between the mythical conjuring of an ancient Caledonian past and the mythical conjuring of an ancient Israelitish past. Indeed there has always been an element of cross-pollenation between British-Israelism and these mainstream, invented traditions. The prominent Ulster Israelist Clifford Smyth builds on the dual influences of Edward Hine and John Sobieski in his lectures on the subject of the Israelitish traditions of the Scottish kilt.[45] Edith Clements used the belief that kilt-wearing was an ancient custom (rather than a nineteenth-century English novelty) in her theories regarding the Tyrian ancestry of the Scots. The 'invading nobility' who arrived in ancient Ireland from Asia Minor, she claimed, had been 'attired in garments made from Tyrian dyed cloth and rich brocades decorated with Greek and Eastern designs.'[46]

Genealogical connection with the past, whether real or mythological, lies at the heart of Walker Connor's analysis of national identity. In his *Ethnonationalism*, Connor identifies 'myths of ancestral origin' as a key motivating factor in the formation of salient national identities. Part of Connor's contribution has been to accentuate the more phenomenological nature of nationalism, demonstrating the importance of intangible qualities – like feelings of belonging, predictability, stability and (what social psychologists call) entitativity – over more material factors.[47] Connor's appreciation of the power of myth and story in promoting a sense of national entitativity is not lost on Anthony D. Smith. 'Myth refers not to a simple fiction,' Smith writes, 'but to a widely believed tale that legitimates present needs and concerns by reference to a heroic collective past that inspires emulation.'[48] 'In the making of nations,' Smith elsewhere claims 'it is not factual history but felt history that counts.'[49] The arch-nationalist Enoch Powell acknowledged that this was the case when he said that the 'life of nations no less than that of men is lived largely in the imagination.'[50] Even within British-Israel circles, believers were no less aware of the power of the stories they themselves were telling. In an article written in 1968, Gladys Taylor wrote that 'many speak disparagingly of tradition, that store of hero-tales and folklore preserved in all parts of the world.' Those who did, she claimed, were failing to appreciate that such tales constituted the 'racial memory' of a people.[51]

What follows, therefore, is in part an exploration of the distinction between a constructed classical past and a constructed Biblical past. What differences can we discern between the attitudes of a group which claims descent from Israel and a group which claims descent from Ancient Greece or Rome? 'Racial memory' tells us not about factual history but rather about felt history.[52] Amongst the first listed members of the Metropolitan Anglo-Israel Association was the 'Duke of Mantua.'[53] This appellation in fact refers to Charles Ottley Groom Napier. Napier was a geologist and mineralogist who became a prominent figure in the Geological Society of

London in the mid-nineteenth century. In his middle age, Napier began to style himself as the Duke of Mantua and commissioned the genealogist John O'Hart to draft a lengthy exposition of his lineage through the royal house of Mantua to King David. O'Hart, himself, claimed that the Irish were descendants of the Milesians. In Napier we find the personal embodiment of invented tradition. For Napier, the sense of a stable and authentic identity in the present could only be guaranteed with the invention of an ancient past.[54]

National election

One oft-cited aphorism describes British-Israelism as a form of 'jingoism with Biblical sanction.' There is much to recommend this description of British-Israelism. However, it fails fundamentally to fully appreciate the complexity of the British-Israelist conception of national election. As such, British-Israelists have continually have rejected the claim that national election serves to vindicate or validate jingoism. This rejection has been a perennial theme of British-Israel apologetics for a century and more. 'Many people object to the idea of a chosen race without pausing to think,' wrote A.J. Ferris in 1934:

> Their objection would be justified if God has selected Anglo-Saxons at the expense of other nations. But this is not the case. God has not just selected the Anglo-Saxon race in the twentieth century, but has been training and moulding the race for the last 3,000 years. The present eminent position of Britain and America in the world is not due to any superior ability of their own.[55]

Ferris' contention here is that, although Britain has been in God's plans for three thousand years, this period has not been one of unrelenting eminence. Britain had experienced periods of 'training' and 'moulding' at regular intervals. In a letter to *The Cornishman*, dated 14 August 1941, one R.G. Simpson declared:

> We believers in British Israel identity in no way deny that it is the will of God to extend His blessings to all nations and to all races . . . but to Israel, the servant nation among the nations, He appointed the national task of administering national blessings in the international world, a service clearly being afforded by Britain at the represent time.[56]

British-Israelists certainly do not believe that all Britons were saved *or* that only Britons would be saved. Nor do British-Israelists believe that the promise made by God to Britain-Israel was immutable. In 1942, the pseudonymous 'A.R.H.' published a detailed response to Dom Bede Frost who had, at an event sponsored by Archbishop George Bell, accused British-Israelists of espousing racist ideas. 'British-Israelism does not bolster up nationalism,' wrote the author 'but proclaims the ideal of the national life dedicated to the service of all mankind.'[57]

This rejection of the 'Smith model' was most pronounced during the years of the Second World War and the period immediately following it, when British-Israelists became increasingly skittish about possible associations being made between their movement and Nazi ideology. British-Israelists during the period of the war tried to dissociate themselves from the claim of British or white racial superiority. British-Israelism is not 'narrow nationalism or flag-wagging,' Charles McKelvey wrote.[58] One commentator stressed that 'it is perfectly clear from the teaching of the Bible that the Chosen Nation was not selected to be the *Herrenvolk* or Master Race but on the contrary to be a servant and witness.'[59] L. Buxton Gresty lamented the 'master race doctrine' in 1952, writing that

> the present generation has endured the sorrowful upheaval through the Master Race doctrine . . . Hitler worked upon the idea . . . until it so nauseated the democratic world that he and his fellows were rightly and roundly condemned by the sane people of all nations.[60]

William Graham dealt harshly with those who tarred Nazis and British-Israelists with the same brush. Nazism was 'conceived in the spirit of greed and animated by pride and arrogance,' whereas British-Israelism was 'conceived in the spirit of humility and sacrifice and elected for the serving of humanity.' Opponents of British-Israelism tended to 'make play on the word *chosen*,' in order to suggest that British-Israelists were 'emulating Germany and preaching a Herrenvolk doctrine.' Such attacks were 'designed to mislead the uninformed.'[61]

The post-war years saw a sustained period of decline in British imperial prestige and power. This period corresponded with a renewed commitment, amongst British-Israelists, to the argument that national chosenness and election could not be reduced to mere status or supremacy. If Britain was to be marginalised and pauperised – through the process of de-imperialisation – most believed that this was simply an opportunity for the renewal of Israel's 'splendid isolation.'[62] Biblical Israel was not a great imperial power. It was charged by the Lord God not to make a great empire but to maintain the coherence, the authenticity and the sovereignty of the people. P.T. Egerton imagined those who sought to undermine British-Israelist teaching, erroneously equating British-Israelism with British Imperialist chauvinism:

> 'Surely you cannot now believe that Britain is a chosen nation? She is fast becoming a third rate power.' Is there an answer to this? Britain is slowly moving towards an enforced position of isolation. We cannot help ourselves. . . . This is isolation, but it is God's isolationist policy to separate His people from the heathen.[63]

In May 1948, the readers of *Brith* were told, in fact, that Britain-Israel should *actively* shed itself of its imperial dependents. 'We should get out . . . and keep out,' wrote C.S. McKelvey.[64] In light of these texts, the claim that British-Israelism as an ideology is umbilically linked to the British imperialist project is somewhat problematic. It is important at this point to identify some key differences between the concept of national chosenness and the concept of imperialist supremacy.

At the outset it should be noted that conventional distinctions between religion and nationalism are not easily applicable to the phenomenon of British-Israelism. John Coakley, for example, recently made the claim that 'intrinsic characteristics of [religion] push in quite a different direction [from nationalism].' He cites, by way of example, the fact that 'religions are universalistic and transethnic; their orientation is towards the spiritual world rather than towards this world.'[65] Neither of these claims are entirely true of British-Israelism. Perhaps, then, British-Israelism could be characterised as a form of nationalism with metaphysical trimmings. The following characteristics of nationalism, identified by Mark Suzman, certainly have a great deal in common with the central claims of British-Israelism:

1 The world is naturally divided into nations, each with its own unique culture, normally based on language but sometimes on religion or other factors.
2 All people must belong to a nation.
3 All nations must seek full political autonomy.
4 Only within an independent nation can an individual find true spiritual and political fulfilment.
5 Only a world of free and sovereign nations can provide international order and stability.[66]

To take the earlier approach, however, would be to almost entirely occlude the influence of the Biblical tradition and the Protestant tradition on British-Israelism. This would be to occlude the elements of the movement which the members of the movement themselves claim is at the heart of their belief system.

In his writing on the subject of nationalism, Anthony D. Smith has long situated himself in opposition to the position held by modernists like Ernest Gellner, Elie Kedourie, John Breuilly and Benedict Anderson. Gellner presented nationalism as a 'rational response to the changes associated with modernisation and industrialisation.'[67] Nationalism, he believed, had replaced the previous, more local structures of belonging and identity, which were themselves identifiable with 'folk cultures' and religious affiliations.[68] As such, nationalism – for Gellner – is always preceded by the nation. Kedourie followed some aspects of Gellner's argument whilst claiming that the movement towards nationalism and away from pre-nationalistic modes of belonging was a product of the Enlightenment and thus was the project of an elite intelligentsia, rather than being atavistic or plebeian in origin.[69] Breuilly is somewhat more cautious than Kedourie in dissociating national- ism with ethnicity and with atavistic notions of collective belonging. None- theless, he claims that the 'key to an understanding of nationalism lies in the character of the modern state.'[70] Benedict Anderson, meanwhile, provides a slightly alternative view on the emergence of nationalism, positioning the rise of print and of the vernacular at the heart of his account.[71] Anderson notes the necessary finitude of nationalism as one of its main distinguishing features when compared with religion. 'The most messianic nationalists do not dream of a day when all the members of the human race will join their nation,' he writes, whilst it may be – or have been – possible 'for Christians to dream of a wholly Christian planet.' Of course, this understanding of Christianity does not apply easily to Protestantism. For those who subscribe to the Reformed Protestant soteriology, sanctified Christianity is as neces- sarily finite as any nation. This, in part, is the inheritance of a national understanding of election, a bequest of the Biblical history of Israel.

Smith dismisses many of these insights as resulting from – what he calls – 'modernist myopia.' In presuming the modern genesis of nationalism, they obfuscate the role played by religious sensibilities. Instead of assuming that nation-states preceded nationalism, Smith instead claims that nationalism originates in pre-national narratives of belonging which he calls the *ethne*. Smith argues that it is in fact 'impossible to grasp the meanings of nations and nationalism without an understanding of the link between religious motifs and rituals . . . memories and symbols.'[72] Smith does not argue that religious traditions provide the basis for nationalist movements. But nor does he suggest that religious forms of nationalism are simply strategic attempts by nationalists to co-opt religion. Rather, he suggests that nation- alistic sentiments grow organically out of shared identifications with faith and ritual culture, 'producing a new synthesis,' which – in facing the chal- lenges of modernity and indeed post-modernity – 'draws strength and inspi- ration . . . from older religious beliefs, moral sentiments and sacred rites.'[73] A particular focus of Smith's research are those narratives which promote the concept of 'chosen peoples.' Smith identifies two positions within this tendency. The first – which requires that the nation turn outward to con- tribute to the redemption of all humanity – he labels *missional* election. The second – which requires that the people turn inwards and fortify themselves against any corruption of the sacred, holy and unique people – is *covenantal* election. The boundaries and borderlines of the nation – both territory and polity – must be closely guarded. There must be no permeable membranes. Many nations adopt elements of both of these positions or oscillate between the two. As Smith points out, the origins of these narratives originate – for many cultures – in the Bible. The Hebrew Bible presents the separation of the sacred from the profane – food, people, nations, days, land – into discrete categories as a principal concern of the chosen people. Moreover, it presents the survival of the chosen people and their ritual and ethnic identifiers as a divinely mandated task.[74] The act of separating functions as a ritualisation of the separation of peoples. By maintaining a sense of uniqueness, the chosen people simultaneously maintain a sense of continuity with the past which – by extension – promises hope for survival in the future:

> The thought here is that, because we are both ancient and unique, we have within us that which can regenerate us, if only we return, in a true national spirit, to our spiritual roots. . . . The true battle is within. . . . It is not primarily a struggle with the alien oppressor or with adverse circumstances, which are the rods of degradation meted out to us, as the ancient prophets would have said; but with ourselves, a cultural and psychological struggle to overcome inner burdens.[75]

Meanwhile, the threat of inauthenticity, of the submergence of the authentic people in a homogeneous swamp of humanity, remains a constant. In the twentieth century, British-Israelists would read regular warnings of the rise of 'the mass man.'[76]

The model for the British-Israelist chosenness narrative is the Biblical polity of Israel. The Hebrew Bible provides several interlacing narratives which explore the notion of God's preferential option for the people of Israel. Several themes emerge from these sources. The covenant made by God with Abraham is conditional. God expresses His love for His peculiar people, but equally He articulates demands, in the form of a vassal treaty, to which the people of Israel must comply if they are to receive His patronage and protection.[77] In Leviticus, God promises that, should Israel 'abhor His commandments,' He will 'bring upon [them] a sudden terror, wasting diseases and fevers.'[78] The prophetic writings of the Hebrew Bible provide a spate of examples of God punishing and rescinding His obligations to Israel on the basis that Israel has broken the covenant. In Ezekiel 16, Isaiah 24, Hosea 8, Joshua 7 and Jeremiah 11, Israel stands accused of 'foresaking God's commandments.' As such, the nature of Israel's chosenness stands primarily in their having been 'taken from among the nations' not necessarily to enjoy special privileges but rather to be held to a different standard *than* the nations.[79] Indeed, the chosenness of Israel – as described in the Hebrew Bible – does not correspond with an image of national supremacy. Israelite chosenness often brought with it hardship and suffering. Israel falls to the Assyrians, then to the Babylonians and then to the Romans. British-Israelists knew this well. 'Any nation chosen for use by God stands to gain either great blessing or terrible judgement,' wrote Monty White, in 1972, 'depending on how they react to him.' If they react badly, then God will 'use non-Israelite peoples to punish Israel for her sins.'[80] Israel's triumphs lie in her resistance to domination – this being personified in the figures of Daniel and Ezra – rather than in conquering others. Indeed, God's election of Israel often results in God *using* other nations in order to punish His people. God appoints the armies of Assyria to chastise the Northern Kingdom for her infidelity. God uses Nebechudnezzar to punish Judah because Judah had not listened to His word.[81] As Donald Akenson demonstrated in his work on *God's Peoples*, the fundamental unfalsifiability of the claim of chosenness allows it to flourish in all kinds of conditions. Good fortune and misfortune are explicable in the same light.[82]

In the age of Christianity, the election of Israel was believed by most Christians to have been superseded by the election of the Church through the atoning sacrifice of Christ. The origins of this claim lie in St Paul's letter to the Galatians. In the third chapter of Galatians, Paul describes the Law as a 'guardianship' which was in place until the incarnation. After the incarnation 'we are no longer under this guardian,' Paul wrote.[83] As such, there was no longer 'Jew nor Gentile' as distinguished by the Law. The doctrine of supersession was shored up in the patristic era, with stark distinction made between God's 'carnal covenant' with the Jews and the 'spiritual covenant' with the Church. As such, Biblical references to the eschatological destiny of Israel were reattributed to the Church.[84]

British-Israelists reject the principle of supersessionism. They argue that God's election of Israel was never rescinded but was rather consummated in the incarnation. 'Replacement theology,' they argue, was an innovation 'from Rome.'[85] This commitment has required British-Israelists to develop an unorthodox model of soteriology which facilitates a form of justification by faith alongside an emphasised form of national election.

Protestants have held differing views of the nature of national election since the period of the Reformation. One of the most important interventions on this subject was made by John Calvin in his commentary on St Paul's letter to the Romans. Paul, in the ninth chapter of Romans, recalls the first of Malachi, in which the Lord God says: 'Jacob have I loved, Esau have I hated.' In his gloss of this passage, Calvin identifies Jacob as a synecdoche of the people of Israel. God – according to Calvin – opts to elect the people of Israel *as a whole*. But this is not to say that the people of Israel are all equally recipients of salvation. The nation includes the tares as well as the wheat. Secondly, Calvin notes that 'the general election of a people is not always effectual and permanent.' Nor does the national election contain within it the power of regeneration which enables the elect saint 'to persevere in the covenant to the end.' Nowhere – for Calvin – is this more evident than in the falling away of the Jewish people in their failure to recognise the messiah. This does not, for Calvin, necessarily mean that the covenantal relationship with Israel as a whole is rescinded, because national election and the election of grace were *always* non-identical. In short, for Calvin, nations were elected by God to a specific task. This does not correspond with any earthly glory, it did not require that all members of that nation were themselves elect and nor did it suggest that such an election was eternally binding or unconditional.[86]

The history of Reformed Protestantism in the Anglosphere has long been influenced by the Calvinist notion of national election.[87] During the early modern period, the political schism between Catholic and Protestant states in Europe intensified. England was 'thrust into the frontline against the European counter-reformation.'[88] Smith argues that national identities began to develop in line with feelings of allegiance to Protestant kings. This corresponded, in the English context, with the passing of the Act of Supremacy.[89] At the same time, British Protestants became more Biblicist, with 'the Puritan community and its elders,' engaging in 'more intensive study of the Old Testament.'[90] One element that Smith elides in his analysis is the development and proliferation of Reformed Protestant soteriology. Whereas the Church had been presented as truly catholic, in pre-Reformation culture, the influence of Calvinism engendered a view of humanity as strictly divided. This was not an equal division. Humanity, by the eternal decree of election, was divided into a Godly minority and a Godless majority. The notion that England was a nation chosen by God for a special purpose had long been part of English culture, but this narrative moved to the fore as England's involvement in the various religious conflicts of the early modern era intensified. Calvin's concept of an elect nation became increasingly influential during this period, never more so than in the 'last war of religion': the English Civil War.[91] The depiction of the Protestant people of England as Israel and of Cromwell as Moses was a powerful and mobilising image in the seventeenth century.[92] In the hands of the Godly, as Achsah Guibbory points out, 'Israel was redefined in a way that threatened those in power.'[93] Anthony Smith himself notes that:

> [The] return to the Old Testament in the radical Reformist versions, notably Calvinism, reintroduced the covenantal model, so long a theological concept, into the political mainstream. . . . The covenantal ideal and the Exodus narrative, vividly conveyed in the vernacular Bible, came to provide the dynamic for radical change in the quest for individual salvation and collective election – including the election of nations.[94]

Once again, however, this model must be carefully defined against a simplistic model of supremacist nationalism. The vision of the Protestant people as a chosen people, as it was described in Godly literature of the seventeenth century, did *not* assert the claim that Britain would experience unconditional divine favour. Indeed, as Alexandra Walsham, Patrick Collinson, Andrew Camber, Peter Lake and many other historians of this period have demonstrated, the description of Godly sanctity as described by Calvinist clerics in Britain during the seventeenth century was a description of hardship, marginalisation and suffering at the hands of a wicked world. Partly this attitude is rooted in a Reformed Protestant soteriology which promotes the claim that the incarnation and crucifixion of Christ served to atone for the sins of a small minority of the elect, whilst the rest of the world remained mired in sin. As Collinson writes, therefore, Protestants in the early modern period required the affirmation that could be attained through opposition and antagonism to 'the world.'[95] Alexandra Walsham notes that Puritans found the 'experience of persecution' to be 'immensely empowering.'[96] Furthermore, Walsham argues that the experience of being 'the objects of verbal mockery and civil ostracism' was in some sense 'psychologically affirming.' In the interests of pursuing this psychological affirmation, she claims, the Godly tended towards the 'cultivation of crises.'[97] Being chosen, as the words of Puritan minister Stephen Denison to his flock demonstrate, meant suffering, hardship and isolation, not glory and prestige. In 1619, Denison defined 'the Godly' as 'those who are evil spoken of in every place.'[98] As Collinson wrote: 'the experience of oppression, real or imagined, provided necessary evidence of election.' Nor is it true that the self-image of 'the saints' in Protestant culture associated Godliness with power. This 'identity of powerlessness' was a significant component of the experience of many of the Godly, as it was for many of the early Christians and for many of the Jews of the Second Temple period.[99] This same conflation of chosenness with suffering and isolation informed the view that the early Puritan inhabitants of America had of themselves. America was to be a shining city on a hill but, if so, it was to be so in its exemplification of God's unerring justice. It would be a place of hardship and suffering if God so willed, and it would be a place of glory and majesty if God so willed. As James Bratt writes, the nature of national election was, for the American Puritans, 'as much a cause for lament as for celebration.' The providential hardships endured by the seventeenth-century inhabitants of New England were cited as evidence of God's adoption of them as His people.[100] The notion that Protestants who believe their nation to be chosen, believe that their nation is exempt from divine ire is – in other words – wholly false.

In his exploration of the phenomenon of Christian Zionism, Andrew Crome places great emphasis on the distinction between chosenness and supremacy. Crome points out that the model of a nation chosen and blessed by God, immutably and eternally, could lead to fatalism. The Biblical model of chosenness – however – does not make this offer. The chosen people are blessed only contingently on their own obedience. Therefore:

> Although this model guaranteed the nation a prominent eschatological role through prophecy, this did not reduce fear of the loss of this status to mere rhetoric. Anxiety over national election was common, and it could cause serious distress. Conversely, it could also act as a powerful impetus for reform and provide hope for the future . . . this encouraged proponents to political engagement.[101]

The same is true of British-Israelists and helps to cast some light on their social conservativism and political activism. After all, if British-Israelists believed that the covenant between God and Israel was immutable and unconditional, they would be more likely to move towards antinomianism than moralism. As Monty White warned, if Israel did not accept her covenant with God, she would suffer a terrible punishment.

Even during periods when British national prestige was at its nadir, the British-Israelist faith continued unabated. Indeed, British-Israelists accentuated Britain's lowly status, engaging in what David Edgerton calls declinism. This phenomenon was noted in the mid-twentieth century by Professor John Wilson.[102] As such, to use the taxonomy proposed by Anthony Smith, the British-Israelist movement – long understood to be an epiphenomenon of missional imperialism – at times exhibited an enthusiastic covenantal nationalism. This enthusiasm was fuelled by a conviction that Britain's sense of national entitativity and salience was bolstered by hardship rather than being defeated by it. In this, British-Israelism exemplifies what Smith refers to as 'a cult of authenticity.'[103]

Authenticity

All ethno-nationalist movements exhibit an obsession with promoting the authenticity and the salience of the nation over and above the supremacy of the nation. This attitude – according to Smith – is best exemplified by Herder's exhortation to the Prussian people:

> Let us follow our own path . . . let all men speak well or ill of our nation, our literature, our language: they are ours, they are ourselves, that is enough.

Authenticity stands for that which is

> true, genuine, sincere, inward . . . unmixed, pure and essential . . . simple, rude, unaffected . . . original, rooted, pristine and autochthonous . . . particular, distinctive and individual . . . expressive, originating, inner-determined and self-determining.

It stands opposed to all that is 'rootless, stale, anxious, derivative [and] cosmopolitan.'[104] For British-Israelists, authenticity is of foremost concern.

The nature of the chosenness narratives of the Hebrew Bible conforms, in many ways, to this understanding of authenticity. Claims of authenticity speak to clear boundaries and taxonomies, the avoidance of confusing or mixing. Many of the injunctions in the Hebrew Bible abjure the devotee to maintain strict categories: separating the Sabbath from the working week, separating the sacred from the profane, the meat from the milk, the priest from the people and – indeed – the priestly people from 'the nations.' The most influential contribution to our understanding of this attitude as expressed in the sacred literature of the Hebrew Bible has come from the work of Mary Douglas. Douglas demonstrated – most famously in her 1966 work *Purity and Danger* – that concepts of purity in ancient Israel were not primitive modes of food sanitation but were, rather, the symbolic maintenance of boundaries.[105] As recent work by Jonathan Klawans and Daniel Weiss has shown, the desire to maintain separation of different elements should not be read as suggestive of a hierarchy. Sacred and 'common' according to Klawans, should not be equated to 'good' and 'bad.' Klawans points out that the Biblical concept of 'purity' is best bifurcated into more accurate concepts of 'ritual purity' and 'moral purity.' Neither, necessarily, provoke sentiments of abjection: whilst the former is *contagious* it is not, necessarily, valuational; whilst the latter is negatively valued, it is not contagious. As Weiss points out, these themes do not necessarily entail a need to eliminate or eradicate otherness. Impurity is not necessarily something that must be 'expelled' or 'repressed' but rather something that can be 'lived alongside.' Genesis 7 specifically notes that 'unclean animals' are *rescued* from obliteration. Participation in sacrificial worship required separation of the devotee from those aspects of human existence most alien to the Godhead: sex and death.[106] At other times – of course – the Israelites were enjoined to come into contact with sex and death. In performing these duties of separation, the ancient Israelites created – what Klawans calls – 'a productive expression of religious ideals.'[107]

If this is the case, then we can further claim that the presence of the impure is *essential* for the practice of separation. To paraphrase Bauman, impurity is 'the one enemy without which order cannot live.' Furthermore, we can assert that the *act* of separation is the intrinsic good.[108] This may also be extended to the understanding of Israel in the Bible. Read through the lens provided by the analysis of Klawans, Weiss and Douglas, we can understand the covenantal nationalism of biblical Israel as *intrinsically* good in that it maintains a form of order whereby the sacred (in this case the chosen people) is kept separate from the profane (the nations). This is nowhere more obviously expressed in the Hebrew Bible than in the story of the returning people's Passover after the period of exile in Babylon, which is found in the book of Ezra. The Jews who have returned to Jerusalem from exile in Babylon confess to Ezra that they have married people of other nations: Ammonites, Hittites, Jebusites, Perizzites, Moabites and Egyptians. At this news, Ezra tears his cloak in two, pulls hair from his beard and sits down, appalled. Of this passage, Smith writes that:

> For Jews and other covenanted peoples, the sense of ritual and moral exclusiveness always counterbalanced the usual pressures of acculturation and assimilation.[109]

Nowhere does this narrative necessarily entail that the nations should themselves be punished or destroyed for their ways. The abomination described here is the mixture of the sacred and the profane, rather than the existence of the profane.

As we have already noted, these themes of holiness, separation and authenticity proved particularly influential in the radical Protestant movements of the early modern era, when the English Protestant mentality began to emerge. John Norden wrote that 'since the beginning of the church God hath bin farre the least part of the world.' Perhaps even more discomfortingly, God was with the 'least part of each congregation.'[110] Calvinist soteriology stressed the irresistible, unconditional, absolute nature of the divine decree of predestination and the strict, binary and irreducible distinction between the elect and the reprobate. 'Can there be greater antipathy,' asked Joseph Bentham, 'than betwixt God's saints and Satan's slaves? God's darlings and Satan's dross?'[111] This same attachment to the ethic of separation and Godly authenticity informs much British-Israelist literature also, in particular in the British-Israel understanding of nationhood.

Britain is presented, in British-Israelist literature, as priestly, holy and alone. In one article, written for *The National Message* in the 1960s, Michael Hart compared the isolation of the British people, as an island nation, to the isolation of Christ before Pilate; the isolation of Elijah on Mount Carmel; the isolation of Paul before Caesar; of Luther before the Diet of Worms.[112] Separation from the other nations was necessary for the maintenance of authenticity. As such it was an intrinsic good. 'Old Testament authors describe Israel as being a peculiar people,' wrote one British-Israel author, 'the word holy means *separate from*.'[113] 'National culture must be singular,' wrote another in 1929: '[this is] of the utmost importance.'[114]

This attachment to the authentic (unmixed, pure and essential, simple, rude, unaffected, original, rooted, pristine and autochthonous, particular, distinctive and individual) as a central and devotional concern also informed the attitude held by British-Israelists to other nations and other groups. Other groups which helped to maintain the authentic character of the nations, thereby maintaining boundaries between discrete categories, are understood to be good. Other bodies or organisations which sought to erode the boundaries between nations are seen as bad. The Jewish people are regarded as kindred insofar as they maintain marks of authentic identification, but they are treated with suspicion insofar as they relinquish these marks of distinctiveness. So, for example, orthodox Jewish people are praised by British-Israelists for maintaining rituals and practices which define them as singular. Secular Jews are criticised for *merging* Gentile and Jewish practices and sensibilities. As one writer claimed, in 1964:

> Adherence [to the Biblical Law] is in the process of being shaken. If it is destroyed, the very reason for the continued existence of the Jewish community will cease to be for its people will be just like those of any other group or country.[115]

This claim is – not untypically – couched in pseudo-scientific terms in British-Israelist writing. Those who maintain orthodox traditions are sometimes considered to be true inheritors of the lineage of Judah, whilst secular Jews are considered to be the miscegenate descendants of Edom-Israel intermarriage.[116] Anti-Semitism is often considered to be a form of xenophobia. But in British-Israelist literature, Jewish people are praised and honoured when they exhibit behaviours which are perceived to be 'different,' mocked and slandered when they exhibit behaviours which appear to be too similar to Christianity.

There is a secondary reason for this desire to maintain boundaries between nations – particularly in the case of the Jews. Andrew Crome points out that the separation of the Jewish people from the nations plays an important confirmatory role for all Christians who subscribe to a providential reading of geo-politics. This includes Christian Zionists as well as British-Israelists. The maintenance of Jewry as a separate category, a separate nation, not only perpetuates the Biblical topos of Israel's particularity but also serves to support the claim that God *in general* works through nations in order to fulfil His will. Indeed we may say, more broadly, that authenticity anywhere is a bulwark for authenticity everywhere.

Equally, a threat to authenticity anywhere is a threat to authenticity everywhere. For this reason, throughout the twentieth century, the principle targets of British-Israelist ire were those bodies which were perceived as being intent on eroding national authenticity: the League of Nations, the European Union, the United Nations, the Arab League, the USSR, the World Council of Churches and more.[117]

Just as the ancient Israelites had done, British-Israelists see clear parallels between the sacred separation of Israel from the nations and the ritual observances which also served as 'productive expressions' of this important sensibility.[118] So, for example, in 1929, one British-Israelist commentator expressed the view that Protestant observation of the separation of the Sabbath day was a mirror image of Britain's expected separation from the League of Nations:

> [Israel] is a Separation subject. The British have their separate Island homes. . . . By law they separate a seventh of their time for holy things. They fight til they win to maintain separate nationality. They will eventually separate themselves from the League of Nations.[119]

Seventy-five years later, precisely the same parallel was drawn by a British-Israel author in the pages of *Bible Truth* (the journal of the British Israel Bible Truth Foundation): 'a holiday derives from a day separate from all the rest . . . in the same way . . . the peoples of Israel belong exclusively to God.'[120]

British-Israelist apocalypticism

'Come out of her my people.' These words, heard from the host of heaven by St John the Divine, and recorded in the eighteenth chapter of his Revelation, have resounded through the writings of Protestant devotees for centuries.

They appear again and again in British-Israelist descriptions of the relationship between Britain and the UN, the EU and the Catholic Church.[121] The image of the people of Israel, battling the global 'Babylon system,' is central to the eschatology of British-Israelism.

Separation and authenticity form the centre of British-Israelist thought in general and British-Israelist apocalypticism in particular. More often than not, British-Israelists drew connections between the Catholic Church and these agents of *in*authenticity. The Catholic Church – in British-Israelist as in much radical Protestant literature – was presented as Babylon: the imperial power which sought to subdue, to swamp, to deracinate, to assimilate or to submerge Israel.[122] As such, British-Israelists saw Popish intrigue behind many of the projects which appeared to have the same goal in mind. The Pope and the Catholic Church were the 'makers of mass man.'[123] The 'Celto-Saxon nations of the West,' British-Israelists believe, are constantly threatened by those who wish to promote the 'internationalist dogma' which necessarily excludes 'any thought that Almighty God could be dealing with peoples collectively in their nation-state family and racial groupings.'[124] The advocates of this dogma, British-Israelists claim, were the devotees of an apostate World Religion. As such, the European Economic Community represented 'the threat of internationalism and the apostate one world religion under the primacy of the Pope.'[125] The Pope was also perceived to have many 'vehicles of his strategy' including 'the UN, the World Bank, The World Trade Organisation, NATO . . . all working tirelessly to establish their One-World Government.'[126]

All of this proved problematic for British-Israelists during the period of British imperial ascendancy. The Empire – and later the Commonwealth – was a project which appeared to promote rather than prevent the intermingling of the chosen people with the nations. When the age of Empire began to wane, therefore, British-Israelists were more than prepared to welcome this development as a resumption of Israel's sacred separation from the nations and a resumption of covenantal Israelite authenticity. This, for many British-Israelists, assured them that the apocalypse was imminent. From the mid-twentieth century onwards, British-Israelist literature became far more focussed on eschatological themes.

But British-Israelists were not alone in expressing this sentiment in the face of imperial decline. The recent scholarship of David Edgerton, amongst others, has clearly delineated the historical and cultural parameters between two oft-conflated phenomena: British imperialist patriotism and British nationalist patriotism. British-Israelists read these same events through a providential lens and expressed these same feelings in providential language.

Conspiratorial thinking

The last identifying characteristic of British-Israelism which appears to pervade all of the narratives with which the majority of this book will be taken up is an affinity for conspiracy theories. The work of Michael Barkun demonstrates that conspiratorial thinking often elevates the significance of so-called 'stigmatised knowledge.' Stigmatised knowledge may refer to marginalised or pseudo-scientific theories (including astrology, numerology, UFOs or alternative medicines) or to parallel explanations of geo-political or geographical events. Often, those who gravitate towards stigmatised theories are seeking ultimately for master narratives which will explain the apparently chaotic unravelling of history. For this reason, Barkun sees the rise in conspiratorial thinking – which often posits the existence of clandestine forces secretly orchestrating world events – as being effected by the ending of the previous, all-encompassing master-narrative of geo-politics: the Cold War.

Barkun believes that most conspiratorial thinkers are drawn to conspiracies via 'bridging mechanisms,' linking unconventional beliefs with conventional modes of political expression. Interest in one area of stigmatised knowledge soon stimulates interest in 'stigmatised material on a broad range of subjects.' As such, 'stigmatised knowledge is a unified domain, an alternative worldview, rather than just a collection of unrelated ideas.'[127] British-Israelist genealogy could be identified as a form of stigmatised knowledge and – as such – it is not surprising that British-Israelists would also gravitate towards other forms of such thinking. British-Israelists have, for example, consistently given credence to the validity of the Archko Volume.[128] The Archko Volume was a forgery, published at the end of the nineteenth century by an American clergyman named William Dennes Mahan. It purported to include contemporary accounts of the life of Jesus, most notably the details of Jesus' trial before Pontius Pilate. The forgery was poorly done and was soon discovered. Mahan was summoned before an ecclesiastical court and was convicted of falsehood in 1885.[129] Nevertheless, British-Israelists continued to tacitly exonerate Mahan, referring to the Archko Volume long into the twentieth century.[130]

In a similar vein, some elements within the British-Israelist community continued to pay credence to *The Protocols of the Elders of Zion*. As late as 1945, the leader of the SPBI suggested that the notorious hoax was valid. It highlighted a 'subjugation and enslavement of mankind.' McKelvey noted that the text had 'foretold with remarkable accuracy the events and trends in world affairs.' The plot would be 'worldwide in its application,' although the 'impact upon Israel would be less severe than on other nations.'[131] McKelvey mused that 'racial Judah' was 'a great fifth column,' which had brought into existence the United Nations Organisation, the better to fulfil its ends.[132]

Equal credence was lent to an equally discredited document: Jacopo Leone's *The Secret Plan*. The publication of this text became a *cause celebre* in the late nineteenth century. The text purported to be written by a disgruntled monsignor who wished to expose the diabolical schemes for world domination which were being hatched by the Society of Jesus. The book was edited by a Fourierist and member of the Council of the Seine named Victor Prosper Considerant. Considerant referred to the Jesuits as a 'mysterious army at the service of obscurantism, despotism, and social retrogradation.'[133] Not unlike *The Protocols of the Elders of Zion*, this text claimed to expose the secret workings of shadowy forces which orchestrated world politics from behind the scenes. It included a transcript of a 'Secret Conference' of Jesuit priests at which the leader of the group – Luigi Fortis – lays out the Jesuits' plan for world domination:

> We need fear no lack of soldiers, only let us apply ourselves to recruiting them from all ranks. . . . But let us at the same time be vigilant, that no one suspect our design.

A second Jesuit – 'with a soft and drawling voice' – responds to this with the following:

> Yes! Let us incessantly and unweariedly propagate our doctrines among the people; warmed by the fire of these doctrines, they will become changed for us into thunderbolts to strike down these haughty kings.

The National Message compared the book to *The Protocols of the Elders of Zion*. Like the *Protocols*, it was a 'document of darkness' which exhibited the 'modern revolutionary tendencies' of international Jesuitism. It exposed the fact that Jesuits were culpable for the rise of Hitler and the 'murders of Auschwitz, Belsen and Buchenwald.'[134] The text was the basis of Stanley Herron's claim – in 1991 – that 'the Papacy sent disguised Jesuit priests into the Church of England . . . to bring it Romeward.'[135]

But whereas British-Israelists found common cause with the French socialist Victor Considerant in their shared suspicion of the motivations of the global Jesuit conspiracy, they more often than not presented the French Revolution as the product of that same international conspiracy and as an event which created the fountainhead for innumerable other 'internationalist' conspiracies. British-Israelists identify Adam Weishaupt as the originator and orchestrator of a global conspiracy to dismantle national sovereignty in the interests of promoting global government. They point out that Weishaupt – who founded the Illuminati Order – was educated by Jesuits. The ideas promoted by his secret organisation were disseminated first amongst the French revolutionaries and latterly amongst the Bolshevik revolutionaries. As such, they drew a common lineage from Jesuitism to *sans-cullotism* to Bolshevism. This theory was propounded by W.F. Finlayson, in an article of 1976 entitled 'The Satanic Origins of Bolshevism.'[136] Some traced the origins of this 'World Revolution Ideology' further back than the writings of Weishaupt. Clifford Smyth, writing in 1968 on the subject of communism and the occult, claimed that 'further investigation of the official communist philosophy of Dialectic Materialism will reveal that this theory is a rehash of the fundamental tenets of the ancient Mysteries of Egypt.'[137] Others broadened the definition of Weishauptism to include not only Jesuits, French Revolutionaries and Bolshevists but also EU federalists. In 2003, Bob Lomas wrote that 'the European Union is based on the Soviet collectivist totalitarian principle, the origins of which reach back to the doctrine of Adam Weishaupt.'[138]

In the late twentieth century, British-Israelists took to conspiracy theories with greater and greater zeal. Perhaps the most influential figure in this drift towards conspiracy theories was Matthew Browning, who would serve as President of the BIWF until 2007. In BIWF publications of the 1990s, there are frequent references to a new world order, designed to undermine the sovereignty of the Israel nations (not including the state of Israel). Browning critiqued the model of free-market capitalism that allowed for the existence of a wealthy, stateless elite: 'the Warburgs, Rothschilds, Schiffs, Lehmans, Melchiors, Hambros and Mayers.'[139] The 'new world order' and its scion, the 'mass man,' was seen as answerable for any of the ills of British society that British-Israelists identified.[140] On the occasion of the resignation of Margaret Thatcher, Pastor Alan Campbell wrote that 'Thatcher, like so many world leaders before her, had outlived her usefulness to her political masters.' In her opposition to Maastricht, Campbell believed, '[Thatcher] had become an obstacle to the creation of their New World Order.'[141]

Browning believed that representatives of these powerful entities were meeting in Turnberry in 1998, as part of the Bilderberg conference. Another *Wake Up* writer, Alistair McConnachie, was sent to Turnberry to investigate, and he published his report in the magazine in June 1998.[142] From 1991, *The British Israel World Federation Quarterly* began reprinting content that had been originally published in *The Spotlight*.[143] *The Spotlight* was a weekly paper published in the United States by the Liberty Lobby from 1975 until the dissolution of the Lobby in 2001. Its content tended to focus on 'anti-elitist' and 'anti-statist' politics, from a libertarian, nationalist, anti-globalist platform. In the 1980s, it was considered by the Anti-Defamation League to be the most widely read periodical of the 'fringe right.' The Liberty Lobby was established by Willis Carto and Jim Tucker in the early 1970s. It worked to promote ideas and theories which correspond to (what Michael Barkun has called) 'stigmatised knowledge': alternative medicines, JFK assassination conspiracy theories, UFOs.[144] *Spotlight* promoted claims that 'Anne Frank's diary was a fraud' and that 'Jew-Zionist bankers' were conspiring against 'hard-working blue-collar Americans.'[145] Conspiracy theorising often defies categorisation in traditional political terms. So, whilst British-Israelist theorising took on a hue which we might usually associate with the political right, their understanding of the nature of global governance often saw them aligning themselves with arguments and figures from the traditional left. In 2001, Michael Clark complimented Jon Ronson's television documentary, *Secret Rulers of the World*. Clark applauded Ronson for exposing the Bilderberg group: 'a notorious group of bankers, politicians, industrialists and media moguls, which has been meeting annually since 1954 to decide what happens in the world.'[146] Two years later, Matthew Browning suggested that Dick Cheney's business concerns provided the real explanation for the bombing of the World Trade Centre.[147]

There is here, I believe, a connection with a deeper aspect of British-Israelism. Critical perspectives on the phenomenon of conspiracy theorising have developed over recent decades. The phenomenon itself was partly defined by analytic philosophers like Karl Popper, looking for classic examples of unfalsifiable belief systems. In the mid-twentieth century, Adorno's conception of the 'authoritarian personality' helped to shape attitudes to conspiratorial thinking and also facilitated the pathologisation of those who avowed conspiracy theories as paranoiacs. More recently, scholars have taken a more social-psychological approach, with Joseph Uscinski arguing that conspiracy theories provide refuge for those who feel marginalised within conventional structures, offering them an alternative value system. Eric Oliver has shown that conspiracy theories are most commonly found amongst those who see the world in Manichean terms, as a cosmic battle between good and evil.[148]

In both cases, we can identify conspiracy theorising as a form of entitativity. Those who hold to unfalsifiable beliefs tacitly affirm the irreducible nature of their kinship with those who share their stigmatised beliefs. This attitude is qualitatively identifiable with the affirmation of kinship that is shared amongst those who share mystical or gnostic beliefs. Meanwhile, the world is presented in a way which accentuates insiderliness and outsiderliness. Attempts by the out-group majority to dispute the validity of these claims with reference to any conventional, rational laws or norms are inevitably unsuccessful. They are nomological danglers. As such, the shared affirmation of unfalsifiable truth claims serve to confirm and to bolster feelings of entitativity amongst those who share them. Seen in these terms, conspiracy theories are really the gnostic expressions of those who wish to belong in some way.

The conspiracy theories which British-Israelists are drawn to include a kernel of stigmatised knowledge encased in an explanation for their own unverifiability. There is another reason for the apparent correlation between British-Israelism and conspiracy theorizing. As Oliver has shown, conspiracy theories inevitably function as expressions of enmity between a marginal or supposedly marginalised group and an imagined global force. The former – almost inevitably – expresses kinship with some easily identifiable social, ethnic, racial or national group, whilst the latter eschews any sense of belonging in lieu of a globalist, rootless, deracinated inauthenticity.

Conclusion

A complex range of characteristics define the British-Israelist milieu. British-Israelists have a tendency to embrace conspiracy theories and to avow what

Michael Barkun has dubbed 'stigmatised knowledge.' They are almost invariably socially conservative. They believe in a British national character which is composed of Protestantism, monarchism and the rule of law. Although these elements may appear to be disparate, they conform to a particular purpose. Each element serves to accentuate the authenticity of the group and the fidelity of the group to the deity. As such, these elements are not radically different from the ritual practices of the Biblical polity of Israel. This chapter has not described any chronological progression in the story of British-Israelism, but rather has identified perennial characteristics of the movement. In the following section, we trace the history of British-Israelism from its origins in the nineteenth century up to the present day.

Notes

1   Kidd, *The Forging of Races*, 272.
2   Alexander Crawford, *Creed of Japhet* (Beccles: William Clowes, 1891); Alexander Crawford, *Progression by Antagonism* (London: Murray, 1846), 42.
3   Archibald Sayce, *The Races of the Old Testament* (London: Religious Tract Society, 1891), 15.
4   *Brith*, no. 160 (May 1959), 16.
5   John Wilson, *Our Israelitish Origin* (London: Nisbet, 1840), 20–21.
6   Wilson, *Our Israelitish Origin*, 23.
7   *Brith*, no. 325 (February 1973), 11.
8   *Brith*, no. 292 (April 1970), 26–28.
9   *The National Message*, vol. 59, no. 1,686 (May 1980), 67.
10 *The National Message*, vol. 41, no. 1,475 (October 1962), 303.
11 *Daily Mail*, no. 10,870 (26 February 1931), 10.
12 Arthur Keith, 'The Evolution of Human Races: Huxley Memorial Lecture,' in *Journal of the Royal Anthropological Institute*, 58 (1928): 316.
13 Elazar Barkan, *The Retreat of Scientific Racism* (Cambridge: Cambridge University Press, 1992), 51.
14 *Brith*, no. 35 (October 1948), 16.
15 *Brith*, no. 350 (March 1975), 17.
16 *The Times*, no. 59,770 (31 July 1976), 13.
17 Dorothy Abraham, *What Is British Israel?* (London: Covenant Publishing, 1954), 58.
18 *The National Message*, vol. 49, no. 1,562 (January 1970), 4.
19 Eric Reisenauer, '"The Battle of the Standards": Great Pyramid Metrology and British Identity, 1859–1890,' in *The Historian*, 65, no. 4 (Summer 2003): 931–978.
20 Hansard, House of Commons Debate (27 October 1970), vol. 805, coll. 76–168.
21 *The Banner of Israel*, vol. 44, no. 2,245 (7 January 1920), 12.
22 Tudor Parfitt, *The Lost Tribes of Israel* (London: Phoenix, 2003).
23 2 Esdras 13: 40–50.
24 Isaiah 49: 12.
25 *Brith*, no. 351 (April 1975), 15.
26 *The Link*, vol. 4, no. 6 (May 1985), 135.
27 L. Buxton Gresty, *Christ or the Kremlin* (London: Covenant Publishing, 1976), 63.
28 *The Banner of Israel*, vol. 42, no. 2,152 (27 March 1918), 120.
29 Wilson, *Our Israelitish Origin*, 191, 270, 368.

30 Edward Hine, *Fourty-Seven Identifications of the Anglo-Saxons with the Lost Tribes of Israel* (New York: Huggins, 1879), 96.

31 Genesis 49: 13.

32 *Bible Truth*, no. 206 (July 2000), 16.

33 *The National Message*, vol. 31, no. 1,303 (28 June 1952), 270.

34 Helene van Woelderen, *Strange Parallels* (Glastonbury: Real Israel Press, 1971), 1.

35 Adam Rutherford, *Israel Britain* (Harrow: Self-published, 1935); Adam Rutherford, *Iceland's Great Inheritance* (London: Self-published, 1937).

36 Jonas Gudmundsson, *Spadomarnir um Island* (Reykjavik Utgefandi: Timaritid Dagrenning, 1941).

37 Jonas Gudmundsson (ed.), *Leyndardomur Ofdrykkjunnar serprentun ur Timaritinu Dagrenning* (Reykjavik Utgefandi: Timaritid Dagrenning, 1950).

38 *The National Message*, vol. 59, no. 1,682 (January 1980), 11.

39 *Wake Up*, vol. 2, no. 7 (July 1978), 283; *The National Message*, vol. 50, no. 1,580 (July 1971), 214.

40 Arthur Koestler, *The Thirteenth Tribe* (New York: Random House, 1976).

41 *The National Message*, vol. 55, no. 1,634 (January 1976), 31.

42 Edward Shils, *Tradition* (Chicago: University of Chicago Press, 1981), 12.

43 Eric Hobsbawm, 'Inventing Traditions in 19th Century Europe,' in *Proceedings of the Past and Present Society Annual Conference 1977* (London: Past and Present, 1977), 1–25.

44 Hugh Trevor Roper, 'The Highland Tradition of Scotland,' in Eric Hobsbawm (ed.), *The Invention of Tradition* (Cambridge: Cambridge University Press, 1983), 13–41.

45 *Crown and Commonwealth*, vol. 4, no. 2 (Summer 2004), 44.

46 *The National Message*, vol. 55, no. 1,635 (February 1976), 52.

47 Walker Connor, *Ethnonationalism* (Princeton, NJ: Princeton University Press, 1994), 74; Michael Hogg, *Extremism and the Psychology of Uncertainty* (Sussex: Wiley-Blackwell, 2012); Michael Hogg, 'From Uncertainty to Extremism,' in *Current Directions in Psychological Science*, 23 (2014): 338–342; Michael Hogg, 'Uncertainty-Identity Theory,' in *Advances in Experimental Social Psychology*, 39 (2007): 69–126.

48 Anthony D. Smith, *Chosen Peoples* (Oxford: Oxford University Press, 2002), 48.

49 Anthony D. Smith, *The Cultural Foundations of Nations* (Oxford: Blackwell, 2008), 2.

50 Tom Nairn, *The Break Up of Britain: Crisis and Neo-Nationalism* (London: Verso, 1977), 266.

51 *The National Message*, vol. 47, no. 1,547 (October 1968), 330.

52 Smith, *The Cultural Foundations of Nations*, 2.

53 Metropolitan Anglo-Israel Association, *Report for the Proceedings at the First Annual Meeting* (London, 1879), 12.

54 John O'Hart, *Irish Pedigrees* (Dublin: Duffy, 1892), 580–583.

55 A.J. Ferris, *God's Education of the Anglo-Saxon-Israel Race* (London: Marshall, 1934), 63.

56 *The Cornishman* (14 August 1941), 5.

57 A.R.H., *British Israel and the Herrenvolk* (London: British-Israel World Federation, 1942), 1–13 [quotation at 12].

58 *Brith*, no. 38 (December 1948), 3.

59 *The National Message*, vol. 27, no. 1,187 (17 January 1948), 28.

60 L. Buxton Gresty, *Satan Fights for Muscovy* (London: Covenant Publishing, 1952), 9.

61 *The National Message*, vol. 22, no. 1,072 (18 August 1943), 137.

62 *The National Message*, vol. 27, no. 1,207 (23 October 1948), 345–346.

63 *Brith,* no. 39 (February 1949), 15.
64 *Brith*, no. 30 (May 1948), 4–5.
65 John Coakley, 'Religion and Nationalism,' in Daniele Conversi (ed.), *Ethnona-tionalism in the Contemporary World* (London: Routledge, 2002), 213.
66 Mark Suzman, *Ethnic Nationalism and State Power* (Basingstoke: Palgrave Macmillan, 1999), 10.
67 Ben Wellings, *English Nationalism and Euroscepticism: Losing the Peace* (Bern: Peter Lang, 2012), 22.
68 Ernest Gellner, *Nations and Nationalism* (Cornell: Cornell University Press, 1983), 57.
69 Elie Kedourie, *Nationalism* (London: Wiley, 1993).
70 John Breuilly, *Nationalism and the State* (Manchester: Manchester University Press, 1993), 15.
71 Benedict Anderson, *Imagined Communities* (London: Verso, 2003 [1986]), 39–47.
72 Smith, *The Cultural Foundations of Nations*, 8.
73 Smith, *Chosen Peoples*, 23.
74 Amit, *Hidden Polemics in the Biblical Narrative*, 239.
75 Smith, *Chosen Peoples*, 94.
76 *Wake Up*, vol. 2, no. 4 (April 1978), 80.
77 Joshua Berman, 'Histories Twice Told: Deuteronomy 1–3 and the Hittite Treaty Prologue Tradition,' in *Journal of Biblical Literature*, 132, no. 2 (2013): 229–250.
78 Leviticus 26: 16.
79 Ezekiel 36: 24.
80 *Bible Impact*, no. 8 (June 1972), 15.
81 Jeremiah 25.
82 Akenson, *God's Peoples*, 135.
83 Galatians 3: 25.
84 Michael Mach, 'Justin Martyr's *Dialogus cum Tryphone Iudaeo* and the Devel-opment of Christian Anti-Judaism,' in Guy Stroumsa and Ora Limor (eds.), *Contra Iudaeos: Ancient and Medieval Polemics Between Christians and Jews* (Tubingen: Mohr, 1996), 27–85; Paula Fredriksen, *Augustine and the Jews* (New Haven: Yale University Press, 2008), 177–179; Rosemary Ruether, *Faith and Fratricide* (Eugene: Wipf, 1995), 117–181.
85 *Crown and Commonwealth*, vol. 2, no. 4 (Winter 2002), 19.
86 Calvin, *Institutes of the Christian Religion*, Book 3, Chapter 21, Section 7.
87 Alexander Walsham, *Providence in Early Modern England* (Oxford: Oxford University Press, 1999), 289; Edward Vallance, *Revolutionary England and the National Covenant* (Woodbridge: Boydell, 2005), 91–94.
88 Jonathan Scott, *England's Troubles* (Cambridge; Cambridge University Press, 2000), 30.
89 Smith, *The Cultural Foundations of Nations*, 130.
90 Smith, 'Nation and Covenant,' 237.
91 John Morrill, 'The Religious Context of the English Civil War,' in *Transactions of the Royal Historical Society*, 34 (1984): 155–178.
92 Achsah Guibbory, *Christian Identity, Jews and Israel* (Oxford: Oxford University Press, 2010), 33–40; Henry Dawbeny, *Historie & Policie Re-Viewed, in the Heroick Transactions of His Most Serene Highnesse, Oliver, Late Lord Protec-tor* (London, 1659), a4r.
93 Guibbory, *Christian Identity, Jews and Israel*, 20.
94 Smith, *The Cultural Foundations of Nations*, 187.

95 Patrick Collinson, 'The Cohabitation of the Faithful with the Unfaithful,' in Ole Grell, Jonathan Israel and Nicholas Tyacke (eds.), *From Persecution to Toleration* (Oxford: Clarendon Press, 1991), 56; Julie Spraggon, 'Puritan Iconoclasm in England, 1640–1660' (PhD Thesis: University of London, 2000), 18; Andrew Cambers, *Godly Reading: Print, Manuscript and Puritanism in England, 1580–1720* (Cambridge: Cambridge University Press, 2011), 13–14, 22; Alexandra Walsham, 'The Happiness of Suffering,' in Michael Braddick and Joanna Innes (eds.), *Suffering and Happiness in England 1550–1850* (Oxford: Oxford University Press, 2017), 56, 58; Peter Lake, 'Anti-Puritanism: The Structure of a Prejudice,' in Kenneth Fincham (ed.), *Religious Politics in Post-Reformation England* (Woodbridge: Boydell, 2006), 85–87.

96 Alexandra Walsham, *Charitable Hatred: Tolerance and Intolerance in England, 1500–1700* (Manchester: Manchester University Press, 2006), 212.

97 Walsham, 'The Happiness of Suffering,' 58, 56.

98 Stephen Denison, *A New Creature* (London, 1619), 44.

99 Spraggon, 'Puritan Iconoclasm,' 18; Walsham, 'The Happiness of Suffering,' 56–58; Cambers, *Godly Reading*, 13–14, 22. This is not to say that all Puritans sought to *be* powerless, but rather that they often sought to associate themselves with cultural *topoi* of powerlessness. Clearly, many of those who identified as Godly saw ways of validating the pursuit of earthly power, not least the engineers of the Cromwellian commonwealth. Taking power in the context of the Civil War was perceived as a duty, not just an act of Knoxean resistance but a 'crusade' [see Timothy George, 'War and Peace in the Puritan Tradition,' in *Church History*, 53 (1984): 492–503]. Nonetheless, even the language of Holy War situated the Godly combatant in a powerless mode. 'Less of man and more of God,' was a repeated refrain in Godly explanations for victories in the Civil War [Matthew Rowley, 'From Fratricide to Revival: The Creation and Evolution of a Theological War Slogan, 1642–1917,' given at Ecclesiastical History Society Postgraduate Colloquium (Magdalene College, Cambridge University [4 March 2016]).

100 James Bratt, 'Calvinism in North America,' in Martin Hirzel and Martin Sallman (eds.), *John Calvin's Impact on Church and Society, 1509–2009* (Cambridge: Eerdmans, 2009), 52.

101 Crome, *Christian Zionism and English National Identity*, 25–26.

102 Wilson, 'British Israelism,' 48, 55.

103 Smith, *Chosen Peoples*, 38.

104 Smith, *Chosen Peoples*, 39.

105 Mary Douglas, *Purity and Danger* (London: Routledge, 2003 [1966]), 55.

106 Klawans, *Purity, Sacrifice and the Temple*, 49–74 [and in particular 58].

107 Klawans, *Purity, Sacrifice and the Temple*, 73; Jonathan Klawans, *Impurity and Sin* (Oxford: Oxford University Press, 2000), 17, 23–25; Daniel H. Weiss, 'Impurity Without Repression: Julia Kristeva and the Biblical Possibilities of a Non-Eliminationist Construction of Religious Purity,' in Robbie Duschinsky, Simone Schnall and Daniel H. Weiss (eds.), *Purity and Danger Now: New Perspectives* (London: Routledge, 2016), 205–221.

108 Bauman, 'Allosemitism,' 144.

109 Smith, *Chosen Peoples*, 63.

110 John Norden, *A Mirror for the Multitude* (London, 1586), 38–39.

111 Joseph Bentham, *The Saints Societie* (London, 1636), 6.

112 *The National Message*, vol. 47, no. 1,538 (January 1968), 11.

113 *Bible Truth*, no. 209 (January 2001), 9.

114 *Crown and Commonwealth*, vol. 1, Special Edition (2001), 10.

115 *The National Message*, vol. 43, no. 1,494 (May 1964), 147.
116 *The National Message*, vol. 27, no. 1,198 (19 June 1948), 200.
117 *Brith*, no. 368 (December 1976), 28.
118 Klawans, *Purity, Sacrifice and the Temple*, 73.
119 *The New British Israel Pilot*, no. 5 (1 November 1929), 68.
120 *Bible Truth*, no. 209 (January 2001), 9.
121 *News of the New World*, vol. 1, no. 11 (October 1966), 4; *Wake Up*, vol. 7, no. 10 (August 1989), 223.
122 *Brith*, no. 233 (June 1965), 20.
123 *Wake Up*, vol. 2, no. 4 (April 1978), 80.
124 *Wake Up*, vol. 5, no. 4 (March 1981), 6.
125 *Wake Up*, vol. 7, no. 12 (November 1991), 282.
126 *Bible Truth*, no. 207 (September 2000), 24.
127 Michael Barkun, *A Culture of Conspiracy* (Berkeley: University of California Press, 2003), 181.
128 *The Banner of Israel*, vol. 40, no. 2,063 (12 July 1916), 306.
129 Tony Burke, 'Apocrypha and Forgeries,' in Tony Burke (ed.), *Fakes, Forgeries and Fictions: Ancient and Modern Christian Apocrypha* (Eugene: Cascade, 2015), 236–240.
130 *The National Message*, vol. 55, no. 1,643 (October 1976), 301.
131 *Brith*, no. 13 (October 1946), 1–3.
132 *Brith*, no. 4 (January 1946), 13; *Brith*, no. 17 (February 1947), 14.
133 Jacopo Leone and Victor Considerant, *The Jesuit Conspiracy* (London: Chapman, 1848), xxx–xxxi.
134 *The National Message*, vol. 49, no. 1,562 (January 1970), 48–49.
135 *Covenant Voice* (February 1991), 18.
136 *The National Message*, vol. 55, no. 1,636 (March 1976), 74.
137 *The National Message*, vol. 47, no. 1,542 (May 1968), 153.
138 *Crown and Commonwealth*, vol. 3, no. 1 (Spring 2003), 13.
139 'New Covenant Times Supplement,' in *Wake Up*, vol. 12, no. 2 (March 1998), 1.
140 *Wake Up*, vol. 2, no. 4 (April 1978), 80.
141 *Covenant Voice* (April 1992), 25.
142 'New Covenant Times Supplement,' in *Wake Up*, vol. 12, no. 2 (March 1998), 1.
143 *BIWF Quarterly*, vol. 4, no. 2 (April 1991), 19.
144 Barkun, *A Culture of Conspiracy*, 26.
145 *Mother Jones*, no. 6 (April 1981), 6.
146 *Crown and Commonwealth*, vol. 1, no. 2 (Summer 2001), 8.
147 *Crown and Commonwealth*, vol. 3, no. 2 (Summer 2003), 5.
148 Theodor Adorno, Else Frenkel-Brunswik, Daniel J. Levinson, and R. Nevitt Sanford, *The Authoritarian Personality: Part Two* (New York: Wiley, 1950), 611; Joseph E. Uscinski and Joseph M. Parent, *American Conspiracy Theories* (Oxford: Oxford University Press, 2014), 130; Eric Oliver and Thomas J. Wood, 'Conspiracy Theories and the Paranoid Style(s) of Mass Opinion,' in *American Journal of Political Science*, 58, no. 4 (2014): 952–966.

2   A history of British-Israelism in the twentieth century

The pre-history of British-Israelism

The history of British-Israel, if British-Israelists are to be believed, begins in the land of Canaan. The blessings of Israel were divided amongst the twelve sons of Jacob. On his deathbed, Jacob told his sons that they would be appointed to different tasks in God's plan for His chosen people. Reuben would be brought low. Zebulun would provide safe harbour for vessels. The descendants of Isachar would submit to slavery, whilst the descendants of Levi and Simeon would be scattered amongst the other tribes. Judah would continue to rule and the 'sceptre would not depart from [her].' Meanwhile, Joseph would continue to be a fruitful vine. His descendants would be assaulted by enemies but would flourish. Each of the sons of Jacob would father tribes of Israel. The two sons of Joseph, meanwhile – Ephraim and Menasseh – were elevated to the status of being fathers of a tribe.[1] After the conquest of Canaan, land was apportioned to the twelve tribes by the drawing of lots. The southern part of the land was given to Simeon and Judah. Levi was excluded from the lot. The northern parts of kingdom were given to the remaining nine tribes, with separate land allotted to Ephraim and Menasseh.

According to the Hebrew Bible, in the eighth century BCE, the Assyrian conquest of the Northern Kingdom led to the destruction of the Kingdom and the dispersion of the northern tribes. From this point, the lost tribes are seldom referred to in the Biblical record. Esdras envisions the people of the lost tribes, now exiled in the mythical region of Arzareth, returning to Zion in the messianic period.[2] This tradition, initiated around the first century in Palestine, continued to win assent amongst the Jewish and early Christian communities, although often with variant interpretations, 'carried along on separate tracks.'[3] The Targum Pseudo-Jonathan contains the first reference to the river of Sambation, beyond which the land of Arzareth was fabled to be.[4] The name of the river indicated that it was traversable only on the Sabbath day. The ninth century traveller and philologist Eldad Ha-Dani claimed to have encountered the lost tribes in the land beyond the Kush.[5] Subsequent rabbinic and historical texts referred to the lost tribes, with some Jews maintaining the association between a future restoration of the descendants of Jacob and the dawning of the messianic era. This belief would become the 'bedrock' of the 'messianic package.'[6] When these writings were translated and popularised by early modern Hebraists, Jewish messianism stimulated Christian interest in the lost tribes mythology.[7]

Conventional British-Israelist accounts of the journey taken by the Israelites from Assyria to Britain include the following details. The Israelites fled northwards to the Black Sea, settling in the region surrounding Sinope. In 600 BCE they moved to the Carpathian region, which was identified with the country of Arzareth, as mentioned in the book of Esdras. Some stayed in the Carpathians, where they gradually became known as the Scythians. This name was a derivation of the word Sacae – the name with which this group was referred to by Persians according to Herodotus. British-Israelist lore suggests that the word Sacae was itself derived from the name Isaac. Some of the Carpathian Israelites migrated up the Danube into Southern Germany between 600 and 500 BCE. Here, these people used a bastardised Greek version of their original name. Whereas they had once been known as Ghomri – the Assyrian word for Israel – they now became known by the Greek name 'Kimmerioi' and would later become known to English-speaking historians as Cimmerians. The Cimmerians settled in Central Europe in 500 BCE. In around 200 BCE they were pushed westwards out of Germany by invading Scythians towards Holland and Britain. Around this time, therefore, the Scythians and the Cimmerians both reached North-Western Europe, reunited as the nations of Israel. Although they had become 'gentilised' and had neglected their Israelite heritage, they nonetheless carried with them linguistic relics of their past. Those who were descended from the tribe of Dan – for example – named themselves and their land after Dan: the *Dan*ube, the Dar*dan*elles, and the tribe of De *Dan*nan in Ireland. They retained their identification with Isaac even after the invasion of Britain, referring to themselves as Saxons. Those who arrived in Britain via Celtic invasions retained the, by now mutated, version of the name of Ghomri, referring to their country as Cymru.[8]

In the period between the arrival of the Israelites and the arrival of Christianity on British shores, the Israelites of Britain practiced a form of religion which was loosely modelled on the religion of their ancestors in the land of Israel. This religion would later become known as Druidism. British-Israelists sought to demonstrate that Druids had preserved – albeit unknowingly – the religious traditions of the Northern Kingdom before the eighth century. Druidism was identified as 'the faith of all our ancestors who arrived on these shores in pre-Christian time.' Druids practiced many of the rituals which were originated by the priesthood of Israel. In fact, British-Israelists claim 'Israelites and Druids all adored the same God and the rites of all were similar.'[9] In 1929, *The British Israel Pilot* featured several articles which sought to demonstrate that the 'Druids' religion in many ways resembled that of the patriarchs.' Amongst other traditions that they ascribed to both 'the Druids' and 'the patriarchs' were the belief in the immortality of the soul, the belief in the resurrection of the dead, the fact that they 'worshipped under the oak,' and the fact that druids used a 'staff of office.' The latter was identified with the Israelite practice described in Numbers 17. Many of these observations were informed by the writings of George Moore, who founded the Anglo-Israel Association in 1879.[10] Moore was a surgeon and a paediatrician who was first converted to the cause of British-Israelism after reading the work of John Wilson. Moore believed that the roots of British culture could be traced back to the druidical tradition and that these roots had come into full bloom in the context of the Protestant Reformation.[11]

British-Israelists claim, moreover, that the evangel reached British shores and was accepted there at a very early stage in the history of Christianity. This was not an entirely discrete contention. God ordained that His people in Israel were His primary concern, and He never rescinded this promise. As such, at the advent of Christianity, the people of the twelve tribes were the first to encounter the truth of the Gospels. British-Israelists often espouse belief in mythological claims relating to the mission of Joseph of Arimathea and Glastonbury.[12] They also claim that other apostles came to British shores, including St Paul. This pseudo-historical claim was relatively widely disseminated in late-nineteenth-century Britain, owing to the writings of Bishop Thomas Burgess and Richard Williams Morgan.[13] The Catholic church is almost always depicted, by British-Israelists, as the embodiment of Babylon, Israel's perennial foe. As such, the claim that Christianity in Britain pre-existed the arrival of Roman missionaries is essential to the British-Israelist belief that the aboriginal Christianity of Britain was true, non-Babylonian Christianity. From a British-Israelist perspective, these supposed historical events serve to cast light on other aspects of scripture. Conventional British-Israelist exegesis takes the words of Jesus, who commissioned his disciples to deliver the Gospel 'to the Lost Sheep of Israel,' to refer directly to the tribes which had been scattered to the North.[14]

Because of their ancient attachment to the religion of Israel, Britons never fully took to the religion of Babylon – that is Roman Christianity – when it arrived on British shores. At various points in the history of Christianity in Britain, many groups sought to throw off the yoke of Popery. The phenomenon of Lollardism and the early advances of Protestantism in the early modern period are explained by British-Israelists as expressions of Israelite repudiation of Babylon. However, Moore argued, it was only with the full realisation of Godly religion, during the sixteenth century, that the British people 'with a full recurrence to the testimony of the Hebrew Bible . . . separated from all other people by the out-speaking of freedom of their spirit.'[15]

British-Israelism in the long nineteenth century

According to British-Israelist tradition, the first figure, after the Assyrian crisis, to recognise the true identity of Israel was Jacques Abbadie. Abbadie was a French theologian who was appointed as minister of the Huguenot church in London in 1688 before moving to Killaloe, County Clare, in the aftermath of the Glorious Revolution. Abbadie wrote several tracts including one on the subject of 'the triumph of Providence.' This text described the fulfilment of prophecy in the advance of Protestantism. Amongst other claims, Abbadie suggested that 'the tombs of the Lost Tribes were opened with the conversion of the Northern Peoples' from Catholicism. The only possible explanation for the disappearance of the lost tribes, according to Abbadie, was that they had migrated to the British isles. 'Unless the Ten Tribes have flown into the air,' Abbadie wrote 'we must look for them in the North, and in that part of the North, which at the time of Constantine was converted to the Christian faith.'[16]

Richard Brothers' name is usually omitted in British-Israelist accounts of the genesis of their movement. This, at least in part, is presumably owing to the Paddington Prophet's reputation as an eccentric and a dissident. Nonetheless, his ideas are sufficiently similar in character to those of later, more mainstream British-Israelists as to merit mention here. Brothers believed that a minority of British people were – unknown to themselves – descended from the biblical Hebrews. Brothers took to prophesying the King's death and was arrested and imprisoned. Having written *A Revealed Knowledge of the Prophesies and the Times*, Brothers wrote another series of pamphlets whilst incarcerated.[17] Brothers' ideas continued to inspire others long after his death and several movements – centring around the figures of Joanna Southcott, John Wroe and Zion Ward – all made similar claims.[18]

The first figure whom British-Israelists claim as their own in the history of the development of their doctrine is John Wilson. Wilson was an Ayrshire-born historian who was educated at Trinity College Dublin. In the late 1830s he conducted a popular lecture tour. His lectures were later published in a book entitled *Our Israelitish Origin*. The central argument of the book is that the peoples of Northern Europe were descendants from the lost tribes of Israel. Wilson claimed that Britain – along with the other countries of Northern Europe – could claim to be genealogically linked with the Biblical polity of Israel. He set a long-standing precedent by claiming that Britain could be specifically identified with the tribe of Ephraim. However, he emphasised that all Germanic peoples had a shared heritage in their Israelitish past.[19]

Wilson's claims attracted the attention of a young bank clerk named Edward Hine. Hine adapted Wilson's argument, claiming that the lost tribes of Israel could be linked genealogically with England, but not – as Wilson had suggested – with the other nations of Europe. Hine conceded that 'the German can trace their ancestry to the same region' as the Israelites but that there was no reason to believe that Britain and Germany were 'related peoples.'[20] For Hine, and the so-called 'anti-Teutonist' movement, only Britain could lay legitimate claim to being Israel. Wilson's vision of Teutonic unity was scuppered by German unification and militarisation. Germany posed a threat to British imperial power, and this tension would soon combust with the start of the First World War.

Hine spearheaded the routing of the Teutonist tendency. On the other hand, Barkun credits him with adopting and promoting a more irenic attitude towards the Jews. Hine wrote that 'the Jews of the present day,' would be counted amongst 'All Israel,' a claim that Wilson was reticent to concede.[21] Hine originally expected to lead the movement. He wrote extensively and established an organisation called the British-Israel Identity Corporation. However, this organisation collapsed. Hine travelled to America, where his influence – partly via his friendship with the Yale-based military historian C.A.L. Totten – helped to stimulate a growing interest in race-religion. Meanwhile, a fellow anti-Teutonist, the barrister Edward Wheeler Bird, established a London-based British-Israelist organisation – the Metropolitan Anglo-Israel Association – and a British-Israelist newspaper – *The Banner of Israel*.[22] The Metropolitan Anglo-Israel Association held its inaugural meeting in 1878. The last remaining Teutonist organisation, the Anglo-Ephraim Association, was absorbed into the Metropolitan Anglo-Israel Association in the same year.

Other luminaries of this period included Charles Piazzi Smyth and A.B. Grimaldi. Grimaldi was an English clergyman of French descent who laid out an entire genealogy linking Queen Victoria with King David.[23] Piazzi Smyth was a scientist, the Astronomer Royal of Scotland and a pyramidologist. Piazzi Smyth argued that the people of Britain were directly descended from the builders of the pyramids. Furthermore, he argued that the pyramids had been built specifically as a 'storehouse for a divinely inspired metrological system.' The 'pyramid inch' – exhibited by the measurements of the pyramids at Giza – was almost identical to the British inch. As such, the inch was seen as a divinely inspired mode of measurement and a bequest from the ancient Israelites to the modern.[24]

Wheeler Bird shared the leadership of the Metropolitan Anglo-Israel Association with Alfred Julius Cachemaille. Cachemaille was the son of a Swiss minister who was a curate of the Church of England on Sark. His brother, Ernest Peter Cachemaille, was a prominent figure in the Prophecy Investigation Society as well as being a prominent South American missionary.[25] Alfred Cachemaille was a missionary in Mauritius in the 1860s. In the 1870s he settled in Oldham. Upon his death at the age of forty-three, Cachemaille's obituarist noted:

> We are struck by the anomaly of a gentleman who is not by birth of the chosen seed advocating so strenuously the opinion that the British nation is descended from the Ten Lost Tribes of Israel.[26]

Already at this time, British-Israelism was considered to be a vanguard tendency in the ongoing resistance to Catholic emancipation.[27] Many of its donors also contributed to organisations like the Protestant Association. Perhaps the most prominent of these was the Devonian entrepreneur W.H. Peters. Peters was an attendee at the first meetings of the Metropolitan Anglo-Israel Association.[28] He was also a leader of the Protestant Alliance in the West of England and attended their meetings. The stated aim of this organisations was 'to maintain the principles of Protestantism in all their integrity and protest strongly against any further concessions to Popery.'[29] At the inaugural meeting of the Metropolitan Anglo-Israel Association, Peters called upon his audience to return as many Conservatives as possible in the upcoming general election, since 'they are the best Protestants.'[30]

In 1880 the Metropolitan Anglo-Israel Association had 1,500 members.[31] At the same time, a number of other British-Israel organisations were beginning to emerge. One such was the Protestant British-Israel League, based at 30 Imperial Buildings, Ludgate Circus, and organised by Mrs Augusta Cook.[32] They held their annual conventions in Committee Room B of Central Hall in Westminster.[33] Cook was a vocal opponent of Catholic influence in Britain. In 1905, she shared a platform with Dr Charles Hutchinson MP at the Autumnal Conference of the Church Association. Mrs Cook conducted a lantern talk (as part of which she showed images of a Catholic priest elevating a host) and admonished all of the young people present to continue the fight against Catholicism. Her sentiments were applauded and echoed by Hutchinson.[34] The British Israel National Union was founded in 1916, with Douglas Parker as its president.[35] Parker wrote a pamphlet entitled *Why Great Britain Will Never Be Destroyed* during the inter-war years.[36] His Union had its own newspaper, entitled *The Southern Star*. It held some sway in the North and was patronised in part by the Earl of Dysart. The latter sponsored a bid to build a British-Israel hall in Sheffield in 1919 but the plans floundered due to lack of funds.[37] It eventually changed its name to the British Israel Empire Union in 1928.[38] The North of England Anglo-Israel Council was founded on 15 May 1894 and continued to exist until 1946, when it was incorporated into the SPBI.[39]

On 7 May 1919, with Britain's victory in World War I still fresh in the mind, Admiral Lord Fisher (who had served as First Sea Lord during the war) wrote to *The Times* to reiterate his belief in 'identity theory.' 'The only hypothesis to explain why we win in spite of incredible blunders is that we are the lost ten tribes of Israel,' he wrote. The purpose of Fisher's letter was to argue that the location for the headquarters of the new League of Nations should not be Geneva but rather Jerusalem. He had already made this claim at an event at the American Luncheon Club given the previous week to celebrate the visit to London of Mr Josephus Daniels, Secretary to the US Navy.[40] A few days before this luncheon took place, a new chapter in the history of the British-Israel movement had begun.

The foundation of the BIWF

A small notice could be found in the bottom right hand corner of the penultimate page of the 7 May 1919 edition of *The Banner of Israel*. It read:

On May 1st and 2nd a conference was held at Caxton Hall in London, the results of which must we think have a very far-reaching effect.

It was decided (subject to the approval of the difference Associations and Councils) to federate all British Israel Societies into one world-wide Union.[41]

This was to prove the first step in the founding of the BIWF. Eventually ninety separate British-Israel groups would be federated under their banner. It also provided the stimulus for the foundation of new branches of the federation. The Leeds British Israelist Association was founded in September 1920, with ninety people in attendance.[42] On 8 December 1920, the Nottingham Association was founded with a 'satisfactory attendance.'[43] In December 1920, Herbert Garrison spoke to the Birmingham Association and eight hundred people were in attendance.[44] The Southport British Israel Association was organised by Fred Bibby, the Conservative Party's election agent for the Gorton division of Manchester.[45]

In the 21 May 1919 edition of *The Banner*, the minutes of the momentous meeting were summarised. Herbert Garrison had spoken and, in his speech, he had looked back at a long history of British-Israelist thought, as the foundations for a long and prosperous future for the movement. He assessed, also, the health of the movement:

> We have thousands of believers, 70 Associations and you know that it has been claimed that British Israel faith has been the means of converting 5,000 infidels to Christianity.[46]

Garrison – prominent figure in the Royal Colonial Institute – was duly appointed as the first Secretary General of the BIWF. In congratulating him on his appointment, *The Banner* claimed that 'among Mr Garrison's patrons have been Queen Alexandra, the King and Queen of the Belgians, Lord Kitchener, Lord Roberts, the Prime Minister and a host of other public men and women.'[47] Garrison conducted a series of lecture tours in the 1920s and 1930s. One, entitled *Our World-Wide Empire*, was accompanied by 'over one hundred fine lantern pictures from the best collection in existence.' A second, conducted in 1926, was entitled *The Greatest Biblical and Racial Discovery of the Age*.[48] Admission was two shillings.[49] Garrison continued to serve as secretary of the movement until his death in 1935.

The inaugural congress of the movement that he led was held in July 1919. Twenty thousand people attended the congress.[50] Amongst them was Princess Alice, the Duchess of Athlone, the Countess Dowager of Radnor, the Duke of Buccleugh, the Earl of Meath, the Earl of Dysart, Lord Gisborough and Major General Hadfield. The latter served as president of the movement for the first two years. Hadfield was succeeded as president by Lord Gisborough. Gisborough was the MP for Liverpool Abercromby, who combined his duties as the president of the BIWF with his leadership of the United Protestant Council. On 11 April 1923, Gisborough submitted a petition on behalf of the Council to the Prime Minister Andrew Bonar Law. The petition called for a realignment of the British state's relationship with the Papacy, for the withdrawal of the King's envoy to the Vatican and for the cancellation of the King's visit to Rome to meet with the Pope.[51] As chairman of the Political Committee of the Junior Constitutional Club, during this period, Gisborough was also acquainted with a host of other influential figures, including Viscount Long, then leader of the Irish Unionist Party.[52]

For most of the inter-war years the presidency of the BIWF was held by Major James Knowles. He was joined by a number of other prominent military figures in organising the United Services Organisation of the British Israel World Federation. Amongst their numbers they could count the Irish-New Zealander war hero Charles Mackesy. As commander of the Auckland Mounted Rifles, Mackesy led the force which occupied the Jordan Valley during the Palestinian campaign of World War I. At the start of the twentieth century, Mackesy toured New Zealand speaking on British-Israel theory.[53]

Perhaps the most influential figure of this period was John J. Morey. Morey 'established more branches than anyone else' during these years. He was prominent in particular in West London.[54] Morey was an anti-Semitic conspiracy theorist, who believed that 'seven million German Jews in the United States' had the power to 'shake the world.' They were a 'synagogue of Satan' who could devalue the pound with a word or an order.[55]

At this point in the history of the movement, the Covenant Publishing Company was founded. It was launched with an authorised sale of ten thousand shares, each priced at £1.[56] Its directors were Brigadier General Coventry Williams, Lieutenant Colonel Vincent Wright and Herbert Garrison. Its first chairman was William Sleeman and its first director was William Pascoe Goard. Goard was an Anglo-Canadian author and Methodist minister. Born in Cornwall, he moved to Canada at the start of the twentieth century. In Vancouver, he served as a minister of the Knox Congregational Church. Barkun credits him with stimulating Howard Rand's interest in British-Israelism whilst on a tour of America in 1929.[57] Goard's lectures were later printed by Rand's publishing house, Destiney Publishing. Some of the titles published by Covenant Publishing – with Goard and Sleeman at the helm – ran into the tens of thousands of copies.[58]

The BIWF secured ownership of an illustrious address at 6 Buckingham Palace Gate. They established offices here in 1924. The house had, during the nineteenth century, belonged to Nathan de Rothschild.[59] It had been in the ownership of William Harcourt, the home secretary at the end of the nineteenth century, but was bought by the philanthropist and chairman of Lloyd's Register, Sir Thomas Lane Devitt. When Devitt died in 1924, the property was auctioned and was acquired by the BIWF. A grand opening was held on 23 June 1924 and was hosted by Lord Gisborough.[60] They would remain at this premises until 1990. The building is less than a hundred yards from the gates of Buckingham Palace.

At the same time, the movement expanded its property portfolio, establishing a college for the passing on of 'British Israel Truth' at Harrow Weald in 1932. The building that they acquired was a manor house. It was originally bought by the federation for a cost of £15,000. Lecturers at the college included the Reverend Dr William Pascoe Goard, Dr Courtney James, Dr Norman James, Clifford Parker, Rupert Thomas and Reverend Alban Heath. Heath was the principal of Dower College in South Africa.[61] In 1937, he wrote a book entitled *The Faith of a British-Israelite*. This text was a call to arms to British-Israelists who had been 'cold shouldered and . . . condemned.' They were, Heath wrote, to 'comfort themselves with the reflection that by standing among the condemned they are in a noble succession whose failures have proved most brilliant successes.'[62] At a four-day conference, staged in Birmingham in 1932, Alban Heath was introduced as a keynote speaker by local councilor F.G. Whittall. Heath declared that Britain was 'the only nation that had ever come anywhere near to filling the programme of God.'[63]

The Orange Street Congregational Church has served as the unofficial chapel of the British-Israel movement from the early twentieth century to the present day. The church is located on a street behind Trafalgar Square in the centre of London. It was built on the site of a Huguenot chapel. Since the start of the twentieth century it has hosted a Congregationalist community who hold, as a central tenet of their beliefs, the doctrine of British-Israelism. With the dissolution of the Congregationalist Church in England in 1956, the church became an independent body, refusing to join the United Reform movement. The current pastor of the community is Anthony Martlew who – with wife Valerie – has regularly contributed to British-Israel publications and spoken at BIWF events.[64] Many such events have been hosted at Orange Street.[65]

The Banner of Israel was first circulated at the end of the nineteenth century. At the inception of the BIWF a new magazine was introduced, bearing the title *The National Message*. With the increase in circulation of *The National Message*, the profitability of *The Banner* went into decline. In 1926, the latter was absorbed by the former. The magazine took up offices in Red Lion's Court off Fleet Street.[66] It was edited by a number of prominent Israelists including Leslie Pine. Pine was a scholar and an historian who served as an intelligence officer in the Second World War. After the war, he served for fifteen years as executive director of Burke's Peerage publishing company as well as the editor of the almanac itself. Pine was also a barrister, a freeman of the City of London and a parliamentary candidate for the Conservative Party. His obituary in *The Times* described him as 'tireless' in his attempts 'to interest his compatriots in their descent.[67]

In the pre-war years, the British-Israel movement became the focus of attention for groups on the far-right. In 1934, a waiter and anti-Semitic conspiracy theorist named Charles Ashton firebombed the headquarters of the BIWF at Buckingham Gate. Ashton had previously attacked the cleaning lady of the Princess Drive Synagogue in Toxteth and was the leader of the National Association for the Resistance to Jewish Monopoly.[68] He believed that the BIWF was a clandestine body established to further the interests of international Jewry on British soil. When questioned by the police, Ashton said:

> In order to expose these people I had originally intended to inflict a flesh wound on the principal, W. Pascoe Goard, by shooting him with a revolver, but as I could get no ammunition for it, I had to modify my tactics and thought of setting fire to the place.[69]

Ashton's footprint in the political life of Britain during the pre-war years was very small, but his activities brought the British-Israel movement into the headlines.[70] His fear concerning the power of the British-Israelists was shared by other conspiratorially minded patriots on the other side of the Atlantic. In the early 1940s, Nazi-sympathising Congressman Jacob Thorkelson spoke regularly on the floor of the House of Representatives of a British-Israelist plot to subvert the sovereignty of the United States. Thorkelson believed the global membership of the BIWF to number in the millions.[71] In 1945, a number of concerned citizens organised themselves in opposition to America's joining the United Nations. Amongst these was Helen V. Somers, who expressed her concern before the Committee on Foreign Relations of the American Senate that the 'United Nations World Charter,' would 'change our form of government by setting up a world government.' Somers warned that shadowy organisations were set on the destruction of the United States and she counted the BIWF amongst them. The 'world movement of the British Israelites,' she warned:

> is identical with the Andrew Carnegie-Cecil Rhodes-Theodore Hertzl plan to return the United States to the British Empire. The British-Israel literature boasts of Britain being mighty and that she will be mightier to rule the world. What is to happen then to our beloved United States? Where will we be? Can't you see? Gone with the wind – No; not if the women of this country have anything to say about it. Never. We will not betray our country to any foreign power.[72]

Somers was part of a movement whose views were most comprehensively documented in Catherine Palfrey Baldwin's *And Men Wept*. Baldwin purported to have uncovered numerous conspiracies designed to facilitate the reabsorption of the United States into the British Empire. Howard Rand was identified as a minion of this cabal, which was based in Buckingham Gate. Baldwin contended, amongst other things, that the army of British-Israelites numbered two million. 'The teaching for which the Federation stands,' she wrote, in 1955, 'is spreading like wildfire through the English speaking world.'[73]

The Scottish engineer David Davidson served as deputy president of the BIWF during this period. He spoke at Westminster Central Hall in 1934.

A full transcript of his speech was presented on page twenty of *The Daily Telegraph* on 5 October 1934.[74] Davidson was famous in the inter-war years for his work on the subject of Pyramidology. Like Piazzi-Smith before him, Davidson believed that the discovery of the pyramids and their dimensions confirmed the claims of British-Israelism. He was influenced in this – and in his conversion to British-Israelism – by Herbert Aldersmith. With Aldersmith, Davidson wrote *The Great Pyramid: Its Divine Message*. This book sold seventeen thousand copies in the 1940s and 1950s.[75]

During the years of the war, the BIWF continued to be led by military personnel, including Commander Ronald Studd. Studd was appointed Honorary Secretary of the BIWF by then president Robert Llewellyn Williams in 1943. His father was a well known philanthropist, Kynaston Studd, who had served as the Lord Mayor of London. Several of his brothers were well-known cricketers. Ronald Studd was the director of the Polytechnic Touring Association, an organisation which encouraged students to travel in mainland Europe.[76]

Post-war schisms

The connection between the BIWF and the military continued during the post-war period. During this period, leadership of the BIWF passed into the hands of Commander Donald Macmillan. Macmillan had served in the British India Company and was captured by Germans in 1914. He joined the Royal Navy at the outset of World War II and was posted to special research at the Admiralty. At the end of the war, he resumed his appointment with the Southampton Docks and Harbour Board and was awarded an MBE in 1955.

Another prominent figure of this period was Brigadier General Sir Standish Craufurd. Craufurd was the commander of the 1st Gordon Highlanders at the Somme. He was captured during the Boer War. He wrote for *The National Message* during this period. In 1946, Craufurd wrote an article in which he imagined the Jewish people, following the destruction of the Second Temple, moving into Europe as 'a continuous stream of inconspicuous pilgrims filtering through to find sanctuary with kinsmen separated by long centuries.'[77]

The movement continued to grow. Around 1950, circulation for *The National Message* peaked at around 100,000.[78] The BIWF maintained hundreds of branches across the country. But the movement was also afflicted with its first schisms. In 1945, several branches of the BIWF based around London, under the leadership of pastor Charles McKelvey, broke away from the federation in order to form the SPBI. They published the first edition of their magazine, *Brith*, in September 1945.[79] The SPBI bought and established a headquarters at 8 Snakes Lane, Woodford Green. They publicised their movement by taking out advertisements in local newspapers across the United Kingdom. The advertisements asked the crucial question: 'What is a

British-Israelite?' Beneath a short outline of British-Israelist doctrine, read the following statement:

> If you believe these facts, then you are a British-Israelite. British Israel is not a sect. It is interdenominational.[80]

They organised a Bible College from a premises on Barnabas Road in Woodford Green. The college remained in operation until the 1990s.[81]

After the schism, Harold Stough took on the position of secretary of the BIWF.[82] Stough was an American, the son of a revivalist preacher named Henry Stough. He moved to Britain in the 1930s and served as a deacon at the Orange Street Congregational Church. He would later be appointed pastor of the Church (a position he held until his death in 2004). In September 1950, Stough and Rear Admiral Sir Errol Manners convened an 'emergency meeting' of the Bath branch of the BIWF. At the meeting, Stough warned his audience: 'history is fast being wound up, and we must look for the second coming of Jesus Christ.' His concern at this meeting was to answer what he considered to be the key questions of the day: 'why this crisis? Will Britain survive? Is there a way out?'[83]

The 1960s were a booming period for British-Israelist magazines. *The National Message* was established in its offices in the Fleet Street area. The BIWF also established a new magazine from its South African headquarters. It was entitled *The Ambassador* and remained in print for the last years of the 1960s. It competed for the South African audience with the Federation of Covenant People's journal *News of the New World*. In the late 1960s, the SPBI began publishing a magazine directed towards the youth. It was entitled *Toren* and included within it material which was designed to stimulate the young British-Israelist. There were articles on 'Health and Hygiene in Israel' and 'A Top Ten of the Ten Commandments' alongside a 'Puzzle Corner' and advertisements for the annual youth conferences to be held at High Leigh in Hertfordshire.[84]

The SPBI reached out to the youth in the 1960s, organising a series of youth conferences. They advertised for sixty places but were over-subscribed.[85] Alongside McKelvey, a new generation of British-Israelists took on more responsibility during this period. Norman Court was initially the treasurer of the SPBI and subsequently became the editor of *Brith* magazine. He also served as the president of the Society of the Somerset Folk. Court, along with other members of the society, was a leading figure in the Anglican Free Communion.

In the BIWF, L. Buxton Gresty began to contribute more frequently to the *National Message* and to *Wake Up*. Gresty was determinedly anti-Communist, and many of his contributions addressed the eschatological conflicts that were expected to emerge between Israel and the Soviet Union. The 1950s and 1960s marked the high point of 'the British nation,' according to David Edgerton, and they also marked the zenith of British-Israelist success. Britain had entered her chambers. The move towards a more 'global Britain,' which would emerge gradually over the proceeding decades, would not be as kind to British-Israelism.

Decline as a mass movement

In 1971, Wilfred S. Reynolds was elected president of the BIWF. Upon his appointment, he warned that the financial situation of the BIWF was 'difficult and was worsening.' He warned that too many readers of *The National Message* were not converting their interest in the movement into a firm commitment to the organisation. Renewed financial commitment to the BIWF was a valuable act of witness, he reminded his readers.[86]

Despite Reynold's complaint, this period saw an expansion of the federation's portfolio. Two new properties were bought. In 1970, the BIWF purchased a premises at Glastonbury and named it Mount Avalon. Mr R.A. Griffiths was appointed warden of Mount Avalon. The dedication ceremony at Easter 1970 was attended by Patience Strong and Harold Stough along with the Mayor of Glastonbury, Councillor Cecil Hamilton Miller. Hamilton Miller was a solicitor who prosecuted concentration camp guards from Belsen in the aftermath of the Second World War. Patience Strong, in her address, said the following:

> I have always wished that the Federation could have its own place here in Glastonbury, a place which I consider to be a jewel of greater value to Christendom than Rome or Canterbury, and in matters relating to sacred associations, second only to Jerusalem.[87]

On Good Friday 1976, the BIWF held an Easter Festival in Glastonbury Town Hall. It was opened by Patience Strong and the speakers included Ted Broad, Bob Danvers Walker and Harold Stough.[88] In a shared initiative with the SPBI, the BIWF also bought a property in Battle, Sussex, as a retirement home 'for elderly and lonely BIs.' The building was named Saxon Homes. It remained in operation for over twenty years.[89] Attendance remained healthy at British-Israel meetings during the 1970s. In 1975, the SPBI was still opening new centres in mainland Britain. In the same year, Cyril Miles embarked on an illustrated lecture tour around the British Isles.[90] The circulation of *Brith*, a magazine promoted by the SPBI, was stable at two thousand copies per month in 1976.[91] But at this point, further schism divided the society. In 1974, McKelvey left the movement to establish the BIBTF. Within two years, McKelvey had died, leaving the new organisation in the hands of Reverend Ted Broad. As a result, the SPBI changed its name, becoming the Covenant People's Fellowship, announcing a new constitution in August 1976.[92]

During this period, the BIWF became more and more intertwined with elements on the anti-immigration right. *The National Message* published a number of editorials praising Enoch Powell. When Powell was pushed to the fringes of the Conservative Party, in the months and years that followed his 'Rivers of Blood' speech, the editors of *The National Message* applauded his tenacity. 'Mr Powell is a loner,' they wrote, 'who fights only on principle. There is, however, so much chicanery and dishonesty in most parts of the community that any person of principle is suspect.'[93] At the same time, Kenneth McKilliam's role in the organisation began to develop. McKilliam was born and raised in Sydney and studied in London before working as an educational and community development officer in Africa. He was once a board member of the BIWF, and he continued to speak at British-Israelist events until he was in his seventies.[94] McKilliam was a virulent anti-Semite and promoter of conspiracy theories. He wrote a number of texts – *Is Our Nation Being Destroyed?*, *High Treason* and *Revealing the Anti-Christ* – which sought to demonstrate that seemingly democratically elected governments were in fact serving as puppets of a global Jewish conspiracy.

At this point, Mary Stanton entered the movement. In 1971, Stanton wrote to twelve prominent British-Israelists, including Norman Court – the then-editor of *Brith* – informing them that she had had a religious experience and had been informed that they were the twelve apostles reincarnated. The following year, Stanton related her experiences in a book, entitled *The Resurrection of the Dead and the Coming Judgment*.[95] Court was swift to distance himself from Stanton, but – writing in 1972 – he lamented that 'several' of the other twelve individuals had 'fallen into the trap' and were 'now committed to what this lady writes and accept what they have been told.'[96] Stanton – who was formerly known as Stephanie Harris – was a friend and collaborator of Lady Jane Birdwood, the wife of Lord Christopher Birdwood. Jane Birdwood was active in anti-Communist movements during the Cold War. In the late 1970s she helped to fund and to organise Christian Attack and an organisation known as The Free Society. The latter – not unlike the BIWF – combined anti-immigration populism with apocalyptic sentiments. At least some members of The Free Society also embraced British-Israelism. One document, released jointly by McKilliam and Stanton made use of some well-established conspiratorial, anti-Semitic tropes:

> Do you know about the Satanic Communist/Zionist Conspiracy to turn us all into slaves under the World Government of the International Bankers? Let us wake up and do something about it before the trap is sprung forever. . . . Only the Lord Jesus, who drove the money-changers out of the Temple, is stronger than Satan. Let us turn to Him, the Creator and Owner of all things, in bitter repentance, and claim the deliverance He has offered to us.[97]

Stanton would later bankroll the publication of *Rainbow Ark* magazine during the early 1990s. *Rainbow Ark* was supported by Stanton, along with Anthony Chevasse, and it published articles written by – amongst others – David Icke and Donald Martin. Martin was a leading figure of the British League of Rights and the publisher of a magazine called *On Target*. He also contributed to *Spearhead*, the magazine of the National Front. The activities of Stanton's group were investigated by Martin Kalman and John Murray in an article for *The New Statesman*.[98]

The National Message fell out of circulation in the late 1970s. In the subsequent decades, the BIWF sought to replace it with other titles. *Wake Up*, in a new smaller format, was published until 1981. *The Message* remained in publication throughout the 1980s, but was replaced later by *BIWF Quarterly* until 2000, then by *Crown and Commonwealth* from 2001 to 2006 and lastly by *The Covenant Nations* which has remained in publication since 2007. The SPBI introduced a new magazine – *Bible Impact* – in 1971, but it would only remain in circulation for two years. *Brith*, meanwhile, was replaced by *Covenant Voice* in 1982 and by *Covenant Viewpoint* in 1994. From the late 1970s, the Covenant People's Fellowship branched out and began to produce recorded material. A 'tape recorded ministry' was established, whereby British-Israelists could order cassettes recordings of sermons on subjects ranging from 'communism or Christ' to 'the Way Ahead' to 'Israel's Companion.'[99]

A second area which opened up for British-Israel expansion during the 1970s and 1980s was Loyal Ulster. Prominent Ulster-based Pentecostalists, Presbyterians and members of the Church of God movement gravitated towards British-Israelism during the Troubles. A new Covenant People's Fellowship centre opened in Newtownabbey, Antrim, on 30 January 1975.[100] Another new centre at Armagh Orange Hall was opened by Francis Thomas under the auspices of Pastor Eric Briggs on 19 November 1975.[101] The BIWF began to hold annual conventions in Ulster at which the leadership of the movement were typically in attendance. In 1980 the speakers at the annual Ulster convention were Margaret Kilner, Harry Johnston and Francis Thomas.[102] James McCook, pastor of the Church of God in Ballymoney preached during the Summer Bible School and Convention of the Covenant People's Fellowship.[103] By March 1989, half of all meetings held by the Covenant People's Fellowship were in Northern Ireland. Three meetings per week were held at the West End Mission on the Shankill Road. A tour of the province was arranged by Francis Thomas that year.[104] Despite these advances, the number of meetings in mainland Britain were beginning to decline. In 1978 the number of monthly meetings of the BIWF had declined to eighty.[105] Ten years later, the number of meetings had dropped again to thirty.[106] 'Our centre in Brighton has suffered a setback,' *Brith* reported in 1975, whilst going on to say that 'our membership in the Emerald Isle is growing.'[107] By 1980 the Covenant People's Fellowship was holding twenty meetings per month.[108] At their annual report for the year 1982, the Covenant People's Fellowship announced that meetings in Bournemouth and Yeovil had been discontinued whilst 'happily' two new meetings had been established in Coleraine and Ballgowan. Two hundred people were registered at the former meeting. The second was attended by John Dunlop MP.[109]

The 1980s saw the ascent of Victor Harper to the presidency of the BIWF. Harper had formerly been the chaplain of the organisation. His presidency was marked by further schism in the movement. In 1984, *The Guardian* reported that the 'small but ancient' BIWF was 'trying to recover from an acrimonious internal dispute.' The running of the federation by Victor Harper had been called into question by his deputy Victor Bowsher. Bowsher alleged that funds had been poorly allocated and that board meetings were chaotic with 'screaming invective . . . the order of the day.'[110] In response to these upheavals, Patience Strong (one of the most high-profile members of the federation during this period) established a parallel organisation – the Ensign Trust – for the purpose of disseminating British-Israel truth.[111]

By the late 1990s, the BIWF had become increasingly concerned with promoting conspiracy theories and Euroscepticism. The former was a key interest of the man who had replaced Harper as president, Matthew Browning. The latter occupied the attentions of the man who would be his successor, Michael Clark. Browning was a Scot who was inculcated into the British-Israel tradition by Hew Colquhoun. He was a soldier and later became a schoolteacher. Browning passed the leadership of the BIWF to Michael Clark in 2006, having been president for nineteen years.[112] Clark divided his work between leading the BIWF and leading (along with Geoff Southall) the Democratic Party. This was essentially a rump movement of the Referendum Party which came into existence with the collapse of the latter in 1997. The Earl of Burford, who drew public ridicule in 1999 when he declared the House of Lords Act to be treasonous, stood as a candidate for the party in the 1999 by-election in Kensington. Southall and Clark submitted a letter as written evidence to the House of Commons Committee on the European Union on 6 November 2007. The letter declared that the UK 'system of government aspires to a higher authority than that of man, whereas the European System is dictated by the Will of Man, a direct product of the French Revolution.'[113] This language was highly reminiscent of the criticisms levelled by Clark at the European Union in the pages of BIWF publications. On 17 October 2001, the day of the third reading of the Treaty of Nice, Clark organised a protest in Parliament Square. The protestors carried banners which proclaimed that the Queen had sworn a coronation oath which forbad her from surrendering power to an external authority.[114]

The 2000s saw the BIWF move away from the capital city for the first time. In 1990, the organisation had moved from Buckingham Gate to a new headquarters at 121 Deodar Road in Putney. In 2003, they moved again, from Putney to Low Etherley on the outskirts of Bishop Auckland. Along with Clark, the BIWF was organised in the 2000s by David Aimer and Martin Lightfoot. Aimer – a 'former Rhodesian' – is principal of the National Bible College which is now based in Bishop Auckland.[115] The leadership of the BIBTF and the Covenant People's Fellowship, in the 1990s and 2000s, was equally dominated by a relatively small number of figures. In the 1980s, the leadership of the Covenant People's Fellowship was taken on by Kenneth Whittaker, whose wife Ena was also a prominent figure in the movement.[116] Leaders of the BIBTF today include Paul Boyd-Lee and Dr. Michael Bennett. Boyd-Lee continues to play a role in the synod of the Church of England and was an Archbishop's council member of the Archbishopric of Salisbury in the early 2000s. Boyd-Lee has served as the secretary of the BIBTF for the past thirty years. During a substantial part of that time, the president of the BIBTF has been Dr Michael Bennett. Bennett's father Stanley was a Bible Pattern preacher in Kent during the 1940s and 1950s. Bennett himself studied botany and was appointed keeper of the Jodrell Laboratory Gardens in the mid-1990s. After an illustrious career at Kew, he was awarded an OBE in 1996 and was made an honorary research fellow at Kew upon his retirement in 2006.[117]

Decline continued in the late 1990s and early 2000s. In 2005, *Bible Truth* claimed to have one thousand readers. Meanwhile, the BIBTF had 148 paying members.[118] The following year it reported 160 members.[119] The BIWF also suffered decline in this period. The number of members fell from 700 in the early 1990s to 311 in 1998.[120] Despite this, the BIWF retained some of its more high-profile support. At this point, patrons include Viscount Allenby of Meggido, who was deputy speaker of the House of Lords, and Nelson McCausland who – until recently – was culture secretary in the Northern Ireland Executive.[121]

More and more, British-Israel movements appear to be attaining an infusion of support and enthusiasm from their sister organisations across the Atlantic. In 2017, 2018 and 2019, the Covenant People's Fellowship held conventions at the High Leigh Centre. In more recent times, mainstays of the British-Israelist movement in the UK (Anthony Martlew, Michael Bennett, Robert Phillips, Colin Farquhar, Norman Pearson, Cora Birch) have been joined on the dais by Pastor Kenneth Kemble of Aletheia Ministries (which is based in San Antonio, Texas) and Brooks Alden of the Association of Covenant People in Vancouver.[122]

Other British-Israel movements

From the outset of the formal organisation of the British-Israel movement under the auspices of the BIWF, the latter encouraged cross-pollenation with other Protestant denominations which held British-Israel principles. The most significant of these relationships was with members of the Elim Church. Throughout the history of British-Israelism, some of its most prominent advocates have been drawn from the ranks of the Elim community. Elim was first founded in 1915 by George Jeffreys. It emerged as one of the most popular embodiments of Pentecostal revival during the first decades of the twentieth century. Jeffreys was a prodigious evangelist. He began his ministry in Ulster before moving to England, where he founded congregations in Essex, Clapham and Nantwich. In 1939 George Jeffreys' commitment to the doctrines of British-Israelism began to create irreconcilable differences in the ranks of the Elim community.[123] In response, Jeffreys left the church that he had founded and established the Bible Pattern Church Fellowship. This community was headquartered at the Kensington Temple, a building which had originally been built as a Congregationalist chapel on Hornton Street in 1848. Its annual convention was held at Westminster Central Hall. These conventions were known to attract tens of thousands of worshipers. Jeffreys continued to write on the subject of 'the Kingdom message.' In 1935 he wrote a pamphlet entitled 'Three Schools of Thought on the Israel Question,' which was published by the Covenant Publishing Company. When he died, in 1962, Jeffreys' obituary was written by Commander Donald Macmillan – then president of the BIWF – in the pages of *The National Message*.[124]

Amongst the first to follow Jeffreys was John Leech. Leech was a King's Counsel. He was also a friend of Jeffreys and eventually a leader within the movement that Jeffreys founded. He preached at the Elim rally at Crystal Palace in 1933, as well as at the Kensington Temple, and was appointed commissioner of the Elim Crusaders in 1934.[125] Leech's British-Israelism was the source of George Jeffreys' own adherence to the doctrine.[126] Jeffreys himself wrote that 'the . . . eminent barrister at law, Mr John Leech introduced me to [the Israel].'[127]

An early disciple of Jeffreys' was Edward Oastler Steward. Steward joined the Elim Church in 1926. At the foundation of the Bible Pattern Church Fellowship, Steward migrated with his mentor to the new organisation. He was appointed to the Advisory Body and then to the Coordinating Council of the Church. During the post-war years he travelled across Europe promoting revivals on behalf of the Bible Pattern Church. In 1950, he became a lecturer on behalf of the BIWF, organising BIWF meetings in the UK before his retirement in 1969.[128] Another figure who straddled his membership of the broader Elim community and the BIWF was Ansley Rash. Rash had been ordained in the Elim Church in the 1940s. He later trained at the BIWF College at Harrow Weald and became BIWF commissioner to Ireland between 1945 and 1956. He was appointed commissioner of the Canadian BIWF during the 1960s.[129] Up to the present day, the connection between Elim and the British-Israel tradition persists. One of the most influential figures in the movement today – Pastor Robert Phillips – serves as the minister of the Elim Free Bible Pattern Church on Edwards Street in Carlisle.

Outside of the UK, a large number of churches gravitated towards British-Israel doctrines during the twentieth century. Many of these can be associated with the Christian Identity tradition and the various religious manifestations of far-right white supremacism. Amongst these, we may include the Lord's Covenant Church, the Anglo-Saxon Federation of America, the Phineas Priesthood and the Church of Jesus Christ Christian.[130] At times, UK-based British-Israelists have actively sought to build ties with elements of the Christian Identity movement. The Church of Israel is a denomination of Mormonism which has adopted the principles of British-Israelism. It was founded in 1972 by Pastor Dan Gayman. The church has been identified by the Anti-Defamation League as an extremist, anti-Semitic group. An article in *Wake Up*, written in 1991, celebrated the anniversary of the establishment of the Church of Israel, calling Gayman 'a very active and outward looking minister.'[131]

A fuller exploration of the development of these various movements can be found in the work of Michael Barkun. Given the scope of this work, a detailed exploration of non-UK-based forms of British-Israelism are not warranted. However, it *is* worth noting the British-Israelist inclinations of the Worldwide Church of God (WCG). Whilst the majority of adherents to the teachings of Herbert Armstrong are based in the United States, in the mid-1960s the church attempted to create an outpost in the United Kingdom. This led to a much increased interaction between the BIWF and members of the Worldwide Church.

The WCG was founded in 1934 by Herbert Armstrong, a radio evangelist.[132] Armstrong cautioned that the world would end in 1975 and exhorted his listeners to avoid materialism, to practice Sabbatarianism and to avoid using conventional medicine. Armstrong's message was disseminated via his radio programme and via the publication of a free magazine entitled *Plain Truth*. In 1954, Armstrong published a book entitled *The United States and Britain in Prophecy*. Six million copies of the book were sold. The book expressed Armstrong's belief in the principles of British-Israelism. Armstrong was principally influenced by a text that he had read in the 1920s: J.H. Allen's *Judah's Sceptre and Joseph's Birthright*. This text promoted a range of British-Israelist claims, including that 'the people of God whom He calls Israel . . . are not Jews' and that 'the Holy Spirit has never, either in Biblical history nor in prophecy called the Jews.'[133] During the 1960s, membership of Armstrong's church expanded rapidly and the church established nine hundred congregations across the United States. In 1960, the church acquired a property at Brickett Wood in Hertfordshire. The property was converted into a campus of Ambassador College, a degree-granting college funded by the church and headquartered in Pasadena. This development brought the WCG to the attention of the BIWF. The leadership of the BIWF expressed scepticism about the orthodoxy of Armstrong's views and, throughout the 1960s, several editorials in *The National Message* were devoted to cautioning readers against membership of the church. In 1964 Eric Last, a lecturer at Kensit Memorial College, wrote an article for *The English Churchman*, warning of the heterodoxical nature of Armstrongism – particularly in its anti-Trinitarianism – and this was later reprinted in the pages of *The National Message*. Nonetheless, elements within the movement remained congenial to some aspects of Armstrong's doctrines, most obviously (of course) Armstrong's own British-Israelism.[134]

Conclusion

The narrative which links the progress of the British-Israel movement with the rise of the British Empire is too superficial. In reality, we find that the British-Israel idea continued to attract adherents long into the twentieth century. As recently as the 1970s, the BIWF was continuing to expand, announcing new magazines and establishing new outposts. In particular, in the province of Northern Ireland, British-Israelism experienced a surge in popularity in the 1980s. It should also be clear from the preceding evidence that British-Israelism attracted adherents from many different sectors of British society. Whilst it has declined in the past twenty years, this decline is broadly in line with a wider decline in church attendance in the UK. As such, a close examination of the history of British-Israelism can provide us with an insight into a particular moment in the history of British nationalism more broadly. In the proceeding chapters, our attention will turn to specific areas to which British-Israelists applied their theories over the course of the twentieth century, beginning with British-Israelist attitudes to the Jewish people and to Jewish religion.

Notes

1 Genesis 48.
2 2 Esdras 13: 40–50.
3 Zvi Ben-Dor Benite, *The Ten Lost Tribes: A World History* (Oxford: Oxford University Press, 2009), 144.
4 Yoel Perez, 'Sambation,' in Raphael Patai (ed.), *Encyclopaedia of Jewish Folklore and Tradition* (Abingdon: Routledge, 2015), 467–468; Benite, *The Ten Lost Tribes*, 87–88.
5 Benite, *The Ten Lost Tribes*, 86.
6 Moshe Idel, *Messianic Mystics* (New Haven: Yale University Press, 1998), 58–63; Benite, *The Ten Lost Tribes*, 83.
7 Christopher Hill, 'Till the Conversion of the Jews,' in Richard Henry Popkin (ed.), *Millenarianism and Messianism in English Literature and Thought 1650–1800* (Leiden: Brill, 1988), 12–36; Benite, *The Ten Lost Tribes*, 170–198.
8 W.E. Filmer, *A Synopsis of the Migration* (Covenant Publishing: London, 1966); *Brith*, no. 351 (April 1975), 27.
9 *The National Message*, vol. 47, no. 1,543 (June 1968), 185.
10 *The British Israel Pilot*, no. 91 (15 July 1929), 5.
11 George Moore, *The Lost Tribes and the Saxons of the East and West* (London, 1861), 357.
12 *The National Message*, vol. 57, no. 1,662 (May 1978), 157.
13 Thomas Burgess, *Tracts on the Origin and Independence of the Ancient British Church* (London: Rivington, 1815); Richard Williams Morgan, *St Paul in Britain* (London: Parker, 1861); Joanne Pearson, *Wicca and the Christian Heritage: Ritual, Sex and Magic* (Abingdon: Routledge, 2007), 35.
14 Matthew 10; Matthew 15.
15 Moore, *The Lost Tribes and the Saxons of the East and West*, 357.
16 Cited in Chester Quarles, *Christian Identity: The Aryan American Bloodline Religion* (Jefferson: McFarland, 2003), 31.

17 Deborah Madden, *The Paddington Prophet* (Manchester: Manchester University Press, 2010).
18 Philip Lockley, *Visionary Religion and Radicalism in Early Industrial England from Southcott to Socialism* (Oxford: Oxford University Press, 2013), 1–24.
19 Wilson, *Our Israelitish Origin*.
20 Hine, *Fourty-Seven Identifications of the Anglo-Saxons with the Lost Tribes of Israel*, 96.
21 Hine, *Fourty-Seven Identifications of the Anglo-Saxons with the Lost Tribes of Israel*, 2.
22 Barkun, *Religion and the Racist Right*, 3–17.
23 A.B. Grimaldi, *The Queen's Royal Descent from King David the Psalmist* (London: Banks, 1885).
24 Charles Piazzi Smyth, *Our Inheritance in the Great Pyramid* (London: Isbister, 1874); Reisenauer, 'The Battle of the Standards,' 931–978.
25 *Acton Gazette* (28 November 1902), 8.
26 *The Guernsey Star*, vol. 70, no. 37 (31 August 1882), 4.
27 Denis Paz, *Popular Anti-Catholicism in Mid-Victorian England* (Stanford: Stanford University Press, 1992).
28 Metropolitan Anglo-Israel Association, *Report for the Proceedings at the First Annual Meeting*, 12.
29 *The Protestant Magazine*, vol. 9, no. 2 (February 1847), 45.
30 Metropolitan Anglo-Israel Association, *Report for the Proceedings at the First Annual Meeting*, 12.
31 Metropolitan Anglo-Israel Association, *Report for the Year Ending 30 April 1880* (London, 1880), 9.
32 *Quarterly Notes of the British-Israel League*, vol. 6, no. 4 (October 1916), 133.
33 *Quarterly Notes of the British-Israel League*, vol. 6, no. 4 (October 1916), 105.
34 *Hastings and St Leonards Observer*, no. 2,501 (18 November 1905), 7.
35 *The Banner of Israel*, vol. 40, no. 2,057 (31 May 1916), 238.
36 Douglas Parker, *Why Great Britain Will Never Be Destroyed But Will Stand Forever* (Sowerby Bridge: Edwards, 1922), 1–4.
37 *The Banner of Israel*, vol. 40, no. 2,075 (4 October 1916), 404.
38 *The British Israel Herald*, vol. 5, no. 53 (May 1928), 82.
39 *Brith*, no. 16 (January 1947), 7.
40 *The Times*, no. 42,093 (7 May 1919), 13; *The Banner of Israel*, vol. 43, no. 2,210 (7 May 1919), 171.
41 *The Banner of Israel*, vol. 43, no. 2,210 (7 May 1919), 171.
42 *The Banner of Israel*, vol. 45, no. 2,298 (12 January 1921), 18.
43 *The Banner of Israel*, vol. 45, no. 2,299 (19 January 1921), 22.
44 *The Banner of Israel*, vol. 45, no. 2,299 (19 January 1921), 27.
45 *Manchester Guardian*, no. 23,463 (26 October 1921), 18.
46 *The Banner of Israel*, vol. 43, no. 2,212 (21 May 1919), 179.
47 *The Banner of Israel*, vol. 43, no. 2,213 (28 May 1919), 197.
48 *Lancashire Evening Post*, no. 12,451 (27 November 1926), 1.
49 *Kent and Sussex Courier* no. 4,947 (17 October 1930), 10.
50 Wilson, 'British Israelism,' 43.
51 'Letter from Lord Gisborough, United Protestant Council,' The Parliamentary Archives, BL 114/11/5.
52 'Papers Relating to the General Administration and Funding of the Junior Constitutional Club,' Wiltshire and Swindon Historical Centre, 947/880.
53 *Ballurat Star*, no. 14,425 (22 June 1902), 5.
54 *The National Message*, vol. 49, no. 1,562 (January 1970), 12–13.
55 *West Sussex County Times* (17 December 1927), 10.

56 *The National Message*, vol. 1, no. 25 (24 June 1922), v.
57 Barkun, *Religion and the Racist Right*, 30.
58 The Roadbuilder, *The Destiny of Britain and America* (London: Covenant Publishing, 1921), i.
59 Bedfordshire Archives, Hospital Records, Daneswood Archives, 6.
60 *Northern Whig*, no. 36,013 (31 January 1924), 8; *The Times*, no. 43,663 (28 May 1924), 24; *Grantham Journal* (28 June 1924), 6.
61 *Belfast Telegraph* (13 February 1932), 2.
62 Alban Heath, *The Faith of a British Israelite* (London: Covenant Publishing, 1937), 88.
63 *Birmingham Daily Gazette* (8 March 1932), 3.
64 *Toren*, vol. 6, no. 1 (April 1969), 2–3; *Covenant Viewpoint* (Autumn 2017), 2–3.
65 *Bible Truth*, no. 241 (May 2006), 24; *Bible Truth*, no. 204 (April 2000), 24.
66 *The National Message*, vol. 43, no. 1,495 (May 1964), 140.
67 *The Times*, no. 62,774 (21 May 1987), 20.
68 National Archives, Metropolitan Police Office, 3/1257.
69 *Daily Express*, no. 10,504 (9 January 1934), 7.
70 *Derby Daily Telegraph*, vol. 94, no. 16,386 (1 February 1934), 1; *Evening Telegraph* no. 19,831 (19 January 1934), 6; *Evening Telegraph*, no. 19,852 (13 February 1934), 5.
71 Remarks of J. Thorkelson, Congressional Record, Proceedings and Debates, 76th Congress, 3rd session (19 August–5 September 1940), 1–28.
72 'Testimony of Mrs. Helen V. Somers on the United Nations Charter Before the United States Senate Foreign Relations Committee,' in *Hearings Before the Committee on Foreign Relations of the United States Senate, Seventy-Ninth Congress, First Session on the Charter of the United Nations for the Maintenance of International Peace and Security Submitted by the President on July 2 1945* (Washington, DC: Committee on Foreign Relations, 1945).
73 Catherine Palfrey Baldwin, *And Men Wept* (New York: Our Publications, 1955), 28.
74 *The Daily Telegraph*, no. 24,764 (5 October 1934), 20.
75 *The National Message*, vol. 31, no. 1,294 (23 February 1952), 84.
76 *The National Message*, vol. 22, no. 1,070 (7 July 1943), 110.
77 *The National Message*, vol. 25, no. 1,156 (23 October 1946), 310–311.
78 *Wake Up*, vol. 7, no. 10 (August 1989), 238.
79 *Brith*, no. 1 (September 1945), 15.
80 *Long Eaton Advertiser*, no. 3,955 (15 November 1957), 2; *Eastbourne Gazette*, no. 5,152 (19 February 1958), 2; *Belfast Telegraph* (5 February 1977), 4.
81 *Covenant Voice* (January 1990), 29.
82 *Crown and Commonwealth*, vol. 4, no. 1 (Spring 2004), 15.
83 *Bath Chronicle and Weekly Gazette*, vol. 195, no. 10,168 (16 September 1950), 16.
84 *Toren*, vol. 3, no. 1 (January 1966), 14; *Toren*, vol. 2, no. 1 (January 1965), 24; *Toren*, vol. 3, no. 1 (January 1966), 24.
85 *Brith*, no. 183 (April 1961), 28.
86 *The National Message*, vol. 50, no. 1,581 (August 1971), 253.
87 *The National Message*, vol. 49, no. 1,566 (May 1970), 144.
88 *The National Message*, vol. 55, no. 1,637 (April 1976), 121.
89 *Brith*, no. 319 (August 1972), 31.
90 *Brith*, no. 350 (March 1975), 28.
91 *Brith*, no. 366 (October 1976), 31.
92 *Brith*, no. 364 (August 1976), 16–25.
93 *The National Message*, vol. 49, no. 1,568 (July 1970), 223.
94 *The National Message*, vol. 59, no. 1,686 (May 1980), 79.
95 Mary Stanton, *Announcing the Resurrection of the Dead* (London: Self-published, 1972).

96 *Brith*, no. 319 (August 1972), 3.
97 Kenneth McKilliam and Mary Stanton, *Free Society* (London, 1972 [Handbill]).
98 *The New Statesman and Society*, no. 358 (23 June 1995), 18.
99 *Brith*, no. 355 (August 1975), 29.
100 *Brith*, no. 349 (February 1975), 29.
101 *Brith*, no. 355 (November 1975), 13.
102 *Brith*, no. 414 (November 1980), 11.
103 *Covenant Voice* (September 1989), 28.
104 *Covenant Voice* (January 1989), 2; *Covenant Voice* (September 1989), 2.
105 *The National Message*, vol. 57, no. 1,661 (April 1978), 125.
106 *BIWF Quarterly*, vol. 2, no. 4 (October 1989), 15.
107 *Brith*, no. 355 (August 1975), 30.
108 *Brith*, no. 413 (October 1980), 2.
109 *Annual Report of the Covenant People's Fellowship for 1982* (Woodford Green: Covenant People's Fellowship, 1982), 5.
110 *The Guardian* (14 July 1984), 3.
111 *The Guardian* (30 July 1984), 3.
112 *The Covenant Nations*, vol. 1, no. 1 (November 2007), 14.
113 'Letter from Geoff Southall and Michael Clark, the Democratic Party Limited,' House of Commons Select Committee on European Union, Written Evidence, https://publications.parliament.uk/pa/ld200708/ldselect/ldeucom/62/62weg19.htm.
114 *Crown and Commonwealth*, vol. 1, Special Edition (2001), 23.
115 *Crown and Commonwealth*, vol. 2, no. 3 (Autumn 2002), 10.
116 *Covenant Voice* (December 1992), 28.
117 Ray Desmond, *Kew: The History of the Royal Botanic Gardens* (London: Harvill, 1995), 382.
118 *Bible Truth*, no. 236 (July 2005), 13.
119 *Bible Truth*, no. 242 (July 2006), 19.
120 British Library, *British Israel World Federation Annual Accounts and Reports* (1993), 1; British Library, *British Israel World Federation Annual Accounts and Reports* (1999), 9.
121 British Library, *British Israel World Federation Annual Accounts and Reports* (1998), 1.
122 *Covenant Viewpoint* (Autumn 2017), 2–3.
123 William Kay, 'George Jeffreys: Pentecostal and Contemporary Implications,' in *Religions*, 9, no. 2 (2018): 60–71.
124 *The National Message*, vol. 41, no. 1,469 (April 1962), 111.
125 Bryan R. Wilson, *Sects and Society: A Sociological Study of the Elim Tabernacle* (Los Angeles: University of California Press, 1961), 51.
126 Kay, 'George Jeffreys: Pentecostal and Contemporary Implications,' 60–71.
127 *Brith*, no. 410 (July 1980), 8.
128 Poch, *Who Hath Believed Our Report*, 1.
129 *The National Message*, vol. 49, no. 1,562 (January 1970), 46.
130 Michael McFarland and Glenn Gottfried, 'The Chosen Ones: A Mythic Analysis of the Theological and Political Self-Justification of Christian Identity,' in *Journal for the Study of Religion*, 15, no. 1 (2002): 125–145.
131 *Wake Up*, vol. 8, no. 8 (September 1991), 179.
132 David V. Barrett, *The Fragmentation of a Sect: Schism in the Worldwide Church of God* (Oxford: Oxford University Press, 2013).
133 John Allen, *Judah's Sceptre and Jacob's Birthright* (Boston: Beauchamp, 1917), 71.
134 *The National Message*, vol. 43, no. 1,496 (July 1964), 211.

3   British-Israelism and the Jews

In the spring of 1926, the Board of Deputies of British-Jews conducted an informal inquiry into the dealings of the BIWF. Members of the board had been alarmed by statements made by John Morey at a meeting of the Ealing branch of the BIWF in mid-March of that year. George Lowe, secretary of the Board of Deputies, wrote to the then president of the BIWF – Herbert Garrison – in order to establish whether or not the BIWF was institutionally anti-Semitic. Garrison protested, in response, that there was 'no truth whatever in the statement that our council favors a policy of anti-Semitism.' He went on to say that 'new members are joining daily,' and 'the vast body of our members stand entirely and loyally by the council.' Morey, meanwhile, echoed Garrison's sentiments. 'We are not anti-Semitic, only anti-Bolshevist,' he wrote, in a private letter to Lowe dated 28 July 1926, 'we are only in opposition to the Bolshevik Jew because he has declared himself as determined to destroy Christianity.' Lowe pressed Morey on some of his associations with avowedly anti-Semitic groups. Morey responded, on 3 August 1926, declaring that the BIWF *could not* be anti-Semitic, given that: 'we teach the reunion of Israel and Judah.'[1] After all, as British-Israelists claimed: '[if] Israel and Judah are promised a reunion . . . then they must *both* exist on this earth.'[2]

This brief interaction exhibits the complexity of the relationship between British-Israelism and the Jews. Throughout the twentieth century, British-Israelists have frequently traded in anti-Semitic canards and slurs. They have, at the same time, declared their kinship with the Jewish people, who they perceive to be (at least in part) the true descendants of the tribes of Judah and Benjamin. They have lamented the lot of the Jewish people when the Jewish people have faced adversity, persecution and genocidal violence. They have celebrated – and have at times even adopted – aspects of Jewish religious life.

The following will seek to untangle the philo-Semitic and anti-Semitic ideas which lie intertwined at the heart of British-Israelist thought. British-Israelists, in their attitudes towards individual Jews and towards the Jewish people as a whole, exhibit a tendency towards allosemitism as defined by Zygmunt Bauman. At times they exhibit anti-Semitic attitudes and at other times they exhibit philo-Semitic attitudes, but at all times they appear 'unable to interact with Jews on their own terms.'[3] Partly this inability is rooted in British-Israelists' attachment to authenticity. The authenticity of the Jewish people, for British-Israelists, lies in their otherness.

Philo-Semitism, Anti-Semitism and allosemitism

Several scholars have pointed out the close interaction between white-nationalist anti-Semitism and the doctrine of British-Israelism. Richard Pierard, for example, has written that the seeming eccentricity of the doctrine 'masks a sinister and malevolent trend towards racial violence . . . a mandate for the destruction of the Jews.'[4] Some anti-Semitic, extremist ideologies have certainly made use of British-Israelist doctrines over the course of the twentieth century. This is most notable in the American context, where individuals like the Richard Hoskins (architect of the Phineas Priesthood movement) and Howard Rand (of the Anglo-Saxon Federation of America) adopted British-Israelist ideas and wedded them to anti-Semitic bigotry.[5] Before its collective *metanoia* in the late 1980s, the WCG, led by Herbert Armstrong, also espoused a form of British-Israelism with avowedly white supremacist elements. Armstrong promoted 'the astounding fact,' that 'our white, English speaking peoples – and not the Jews – have inherited the national and physical phases of the promise.'[6] In the United Kingdom, also, British-Israelist theories have been used as a fig leaf for anti-Semitism. Kenneth McKilliam was once a board member of the BIWF.[7] McKilliam was an open anti-Semite, and his work has subsequently been embraced by far-right extremists in the United Kingdom including Simon Sheppard, the founder of Redwatch.[8]

At the same time, British-Israelists were prone to making philo-Semitic declarations. This was especially true in the first half of the twentieth century. Thomas Rosling Howett offered an exploration of the relationship between the Aryan theorising of Max Muller and the theories of British-Israelism. Howett's text bares all the hallmarks of objectifying philo-Semitism. 'The Jews,' according to Howett, are 'studious, industrious and thrifty.' They are 'religious, law-abiding, pure in habits, phenomenally chaste, beautiful in their homelife.' They are 'healthy and long-lived.'[9] T.W. Plant, former president of the British-Israel National Union, made a number of assertions, in his address to the inaugural meeting of the BIWF, regarding the characteristics of the 'Jewish Race.' Jews, Plant believed, were an 'exceptionally intelligent, intellectual race, keenly alive to logic and to their own history.'[10] In 1931, Grace Norton wrote to a Norfolk newspaper expressing equally philo-Semitic sentiments. She claimed to have close personal relationships with 'leading Jews' in East London. She had been invited to weddings, bar mitzvahs and circumcisions. 'I have always been treated with the greatest respect, kindness and love,' Norton wrote.

In addition to espousing philo-Semitic attitudes, particularly in the twentieth century, British-Israelists have often publicly disavowed anti-Semitism.

Grace Norton argued that the 'first concern' of British-Israelists should be 'for the Jews' welfare.'[11] Thirty years later, with a reported spike in anti-Semitic violence reported in West Germany, British-Israelists again expressed solidarity with their Jewish kinfolk. They warned that anti-Semitism had 'an insidious appeal,' to Germans and that the Nazis could 'climb back into power on the backs of an anti-Jew inflamed Western German people.'[12]

In 1970, *The National Message* featured an article debunking the *Protocols of the Learned Elders of Zion,* calling it a 'slanderous forgery' and 'an evil seed sown in the mind of Hitler.'[13] Throughout the 1960s and 1970s, repeated efforts were made by representatives of the major British-Israelist organisations to distance themselves from the perceived excesses of Armstrongism, particularly in light of the establishment of an outpost of Ambassador College at Bricket Wood in Hertfordshire.[14] Whilst British-Israelist publications did not shy away from their association with Howard Rand's Anglo-Saxon Federation, they maintained that anti-Semitic elements within Rand's movement were a distortion (a heresy indeed) to be eschewed:

> Neo Nazi and other white revolutionary supremist [*sic*] groups have distorted the racial aspects of Christian Israel beliefs into a philosophy of anti-Semitism and white superiority, claiming scriptural justification for their intolerant and often violent attitudes.[15]

At the Annual Congress of the Covenant People's Fellowship in 1990, a motion was tabled which stated that 'The Celto-Anglo-Saxon peoples are *not* a superior race.'[16] The *BIWF Newsletter* of January 2007, meanwhile, lamented the rise of 'extremist' groups, combining anti-Semitic and British-Israelist beliefs, particularly in the USA.[17] In 2008, the *Northern Echo* reported on efforts by the National Bible College (an adjunct organisation to the BIWF) to join an archaeological dig in Israel. The *Echo* interviewed Martin Lightfoot, who made the claim that the BIWF was 'an interdenominational organisation very much in harmony with the Jewish community.'[18] Individuals like Jacob Thorkelson and Charles Ashton – who both attacked the BIWF in the 1930s – perceived the British-Israelist movement to be too philo-Semitic.

These opponents of British-Israelists believed they were attempting to facilitate a Jewish monopoly on global power.[19] This view was shared by Christian-Identitarians who occasionally accused traditional British-Israelist thinkers of being manipulated by Jews or – indeed – of being Jewish themselves.[20] In one sense, their perception of British-Israelism as philo-Semitic has some grounding. British-Israelists express the belief that white, Anglo-Saxon peoples share a kinship with the Jewish people of some kind. Many British-Israelists also look forward to an eschatological date at which the Jewish people will reign alongside the peoples of British-Israel in Jerusalem. Whereas other anti-Semitic groups have denied or even celebrated the Holocaust and other examples of anti-Jewish violence, historically, many British-Israelists have spoken out against the persecution of Jewish people, whether in Tsarist Russia, in Nazi Germany or in the Arab world.[21]

At times, indeed, British-Israelists have explicitly highlighted points of commonality between Jews and Britons in an effort to accentuate claims of shared kinship. So, in 1918, B.H. Norton offered an inventory of characteristics which linked British and Jewish identities, including the shared objection to idolatry, shared monotheism and shared affinity for monarchical systems. Norton concluded:

> These relics of similarity must be more than a coincidence and may help those in doubt to see a greater reasonableness than before in the identity of Israel with the Anglo Saxons by this extra light from the tribe of Judah.[22]

Zygmunt Bauman writes that philo-Semitic and anti-Semitic Christians, alike, share a common commitment to the 'othering' of 'the Jew.' Bauman cites the example of Friedrich Rühs who, observing the process of Jewish de-ghettoisation in early-nineteenth-century Germany, expressed relief that Jewish people would always be distinctive, inimitable and distinguishable. Rühs 'could not bear the idea of the Jew melting inconspicuously into the crowd,' Bauman writes: 'Jews were different and their difference mattered.'[23]

Furthermore, Bauman contended that animosity towards Jews was not the product of 'heterophobia' but rather of 'proteophobia': not the fear of 'the unfamiliar,' but rather the fear of 'something or someone that does not fit the structure of the orderly world, does not fall easily into established categories, emits contradictory signals and . . . blurs the borderlines.' The Jew, according to Bauman, is 'ambivalence incarnate.' How did this come about? Bauman suggests that the Jewish people were presented in Christian, supersessionist thought as 'living fossils.' In the patristic era, Christian scholars promoted the claim that Jews were '*scrinaria*,' the bearers of a prophetic corpora, the witnesses to a providence that they themselves could never understand. As such, Jews simultaneously stood for divine chosenness and abjection: 'more un-pagan-like than Christians and yet more pagan than ordinary heathens.' Combining both of these elements, Bauman reaches the conclusion that order and ambivalence are mutually interdependent. 'Ambivalence,' he writes 'is the *cause* of all ordering concerns . . . [it is] the one enemy without which order cannot live.' As such, the topos of the Jew is troublingly contradictory and *therefore* necessary.[24]

This theoretical tool has been put to use in Andrew Crome's analysis of the phenomenon of Christian Zionism. Like British-Israelists, Christian Zionists sometimes appear to defy the bright-line distinction between anti-Semitism and philo-Semitism. Many Evangelicals advocate greater support for the Jewish people. But their support is predicated on the contention that the Jewish people are in a state of estrangement from God, resulting from the deicide, which can only be resolved at a providentially appointed moment when they will be forgiven and then will convert to Christianity.

Crome analyses Christian Zionism from its roots in the Judeocentric millenarianism of Thomas Brightman and Henry Finch, to Evangelical expressions of support for the state of Israel in the twenty-first century. His analysis suggests that Zionism and British, covenantal nationalism are mutually reinforcing ideologies. He disagrees with Anthony Smith's claim that the identification of Britain as a providentially preferred nation led necessarily to a *doppelgänger* affect, whereby Britain sought to 'supplant the Jews as the chosen people.'[25] British 'chosenness,' Crome argues, was in reality *complimentary* to the chosenness of the Jewish people for three important reasons. Protecting and preserving the Jewish people from harm and ultimately facilitating their restoration to Palestine was seen as the missional component of their divine appointment. Secondly, the apparently providential role of the Jewish people – evidenced by the continued dissimilarity of the Jewish people from 'the nations' – serves to reassure covenantal nationalists of their fundamental belief that God 'works through particular nations' his ends to accomplish. Thirdly, Crome echoes a point made earlier by Adam Sutcliffe and Jonathan Karp in the introduction to their *Philosemitism in History*. Judeocentric millenarians and Christian Zionists, as Crome, Karp and Sutcliffe demonstrate, typically *do not* look forward to the conversion as an erasure of Jewish particularity. On the contrary, the innovation of Brightman and Finch's eschatology lay in its claim that the Jewish people would continue to be a distinctive people even after their conversion and, furthermore, that the Jewish people would rule over the crowned heads of the world (including the crowned head of England).[26] For Judeocentric millenarians, the desire for the authenticity of the Jewish people – and the fear that the authenticity of the Jewish people may be eroded – inspired both philo-Semitic and anti-Semitic feeling, words and actions.

To what extent is this relevant to our analysis of British-Israelism? After all, Crome suggests that British-Israelism *does* seek to 'sublimate Jewish identity into Englishness' and as such belongs to a category apart from Christian Zionism.[27] This assumption is understandable but is not strictly accurate. British-Israelist doctrine does not – as Crome suggests – seek the erasure of Jewishness (either from a philo-Semitic or anti-Semitic motivation) any more than Christian Zionism does. British-Israelists did *indeed* attempt to maintain the otherness of 'the Jew.' Moreover, the 'attitude of radical ambivalence' that forms the basis of allosemitism is as pervasive in British-Israelist ideology as it is in Christian Zionist ideology. There are, however, aspects of British-Israelist belief and practice which speak to a complimentary desire for *auto*semitism: for accentuating the similarities that exist between 'Christian Israel' and 'Jewish Israel.' As such, British-Israelists are engaged, more than most Christians, in a perpetual process of defining and negotiating the boundary between Christians and Jews: at once seeking to adduce to themselves a continuity with the Jewish people (as singular and therefore authentic) whilst seeking to mitigate this process by accentuating and doctrinally codifying the distinctiveness between themselves and the Jews. In the British-Israelist context, this claim is grounded in the pseudoscience of racial theory. The prophet Ezekiel envisioned the people of God as two sticks, joined together. This image was widely referred to by British Israelist writers. In 1931, one such writer noted that

> In Ezekiel's figure of the joining of the two sticks, we see that Judah is to remain a distinct entity until that time, which is yet in the future, when they will be joined again to Ephraim Israel under one crowned Head. . . . This again shows Judah as a separate entity, not as being commingled with the other tribes, and as that is the condition of the Jews at this time it is clear that they are the people referred to in this passage.[28]

In these intertwining sticks, both difference and closeness are exhibited, the former in the latter. Jews must be kept close to Israel, intertwined with Israel, but only in order that the difference between Israel and Judah can be most clearly expressed. The same is true of the autosemitic and allosemitic tendencies within British-Israelist thought. Whilst they may appear to represent opposite impulses, they do in fact form a single helix of identity formation.

British-Israelist genealogy

British-Israelists subscribe to a range of beliefs regarding the genealogical origins of different ethnic groups. These genealogies draw upon the dual authority of the Bible and racial pseudo-science. Within these genealogical schemata, British-Israelists allot distinctive but synergetic roles for 'the Jews' and for 'Israel.'

The primary claim of British-Israelism – originating in the writing of John Wilson, Edward Hine and others – is that the Anglo-Saxon people of Britain are descended from the lost tribes of Israel. Within this broad assertion there are varied opinions. Most British-Israelists claim that the people of Britain are of the tribe of Ephraim. The United States, meanwhile, is often associated with the tribe of Menasseh. According to the Biblical narrative, Menasseh and Ephraim were the sons of Joseph and – as such – these two tribes formed the house of Joseph. On this basis, Britain, the United States and the Commonwealth nations of Australia, New Zealand and Canada represent the 'company of nations' prophesied by Jacob in Genesis 48.[29]

The Jewish people are described, by most British-Israelists, as the descendants of the tribe of Judah and of Benjamin.[30] According to the second book of Kings, the tribes of the Northern Kingdom were forcibly resettled by Assyria and from that point on were separated from the tribes of Judah, Benjamin and Simeon, who were subsequently referred to as 'Jews.'[31] As such, the fortunes of the Jewish people are explained by British-Israelists as conforming to the prophecies in the Hebrew Bible relating to those tribes in particular, rather than to Israel as a whole. For example, British-Israelists pay close attention to Zechariah 11 (in which the Lord God breaks the staff of union between Israel and Judah), which they claim describes the final severance of Judah from the tribes, coinciding with the rejection of Christ by the Jewish people. Hosea 1, in which the prophet foresees Judah and Israel coming together – they suggest – promises a reconciliation between Israel and the Jews. Zechariah 12:7 ('the Lord will save the dwellings of Judah'), meanwhile, is used by British-Israelists to explain the role of the Jewish people in the approaching, apocalyptic conflict which will take place before the reconciliation of the tribes.[32]

British-Israelists place great emphasis on the historical use of the term 'Jew.' Before the Assyrian crisis, they note, the word 'Jew' was not used to denote the people of Israel:

> It was in Babylon that the people of Judah had their name changed to Jew and accepted the change to such an extent that even those who returned to Palestine preferred to remain known as Jews instead of reverting to the old name Judah.[33]

Abraham, Isaac, Jacob and Moses, they therefore claim, 'were not Jews.' Neither, according to the same logic, was Jesus. As Roy Simpson wrote in 1980: 'if Jesus were a Jew because He was a descendant of Abraham, then the Arabs must be Jews, because they are also sons of Abraham.'[34] Some British-Israelists, meanwhile, claim that the word 'Jew' has a solely religious, rather than ethnic, meaning. It referred to the 'remnant of the tribe of Judah,' when combined with 'others who adopted the Talmud religion.'[35]

Some British-Israelists point to a perceived discrepancy between the physiognomy of Biblical Jews and modern-day Jews. They argue that 'Anglo-Saxon' people conform, physiologically, to the description of the Israelites in the Hebrew Bible, whilst 'Jews' do not.[36] This issue was raised by H. Morton Niblett in a letter to *The Banner of Israel* in 1919. The editors responded:

> The difference between Jewish and English features was one of the first – probably the very first – objection raised against our identity with Israel. . . . What we call the Jewish features are not the primitive features of the Jews. . . . The old Hebrews were not distinguished by any facial peculiarities. . . . And the great painter Holman Hunt, who studied this point in Palestine, made the noteworthy declaration that, after careful observation, he believed that the ancient type of the Hebrew nation approached nearer to the Anglo-Saxon than to any other.[37]

Niblett was referring to a speech given by Holman Hunt at Exeter Hall in London on 2 May 1900. Holman Hunt was a founding figure of the pre-Raphaelite Brotherhood. In 1853, he travelled to the Middle East to seek inspiration for a series of religious paintings, the most notable being *The Light of the World*. In his speech at Exeter Hall, he explained his decision to portray Christ with seemingly 'European' physical features. Holman Hunt said that, during his time in Jerusalem, he 'looked with great attention at all the Jews' and noticed that – although 'a certain proportion were dark, and were readily recognisable to an Englishman as Jews,' – he nevertheless found other Jews 'who were fair, and who might have passed without being so recognised.'[38]

British-Israelists offer a twofold explanation for the apparent physical dissimilarity between the Jewish people (as a perceived ethnic group) and the Anglo-Saxon people. Firstly, it can be identified as the consummation of a prophecy found in Isaiah 3:9. In this passage, the prophet suggests that the 'expressions on the faces' of the people of Judah 'testify against them.' This has been taken by British-Israelists to denote a change in Judahite physiognomy as a result of their rejection of Christ.[39] Secondly, it can be accounted for as a result of the miscegenation of Judah.[40] In one account, Everard Taylor hypothesised that the true descendants of the tribe of Judah constituted only 14% of modern-day Jewry: '14% of this 12 millions gives some 2 millions of Biblical Jews of Judah, Levi and Benjamin.'[41] As such, most British-Israelists do not believe that modern-day Jewry is identifiable *directly* with the lineage of Judah or Benjamin. Firstly, British-Israelists believe that the people of Judah intermarried with the people of Edom, the descendants of Esau. This 'corruption' was supposed, by British-Israelists to have taken place during the period of the Hasmonean dynasty. Jewry had been 'contaminated,' when John Hycarnus 'forcibly and disastrously incorporated' the Edomites 'including the Amelekites, sons of Esau' who were a 'predatory, ruthless race, destined to be an evil disruptive force, epitomised by Herod.' This group 'carried a perpetual strain of evil exercised particularly against God's power.'[42] The intermarriage of Judah with Edomites had 'befouled Jewry.'[43] At the Covenant People's Fellowship Summer Convention in 1976, Christine Sumner referred to Josephus as a source for this claim. Josephus records that John of Giscala stirred up fears that the High Priest would send for Roman assistance in ending the Zealots' occupation of the Temple, leading the Zealots to send to the Idumeans for help. According to Sumner, 'from this time on, the Edomites ceased to exist as a separate nation, they took over the name of the Jews and were scattered throughout the nations.'[44]

The legacy of the Jewish people's Edomite heritage, according to British-Israelists, is a tendency amongst Jewish people towards violence and treachery. 'The Jews, mixed with the seed of Esau have continually produced the thorns of violence throughout history,' wrote William Finlayson. 'The first advent of Jesus,' he continued, 'was greeted by the massacre of the innocents by the Edomite Jew King Herod.'[45] British-Israelists see the influence of the Esau-Edom line as being responsible for the Jewish people's infidelities:

primarily the non-recognition by Jewish people of Jesus Christ as the Messiah.[46] At the inaugural meeting of the BIWF, Colonel Gosset asserted that 'British-Israelism is not a Jewish question, for to the Jews belong the curses for having crucified our saviour.'[47] As such, British-Israelists maintain that Edomite Jews – rather than Judah – were responsible for the death of Christ. Indeed, when, in 1965, the Vatican published a document entitled *Nostrae Aetate*, which included a statement repudiating the association of Jews with deicide, this move was swiftly condemned and mocked in the pages of *Toren*, the magazine of the SPBI youth movement.[48]

In addition, many British-Israelists have co-opted Arthur Koestler's Khazar hypothesis in the interests of demonstrating the distinction between Israel and Jewry.[49] Even before the publication of *The Thirteenth Tribe*, in 1948, W.A. Jordan wrote that 'Ashkenazim Jews are descendants of foreigners and they are Jews by religion only and not descent.'[50] In 1952, Buxton Gresty wrote that 'a whole people [went] bodily over to Judaism in the seventh century, when the Chazars ... accepted the Jewish faith.'[51] In 1977, Roy L. Simpson explained that the Middle East had become 'the main theatre of world conflict,' because 'the major proportion who call themselves Jews are, in fact, of Gentile stock.'[52] On 26 March 1978, *The Sunday Times* published a letter from L.G. Pine, then editor of *The National Message*, in which Pine expressed regret about the publication by the former of an article entitled 'The Genius of the Jews.' The author, according to Pine, was guilty of 'perpetuating the fiction of a Jewish race.' The Jews were not a race, Pine wrote, but rather 'an amalgamation of many races.'[53] In 1980, a letter from a British-Israelist, extolling the virtue of Arthur Koestler's research, was published in the *Church News*. The letter suggested that '90% of Jewry are Ashkenazim who were converted to Judaism in the 9th century.'[54] Noel Hunt went even further, in 1990, contending that '95% of all Jews in the world . . . are Ashkenazi.'[55] 'There is not much doubt,' claimed Paul Johnson, 'that the Ashkenazi Zionist Jews are subconsciously seeking to recreate the kingdom of the Khazars.'[56] Making the bold claim that 'nobody really knows what anti-Semitism is,' Raymond Capt reached the conclusion that criticism of Jews and Judaism could never be anti-Semitic since 'the Jews who protest loudest about anti-Semitism are not even Semites themselves, but are Japhethites.'[57]

British-Israelists, furthermore, have long been scornful of the claims made by Falashas and other 'non-white' Jews regarding their lineage. Writing in 1985, one British-Israelist was withering in their criticism of the decision taken by the state of Israel to 'rescue' Ethiopian Jews from Sudan during the civil war of 1983. 'The multi-racial Israeli State' had 'trouble in store.'[58] The existence of 'the black Jew, the yellow Jew, the brown Jew and the Slav Jew' was sufficient evidence for McKelvey that 'the House of Judah [had] become lost in world-wide Jewry.'[59] The development of a 'multi-racial' Jewish state in Israel proved particularly galling to British-Israelists. 'The inflow of European Jews has almost ceased,' wrote Buxton Gresty in 1964, '[but] there is a flood of immigration from such countries as Iraq, Yemen, India, Egypt and North Africa. . . . These multi-racial, polyglot Orientals now form half the total population of [Israel].'[60] Francis Thomas also noted the lack of ethnic continuity amongst the population of the Jewish state:

> In 1951, of the population of Israeli the number of Jews was 1,061,000 of whom 665,000 came from European countries, 290,000 from Asian countries, 100,000 from Africa and 6,000 from North and South America. 334,000 were born in Palestine and 170,000 were Arabs. . . . To suggest that this agglomerate are the Chosen People of God is an insult to common sense.[61]

Diversity was considered by British-Israelists to be the main cause of Israel's problems. 'Their main error,' according to one British-Israelist was that 'the Zionist accepted as true Jews, all those who call themselves Jews . . . and so Jews of all colours are entering Palestine.'[62]

For these reasons, British-Israelists make a distinction between 'Judah-Jews' and 'Gentile-Jews.' The former represented a caucus within Jewry that shared close kinship with the people of Britain-Israel and which would reign with Britain in Palestine at some point in the eschatological future. The latter represented a diabolical and violent ethnic group within Jewry, to use Bauman's phrase, 'more pagan than ordinary heathens.'[63]

The ideological claim that Jews can only equivocally be associated with the Biblical polity of Israel forms the basis of British-Israelist attitudes towards the Jewish people. The Jews are considered to be only *partly* of Israel in the sense that other groups also constitute the majority of Israel. The Jews are also only considered to be *partly* of Israel in the sense that Jewry is a product of the intermarriage of the tribespeople of Judah and Benjamin with other – non-Israel and *anti*-Israel – ethnic groups. The latter, in particular, serves to undergird logically the most anti-Semitic claims avowed by British-Israelists. Here is proteophobic anti-Semitism presented in the guise of genealogical determinism. The Jews represent a confluence of the sacred and profane, not only conceptually but also biologically. Bauman wrote that Jews were not foreign, but rather were 'unlike foreigners.' In the allosemitic attitude, 'endemic to Christianity,' Jews were understood to be 'outside even when inside.'[64] British-Israelists express affection for – indeed affinity and fraternity *with* – Jews. This is explained as being the result of close, genealogical and ethnic connections between Israel and the Jews. In this they are easily distinguishable from those anti-Semites who seek the destruction of Jewry and who describe Jewry as being ethnically inferior to white 'Anglo-Saxons.'[65] Nonetheless, British-Israelists are cautioned that Jewry is an ethnic Trojan horse carrying within it elements which are anathema to God and to the people of God.

British-Israelist responses to anti-Semitism

In Thomas Howett's description of the relationship between Judah and the other tribes, he noted that anti-Semitism is largely a Russian and German phenomenon and suggested that it originated in the envy felt by German and Russian Christians of their more successful Jewish neighbours. But – Howett wrote – the Anglo-Saxon peoples were distinguished from their neighbours in their readiness to harbour those fleeing from anti-Semitic prejudice and violence:

> Thank God there is room enough in the broad domains of the Anglo-Saxons for more than 7,000,000 of our kindred of the house of Judah. . . . It is remarkable that the owner of these vast possessions is the one race in all the earth that befriends the Jew. This, with our identity with the lost tribes of Israel, is the key for the solution of this mighty and world-wide problem. Citizenship with the Anglo-Saxons is the destiny of the Jew.[66]

In July 1916, Alex Mason wrote to the editor of *The Banner of Israel*. He contended that 'amidst the clamour of this great war, no people is being more persecuted than the Jew.' He described the starvation and persecution meted out to the Jewish population of Russia. 'Black clouds are hovering over this much distressed people,' Mason wrote, before calling the editors attention to parallel experiences of persecution recounted in the Hebrew Bible.[67] The following week, the editorial of *The Banner of Israel* predicted British success in Palestine and expressed hope and conviction that a victory over the Ottomans would 'enable us to ameliorate in some measure the sufferings of our Jewish brethren.'[68] At the end of 1918, M. Vincent Cox described the lacrimose history of the Jewish people:

> Only in the British Empire and in the United States have they enjoyed an equal degree of liberty with the dwellers in those countries. In Russia, their condition has been one of servitude. In Germany, the *soi disant* chosen nation, anti-Semitism has been a national characteristic.[69]

This was not a sentiment atypically expressed amongst British-Israelists in the early twentieth century. Unlike other, avowedly anti-Semitic, movements, British-Israelists supported Britain's role in the Second World War. Many considered Nazism to be a diabolical attempt to eradicate the influence of Britain-Israel in Europe and in the world. Most did not deny that the Holocaust took place and saw it as evidence of the devil's desire to eradicate the 'Israel peoples' from the earth. 'We are rightly horrified by the atrocities committed by the Nazis against the Jews in Europe,' wrote C.F. Parker in 1945, 'and we feel a sense of intense shame at the very suggestion that we are following their methods.'[70] To deny the Holocaust or to caveat the significance of the horror was therefore considered to be an act of disloyalty. 'We who believe we are part of the non-Jewish Israel,' wrote Helene Woelderen in 1965, 'should never believe anti-Jewish propaganda, but should realise the . . . immense loss and sorrow the Jews on the continent suffered.'[71] British-Israelists like Arthur Eedle continued to refer to the Holocaust as one of the most 'monstrous' events in history.[72] In 1974, *The National Message* referred to Nazism as 'the incarnate evil of the age,' which 'sent cold shivers down the spine of every thinking individual.'[73] For many British-Israelists, the horrors of the Holocaust were sufficient reason for the desire amongst Jews for a national home. Writing in 1957, John Shenton expressed understanding for the pioneers of post-war Zionism.[74]

Where expressions of sympathy for the victims of the Holocaust were offered, however, they were often caveated with the claim that the sins of the Jewish people – most notably the deicide – were the indirect cause of the hardships that they had endured.[75] As John Shenton wrote, the rejection of Christ was only one cause of the ire which had been visited upon the Jews of Europe. 'Events in Europe,' he wrote, 'have taught [the Jews] a most painful and chilling lesson. They could not lose themselves among the nations.' Shenton suggested that the integration of Jews into European society and their loss of authenticity led ultimately to their destruction.[76] Some British-Israelists believed that the Holocaust was a providential event. In the immediate aftermath of the Holocaust the editors of *Brith* magazine suggested that the 'God [had] ordained that [the Jews] should be scattered amongst every nation . . . and be hounded and persecuted by nations.'[77] Some considered the Holocaust to be a partial fulfilment of the prophecies of woe that are found in Matthew 23. Nazism, therefore, was to be seen in the same providential light as the destruction of the temple.[78]

British-Israelism and anti-Semitic conspiracy theory

In 1921, at the second annual conference of the BIWF, the then secretary of the organisation – Merton Smith – 'gave staggering figures for the world's war indebtedness,' adding that 'nearly the whole of this amount was owing to the Jews.'[79] This conspiracy theory had some currency during the inter-war period and had been often peddled by Henry Ford in the pages of *The Dearborn Independent*.[80]

Five years after Merton Smith's speech – on 26 March 1926 – Charles Emanuel, solicitor and secretary of the Board of Deputies, wrote a letter to *The Middlesex County Times* highlighting the errors made by John Morey in a speech to the Ealing branch of the BIWF. Morey – it was claimed – had suggested that the Bolshevik revolution was backed by a shadowy conspiracy of international Jewry. He provided a list of names of prominent Jewish Bolsheviks. In Emanuel's response, he pointed out that – of the long list of Jewish Bolsheviks provided by Morey – only a handful were actually Jewish.[81] Of those none were religiously so. Morey, in response, protested that it was unfair that decent, patriotic anti-Bolshevism should be tarred with the brush of anti-Semitism. The claim that a Jewish cabal stood behind the Bolshevik revolution was not exclusive to British-Israelist literature. Morey himself, apparently, relied on the literature produced by the Britons Publishing Society and in particular a pamphlet published by that organisation titled *Jewish Bolshevism*. The pamphlet included a foreword by Alfred Rosenberg.[82] Whilst Morey believed that a cabal of Jews had orchestrated the Russian revolution, he also believed that the Jews were manipulating the levers of capitalism.[83]

During the 1940s, C.S. McKelvey, the leader of the SPBI, continued to perpetuate conspiracy theories relating to the 'International Jew.' In an early edition of *Brith* – the SPBI monthly – McKelvey gave credence to *The Protocols of the Elders of Zion*, suggesting that it probably was not a fabrication.[84] Some British-Israelists turned their attentions away from the Soviet Union and towards another avowedly internationalist body, the United Nations. McKelvey believed that 'racial Judah' was 'a great fifth column,' which had brought into existence the United Nations Organisation, the better to fulfil its ends.[85] McKelvey's contention was evidenced by the findings of the 1947 UNO Commission on Palestine. 'All across Europe intense underground whispering campaigns are going on,' McKelvey claimed, and 'they are fomented by the Zionist organisations and backed by Jewish money, besmirching the fair name of Britain.'[86] 'Jewry in fanatical madness is trying to create a puppet state,' he continued, 'that it might govern the world through blood stained gold.'[87] The extent of international Jewry's power extended beyond the political sphere. McKelvey believed that Jews were also controlling a vast international, Babylonian conspiracy, based in four discrete centres: Hollywood, Rome, Moscow and Washington.[88]

Fear of attempts by international Jewry to subvert the sovereignty of independent nation-states continued throughout the late twentieth century. In the 1970s, the BIWF counted amongst their number unapologetic anti-Semites like Kenneth McKilliam. McKilliam was listed as a board member of the BIWF until 1990.[89] In his book *The Annihilation of Man*, published in 1972, McKilliam pointed to the role played by Alger Hiss and other prominent Jewish figures in the foundation of the United Nations; McKilliam wrote that 'the UN is a Jewish ideal.' Like McKelvey, McKilliam saw the foundation of the state of Israel as a strategy of the 'world government,' which had established its 'seat' in Jerusalem.[90]

The building of bridges between the BIWF and American conspiracy theorists during the 1990s gave rise to a host of anti-Semitic conspiracy theories. British-Israelists were told that a shadowy cabal of 'Warburgs, Rothschilds, Schiffs, Lehmans, Melchiors, Habros and Mayers' were secretly in charge of the global economy. This tendency towards conspiracy theorising was facilitated by the presidency of the BIWF of Matthew Browning. Browning sent Alistair McConnachie to Turnberry in 1998 to cover the Bilderberg conference.[91] McConnachie was embroiled in a scandal three years later which led to his expulsion from the UK Independence Party. He wrote to Christopher Skeate, press officer for the party, expressing his view that 'gas chambers were not used to execute Jews.' He took aim at the Board of Deputies of British Jews for, as he claimed, closing down discussion around the historical evidence for the Holocaust. When this correspondence was made public, several prominent members of the party stepped down from their positions in protest.[92]

It is clear, in other words, that the British-Israelist movement was associated, throughout the latter half of the twentieth century with a conspiratorialist, anti-Semitic milieu. British-Israelist conspiracy theories typically focus on international organisations – whether clandestine organisations (like the Bilderbergers) or public organisations (like the UN) – which are believed to be seeking to undermine the sovereignty of the United Kingdom and the particularity of British culture.[93] For British-Israelists, these theories often centred around the figure of the 'international Jew,' thus trading off a centuries old, anti-Semitic canard. What makes British-Israelist conspiratorialism distinctive, however, is the belief that the 'true' Jews, the legitimate descendants of the tribe of Judah, are equal victims of attempts by Esau-Edom and Babylon to upend the divine order and obscure the God-given chosenness of Britain-Israel and Judah. In keeping with Bauman and Crome's analysis, the kind of anti-Semitic conspiratorialism peddled by British-Israelists is almost exclusively directed at agents – real or imagined – who are attempting to dismantle the structures – national, cultural, political – which provided a sense of (what Anthony Smith calls) 'national authenticity.' The result is twofold: British-Israelists turn their ire on the – perceived – Jewish agents of this process, whilst at the same time carefully ensuring that 'Israel-Judah' are exonerated from the stigma of association with this process.

British-Israelism and Judaism

'Who and what are Jews today?' asked P.F. Greenfield, writing in 1968:

> Recently . . . a Jewish Rabbi, interviewed in Sydney, stated that Judaism was a religious concept which anyone could adopt as a 'way of life.' This would indicate that a Jew is a person who practises the Judaistic way of life which, by the way, is no longer in accordance with the Law as set down by Moses.[94]

With the belief that Jewishness was 'a sociology' rather than a coherent ethnic group, British-Israelists came to see religion as the key distinguishing feature of Jewish nationhood. With the belief that religious practice was an essential component of the ethnic character of Jewish people, many British-Israelists were drawn into a complex negotiation of the relationship between Jews and Judaism and indeed their *own* relationship with ostensibly Jewish devotional practices.

From the twentieth century onward, British-Israelists expressed concern about the rise of secular Jewish identity. It was feared that the development of this phenomenon would lead to the abandonment of Judaism and – as such – of the erosion of Jewish authenticity. In 1917, Ralph Darlington wrote that the Jewish people of Europe 'have become so heterogeneous that they have ceased to be a nation.'[95] These fears persisted. The Biblical law was 'in the process of being shaken.' Should the Biblical law ultimately be 'destroyed,' British-Israelists feared that 'the very reason for the continued existence of the Jewish community will cease to be.'[96] In 1970, John Hulley noted with concern that the Israeli Interior Ministry had registered 'two children of a Jewish Lieutenant Commander and his Gentile wife, both atheists, as being of the Jewish Peoplehood but of no religion.'[97] After all, British-Israelists saw the maintenance of Jewish authenticity to be the foremost concern, not only of all Jews but of all Israel. Without Judaism, they argued, the Jewish people would 'be just like those of any other group or country.'[98]

Anxiety that the authenticity of the Jewish people would be lost with the loss of Judaism led British-Israelists to attack those Jewish groups who practiced reformed modes of Judaism. An article published in *Brith* in 1949 identified 'three groups' within 'modern Jewry': orthodox, reform and secular Jews. Whilst the orthodox Jew 'adheres closely to Judaism and looks forward to the coming of the Messiah,' the reform and secular Jews 'no longer believe.' The claim that Orthodox Jews represented the true descendants of the Biblical promise was combined with the claim that reform, liberal or secular Jews were not 'of Israel.'[99] This explained their attachment to causes which were counter to the interests of Israel. 'Zionists are either atheistic Jews or religious Jews of the Liberal Schools,' McKelvey wrote in 1971.[100] 'Political Zionism is not Judahite in origin,' wrote C.F. Parker, 'since it is rejected by Orthodox Jews.'[101]

At the same time that British-Israelists denounced secular Jews for not maintaining those practices which had been appointed by God in order to set them apart from the nations, they also began the process of investigating, exploring and debating the validity of revitalising apparently Jewish practices. The abandonment of the ritual law is traditionally explained in supersessionist terms. The claim that Christians were not bound to the ritual or judicial laws of the Hebrew Bible can be dated to the patristic era. The ritual law, according to Aquinas, had been disbanded by the atonement. As such, observation of the law was not only dead but deadly.[102] At various points in the history of Christianity, the renovation of Judaising practices has been condemned as a form of heresy.[103] Since British-Israelists denied the supersession of the Mosaic covenant, the question of whether the full law should be acknowledged by the people of Israel was reopened. In 1952, Hugh MacKintosh suggested that there was 'a growing body of opinion which is beginning to wonder if, after all, the Law as given to Israel should not be taken at its face value.'[104]

Some British-Israelists believed that many of Britain's problems in the post-war era could be alleviated if Britons were prepared to embrace the Levitical dietary laws. 'Is there any day in any year in any ordinary household where Pig Products are not used?' asked one. 'Yet pig is one of the forbidden foods!'[105] Charles McKelvey, the charismatic leader and founder of the SPBI, adopted several aspects of Jewish food laws. In 1950, he wrote of the 'national sin' being perpetrated by the Smithfield Butchers and the National Food Board.[106] Typically, Peter's vision of the pure and impure meats, recorded in Acts 10, is cited as the explanation for Christian dereliction of the Levitical dietary laws. McKelvey stressed that 'this passage should not be used to show that food laws have been cancelled.' Indeed, McKelvey extended the provision of the food laws. He argued that Israel should avoid not only those biblically proscribed foods but also any foods which contained artificial or synthetic additives. 'Israel must eat pure and unadulterated foods,' he wrote:

> SATAN IS THE DEFILER and we have no doubt that Satan succeeded in defiling some of God's creatures . . . by some devilish system of crossing or hybridising. . . . God created plants and animals and He intended them to remain as He made them. To this end, He forbade cross-breeding and hybridising.[107]

Later, McKelvey would emphasise that these laws were ordained *not* as moral injunctions but rather as a providential means of separating Israel from her neighbours. 'If any animal dies of itself, it shall not be eaten by any in Israel,' he wrote, but 'it may be given to the Gentiles in the land or sold to the Gentiles outside of the land.'[108] In 1969, Valerie Martlew repeated the call to kosher living in a BIWF publication. Whilst acknowledging that most British housewives would find it difficult to locate a kosher food store, she encouraged her readers to continue to enquire after kosher meats.[109] Again, in 1991, British-Israelist writers cautioned that 'Pig Meat should be banned.' 'It is with a great sense of relief,' Reginald Cox wrote, 'that the Scripturally orientated Christian reacts to the knowledge that the . . . Common Market countries suddenly have become so nervous about the eating of pigs.' 'Would it not be good sense as well as good politics,' he goes on to ask, 'to ban pig meat as human food?'[110]

Some British-Israelists continue to observe the dietary restrictions described in the books of the law. In 2017, Vivien Cooksley's *The Biblical Food Laws* was published by Covenant. In it, Cooksley laments that 'many foods have been devalued, altered or contaminated by man.'[111] In 2017, Professor Michael D. Bennett, leader of the BIBTF, recalled a period of convalescence that he spent in hospital following an operation. He spoke to a fellow patient about his beliefs:

> A notice above every bed stated the consultant's name and also the patient's name and permitted diet. A man in the ward noted that mine

said 'no pork, no seafood', so he asked me if I was Jew. When I replied 'No' he asked 'then, why are you keeping the Jewish food laws?' I told him the food laws are for Israelites, and are also kept by many Christians like me who believe they are Israelites and want to obey God's laws. . . . He encouraged me to stand firm in my faith to Bible truth. We shook hands. I thought how strange to have such an honest conversation invited by a complete stranger in hospital, while outside it is hard to have one on this subject with fellow Christians who deny God's food laws and are often quick to oppose any who seek to keep them (and serve ham sandwiches at every church event!).[112]

If we are to read these passages as suggesting that the food laws remain valid insofar as they forbid the consumption of things mixed, 'altered and contaminated,' or 'hybridised,' then it represents an intriguing interaction between the thought of the British-Israelists and the Levitical authors. The British-Israelists express a fundamental concern for the maintenance of separation amongst different elements: racial, cultural, and (occasionally) comestible. Mary Douglas famously argued that Levitical dietary laws were an expression of a taboo, invoked against entities which defied boundaries. Pigs – as animals which could not be categorised along with ungulates because (despite their cloven hooves) they did not chew cud – were therefore considered unclean. This apparent intolerance of 'mixed' categories clearly informs McKelvey's teachings on dietary purity. Like the Levitical authors, he believed that the diet of Israel functioned as a synecdoche to her broader project of *separating* herself from the nations. This process was twofold: the act of separating foods functioned as an attempt to separate the observers of this practice from those who did not observe it.[113] In this regard, British-Israel is separated *with* the Jews, *from* the nations.

British-Israelist autosemitism was not confined to observation of the Levitical dietary laws. In an obituary, published in *Brith* in 1952, a recently deceased British-Israelist farmer – Mr. Lee of Capel – was remembered to have 'as far as possible always farmed according to the Law.'[114] Whether this means that Mr. Lee kept a Jubilee year in accordance with Leviticus 25, or that he abstained from wholly reaping the corners and gathering the gleanings, in accordance with Leviticus 19, is unclear. In 1960, John Hutt wrote of the moral ill of 'continuous cropping' in modern Britain.[115] In 1980, David Cox wrote an article for *Brith* in which he suggested that the Biblical laws on tithing should be reintroduced for all Israel.[116] In addition, some British-Israelists actively contended for the revitalisation of Jewish festivals and feast days. In 2015, Lynne Gray wrote an article in *Bible Truth*, explaining the purpose of Yom Kippur, Shavuot and Passover, and suggesting that 'in keeping the feasts, the Israelites would constantly have in focus all aspects of the Godhead (Trinity), and have a realization in their daily lives.'[117] In this, Gray was associating herself with a periodically observed but venerable tradition within British-Israelist circles. In 1908, *The British*

Israel Ecclesia published guidelines for its readers on the observation of Jewish festivals. Passover was to be honoured, the editor of the magazine wrote, since it was 'Jehovah appointed, Messiah and Apostolic observed.' A British-Israel Passover celebration was held at 6:51 pm on Tuesday 14 April 1908 at Canfield in Essex. *The British Israel Ecclesia*, incidentally, dated its editions using the Jewish calendar.[118]

Even circumcision, the centerpiece of Jewish ritualised ethnicity, was mooted by some British-Israelists. Typically, British-Israelists do not recognise the circumcision as a sign of the covenant between God and Israel. It is considered a tacit denial of the incarnation and thus blasphemous.[119] However, at various stages in the history of British-Israelism, controversies have arisen on this subject. So, in 1917, Daniel Whitelaw Senior wrote to Colonel G.W. Deane to refute his claim that circumcision was a condition of the covenant.[120] Deane replied in February of that year that 'circumcision was in force and existence for generations before the covenant of Moses was ever heard of' and, as such, that 'its abolition must be dealt with in relation to the Abrahamic as well as the Mosaic covenant.'[121]

This complex relationship between allosemitism and autosemitism is an intriguing offshoot of the discussion established in Bauman and developed in Crome. British-Israelists sought to accentuate their affinity with and their fraternity with the Jewish people by adopting Jewish (or in British-Israelist terms 'Hebraic') practices. They thus presented themselves as separate from the nations, *with* the Jews. We know, from their own words, that they considered ritual adherence to be an identifying characteristic of genealogical authenticity. But at the same time, they recognised *only* those Jews that were distinguishable, in their practices, from Christians, as true descendants of the Biblical polity. Therefore, the Jewish people *must* be housed within the 'big tent' of Israel, but they must simultaneously be identifiable *amongst* the other people of Israel. As such, British-Israelists were perennially engaged in a process of negotiation of the boundaries between Israelites and Jews. The question of singularity, distinctiveness and – by extension – authenticity was always at the forefront of British-Israelist thought.

Jewish British-Israelists

In 1925, it was reported in the *British-Israel Star and Circle* that the prominent Zionist activist Max Nordau had made the following declaration: 'We Jews thought that the Messiah would be an individual but I feel now as if it were a collective entity and that its name might be the British Nation.'[122] In this Nordau was repeating claims which had been made by a tiny minority within the Jewish community for many years. In the late nineteenth century, the editor of *the Jewish Chronicle* wrote:

> At the present time it appears to us that the design Providence seems to work at, would be best promoted if in the dissolution of the Turkish

Empire, which cannot be far off, England was impelled to extend her protecting hand over Syria. No contingency would be hailed by the Jewish people with greater satisfaction than such a turn of affairs in the East. England has given so many proofs of her friendly feeling toward the Jews that they could not wish to see the land of their forefathers under a safer keeping than that of Great Britain.[123]

British-Israelists pounced on these seeming affirmations of the providential role of the British in relation to the Jews. But it was not the only occasion when the testimony of Jews appeared to confirm British-Israelist truth.

Over the past one hundred fifty years, several notable figures within the British-Israelist movement have emerged from Jewish stock. The first example of a Jewish British-Israelist was probably Moses Margoliouth.[124] Margoliouth's correspondence attests to a strong sense of Jewish identity which persisted after his conversion to Christianity.[125] Margoliouth was raised as a Jew in Suwalki in Poland. Having moved to Liverpool, he converted to Christianity and – in 1840 – he began his training for ordination at Trinity College Dublin. He became a teacher of Hebrew at the Liverpool Institution for Inquiring Jews. By 1846 he had become convinced of the truth of British-Israelist doctrine and he published a book entitled *The History of the Jews in Great Britain*. Margoliouth believed that the 'ends of the world,' mentioned in Isaiah 62:11, referred to the British Isles and was 'a common appellation for these islands in remote ages.'[126] Margoliouth was joined in this conviction by a Russian emigré named Elieser Bassin. Bassin was born to a wealthy family in Russia and, having first settled in Edinburgh, moved to the capital and became associated with the London Jews Society: a philo-Semitic, conversionist organisation.[127] In the 1870s, when Bassin was in his late thirties, he read the writings of Edward Hine and became convinced that British people had arrived in the British Isles in 720, by way of Spain and Ireland. Bassin claimed that 'most of my Jewish Brethren still believe that the Ten Tribes exist, somewhere, as a powerful nation, having a king of their own, hidden from the sight of men until the coming of the Messiah.'[128]

Many early British-Israelist sources refer to the testimony of Rabbi Marcus Bergmann.[129] Bergmann was an Hasidic Jew, born in Wieruszów, who moved to London in 1866. Whilst in London, he had a religious experience and converted to Christianity, with the guidance of Reverend Dr Ewald. In one of his testimonies, Bergmann apparently expressed his commitment to the belief that 'the Hebrew Scriptures pointed to the British Isles as the home of Israel.' He claimed to have overheard a boy describing British-Israel doctrine and elucidating a passage from Isaiah 49, when he realised that 'Christ is given to Britain.'[130]

In Pastor Alan Campbell's defence of British-Israelist doctrine, he cites the example of Cyril Leach, a Jew who became convinced of the truth of

British-Israelist doctrine at the start of the twentieth century. Leach was an orthodox Jew 'from a line of Rabbis . . . known far and wide in Palestine for their piety, charity and wide learning.' He gave an account of his conversion experience:

> One day a book was lent me, setting out what appeared to me at the time a preposterous idea, that the Saxon race is the continuation of the Northern Kingdom of Israel. To my intense surprise I found that prophecy after prophecy had materialised and was in the process of materializing in the Saxon people. I now saw quite clearly that it is discrediting God's Holy Name, and His reputation as a God who fulfils His promises, to assert that the Jews form the whole Seed of Israel.[131]

Leach's testimony has been cited by Alan Campbell as 'an acid test' for the authenticity of British-Israelist truth.

British-Israelists actively courted Jewish converts in this period. In 1902, the Reverend S.J. Carlton established the Bethesda Mission to the Jews, at Ebenezer Hall, Commercial Road, the only mission society which specifically sought to convert Jewish people to the British-Israelist point of view. Its motto was 'As British Israelites our chief duty is to preach the Gospel to the tribe of Judah.'[132] The Bethesda mission to the Jews advertised in the pages of the *British Israel Pilot*.[133] The mission met Jewish immigrants at the London docklands and distributed literature in Yiddish as well as English. They also provided medical support for the local Jewish community.[134]

Aside from those Jews who explicitly expressed a belief that the doctrines of British-Israelism were correct, British-Israelists frequently refer to Jewish figures who expressed sympathy for and encouragement to the British-Israelist movement. So – for example – a rabbi in Brighton reported to Henry Marchant in 1918 that he had 'fallen on his knees, thanked God and wept for joy,' when he heard that the British had taken Jerusalem.[135] In 1920, a correspondent wrote to *The Banner*, referring to the fact that he had lent 'several numbers [of the magazine] to a Jew and today I lent him some of the March numbers, always marking the places which I want him to read.'[136] These exemplars shouldn't be taken as apologists for British-Israelism. It is nonetheless significant that British-Israelists saw the testimony of supposedly sympathetic Jews as a vindication of their beliefs.

Leach, Margoliouth and Bassin exemplify a form of Jewish British-Israelism which is mediated through a process of conversion to Christianity. Less common are figures who maintain their affinity with Jewish religion in some form whilst at the same time avowing a belief in the genealogical claims of British-Israelism. One example of this can be found in the pages of an edition of *Toren* (the SPBI youth magazine) from September 1965. The magazine included a letter from one Michael Green: a twenty-four-year-old

British Jew who claimed to have read British-Israelist literature and to have been convinced of the validity of the doctrine:

> I searched the scriptures and began to see how blind I had been. Thanks to a B.I. believer I gradually began to piece together the puzzle. I found out that I was a descendant of the Southern house and that many years ago the Ten Tribes left Assyria and travelled across Europe finally ending in Britain. . . . Since then I have never stopped searching the Scriptures for information on British-Israel teaching.[137]

A more prominent example of this form of Jewish British-Israelism is Yair Davidiy. Davidiy is a self-described 'orthodox Jew,' living in Israel, who has written extensively on the themes of British-Israelism. He has established an organisation called Brit Am, based in Jerusalem. Davidiy's contentions are similar to those of mainstream British-Israelism. He believes that Britain represents the tribe of Ephraim, whilst the Jews represent the tribe of Judah. Unlike many British-Israelists, Davidiy rejects the claim that Esau-Edom is represented in modern Jewry. On the contrary, Davidiy has claimed that the nation of Germany is identifiable with the Esau-Edom strain, thus explaining the rise of Nazism. Moreover, in response to the use of the Khazar hypothesis as part of anti-Semitic, British-Israelist ideology, Davidiy has made the claim that Khazar's were indeed converts to Judaism, but that they were *also* themselves descendants from the lost tribes of Israel.[138] Davidiy's work is supported in part by the Maccabee Institute and by its director Rabbi Avraham Feld.[139] Davidiy himself is adamant that membership of Brit Am is not only congruent with Orthodox Jewish observation but that it is 'best suited' to Orthodox Jews.[140]

For several decades, British-Israelists have sought to build bridges with Yair Davidiy and with the Brit Am community. In 1996, an edition of *Wake Up* referred readers to Davidiy's work.[141] In the late 1990s, Clifford Smyth – a prominent British-Israelist, BBC Northern Ireland pundit and erstwhile Democratic Unionist politician – made contact with Davidiy and was encouraged by the leadership of the BIWF to promote this relationship. In 1998, Smyth reported to the leadership of the BIWF that 'visitors representing Yair Davidiy' had been hosted at his house and that 'these contacts have been challenging and rewarding.'[142] The following year, Smyth reported that he 'has contacts with Mr. Davidiy and his Jewish associates in Israel on a weekly basis.'[143] This relationship has continued to flourish. In 2009, pictures of Smyth, standing in a Loyalist neighbourhood of Ballymena, below a flag which incorporated the Red Hand of Ulster and the Star of David, were published on Davidiy's personal website.

Accounts of Jews who were or are receptive to British-Israelist ideas came to form a vital part of the British-Israelist argument. Their Jewishness was not an impediment to their credibility as witnesses to British-Israel truth. Here, therefore, we find a significant cleavage between the attitudes of white supremacist groups and the attitude of British-Israelists towards the Jewish community. The nature of the relationship between British-Israelists and the Jews shares some similarities with the relationship between the philo-Semites of the Victorian era and the Jews. As Karp and Sutcliffe point out, Judeocentric millenarians did not seek the erasure of Jewry at the point of restoration. From the era of Brightman onwards, Judeocentrists believed that the Jews would remain a separate polity even after their conversion to Christianity and indeed that they would reign from Jerusalem as a trans-formed and glorified nation of Christian Jews. The logic of British-Israelism does not allow this. For British-Israelists, faith and race, ethnicity and ethics are tightly wound together, such that the infidelity of the Jews is identified as evidence that the Jews are not truly of Israel. As such, the otherness of the Jews as a polity is inextricable from their faith. Nonetheless, British-Israelists believe that the Jews are at least partially of Judah. As such, their testimony retains some prophetic value. This is, in part, why British-Israelists do not appear to be as zealous for the conversion of the Jews as some fundamental-ist Christians in the Victorian era. Nonetheless, they value the conversion of the Jews to British-Israelism, even if it is not accompanied with a conversion to Christianity.

Conclusion

In 1999, at the Annual General Meeting of the BIWF, President Matthew Browning told his fellow board members a story. He told them that he had once been asked to bless a marital union between a Jewish man and a Christian woman:

> The young man was of Jewish background – of appearance not at all unlike ourselves – and the Rabbi would not marry them unless his intended was prepared to take a year's instruction in Judaism. Nonethe-less, they were anxious that there be a blessing upon their union. Hence at this time of the Age-end, we had a child of Judah and a child of Ephraim-Israel coming together, symbolising in parable, as it were, the prophecy of the two sticks of Ezekiel 17, and the healing of the breach between Jacob's two families.[144]

It is not difficult to find anti-Semitic stereotypes, slanders and hate speech in the corpus of British-Israelist literature. Nor – indeed – is it difficult to find philo-Semitic arguments and ideas. As such, the best way to understand British-Israelism is as a form not of anti-Semitism nor of philo-Semitism but rather as a form of allosemitism. British-Israelism is distinguished from other allosemitic phenomena, however, in that it combines allosemi-tism with autosemitism. The claim that the former would lead to the lat-ter should not be surprising. The reification of 'the Jews' as an entitative, recognisable and distinctive group undergirds the essential claim that God works through nations and peoples – continuously and not only in the Biblical past. This attitude is no better expressed than in an article written by C.F. Parker for *The National Message* in 1948. 'For both Jews and Britons,' he wrote, 'isolation from the world around has helped to produce a unique mentality.'[145] But the otherness of the Jewish people is rendered all the more salient by its proximity. This was a point that Bauman made in his essay. Bauman reached the conclusion that order and ambivalence are mutually interdependent. 'Ambivalence,' he writes, 'is the *cause* of all ordering concerns . . . [it is] the one enemy without which order cannot live.' For this reason, British-Israelists did *not* simply engage in a process of 'othering' Jews, but rather engaged in a constant process of comparison and contradistinction. As Parker suggested, 'the Jews' were 'isolated' and therefore were 'unique.' But it was in their 'uniqueness' that they were most similar to 'the Britons.' In 1917, one British-Israelist described the authenticity of the Jewish people:

> Down the centuries the stream of Jewry flows through all nations, preserving a separatism, an identity of physical and mental characteristics, and an individuality of outlook that has no parity in the story of any other people.[146]

This uniqueness amongst the nations was to be admired, emulated even, but never compromised.

Notes

1 'Correspondence with the British-Israel World Federation Concerning Lectures and Meeting,' London Metropolitan Archives, ACC/3121/B/04/B022.
2 *The Banner of Israel*, vol. 44, no. 2,254 (10 March 1920), 84.
3 Crome, *Christian Zionism and English National Identity*, 23.
4 Pierard, 'The Contribution of British-Israelism to Antisemitism,' 45–68.
5 Douglas E. Cowan, 'Theologizing Race: The Construction of Christian Identity,' in Craig Prentiss (ed.), *Religion and the Creation of Race and Ethnicity* (London: New York Univeristy Press, 2003), 112–124; Barkun, *Religion and the Racist Right*, 96, 279–280.
6 Herbert Armstrong, *The United States and British Commonwealth in Prophecy* (Pasadena: Ambassador, 1967), 15.
7 *The National Message*, vol. 59, no. 1,686 (May 1980), 79.
8 Kenneth McKilliam, *The Annihilation of Man* (Devon: Britons, 1972).
9 Howett, *Anglo-Israel*, 144–145.
10 *The Banner of Israel*, vol. 43, no. 2,220 (16 July 1919), 250.
11 *The Homeland Pilot*, no. 23 (May 1931), 79.
12 *The Covenant Message*, vol. 29, no. 2 (February 1960), 45.
13 *The National Message*, vol. 49, no. 1,562 (January 1970), 48.
14 *The National Message*, vol. 43, no. 1,496 (July 1964), 210.
15 *The Link*, vol. 4, no. 5 (April 1985), 108.
16 'The Covenant People's Fellowship Annual Report for 1990,' British Library, P881/444, 12.

17 *The BIWF Newsletter*, no. 1 (January 2007), 6.
18 *Northern Echo* (24 March 2008), 18.
19 National Archives, Metropolitan Police Office, 3/1257.
20 *End Time Revelation Newsletter*, no. 1 (October 1976), 2.
21 *The Banner of Israel*, vol. 40, no. 2,065 (26 July 1916), 303; *Toren*, vol. 2, no. 3 (March 1965), 9; *Bible Truth*, no. 254 (April 2009), 27; *The National Message*, vol. 53, no. 1,620 (November 1974), 336.
22 *The Banner of Israel*, vol. 42, no. 2,159 (15 May 1918), 183.
23 Bauman, 'Allosemitism,' 143–156.
24 Bauman, 'Allosemitism,' 143–156.
25 Smith, *Myths and Memories of the Nation*, 214.
26 Thomas Brightman, *A Commentary on the Canticles* (London, 1644), 1051; Thomas Brightman, *A Revelation of the Apocalyps* (London, 1611), 554; Henry Finch, *The Worlds Great Restauration or the Calling of the Jews* (London, 1621); Adam Sutcliffe and Jonathan Karp, 'Introduction,' in Adam Sutcliffe and Jonathan Karp (eds.), *Philosemitism in History* (Cambridge: Cambridge University Press, 2011), 3; Crome, *Christian Zionism and English National Identity*, 12; Andrew Crome, ' "The Proper and Naturall Meaning of the Prophets": The Hermeneutic Roots of Judeo-Centric Eschatology,' in *Renaissance Studies*, 24, no. 5 (2010): 734; Philip Almond, 'Thomas Brightman and the Origins of Philo-Semitism: An Elizabethan Theologian and the Return of the Jews to Israel,' in *Reformation and Renaissance Review*, 9, no. 1 (2007): 3–25.
27 Crome, *Christian Zionism and English National Identity*, 196.
28 *The New British Israel Pilot*, no. 22 (1 April 1931), 59.
29 *The Link*, vol. 4, no. 6 (May 1985), 135.
30 *The Banner of Israel*, vol. 42, no. 2,141 (9 January 1918), 17.
31 2 Kings 17–18.
32 *The National Message*, vol. 53, no. 1,619 (October 1974), 304.
33 *Brith*, no. 3 (November 1945), 14; Brith, no. 379 (December 1977), 21.
34 *Brith*, no. 408 (May 1980), 21.
35 *Brith*, no. 67 (June 1951).
36 *The National Message*, vol. 35, no. 1,395 (February 1957), 54.
37 *The Banner of Israel*, vol. 43, no. 2,244 (31 December 1919), 455.
38 Reprinted in *Covenant Nations*, vol. 3, no. 4 (2014), 11.
39 *BIWF Quarterly*, vol. 4, no. 1 (January 1991), 13.
40 *The National Message*, vol. 35, no. 1,395 (February 1957), 55.
41 *The National Message*, vol. 59, no. 1,683 (February 1980), 22.
42 *Wake Up*, vol. 2, no. 7 (July 1978), 283.
43 *The National Message*, vol. 50, no. 1,580 (July 1971), 214.
44 *Brith*, no. 370 (March 1977), 23.
45 *Wake Up*, vol. 8, no. 6 (January 1991), 135.
46 *The National Message*, vol. 27, no. 1,197 (5 June 1948), 177.
47 *The Banner of Israel*, vol. 43, no. 2,220 (16 July 1919), 249.
48 *Toren*, vol. 2, no. 5 (September 1965), 15.
49 Arthur Koestler, *The Thirteenth Tribe* (London: Bridger, 1976).
50 *Brith*, no. 10 (July 1946), 13.
51 Gresty, *Satan Fights for Muscovy*, 62; Gresty, *Christ or the Kremlin*, 52.
52 *Brith*, no. 379 (December 1977), 22.
53 *The Sunday Times*, no. 8,070 (26 February 1978), 14.
54 *The National Message*, vol. 59, no. 1687 (June 1980), 94.
55 *Wake Up*, vol. 8, no. 4 (August 1990), 91.
56 *Wake Up*, vol. 8, no. 4 (August 1990), 95.
57 *Bible Truth*, no. 231 (September 2004), 8–11.

58 *The Link*, vol. 4, no. 4 (February 1985), 95.
59 *Brith*, no. 3 (November 1945), 16.
60 *The National Message*, vol. 43, no. 1,490 (January 1964), 26.
61 *Brith*, no. 354 (July 1975), 5.
62 *Brith*, no. 299 (November 1970), 7.
63 Bauman, 'Allosemitism,' 150.
64 Zygmunt Bauman, *Modernity and the Holocaust* (Cambridge: Polity, 1989), 53.
65 Cowan, 'Theologizing Race,' 112.
66 Thomas Rosling Howett, *Anglo-Israel* (Philadelphia: Spangler and Davis, 1892), 143.
67 *The Banner of Israel*, vol. 40, no. 2,064 (12 July 1916), 301.
68 *The Banner of Israel*, vol. 40, no. 2,065 (26 July 1916), 303.
69 *The Banner of Israel*, vol. 42, no. 2,179 (9 October 1918), 341.
70 *The National Message*, vol. 24, no. 1,130 (24 October 1945), 199.
71 *Toren*, vol. 2, no. 3 (March 1965), 9.
72 *Bible Truth*, no. 254 (April 2009), 27.
73 *The National Message*, vol. 53, no. 1,620 (November 1974), 336.
74 *The National Message*, vol. 35, no. 1,398 (April 1957), 98.
75 *The National Message*, vol. 27, no. 1,189 (14 February 1948), 61.
76 *The National Message*, vol. 35, no. 1,398 (April 1957), 98.
77 *Brith*, no. 13 (October 1946), 10.
78 *Brith*, no. 12 (September 1946), 16.
79 *The Banner of Israel*, vol. 45, no. 2,324 (13 July 1921), 242.
80 Henry Ford, *The International Jew, the World's Foremost Problem: Articles Appearing in the Dearborn Independent* (Dearborn, MI: Dearborn Publishing, 1920).
81 *Middlesex County Times*, vol. 63, no. 4,072 (6 March 1926), 6.
82 'Correspondence with the British-Israel World Federation Concerning Lectures and Meeting,' London Metropolitan Archives, ACC/3121/B/04/B022.
83 *West Sussex County Times* (17 December 1927), 10.
84 *Brith*, no. 13 (October 1946), 1–3.
85 *Brith*, no. 4 (January 1946), 13; *Brith*, no. 17 (February 1947), 14.
86 *Brith*, no. 23 (October 1947), 6.
87 *Brith*, no. 17 (February–April 1947), 22.
88 *Brith*, no. 17 (February 1947), 14.
89 'British Israel World Federation Annual Accounts and Reports for 1990,' British Library, ZC/9/a/2499.
90 McKilliam, *The Annihilation of Man*, 73, 77.
91 'New Covenant Times Supplement,' in *Wake Up*, vol. 12, no. 2 (March 1998), 1.
92 *The Guardian* (27 February 2001), 10.
93 'New Covenant Times Supplement,' in *Wake Up*, vol. 12, no. 2 (March 1998), 1.
94 *The National Message*, vol. 47, no. 1,541 (April 1968), 114.
95 *The Prophetic News and Israel's Watchman*, no. 8 (August 1917), 127.
96 *The National Message*, vol. 43, no. 1,494 (May 1964), 147.
97 *The National Message*, vol. 49, no. 1,564 (March 1970), 70.
98 *The National Message*, vol. 43, no. 1,494 (May 1964), 147.
99 *Brith*, no. 40 (March 1949), 3–5.
100 *Brith*, no. 301 (January 1971), 23.
101 *The National Message*, vol. 27, no. 1,198 (19 June 1948), 200.
102 Ruether, *Faith and Fratricide*, 117–181; John Gager, *The Origins of Anti-Semitism* (New York: Oxford University Press, 1983); Daniel Boyarin, *Borderlines: The Partition of Judaeo-Christianity* (Philadelphia: University of Pennsylvania Press, 2004); Thomas Aquinas, *Summa Theologica*, First Part of the Second Part, Question 104, Article 3.

103 Petri Luomanen, *Recovering Jewish-Christian Sects and Gospels* (Leiden: Brill, 2012), 17–45; Eusebius, *Life of Constantine*, trans. Averil Cameron and Stuart G. Hall (Oxford: Oxford University Press, 1999), 178; John Falconer, *A Briefe Refutation of John Traske's Judaical and Novel Fancyes* (St. Omer, 1618); Arthur Squibb, 'A Faithful Testimony Against the Teachers of Circumcision Who Are Lately Gone into Germany,' in Edward Stennet (ed.), *The Royal Law Contended for* (London, 1666), 45–47.

104 *The National Message*, vol. 31, no. 1,291 (26 January 1952), 32–33.

105 *The Covenant Message*, vol. 29, no. 2 (February 1960), 73.

106 *Brith*, no. 51 (February 1950), 8.

107 *Brith*, no. 4 (January 1946), 5–7.

108 *Brith*, no. 51 (February 1950), 8.

109 *Toren*, vol. 6, no. 1 (April 1969), 2–3.

110 *Wake Up*, vol. 8, no. 7 (July 1991), 148.

111 Vivien Cooksley, *The Biblical Food Laws* (Bishop Auckland: Covenant Publishing, 2017), 22.

112 *Bible Truth*, no. 288 (October 2017), 14.

113 Douglas, *Purity and Danger*, 55; Klawans, *Impurity and Sin*, 17, 23–25; Weiss, 'Impurity Without Repression,' 205–221; David Kraemer, *Jewish Eating and Identity Through the Ages* (London: Routledge, 2007), 30–33.

114 *Brith*, no. 77 (May 1952), 20.

115 *The Covenant Message*, vol. 29, no. 2 (February 1960), 74.

116 *Brith*, no. 407 (April 1980), 22–24.

117 *Bible Truth*, no. 279 (July 2015), 10.

118 *The British-Israel Ecclesia*, vol. 3, no. 25 (March 1908), 500.

119 *The Banner of Israel*, vol. 41, no. 2,088 (3 January 1917), 31.

120 *The Banner of Israel*, vol. 41, no. 2,094 (14 February 1917), 68.

121 *The Banner of Israel*, vol. 41, no. 2,094 (14 February 1917), 68.

122 *British Israel Star and Circle*, no. 39 (March 1925), 42.

123 Quoted in Howett, *Anglo-Israel*, 149.

124 *Wake Up*, vol. 2, no. 7 (July 1978), 152; David S. Katz, 'Margoliouth, Moses [1815–1881],' in *Oxford Dictionary of National Biography* (Oxford: Oxford University Press, 2004; online edition). www.oxforddnb.com/view/article/18055

125 Lambeth Palace Archives, Tait 145, ff. 371; Lambeth Palace Archives, Tait 250, ff. 93–97; Lambeth Palace Archives, Tait 124, ff. 1–10; Lambeth Palace Archives, Tait 116, ff. 358; David B. Ruderman, 'Moses Margoliouth: The Precarious Life of a Scholarly Convert,' in *Jewish Quarterly Review*, 109, no. 1 (2019): 84–117.

126 Moses Margoliouth, *The History of the Jews in Great Britain* (London: Bentley, 1846), 25; *Bath Chronicle and Weekly Gazette*, vol. 150, no. 7,726 (26 September 1907), 4; W.T. Gidney, *The History of the London Society for Promoting Christianity Among Jews* (London: London Society for Promoting Christianity Among Jews, 1908), 16; Michael Darby, *The Emergence of the Hebrew Christian Movement in Nineteenth-Century Britain* (Leiden: Brill, 2010), 135–140.

127 'Naturalisation Certificate of Eliezer Bassin,' National Archives, HO 334/12/4226; Todd Endelman, *The Jews of Britain: 1656–2000* (London: University of California Press, 2002), 285.

128 Elieser Bassin, *The Lost Ten Tribes* (London, 1884),

129 *The Banner of Israel*, vol. 43, no. 2,217 (25 June 1919), 226.

130 W.E. Oldroyd, *The Case for British-Israel* (London: Marshall Brothers, 1922), 8.

131 Denis Hanan, *British Israel Truth* (London: Covenant Publishing, 1932), 11.

132 *The Banner of Israel*, vol. 44, no. 2,287 (27 October 1920), 371.
133 *The Pilot*, no. 92 [misnumbered 91] (15 August 1929), 32.
134 Gerry Black, 'The Right School in the Right Place: The History of the Step-ney Jewish School, 1864–2013,' in *Jewish Historical Studies*, vol. 45 (2013): 131–144; Lara Marks, 'Irish and Jewish Women's Experience of Child-birth and Infant Care in East London 1870–1939: The Responses of Host Society and Immigrant Communities to Medical Welfare Needs' (DPhil Thesis: Wolfson College, Oxford, 1990), 347.
135 *Banner of Israel*, vol. 42, no. 2,171 (March 1919), 289.
136 *The Banner of Israel*, vol. 44, no. 2,267 (9 June 1920), 201.
137 *Toren*, vol. 2, no. 5 (September 1964), 17.
138 Yair Davidiy, *The Khazars: Tribe 13* (Jerusalem: Russel-Davis, 1993).
139 Yair Davidiy, *Ephraim: The Gentile Children of Israel* (Jerusalem: Russel-Davis, 1995), a–j.
140 Yair Davidiy, *Germany and Edom* (Jerusalem: Russel-Davis, 2015), 34, 39, 146, 162.
141 *Wake Up*, vol. 11, no. 3 (May 1996), 55.
142 'British Israel World Federation Annual Accounts and Reports for 1998,' British Library, ZC.9.a.2499, 13.
143 'British Israel World Federation Annual Accounts and Reports for 1999–2000,' British Library, ZC.9.a.2499, 15.
144 'British Israel World Federation Annual Accounts and Reports (1999–2000),' British Library, 15.
145 *The National Message*, vol. 27, no. 1,186 (3 January 1948), 9.
146 *The Prophetic News and Israel's Watchman*, no. 12 (December 1917), 185.

4 British-Israelism and the British Empire

British-Israelism is often associated, by historians, with British imperialism. This was what Goldwin Smith had in mind when he described the doctrine as 'jingoism with Biblical sanction.' It is a view which has been echoed in more recent scholarship. Colin Kidd referred to British-Israelism as having provided 'justification for the wide-reaching claims of British imperialism.'[1] Michael Barkun identified British-Israelism's foundational doctrine as the belief that 'the Empire was a sign of God's special favour.'[2]

Writing in the 1960s, Professor John Wilson urged caution when it came to reducing the British-Israelist movement to a form of 'sanctified imperialism.'[3] Wilson wrote that the movement appeared to be flourishing – and indeed to be making converts – during a period in which Britain's claim to imperial prestige was waning. 'Britain's international circumstances,' he wrote, in 1968 'are not such that recruits are likely to be swept on a tide of emotional imperialism.'[4]

How, then, do we assess the relationship between the Empire and 'the national message.' It would be misleading to deny that the movement – at least at its outset – decked itself in the finery of imperial prestige. It would be equally misleading to suggest that the racism which fed the British Imperial imagination, did not also feed the British-Israelist imagination. Long into the twentieth century, British-Israelists continued to express the belief that 'the descendants of Ham . . . were to be servants of servants.'[5] But by the middle of the twentieth century, British-Israelism appeared to be far more immersed in nationalism than imperialism. This – according to the work of David Edgerton – was symptomatic of a cultural shift in the country more widely. The tenor of British patriotism shifted from the missional to the covenantal tone; expressions of patriotic concern shifted in focus from prestige to what Anthony Smith would call authenticity. During this period, British-Israelists developed a carefully constructed understanding of providential history, which explained why Britain's status as a global power was rapidly declining. At the same time – in their own literature – they accentuated the severity of Britain's decline. Analysis of the words that were written by British-Israelists on the subject of Empire brings us back to a careful consideration of the distinction between chosenness and supremacy. A combination of the former and the latter informed the ways in which British-Israelists responded to the decline of the Empire, how they interacted with the erstwhile dominions of the Commonwealth and how they responded to the phenomenon of Commonwealth immigration in the later decades of the twentieth century. Edgerton argues that the British were forced to create a new national image of Britain in the twentieth century as a response to the changing status of Britain in the world. The Biblical account of national chosenness – explicit in British-Israelist literature and implicit in mainstream, nationalist propaganda – served (I claim) to lubricate this process.

British-Israelism at the height of empire

There is no doubt that during the period of the super-eminence of the British Empire, British-Israelists reveled in the success of the imperial project and – indeed – that they explained this success in providential terms. In 1878, for example, Edward Wheeler Bird suggested that the 'preparation of communications by railway with India,' had been predicted by John of Patmos in Revelation 16, in the vision of a 'way being prepared for the kings of the East.'[6] The architects of the British-Israel movement at the end of the nineteenth century certainly believed that Britain's empire was proof that Britain was Israel. Gertrude Smith, writing at the start of the twentieth century, believed that Britain's 'world power . . . is indeed a wonderful piece of blind evidence to our identity,' since 'in the latter days Isaiah foretold . . . that Israel was to blossom and bud and fill the face of the world.'[7] At times, prophetic significance was read into the nature of Britain's acquisition of the Empire. At these moments, British-Israelists tended to point to the notable differences between the British and other, historical, empires. Reginald Cox, writing at the tail end of the imperial age, suggested that the British Empire stood alone, distinct from the 'world powers of Egypt, Assyria and the four predominant empires of Babylonia, Medo-Persia, Greece and Rome,' in that these other empires had been 'taken and held by military force' and had been 'planned and built by conquerors,' whilst the 'British Empire was never planned,' but 'developed as though by accident.' Indeed, Cox went so far as to claim that 'no British government has ever consciously meditated its expansion' and that 'not one single yard of the British Commonwealth has been added as a result of premeditated aggression.'[8] The difference, according to John Shenton, was that Britain was not a warlike, imperialist country, but was rather a 'servant people.' In building a 'Christian empire,' this 'servant people' had 'shouldered the burden for which it had been called into being.'[9]

British-Israelists also espoused a vision of the Empire – during this period – which was in keeping with what Anthony D. Smith has called 'missional election.' God, they believed, had appointed His chosen people to a particular task in the world. In its crudest terms, this was expressed as a mission to civilise the descendants of the tribe of Ham. 'The duty of Celto-Saxon

Israel,' one commentator mused, 'is to lead and control the heathen, without fear, for their own good and for the good of all.'[10] This view was expressed during the years of the First World War, when the official organs of the British-Israelist movement turned their ire on the Germans. The editors of *The Banner of Israel* responded to atrocities committed in East Africa at the end of 1916 by calling for Britain to redouble her commitment to her 'African responsibilities,' to prevent the 'atrocious conduct of the Germans in East Africa,' and to 'preserve the black races from their terrible fate.'[11]

It must also be said, however, that the tendency to explain the success of the British Empire as evidence of providential favour was not confined solely to the British-Israelists of this period. Indeed, the most mainstream voices could be heard extolling the glory of the empire as a sign of God's favour. At the end of the nineteenth century, the headmaster of Harrow told his charges that it was the job of an English headmaster 'to inspire [his pupils'] faith in the divinely ordained mission of their country and their race.'[12] In view of this understanding of the role of Britain-Israel in world history, British-Israelists actively attempted to expand their influence beyond the borders of Britain and to push into the colonies during this period. When, in 1878, the Anglo-Israel Distribution Fund was established, its constitution promised that the 'sowers of the seed' of British-Israel truth would be stationed 'in Canada, Unites States, South America, East and West Indies, Malta, Egypt, India, Burma, Australia, Tasmania, New Zealand, South and British Central Africa.'[13] Over the next decades, this vision became a reality and fledgling British-Israelist communities were established across the Empire. Even at this early stage, Southern Africa and Canada proved to be the breadbasket of the imperial British-Israel movement. At the beginning of 1918, one missionary living in Johannesburg wrote to inform British-Israelists at home of the success of his ministry in the south of the country, in Natal. The correspondent was pleased to report that he was able to 'bring our belief into prominence through the newspapers,' and from the pulpits of the Anglican Church. Any success that he had had in Natal was only exceeded when he moved to Johannesburg, he claimed.[14] His reports were somewhat vindicated when the Green brothers, diamond miners in the Transvaal, wrote to *The Banner* to confirm that they had been converted to the doctrine and that they were eager to 'help in spreading the good news abroad.'[15]

At the end of 1918, William Bond wrote to *The Banner* to advise of the foundation of a Tasmanian branch of the British Israel Association at 257 Liverpool Street in Hobart.[16] The influence of a network of prominent British-Israelists in this part of the Empire appears to have reached the highest echelons of colonial governance. In 1919, the officers of the Tasmanian branch were entertained by Sir Francis Newdegate at Government House. Newdegate was an Etonian and a graduate of Sandhurst who – after a career in the Grenadier Guards – became a Conservative Member of Parliament and ultimately a colonial administrator. In his latter role he served as Governor of Western Australia as well as Governor of Tasmania. In 1925, a town on the south-west tip of the continent was named in his honour. When Newdegate met the delegation from the British Israelist Association of Tasmania, they presented him with a loyal address. They thanked Newdegate for the 'expressions of trust, confidence and thankfulness, in and to the Almighty God of Israel,' that the latter had used in his thanksgiving oration. The Governor responded gratefully, declaring his long-term interest in the movement and stating that 'as he studied its work further, interest grew upon him.' Newdegate was not a card-carrying British-Israelist. He declared that he 'had not yet reached the stage at which he could consider his mind completely decided' on the issue. However, he mused that the 'mysterious' nature of the expansion of the British Empire was seemingly 'otherwise inexplicable,' if British-Israelism's tenets were false.[17]

As the decades of the twentieth century advanced, and the empire fell into a period of terminal decline, many British-Israelists clung to the belief that their providential task included the enlightenment of the 'gentiles' in Africa and Asia. Even as Britain shed her 'imperial dependents,' British-Israelists continued to claim 'the superior capacity of the Anglo-Saxon race to govern peoples who cannot govern and organize themselves.'[18] The editorial of *The National Message* urged British-Israelists not to relinquish their commitments to the 'Imperial Project.' Britain was Africa's 'trustee.' The 'primary purpose of the rise and development of the British Empire,' was, according to Bernard Bateson, 'a spiritual one.' It was 'for the service of all mankind.'[19]

British-Israelist response to decolonisation

The first waves of decolonisation took place in the immediate aftermath of the Second World War. Ireland was gone already. But the 1940s saw the jewels in the imperial crown fall away one by one. With the election of a Labour government in 1945, the India Office made it clear that Indian independence was its objective. By the summer of 1947 India was independent. Meanwhile, Malayan nationalists who had defeated the Japanese during the Second World War refused to resume their position in the empire and – supported by allies from the Communist bloc – they waged an effective guerrilla war which would last for over a decade, ultimately resulting in the independence of Malaysia. In the Middle-East, Britain's mandate in Palestine was losing its credibility day by day until, ultimately, it was forced to give it up altogether in 1948. The Suez crisis appeared to place a punctuation point on the history of the British Empire. Nasser's decision to nationalise the Suez Canal was expected to severely damage Britain's strategic and economic interests in the region. Britain joined Israel in sending in troops to unseat Nasser from power and to regain control over the canal. But, when President Eisenhower threatened severe sanctions against Britain, British troops withdrew from Suez without having achieved their principle military objectives in any meaningful way. These events demonstrated to the world that Britain was a nation that would from now on take orders rather than giving orders. It was a chastening experience and it led to the resignation of Anthony Eden as Prime Minister.

These changes were greeted with some consternation by British-Israelists. 'It is no wonder,' wrote one, 'that many faint hearts feel that the old Empire is disintegrating.'[20] 'The world is watching with bated breath,' wrote McKelvey, 'who knows what part of the Empire will be next to ask for and receive their separation status?'[21]

As the Empire began to disintegrate, colonial administrators and military personnel began to drift home. British-Israelists developed a prophetic interpretation of these events. The repatriation of hordes of Britons was interpreted by some as an indication that the period of Israel's restoration was at hand. 'Through it all God is gathering his people,' one wrote 'drawing them to their place. Home come the military men, their God-given task done.' This was all seen as a fulfilment of Isaiah 26, in which the prophet foresees the people of Israel returning to the fortified city, to prepare for the eschaton.[22]

Some elements within the British-Israel movement had pre-empted these events, thus mitigating their disappointment. When Egypt was initially granted her independence, in 1946, Charles McKelvey wrote that 'If Britain stays in Egypt she will have to defend Egypt when Russia comes down. . . . This not only means a major war with Russia but a great Russian Victory.'[23] As such, Britain was wise to get out of Egypt, rather than humbled. 'For Britain and her Empire, it means safety,' wrote McKelvey, since 'by getting out of Egypt now she is saving herself from a major war she could not have won.' Britons should be grateful that the 'unseen hand of God has led Britain out before the trouble really begins.'[24]

A second wave of decolonisation began within a generation. In a speech to the South African Parliament on 3 February 1960, Prime Minister Harold Macmillan signalled to the African nations of the British Empire that his government would not stand in the way of their attempts to attain independence. 'The wind of change is blowing through this continent,' he said. In the 'winds of change' speech, Macmillan singled out the government of South Africa for criticism. Macmillan expressed his desire to assist South Africans in their journey towards full manumission but expressed significant reservations about the emergent political system which would become known as *apartheid*.

British-Israelists were initially scornful of the ability of African nations to maintain themselves without the succor provided from the mother country of the Empire. Buxton Gresty expected Africa to 'degenerate into a veritable bobbery of small nations.' This attitude persevered for several decades. In 1980, Francis Thomas looked back at the 'winds of change' speech as a sign of the 'deepening apostasy.' Thomas lamented that Macmillan had not anticipated the 'far reaching consequences' of decolonisation. Into the 1990s, readers of the *Covenant Voice* were told of a 'lost decade,' in Africa, which had resulted from 'self government.' 'Laziness,' had 'seised the people, who are encouraged . . . that it is more beneficial financially for a man to be unemployed.'[25] Other British-Israelists expressed concern that Britain's exit from Africa left African nations vulnerable to 'the masters of red Russia' and worried that the 'independent black states' might 'fall, through local chaos, into the Communist grip.'[26]

As the 1960s progressed, however, there was a marked shift in the tone expressed by British-Israelists on the issue of Africa. Whereas 'settlers' in Africa had previously been portrayed as the triumphant, missional, imperial delegates of Israel, they were now represented as a nation in exile, beleaguered and embattled. In the first instance, this shift affected British-Israelist attitudes to the British in Africa exclusively. Major Venn Fey was a key exemplar for British-Israelists in this period. Fey was a fourth-generation British landowner who had led a Tracker Combat Team during the Mau Mau uprising. Having relocated to South Africa, he now found himself at odds with the government of his homeland on the issue of imperial responsibility. The *Covenant Voice* heaped opprobrium on Macmillan for 'abandoning' Fey and his like.[27]

British-Israelists in South Africa were still fairly numerous at this point. The movement had set down roots in the country in the early twentieth century and a branch of the BIWF had been established in 1920 under the leadership of A.W. Marris. Their membership was – as might be expected – drawn mainly from the ranks of British South Africans, rather than Afrikaners. The BIWF headquarters was located at number 28 Jorissen Street, Braamfontein. In the month of September 1960, the headquarters hosted meetings and lectures on eighteen out of thirty days, not including prayers, held every Tuesday morning at 10 am and every Thursday afternoon at 1:15 pm. William Finlay was a bulwark of the movement in Johannesburg. British-Israel reading rooms could be found in Bulawayo, Cape Town, Durban, Pietermaritzburg, Pretoria and Salisbury. A funding drive for the movement accumulated a total of £3,966 from a total of one hundred ten donors.[28] Three British-Israelist periodicals – the *Covenant Message*, *News of the New World* and *The Ambassador* – were published in South Africa during this period.

British-Israelists supported the policy of apartheid, and their magazines explained that apartheid laws were – in ethos – no different from the biblical injunctions against miscegenation. An early edition of *The Ambassador*, from 1966, included the following testimony of a sixteen-year-old South African. In this testimony, the author expresses his incredulity at the level of antipathy to the policy of apartheid amongst the international community:

> I am completely unable to understand why there is such an intense effort by people to force an end to segregation which has been a natural and accepted principle throughout history. Evolutionists insist that the human family is merely an advanced form of the animal kingdom but I feel that the animals, if they were capable of expressing an opinion,

would hang their heads in shame at the behaviour of human beings. God instituted a basic law which the animal kingdom has observed since that time – 'after its kind.'[29]

In the UK, many British-Israelists reiterated the claim that apartheid was a biblically mandated system. Principal amongst those who sought to give succor to apartheid-era South Africa was G.H. Nicholson. Nicholson had been a chaplain to the armed forces during the inter-war years.[30] He served as the rector of Burghfield, where he would frequently use his sermons to expound on theories of race and indulge in anti-Semitic tirades. He also acted as an informal pastor for the National Front during the 1960s, and he conducted services at the cenotaph on behalf of the National Front and the Anglo-Rhodesian association.[31] Nicholson was a regular contributor to *The National Message* during the 1960s.[32] More often than not, his contributions to the magazine focussed on the subject of apartheid and on the misguided nature of the 'winds of change' initiative. In 1960, he expressed his amazement and shock 'at the way in which the subject [of apartheid] has been so ignorantly treated.' Nicholson took aim at the Archbishop of Canterbury who had described the apartheid regime as 'a sort of slavery.' Nicholson accused the Archbishop of 'adding to the confusion by not distinguishing between segregation in principle and for the purpose for which it is enjoined in Scripture.'[33]

Nevertheless, British-Israelists were not – at this point – prepared to support the policies of the apartheid government in one particular area. They opposed the withdrawal of British presence in Africa and saw the National Party (which had been in government since the 1950s) as an antagonist of Israel. When the National Party successfully campaigned to remove South Africa from the Commonwealth in 1960, the chief organ of the BIWF in South Africa predicted that the long-term effects of this move would result in a 'longing amongst the ordinary people for a return to the Peace of Israel.' The Afrikaner Nationalists were counted amongst the 'dark forces' which menaced the 'citadel of Pax Britannica' in Africa.[34]

When, in the mid-1960s, Southern Rhodesia descended into civil war, British-Israelists found themselves at a crossroads. In 1965, the Rhodesian government, led by Ian Smith's Rhodesian Front, announced the Universal Declaration of Independence from Britain. In this instance, however, British-Israelists turned their ire on the British rather than the Rhodesian government. The British government – in their insistence on majority rule – had 'abandoned' white Rhodesians. V.F. Conningham called on British-Israelists to express solidarity with the inhabitants of Rhodesia. '[White Rhodesians] have no other homeland,' V.F. Conningham wrote. They were perturbed to see the 'hilarious disorderliness' of newly emancipated Nigeria.[35] Criticism of British government policy on Rhodesia usually was couched in reference to British participation in multi-national treaty agreements such as NATO, the UN and the EEC.[36] Typically, British-Israelist apologists for

Smith's Rhodesia accused the mainstream media of being witting or unwitting collaborators in an anti-Christian propaganda effort. So, in 1966, the Reverend Stephen Pulford wrote that Britain's 'leading politicians have become victims of that subtle form of Communist propaganda,' which promoted 'one-world government, internationalism and multi-racialism.'[37] As British policy towards newly independent Rhodesia became steadily more antagonistic, the tone of British-Israelist literature on the subject became more ardent. 'The British Government's sanctions against Rhodesia are a betrayal and a clear evidence of the enslavement of the British people to the Beast-Babylonian system,' wrote one commentator in the pages of *News of the New World*.[38] British-Israelists supported and promoted the writings of apologists for the Smith administration. In the 1970s, Dr William Finlay – author of *Races in Chaos* – corresponded with the leaders of the Covenant People's Fellowship and – in 1973 – McKelvey travelled to South Africa to visit him.[39] McKelvey spoke, alongside Finlay, in 'one of the largest hotels,' in Natal.[40]

At this point, Lord James Graham held positions of authority in the Smith administration. Graham was the Minister for Agriculture and was a signatory of the Declaration of Independence. At a function in 1966, held to celebrate the first anniversary of independence, Graham confessed to one attendee that he was a British Israelite. The British in Rhodesia, he believed, were of Israelitish origin. On this basis, he argued that due to 'divine assurance' Rhodesia would be 'alright' and that 'the UDI venture was bound to succeed.'[41]

In all of their commentary, British-Israelists presented the struggle of white Africans, not as a struggle between the white and black population, but rather as a struggle between beleaguered Israelites and the international forces of Babylon. This attitude was mirrored in the writing of Father Arthur Lewis. Lewis was the chairman of the Rhodesia Christian Group. He had organised a mission in Rhodesia since the 1950s and had been a stern critic of the role of the World Council of Churches in the decolonisation movement. In 1976, he was elected to the Rhodesian Senate. In 1979 Lewis was denied entry to the United Kingdom. Questions were raised about this decision in the House of Commons by Patrick Wall. Wall was a member of the Monday Club and a parliamentary consultant for the Western Goals Institute.[42] His interventions on the issue were commended by British-Israelists. Lewis himself regularly contributed to *The National Message* during this period. In 1980, on the eve of the first ever free elections to be held in Rhodesia, Lewis warned that the 'World Council of Churches' (through its Programme to Combat Racism) was 'involved . . . in what has become a programme of outright genocide' in Rhodesia. The WCC was in alliance with both the Soviets and the Americans in attempting to destroy the Rhodesian people. 'The Rhodesian Christians,' he promised, would 'keep the machinery of a civilised society going' and would 'hold [their] heads high in the face of [their] incoming masters and the curious array of aliens,' which would be 'foisted upon [them].' He finished his epistle with the following entreaty:

[We] must continue this resistance to the Marxist takeover. Keep in touch with us wherever you are: pray for us, circulate this letter – it may well be the only public voice left to us – and give us every help you can.[43]

At this remove from the end of empire, British-Israelists became more amenable to the idea that Afrikaners, as well as British South Africans, represented a 'covenant people.' In 1985, *The Link* reported that the 'most vulnerable,' people in South Africa were the 'Afrikaner churchmen.' They had been 'outlawed from the World Church bodies.' Afrikaners were identified as an Israel people, who had stood for the Gospel in the face of an 'apostate world.' British-Israelists began to repeat the Afrikaner mythologies which – as Akenson has demonstrated – linked Afrikaner identity with the polity of Israel. In 1991, Michael Clark went so far as to identify the Great Trek as a key event in the history of Israel.[44]

One aspect of the relationship between South African, pro-apartheid campaigners and British-Israelists found its way into the mainstream media during the 1990s. Andrew Smith (alongside General Sir Walter Walker) was one of the key figures in the Western Goals organisation. In the 1980s, he became a prominent member of the Monday Club. At the same time, he was associated with prominent figures in the British National Party including Steven Milson and Gregory Lauder-Fox. As a result of his association with Western Goals and the Anti-Communist League, Smith made contact with Clive Derby-Lewis. Derby-Lewis was a Member of Parliament, representing the South African Conservative Party. He had dedicated his political career to the defence of the apartheid regime. In 1993, Derby-Lewis recruited the services of Polish immigrant Janusz Walus to assassinate the ANC militant Chris Hani. Walus shot Hani as he stepped out of his car, outside his home in Boksburg. Walus was arrested. The gun that he had used was identified as belonging to Derby-Lewis, who was also arrested and sentenced to death. When the death sentence was abolished in 1995, his sentence was commuted to 'life imprisonment.' Derby-Lewis' involvement in the Western Goals Initiative drew the attention of the press in the UK. *The Guardian* published an exposé which linked Derby-Lewis with the Monday Club and established that Derby-Lewis had spoken at fringe events at the Conservative Party conference in 1989. It appeared that this link was orchestrated by Andrew Smith in his role as director of Western Goals.

Andrew Smith combined his active role in the Western Goals Institute and the Monday Club with an active role in the BIWF. In a letter which was later acquired by *The Guardian*, he expressed the belief that:

the British nation and kindred peoples around the world, ie all those of Anglo-Celto-Saxon descent, are the direct lineal descendants of the ten 'lost' tribes of Israel, and that we have a divine mission to spread Christ's Gospel and advance the cause of genuine Bible-based Protestant Christianity.[45]

Whilst the Western Goals Institute did not avow the more unusual claims of the British-Israelists, its stated political aims were not dissimilar. In 1991, Stuart Northolt (who edited the Western Goals Institute's journal *European Dawn*), described the intentions of the Institute in the following terms:

Western Goals works to establish networks and links with conservative groups dedicated to the preservation of the cultures and identities of western nations. We are conservatives who believe in traditional conservative values.

Northolt saw the end of immigration into Britain as an essential part of this project. As we shall see, this concern was shared by the British-Israelists of this period.

British Israel enters her chambers

A tone of providential declinism – quite the reverse of 'jingoism with Biblical sanction' – suffused British-Israelist commentary throughout this period. By the 1970s, every news story appeared to confirm – for British-Israelists – the fact that Britain was no longer at the top table of geo-political prestige. Hearing of Britain's third successive defeat in the Cod War of 1976, Buxton Gresty lamented this 'melancholy problem,' writing that the fisheries dispute 'shows how far we have slipped in the eyes of our neighbours.' It was to be expected, given that Britain had 'departed from her God-given commission.' But Gresty also believed that there was a providential explanation for these developments. The prophets had foreseen that Israel would disappear from 'the front rank of nations' and would be 'insulted' by the weakest nations.[46]

Tom Nairn once wrote that Britain's destiny 'was once an imperial one, but now it has to be something different.'[47] This was apparent, even to the most ardent of British patriots. In a speech in Louth in 1963, Enoch Powell said:

Every nation, to live healthily and to live happily, needs a patriotism. Britain today, after all the changes of the past decades, needs a new kind of patriotism and is feeling its way towards it. The policy which matches such a patriotism is [a policy] which is not ashamed of the nation.[48]

David Edgerton's recent work has drawn attention to a shift that took place in British politics in the middle decades of the twentieth century. At this point in her history, Britain ceased to be a cosmopolitan, free trading state with a fluid attitude to borders (both on and off the island of Britain) and became instead a 'nation,' with nationalist economic policies oriented towards subsistence and self-sufficiency. Along with this shift in economic and social policies (which was facilitated by both the right and the left), Britain embraced a new, nationalistic political culture, with 'national rather than imperial histories, a nationalist critique of cosmopolitan capitalism and a powerfully nationalist declinism.' Many nations were built in the embers of the British Empire during this period. Edgerton contends that Britain 'can usefully be seen as one of the new nations which arose from the dissolution of the one empire.' This was a reimagining of Britain, which – to use Smith's nomenclature – signalled a shift from the missional to the covenantal.[49]

The editors of *Brith* also sought a providential explanation for the retreat of Britain's influence in the world. But for British-Israelists, this transition was explained in explicitly providential terms, with explicit reference to Britain as Israel. They argued that the latter was actually a form of consolidation of Israel. The nations that Britain had attempted to convert were 'reverting to various forms of heathen worship.' As such, the day was nearing when 'the world will be completely divided into the Godless nations and the Christian nations and the Christian nations will be the Anglo-Saxon.'[50] 'Separatism is the way to peace,' trumpeted the headlines in *Wake Up* magazine. The editors claimed that the withdrawal of Britain from the world was a positive thing. Empire-building had been a task which had been allotted to Israel by God, but it had brought with it the problems of cosmopolitanism and the mixing of the races. With the end of empire, Britain had an opportunity to retreat, to separate herself from the world, the better to live in the natural way ordained for human beings by God. The Lord God 'decreed that the races of mankind should live in separate communities,' and the end of the Empire would allow this natural order to resume.[51]

Foremost amongst those making this argument was Charles McKelvey, leader of the SPBI. McKelvey anticipated that the first sign of the end would be the 'isolation of Israel in her chambers.' This would involve 'the Israelite peoples that live in the Chambers of Israel. . . [being] cleansed and made ready for the coming of the Lord.' In a *Brith* editorial which greeted the emancipation of India, McKelvey commented that 'by coming out as we are doing we are but entering into our chambers.' Just as Ezekiel had prophesied, God was 'putting ideas into the Heads of Russian Statesmen that [He] fully intends them to think and upon which they will act to their final destruction.'[52] Indeed, as McKelvey suggested more than once, the most advised course of action, in light of the juncture that had been reached in the unfolding of providence, was for Britain to actively shed her imperial territories.[53]

A third stage in this transition took place at the end of the twentieth century with the death of national Britain. With the shift in focus, in the political sphere, towards a new global Britain, those who had developed a political ideology around the covenantal nationalism of the previous generation found themselves politically homeless. From this, the activist politics of Euroscepticism emerged in the 1990s. For the Eurosceptics of this period, authenticity of a secular kind became just as central a concern as the providential authenticity of the 'national message' had been for the British-Israelists.

British-Israel and commonwealth immigration

A key focus of the providential-declinist commentary of British-Israelists during this period was its criticism of immigration from the Common-wealth. The British Nationality Act of 1948 permitted all citizens of Commonwealth countries to live and work in the United Kingdom without any requirement to secure a visa. This remained the status quo until the passing of the 1962 Commonwealth Immigrants Act. During the 1950s and 1960s, anti-immigration sentiment began to develop from the right of the Conservative Party, resulting in the foundation of the Monday Club in 1961. As the 1960s progressed, other far right, anti-immigrant organisations gained support in the form of the National Front and the first iteration of the British National Party. Foremost amongst these new opponents of Commonwealth immigration was Enoch Powell, whose 'rivers of blood' speech drew many to the cause. Nairn characterised the anti-immigration movement of the 1960s and 1970s as the latest stage in a process of antagonistic self-definition in British nationalist culture. 'Powell realised,' he wrote, '[that] it had become possible to define Englishness vis-a-vis this internal "enemy," this "foreign body" in our own streets.'[54]

British-Israelists shared the view, held by many on the nationalist right during this period, that the policies which had facilitated mass immigration from commonwealth countries were destructive. They aligned themselves, actively, with Enoch Powell and his supporters. Writing in 1968, the editors of *The National Message* claimed that Powell was 'backed by a great majority of the people of these islands' and congratulated him for his courage in 'outlining a growing problem which is facing this country.'[55] British-Israelists were quick to blame all kinds of social disharmonies, during this period, on the newly arrived Commonwealth immigrants. 'Loutish rioting' at Notting Hill Gate in 1976 was described as the inevitable result of the 'ultra-naïve sky-is-the-limit policy on mass immigration followed by successive governments of both parties since the Winds of Change days.'[56] Like Powell, most British-Israelists took the view that objecting to immigration was not racist, but was rather a reasonable response to rapid demographic changes. It was a defensive rather than an aggressive posture. 'It is not a question of attributing racial inferiority,' one commentator wrote, 'it is a genuine fear . . . that within a few generations, [our] grand children will be a minority of strangers in the land of their fathers.' The fear of immigrants was a rational fear, they claimed, and those who criticised others for expressing these fears 'were paying scant regard to the fact that they had this human flood imposed upon them without reference to their own wishes.'[57]

Also, like Powell, British-Israelists maintained that their principal concern was not selfish or nationalistic but humanitarian. They expressed fear that immigrants would be the principle victims of the folly of multiculturalism. 'Mixed racial communities,' wrote Michael Hart, were likely to result in slavery or in a caste system, both of which were deemed to be contrary to the Christian ethic. These arguments were couched in naturalistic language. To be separate was to be natural. To be mixed or miscegenated was identified as unnatural or profane.[58]

In their condemnation of commonwealth immigration, British-Israelists often presented themselves as truth-tellers, prepared to be stigmatised and shot down for expressing their views. Those who 'had the temerity to counsel caution' had been 'violently stigmatised as anti-social, un-Christian and colour-conscious.'[59] In these texts, British-Israelists are presented as experiencing a dual embattlement: firstly against the 'invading' immigrant population, but secondly against the liberal, reprobate majority. Others saw the demographic changes that were taking place in Britain as evidence of something far more sinister. In an article written in 1966, the Reverend Stephen Pulford presented the Commonwealth immigrants as 'invited invaders.' These 'mostly black and coloured' immigrants 'continue to arrive in our already over-crowded island in their organised thousands, in spite of the shortage of houses for our own people,' he wrote. But this was by no means a coincidence. It was, rather, a 'nefarious communist plot by some left wing MPs who are dead set on increasing the inflow of coloureds who are establishing a bridgehead to get the English out of their last colony.'[60]

Beneath all of this – familiar – anti-immigrant rhetoric, British-Israelists had a distinctive message. British-Israelists believed that 'races have a divine spark to preserve their identity' and that the attempt to create a 'multi-racial society' was 'the principal sin of the Antediluvian world.'[61] This viewpoint was summarised by Buxton Gresty in an article written for *The National Message* in 1965. Gresty acknowledged that large numbers of people shared the scepticism of British-Israelists about the rise in immigration. But 'Christians,' he claimed 'have an additional and even more important consideration' than those of mere economics or politics. 'Those who are convinced that the English speaking peoples embody the descendants of Israel' had a responsibility to 'welcome coloured Christians into our worship.' At the same time, however, Buxton Gresty reminded his readers that 'our nation was set apart by God for a special responsibility to mankind at large' and that 'it was not His purpose that His people should be diluted by indiscriminate admixture with other nations.'[62] For this reason, British-Israelists expressed 'strong opposition to' the Race Relations Act in 1965.[63] British-Israelists in America had long voiced these arguments against intermarriage and racial mixing. In the middle decades of the twentieth century, this became a prevailing concern of British-Israelists living in the motherland. Gresty claimed that 'the large-scale mingling of races operates to the general detriment.' As such, he echoed well-established themes of British-Israelist thought.[64]

In 1972, a second wave of immigrants arrived. In August of that year, Idi Amin declared that all 80,000 Asians who were living in Uganda would be forced to leave the country within ninety days. This injunction was later relaxed, allowing 23,000 Ugandan citizens the right to remain in the country. Nonetheless, 27,000 Ugandan Asians, mostly Commonwealth citizens of Gujarati origin, left the country. The UK government decided to offer asylum to the Ugandan Asians, and the Ugandan Resettlement Board was established in order to facilitate the absorption of the Ugandan population. There were some dissenting voices. In August, *The Telegraph* reported 'categorical rejections of any further influx from local authorities' and suggested that 'the situation with regard to housing and education in particular [is] already stretched.'[65] Enoch Powell told the BBC that the attorney general had 'prostituted his office' by misleading the public into believing that Britain had any obligation to the Ugandan Asians.[66] Amongst British-Israelists, these voices were also raised. In 1972, writing in the pages of *Brith*, Noel Court expressed his sorrow in witnessing the hardship experienced by the Ugandan Asians. 'Everyone feels sorry for victims of oppression wherever they are found,' he wrote. Nonetheless, Court was perturbed by the fact that the resettlement programme gave 'preferential treatment to people who really have no connection racially by family ties, culture or language with this country.' For all its good intention, the acceptance of the Ugandan refugees would lead to a host of other problems relating to the 'housing shortage and unemployment.' Alongside these concerns, Court cited the difficulties that would be caused by 'the presence in the land of the heathen religions of the newcomers.' Nonetheless, he was sceptical by November that any political action could be done to reverse the decision and counseled that it would 'be best to commit the whole problem to God.'[67]

In particular, British-Israelists feared that the influx of Asians would increase the likelihood of intermarriage between Israel and non-Israel people. British-Israelists strongly adhere to the belief that relationships between white and non-white people constitute a sin in the eyes of God. The injunction against 'mixed marriage' originated in the sixth chapter of Genesis when the 'sons of God' married with the 'daughters of men.'[68] The argument that the sons and daughters of Israel should not marry the sons of daughters of other nations is most fully expressed in the book of Ezra. The Jews who had returned to Jerusalem from exile in Babylon confess to Ezra that they have married people of other nations: Ammonites, Hittites, Jebusites, Perizzites, Moabites and Egyptians. At this news, Ezra tears his cloak in two, pulls hair from his beard and sits down, appalled.[69]

The commandment to avoid intermarriage with 'strangers' was – according to British-Israelists – no less binding on Israel in the twentieth century than it was in the fifth century BCE. 'Miscegenation is self-evidently wrong,' wrote one, 'and is truly a destruction of God's created order of race.'[70] As such, some British-Israelists claimed that there 'would be no danger from strangers in our midst if our own people were rightly instructed.'[71] It was only the fact that an insufficient proportion of the population of British-Israel understood or knew of the injunction against marrying non-Israelites that meant that mass immigration would prove dangerous to Britain. And dangerous they believed it would be. Israel, after all, was punished for the sin of miscegenation. The Lord God ordained that, should the Israelites intermarry, 'the stranger within thee shall get up above thee very high.'[72] British-Israelists believed that this had taken place in Israel 'when the Idumeans seised power,' and they worried that the same might take place in the UK, should intermarriage become widespread.[73]

The increasing levels of commonwealth migration provided an additional headache for those who were seeking to explain Britain's diminished status in the world in accordance with the prophecies of Isaiah 26. According to the claim that Israel would 'enter into her chambers,' in anticipation of the eschatological denouement, Britain should expect to experience a period of isolation from the world. As such, the preparation times would necessarily involve 'the Anglo Saxon community at present spread over the world,' being 'forced out of all nations and brought back into the chambers.'[74] This prophetic understanding of Britain's changing role was easy to correlate with Britain's withdrawal from her former colonies.[75] But the increase in contact between Israel-Britain and the nations – resulting from Commonwealth migration – was less easy to explain in these terms. McKelvey predicted that 'the great influx of aliens into this land' was 'Satan's last attempt to so contaminate the blood of Israel that the Lord would have to destroy them.'[76]

Beneath all of these crises within the British-Israel community lay an underlying fear that the rise of immigration in the mid-twentieth century was a foreshadowing of the gradual erosion of national authenticity. As David Edgerton writes, racism should not be conflated with imperialism, since – during the 1960s and 1970s – racism was 'increasingly likely to be nationalist rather than imperialist.' This anxiety would continue to plague British-Israelists – and would become their foremost preoccupation – in the twenty-first century. 'Can a separated people survive in a borderless world?' one BIWF member asked, in 2001, '[when] vast numbers from Asia, South America, and the Balkans are flooding into the rich Israel nations,' through the Channel Tunnel?[77]

As this quotation demonstrates, British-Israelists were able, by the end of the twentieth century, to describe migration as a new battle in the cosmic struggle between Israel – which stood for all that was singular, authentic and salient – and Babylon – which stood for Empire, globalisation, miscegenation and the protean. The Siegfried line of this new conflict was Dover: the newly established land border between Britain and Catholic Europe.

Conclusion

On the 25 November 1959, Lord Brooke of Cumnor made the following comment in a debate on the subject of immigration in the House of Lords:

> Britain will make its best contribution to the world if it continues to be a nation of predominantly Anglo-Saxon stock. If for saying this I am branded a racialist, then I am proud to be a racialist.[78]

Many Britons, in this period – including those with power to affect legislation – subscribed to essentially the same mythological belief: that the 'British people' existed and that their preservation as a coherent, authentic and salient group was essential for the wellbeing of the nation and perhaps of the world. There is no more basis for believing in an 'Anglo-Saxon stock' with an essential national character than there is for believing in an Israelitish stock with an essential national character. This belief – whether attached or detached from the empirical, historical claims of British-Israelists – fed populist antipathy to Commonwealth migration in the noonday and the twilight of the twentieth century.

Britain had fundamentally changed, according to David Edgerton, from a cosmopolitan society into a society which was deeply suspicious of cosmopolitanism. Britain had also become a nation of declinists, asserting Britain's greatness by accentuating the heights from which she had fallen. British-Israelists certainly reflected these changes. They provided an account of Britain's retreat from the world which mirrored almost exactly the narratives promoted by Powell and later by Thatcher. The only difference was that British-Israelists couched their account of decline in a providential tenor. It is possible, however, that British-Israelism does more than hold up a mirror to the nation. The cultural resources, the images and stories, which formed the British-Israelist account of Britain's 'retreat into her chambers,' had been at the heart of British culture for hundreds of years, even if they were – by the late twentieth century – impossible for most Britons to name. In the new image of Britain – gloriously isolated – that emerged in the late twentieth century, it is hard not to see the reflection of covenanted Israel, whether that comparison was made explicit or remained implicit.

During this period, British-Israelists turned their attentions away from the empire and (as they did so) they turned their ire towards those entities – the United Nations, the European Union and the Catholic Church – which they saw as seeking to destroy the authenticity of nations. 'We have to stand together,' wrote Francis Sibson in 1960, 'against a United Nations ruled by a majority vote of Black Nationalist Africa, anti-West Asians and the Red Bloc, acting wittingly or unwittingly in concert to overrun the last remnants of the Israel British servant people.'[79] Amongst these events, Britain's increasingly close relationship with the nations of continental Europe provided the most cause for concern.

Notes

1 Kidd, *The Forging of Races*, 213.
2 Barkun, *Religion and the Racist Right*, 9.
3 Kidd, *The Forging of Races*, 213.
4 Wilson, 'British Israelism,' 48, 55.
5 *Brith*, no. 292 (April 1970), 26.
6 *The Banner of Israel*, vol. 2, no. 81 (17 July 1878), 229.
7 *The Banner of Israel*, vol. 42, no. 2,146 (13 February 1918), 94.
8 Reginald Cox, 'The Enduring Commonwealth,' in *The New World Crusade* (London: Covenant Publishing, 1944), 9.
9 *The National Message*, vol. 55, no. 1,643 (October 1976), 295.
10 *The National Message*, vol. 31, no. 1,294 (23 February 1952), 76.
11 *The Banner of Israel*, vol. 41, no. 2,093 (7 February 1917), 78.
12 Cynthia Behrman, 'The Mythology of British Imperialism, 1890–1914' (Doctoral Thesis: University of Boston, 1965), 47.
13 *The Banner of Israel*, vol. 43, no. 2,192 (1 January 1919), 7.
14 *The Banner of Israel*, vol. 42, no. 2,146 (13 February 1918), 68.
15 *The Banner of Israel*, vol. 43, no. 2,192 (1 January 1919), 8.
16 *The Banner of Israel*, vol. 42, no. 2,178 (2 October 1918), 341.
17 *The Banner of Israel*, vol. 43, no. 2,203 (19 March 1919), 104.
18 *The Banner of Israel*, vol. 44, no. 2,267 (9 June 1920), 195.
19 *The National Message*, vol. 31, no. 1,291 (26 January 1952), 28.
20 *Brith*, no. 39 (February 1949), 15.
21 *Brith*, no. 17 (February 1946), 3.
22 *Brith*, no. 292 (April 1970), 98–99.
23 *Brith*, no. 13 (October 1946), 7.
24 *Brith*, no. 13 (October 1946), 6.
25 *Covenant Voice* (February 1991), 22.
26 *The Covenant Message*, vol. 29, no. 2 (February 1960), 47.
27 *The Covenant Message*, vol. 29, no. 4 (April 1960), 128.
28 *The Covenant Message*, vol. 29, no. 9 (September 1960), 358–361.
29 *The Ambassador* (June 1966), 21.
30 *London Gazette*, no. 3,415 (30 April, 1935), 2824.
31 *7 Days*, no. 20 (15 March 1972), 11–15.
32 *The National Message*, vol. 50, no. 1,576 (March 1971), 17.
33 *The Covenant Message*, vol. 29, no. 10 (October 1960), 371.
34 *The Covenant Message*, vol. 29, no. 6 (June 1960), 205; *The Covenant Message*, vol. 29, no. 5 (May 1960), 164.
35 *The National Message*, vol. 45, no. 1,514 (January 1966), 17.
36 *News of the New World*, vol. 1, no. 5 (April 1966), 3.
37 *News of the New World*, vol. 1, no. 5 (April 1966), 11.
38 *News of the New World*, vol. 1, no. 3 (February 1966), 6.
39 *Brith*, no. 365 (September 1976), 10–11.
40 *Brith*, no. 328 (May 1973), 30.
41 *The Guardian* (24 February 1992), 35.
42 Hansard, House of Commons Debate (22 January 1979), vol. 961, c35W.
43 *The National Message*, vol. 59, no. 1,685 (April 1980), 50, 58–59.
44 *Wake Up*, vol. 8, no. 9 (November 1991), 208.
45 *The Guardian* (24 April 1993), 25.
46 *The National Message*, vol. 55, no. 1,634 (January 1976), 17.
47 Nairn, *The Break Up of Britain*, 274.
48 Enoch Powell, 'Speech at Louth, 8 March 1963,' POLL 4/1/1 [cited in Paul Corthorn, *Enoch Powell* (Oxford: Oxford University Press, 2019), 55].

49 Edgerton, *The Rise and Fall of the British Nation*, 26.
50 *Brith*, no. 326 (March 1973), 11.
51 *Wake Up*, vol. 8, no. 7 (July 1991), 160.
52 *Brith*, no. 13 (October 1946), 7.
53 *Brith*, no. 30 (May 1948), 4.
54 Nairn, *The Break Up of Britain*, 274.
55 *The National Message*, vol. 47, no. 1,543 (June 1968), 166.
56 *The National Message*, vol. 55, no. 1,643 (October 1976), 294.
57 *The National Message*, vol. 55, no. 1,644 (November 1976), 324.
58 *The National Message*, vol. 43, no. 1,497 (August 1964), 230.
59 *The National Message*, vol. 41, no. 1,467 (February 1962), 47.
60 *The Ambassador* (April 1966), 23.
61 *Wake Up*, vol. 8, no. 2 (March 1990), 42.
62 *The National Message*, vol. 43, no. 1,502 (January 1965), 10.
63 *The National Message*, vol. 47, no. 1,543 (June 1968), 166.
64 *The National Message*, vol. 43, no. 1,502 (January 1965), 10.
65 *The Daily Telegraph*, no. 36,474 (23 August 1972), 14.
66 *The Guardian* (28 August 1972), 16.
67 *Brith*, no. 322 (November 1972), 16.
68 Genesis 6: 1–4.
69 Ezra 9: 1–5.
70 *Wake Up*, vol. 8, no. 2 (March 1990), 47.
71 *The National Message*, vol. 50, no. 1,583 (October 1971), 300.
72 Deuteronomy 28:43.
73 *The National Message*, vol. 50, no. 1,583 (October 1971), 300.
74 *Brith*, no. 326 (March 1973), 12.
75 Isaiah 26: 1–3, 20–21.
76 *Brith*, no. 326 (March 1973), 12.
77 *Crown and Commonwealth*, vol. 1, no. 1 (Spring 2001), 19.
78 Hansard, *House of Lords Debate* (25 November 1959).
79 *The Covenant Message*, vol. 29, no. 4 (April 1960), 133.

5 British-Israelism and Ireland

The complex, cultural negotiation of the relationship between Ireland and Britain, between the Irish and the British, has been a perennial feature of British life over the past several centuries. The nineteenth century brought the question of Irishness to the fore. The Act of Union required Ireland to be brought into the heart of the family of nations. However, the alien nature of Irish religion meant that Ireland would have to be reformed or would never fully belong. When it became clear that the former was impossible, it became imperative for the lines to be drawn, in a racial sense between the Irish and the British. The Irish were 'savages,' were 'more like squalid apes than human beings.'[1] But for all the Irish were presented as fundamentally other – chaotic, Catholic, childlike, crapulent – it was nevertheless impossible for Britain to relinquish her. This complex relationship of entanglement and antagonism led to decades of riot, revolution and trouble.[2]

British-Israelist belief often mirrors the predominant beliefs of the day. In most cases, however, the beliefs of British-Israelists – regarding religion, politics or culture – are contextualised in racialist terms. The question of whether Ireland – so close to Britain and yet so different – could be considered an Israel nation provided the basis for an ongoing struggle amongst British-Israelists about the importance of Ireland (and in particular the importance of Ulster) in the unfolding plan for God's people.

'Are the Irish Israel?'

The question of whether the Irish constituted an Israel nation provided British-Israelists with a perennial problem during the twentieth century. British-Israelist tradition ascribed an important role to Ireland in the history of the Israel people. At the same time, several problems thwarted the full recognition of Ireland as an Israel nation. Principal amongst these problems was the apparent unwillingness of the Irish people to remain part of Britain. Secondly, the Irish people remained in thrall to Babylonish religion – that is to say Catholicism – whilst the Israel nations embraced true Christianity. Thirdly, the Irish people – according to the pejorative stereotypes which many British-Israelists subscribed to – did not exhibit the racial character which was proper to Israel nations.

In the very earliest iterations of British-Israelism, three sites were identified as sacred to British-Israelists: Glastonbury, Westminster Abbey and the
hill of Tara. The last of these was identified as the seat of 'great dynasties
which went back into the dim past of Irish history.' Speculations abounded
as to the special significance of this place:

> Perhaps somewhere under the ground lies hidden the Ark of the Cov-
> enant, the Tables of the Law, and perchance other relics which, if
> unearthed, would open up vast treasures of information concerning the
> migrations of Israel from Palestine to the isles of the Sea.[3]

The origins of this story can be found in F.R.A. Glover's 1861 text entitled
England the Remnant of Judah. It was reiterated by Grimaldi in his *Pedi-
gree of Queen Victoria*, by Walter Milner in his *The Royal House of Britain*
and again in J.H. Allen's *Judah's Sceptre and Joseph's Birthright*.[4] Glover
relied to some extent on the *Chronicles of Eri*, a pseudepigraphical history
published by Roger O'Connor in 1822. This text in turn drew on the medieval chronicle *Lebor Gabála Erenn* which detailed the mythical Milesian
invasion of Ireland. The early modern *Annála Ríoghachta Éireann* tell of
an ancient queen of Ireland named Tea Tephi who was married to the Milesian King Erimon. Tea Tephi became the focus of British-Israelist curiosity
during this period. If it was the case that the tribe of Judah (including the
British royal family) had arrived in Britain via Ireland, then the question of
the origins of the Irish people was almost as important as the question of
the origins of the British people. This was recognised by Noel Court in the
1970s. Writing in *Brith*, Court reminded his readers that 'in spite of current
events' the people of Ireland 'hold the key to the unravelling of the drama of
the illustrious Davidic lineage.'[5]

Glover was chaplain to the consulate of Cologne. In *England, the Remnant of Judah*, he sought to prove that 'England is in possession of Jacob's
pillow' and that 'there must have been a royal seed of Judah to set upon
it.' This was a reference to the coronation stone, which British-Israelists
believed was identical to the stone that Jacob rested his head upon according to Genesis 28.[6] In part, Glover's claims were based on a belief that the
prophet Jeremiah had come to Ireland to 'plant and build' that which he
had 'plucked up' and 'rooted out' in his own land. In other words, Glover
believed that the prophet Jeremiah had brought the Jacob Stone and a member of the royal house of Judah to Ireland.[7] The latter was understood to be
a daughter of King Zedekiah named Tea Tephi. The story of Tea Tephi is
crucial to British-Israelist understanding of the role of Ireland. Jeremiah 43
attests that Zedekiah had daughters who survived the Babylonian conquest
of Judah.[8] Tea Tephi was believed to have migrated north through Spain. She
married Eremon, a High King of Ireland. Of this original ancestor, the royal
house of Great Britain is a scion. Glover contended that Ollamh Fodhla – a
mythical king of Ireland whose reign is documented in the eleventh-century

chronicle the *Lebor Gabala Erenn* – employed Jeremiah to teach the law from a scholarly institution which he founded in Meath. The hill became known – in reference to the Hebrew word for Law – as Tara.

In 1882, the circulation of rumours about the Biblical history of the Hill of Tara gave rise to a popular movement for its excavation. These were reported on in the pages of *The Illustrated Police News* as a potential and 'novel method of giving peace to Ireland.' Should Tara be excavated, perhaps it would 'settle all dispute and inaugurate a new era of lasting tranquility,' by proving that 'Celt and Saxon are alike descended from Jacob.'[9] 'Tara will be opened at a period of Revolution in Ireland,' promised Harrison Oxley.[10]

In 1889 these words were matched with action and an expedition of British-Israelists went to Tara in order to conduct an archaeological dig. The group was led by the Reverend Denis Hanan, a rector from Tipperary and a member of the British Israel Association. Hanan had read F.R.A. Glover's book and argued – in addition to Glover's claims – that Tara was likely to be the site of the Ark of the Covenant. At a lecture given in Belfast that year, Hanan used diagrams to show that the dig would be 'conducted in a way that would not cause the least injury to the historic site.'[11] Nevertheless, the dig became an issue of national controversy amid the febrile atmosphere of antebellum Ireland. Nationalist members of the House of Commons 'bombarded the Chief Secretary with a series of questions on the issue.'[12] A counter demonstration was organised and it brought to its call the most prominent members of the nationalist movement. This included Arthur Griffith (future President of Dáil Eireann), the poet William Yeats and the suffragette and nationalist Maud Gonne. Gonne staged her own inimitable protest against the excavation, singing a rendition of 'A Nation Once Again' before a bonfire atop the hill.[13]

In the aftermath of the Tara excavation, a pamphlet was published by one Walter Milner. Milner was a clergyman who served as vicar of the Crown Parish of Sunk Island. His pamphlet, entitled *Tara Vindicata*, promised to demonstrate the validity of the 'Hebrew episode in Irish history.' The pamphlet was published by Banks and Son of Fleet Street on behalf of the British Israel Association. Milner believed that the descendants of Tea Tephi – and ultimately the descendants of King David – included the Royal Family of Great Britain. This descent was traced through Ugaine the Great, the son of Tea Tephi and Eochaid Buaidhaig. Milner was particularly excited by the fact that Prince David – the future King Edward VIII – was himself the hundredth generation of King David's line:

> Prince David will have lived a generation in 1924. The interval is exactly a hundred generations. In the present paper we have verified the hypothesis . . . deducing our Royal House from Jerusalem through Tara.[14]

The stories of Tea Tephi and Tara led some to the conclusion that the Irish language was heavily inflected with Hebrew influence. One correspondent to *The Banner of Israel* proposed that 'the Irish Fer = a man, and the Latin Vir = a man, are both only another form of the Hebrew *Bar*.'[15] Others drew comparison between purportedly ancient Irish customs and the customs of Biblical Israel. R.M. Maguire, writing in December 1917, drew attention to certain cultural commonalities shared between the ancient Irish and the ancient Israelites. 'Like Israel, when settled in Canaan,' he wrote 'the ancient Irish had places of refuge for a homicide.' 'Like the ancient Israelites,' he continued, 'the Irish both before and after the Christian era, believed in the right of the next of kin to avenge the blood of slain persons.'[16]

At the same time that these claims were being made about the 'Hebrew episode in Irish history,' parallel claims were made about the ethnic origins of the Irish. The notion that the Irish were also descendants of Israel was troubling to those who believed that Britain's Israel heritage was the explanation for her embrace of Protestantism. Ireland, if she was truly of Israel, appeared to be anomalous in her tenacious attachment to Babylonian Romanism. Indeed, Catholicism was just *one* example of the Irish people's un-Israelitish national character. One exasperated British-Israelist lamented that the Irish were unable to 'renounce the drink by which they are so readily affected' and were unable to 'take off their coats and work' and expressed the belief that if 'Roman Ireland had but half the grit and perseverance of Protestant Ulster, they soon would proportionally begin to rival them in prosperity.'[17]

In response to this problem, many British-Israelists, during the early part of the twentieth century, devised an alternative theory. Whilst the aristocratic class of Israelites had been brought to Ireland and provided, thereby, the Davidic seed for the British royal line, the majority of the Irish were not descendants of Israel but, rather, were descendants of Israel's sworn enemy Canaan. As Hine had pointed out, the fact that the roots of the Semitic races were found in the Middle East did not mean that all of the Semitic races were of Israel. In reality, many of them may be the descendants of Israel's long-standing, divinely appointed adversaries.[18] In a lecture given by E.S. Jacques at Southport on 28 September 1920, the speaker asked the question 'why can we not rule Ireland?' In answer he made the following claim:

> It is known that the South and West of Ireland is inhabited by Canaanites. In Numbers 33 the Israelites are commanded to drive out the idolatrous Canaanites. The command was not obeyed and idolatry spread.[19]

This claim was accepted by British-Israelists during the early part of twentieth century. An editorial in *The Banner of Israel* in 1920 explained that 'the Canaanites' were 'one branch of the great Semitic stock,' along with the Phoenicians. As such, it was deemed natural that the great traders of Phoenicia would have brought both Israelites and Canaanites 'attracted by the Phoenician enterprise' with them on their trading missions to Britain for 'their own immigration purposes.'[20] The claim that Ireland was in fact home to *two* groups of people – one Israelite and one Canaanite in origin – was extrapolated upon by one Mrs Bristowe, in the summer of 1919, in a lecture at the Ewart Library in Dumfries. Mrs Bristowe explained that 'in early Irish history we read of the country being divided between two races of men of different languages, habits and laws and animated with deadly hatred towards each other.' One was 'free,' whilst the other was 'servile.' This belief continued to gain traction in British-Israel circles well into the mid-twentieth century.

The belief that the majority of the Irish were in fact racially distinct from the people of Israel and – indeed – that they were racially inclined to be antagonistic towards Israel informed British-Israelist beliefs about the correct policy in Ireland. Bristowe depicted the Irish problem as a curse, placed on Israel by God for her infidelity. She based this claim on a promise made by God to Israel, recorded in Numbers 33. God instructed the Israelites, upon occupying Canaan, to drive out the inhabitants. If they failed to do so, God promised, the former inhabitants of the land would 'remain as barbs in your eyes and thorns in your sides.' The British had been commanded 'to destroy a wicked race' in Ireland and because they had failed to do so, this wicked race had become 'as thorns in their sides forever.'[21] This claim was reiterated by E.S. Jacques in his speech the following year:

> The command was not obeyed and idolatry spread. Then was to come the punishment for disobedience. The Canaanites 'shall be pricks in your eyes and thorns in your sides.' There is still trouble before us. Yielding is a mistake as of old. We should meet the Canaanites and their propaganda and put them down with a firm hand.[22]

In 1952, L. Buxton Gresty stressed that the Celts and the Anglo-Saxons were of one race. However, he reiterated the claim that Canaanites had arrived in Ireland before the Israelite Celts. Gresty believed that the first group to spread 'the white race' in the 'isles and coastlands of the west' were 'Iberians.' They had preceded the Celts in reaching Ireland. The 'Iberians,' according to Gresty's research, were mixed with 'the progeny of Ham' and were probably 'descendants of the Hamitic tribes who fled from Canaan at the time of the invasion by Joshua's Israelites.' As such, many of the Irish were not of Israel but rather were of the 'swarthy Iberian' race. This genealogy helped to explain Irish antipathy to Israel's culture, religion and identity.[23] A similar genealogy was proposed by Reginald Cox in 1985. Cox explained that 'the whole island was populated by the same people as those in Great Britain until the influx of Spaniards to Cork in 1601.' 'These people and their religion have no comparable racial claim to Ireland whatsoever,' Cox contended.[24] The Celtic religion of Ireland had been established long before the arrival of Catholicism, and British-Israelists believed that this tradition was closely linked to true Israelitish religion, 'much closer to the revealed truth than the Roman Catholic Church ever was.' However, the non-Israelite demographic in Ireland took to 'replacement theology' when it was brought to the country by Roman missionaries in the early medieval period. Nonetheless, a remnant of Israelitish religion remained in Ireland, thus explaining the opposition 'in the North of that land to any possibility of the Roman order of the day holding sway.'[25]

The claim that the majority of the Irish people were not Israelitish but were rather Canaanite became a truism of British-Israelist thought as the years of the Troubles wore on. In the 1970s, Edith Clements claimed that 'to form an opinion on Irish origins, it is necessary first to consider such knowledge as we have on the ancient Phrygians and Phoenicians.' She pointed out that 'Canaanite Phoenicians established their idolatry wherever they colonised.' This in part explained the Irish weakness for Popery.[26] The suggestion that the Irish were in fact Canaanites, wedded to anti-Israel prejudice and anti-Christian religion, provided the most compelling elucidation of the Irish problem for British-Israelites throughout the twentieth century. As one British-Israelist, writing in 1971, claimed:

> Many of the troubles of latter day Israel have been fomented by this rancid remnant of demoniac hatred which started in the land of Canaan more than three thousand years ago.[27]

These narratives – which linked Britain-Israel to the land of Ireland whilst distancing the people of Britain-Israel from the people of Ireland – simultaneously vindicated Britain's attachment to Ireland and delegitimised the argument for self-governance by the Irish people. Indeed, some – like Reginald Cox – were prepared to argue that the people of Ireland had less 'racial claim to the land' than did the British.[28] Britain-Israel was close enough to Ireland to rule it, but distant enough from it not to be contaminated by Irishness: Popery, rebellion and shiftlessness.

British-Israelism in Ireland in the twentieth century

Loyalist British-Israelism has a long history in Ireland. In February 1917, a branch of the Anglo-Israel Union was founded in Belfast. An advertisement in *The Banner of Israel* read:

> The union has arranged to hold a meeting in the centre of Belfast every Sunday evening. Will those of our readers who have good literature to dispose of please send it to W. Adair of Springfield Gardens.[29]

At one such meeting, on Armistice Day 1919, the Drumbeg Orange Hall was packed to hear the thoughts of William Orr on 'the Approaching End of the Age.' Orr warned that the Philistine race, who had so menaced Israel in antiquity, had not been finally vanquished. 'Like Israel they dispersed,' he told the audience, 'and are today identified by heraldic, historic and etymological evidence as the Phoenician or Fenian Irish.' As had been prophesied, this people had continued to be 'thorns in the flesh against the House of Israel.' This had continued because 'the Divine injunction to destroy them out of the Holy Land had been disobeyed.' Only providence could explain the 'disloyalty and hostility of the Southern Irish': a 'modern manifestation of an old hate.' There was hope however. Prophecy showed that this hatred would some day be 'drastically subdued.'[30] This linguistic association of 'Fenians' and 'Phoenicians' was also repeated on the mainland. In 1911, the *London Daily News* reported that the same claim had been made in a coronation sermon, preached by the rector of St Peter's Trusthorpe.[31]

The Belfast branch of the BIWF was founded in 1928, nine years after the inauguration of the federation itself. In 1931, the *Belfast Telegraph* reported that the group had continued to grow steadily in membership and in terms of attendance at meetings. During the early years of the Belfast branch, there was some coordination between the BIWF centre and the province. Alban Heath and J.J. Morey visited Belfast more than once in order to speak to the Belfast membership. Joseph Cordner was also a speaker during this period.[32] James Niblock was the president of the Belfast branch of the BIWF.[33] He was supported by the work of Maxwell Carnson and of John Leech.[34] Leech and Carnson were prominent in the movement throughout the first decades of partition. On 1 February 1931, Leech was a keynote speaker at the Ulster Hall in Belfast for an event organised by the BIWF. 'The promises [to Israel] have nearly all been fulfilled,' Leech announced 'and the few that remain will be fulfilled shortly. They have been fulfilled in the British, the Anglo-Saxon people, in the company of nations that we call the British Commonwealth.' The meeting was presided over by the Lord-Mayor of Belfast, Crawford McCullagh.[35] He was joined on stage at this event by Maxwell Carnson. Carnson also accompanied him at later engagements in Wellington Hall, at a meeting which was chaired by William Grant MP.[36] Carnson is a mysterious and remarkable figure. He was a Wesleyan minister, a missionary to China, a serviceman in the first World War and a garrison chaplain during the second. He was also a fellow of the Royal Geographical Society and a writer.[37] Amongst his works was *O Pale Galilean*, described by one reviewer as 'a mono-drama written and portrayed by Maxwell Carnson [in which] Mr Carnson will play all eighteen characters.'[38]

As the twentieth century unfolded, more and more prominent Loyalist community leaders aligned themselves with the British-Israelist movement. Pastor Eric Briggs helped to disseminate British-Israelist thought in the province during the middle of the twentieth century.[39] Briggs was pastor of the Bangor Bible Pattern Church. The Bible Pattern Church was founded following a split from the Elim Church in 1939 which resulted from a disagreement about the validity of British-Israelist doctrine. Briggs was also a supporter of James McConnell, the controversial founder of the Elim-affiliated Whitewell Metropolitan Tabernacle in North Belfast.[40] He spoke alongside Gordon Magee, James Graham, K. Mahood and Stanley Herron at a 'Britain is Israel' meeting at the Orange Hall on the Shankill Road in 1950.[41] The movement continued to be orchestrated from the centre, in London, during this time. In 1957, there was 'an enthusiastic meeting of the Londonderry Branch of the BIWF.' This meeting was organised to celebrate the visit of Thomas A. Price, the London commissioner of the BIWF. Price was introduced by Lieutenant J.G. Simmons. In his sermon, Price emphasised the division of the world 'into two camps' which would precede the eschaton.[42] In 1958, as a young pastor, Briggs was invited to toast Colonel McKibbin MP at a dinner celebrating the work of the B-specials.[43]

During the Troubles, Loyalist leaders continued to be drawn to the British-Israelite cause. Perhaps the most notable of these is Robert Bradford MP. Bradford was a Methodist minister who was deeply influenced by the leaders of the Fourth Great Awakening: Billy Graham, Harold Ockenga and Bill Bright.[44] He was an active member of the BIWF and gave an address at the BIWF 55th Congress at Portsmouth in 1974. He spoke at the 58th BIWF Annual Congress in Carlisle in 1977.[45] He also spoke at the Swanwick Convention of 1977, and his sermons and lectures were transcribed and published in BIWF periodicals.[46]

Alan Campbell was a leader in the Open Bible movement in Belfast, throughout the late twentieth century. Initially converted by Ian Paisley, he was eventually expelled from the Free Presbyterian Church for his British-Israelist views. Campbell had long-standing ties with the Covenant People's Fellowship, and he established the Cregagh Covenant Peoples' Fellowship in the early 1980s. He wrote, often, for the *Covenant Voice* during that decade.[47] He was the keynote speaker at the 1989 Antrim Convention of the Covenant People's Fellowship, amongst numerous other speaking engagements.[48] Campbell again spoke at the 1990 convention of the fellowship, which was held at Bangor.[49] He also maintained ties with the BIWF, speaking at the 70th annual Congress at the end of September 1989 in Carlisle.[50] In addition, he was associated with the BIBTF, speaking at the Annual May Convention of the BIBTF at the Orange Street Church on 6 May 2000.[51] During this period, Alan Campbell was appointed as the head of religious education at Newtownabbey Community High School. He was dubbed 'Ulster's most controversial religious education teacher' by *Sunday Life* in 2001. The newspaper had obtained cassette recordings of Alan Campbell's sermons. The sermons included the claim that the Protestant people were 'the Israel people . . . planted here for a purpose, as a light forever in darkest Ireland.' Having been castigated for his views, Campbell referred to himself and to his community of followers as 'despised outcasts . . . cast out because of what we believe and teach.'[52] Video tapes of his sermon were advertised via the *Covenant Voice* magazine.[53] He expressed a firm commitment to the belief that Ulster Protestants had a genealogy which distinguished them from both Irish Catholics *and* English Protestants. 'We Ulster people have an identity of our own,' he claimed, 'and it is separate from the so-called Irish identity that everybody's trying to foist upon us against our will.' The people of Ulster had 'a part to play' in British history, he suggested, 'in showing them *their* origins.'[54]

Perhaps the most high-profile of the British-Israelist leaders within the Loyalist community in recent decades has been Nelson McCausland. McCausland was the minister for culture in the Northern Ireland Executive between 2009 and 2011. He was a member of the Legislative Assembly at Stormont for North Belfast from 2003 to 2017. Although his first foray into politics was as a prospective MLA for the United Ulster Unionist Party, he later joined and stood on behalf of the Democratic Unionist Party.[55] McCausland's commitment to the British-Israelist cause and its tenets can be traced back several decades. In January 1991, the quarterly magazine of the BIWF advertised an evening with Nelson McCausland and Robert Graham. Graham and McCausland were to speak on 'The Approaching Kingdom.'[56] The meeting would be held on 22 July 1994 at Swanwick. In the mid-1990s, Nelson McCausland gave regular talks on British-Israelism to Bible Study groups in the Belvoir Activity Centre in South Belfast.[57] In 2001, he spoke at the annual conference of the BIWF on the subject of Isaiah 62 and the prophecy of the islands at the end of the world.[58] McCausland continued to play a prominent role in disseminating the 'national message' in the North of Ireland and across the United Kingdom after he was elected to public office. In October 2008, he spoke at the 89th Congress of the BIWF.[59] In April 2012, he spoke alongside Michael A. Clarke, Carol Cream, Norman Pearson and David Hilliard at a rally in support of the BIWF in Morecambe.[60] In 2017 McCausland was listed as a voluntary trustee of the BIWF.[61] In April 2019, he spoke at the British-Israelist Annual General Meeting at the Auckland Hotel in Morecambe.[62]

Clifford Smyth, like McCausland, has long been involved in mainstream Loyalist politics in the province. He was elected to the 1973 Northern Ireland Assembly as a representative of the Democratic Unionist Party, but joined the Ulster Unionists in 1976 after his expulsion from the DUP. Smyth is also a regular contributor to the *Belfast Telegraph* and has frequently appeared as a commentator on political and cultural affairs on BBC Northern Ireland. Alongside McCausland, Smyth has been a prominent figure in the Northern Irish hemisphere of British-Israelist activities. In 1989, Smyth was named as the Northern Ireland delegate of the BIWF at its Annual General Meeting. At that meeting, Smyth spoke about the activities that he had been engaged in, seeking to disseminate the message of British-Israelism across the province.[63] In April of 1991, *BIWF Quarterly* advertised a seminar on 'Ulster's Cultural Heritage,' led by Smyth.[64] He was the editorial consultant of the BIWF magazine *Wake Up*.[65] He also spoke at a BIWF rally at Chimney Corner in Belfast on 17 September 2016 and in Morecambe on the 21 April 2017.[66] In September of the same year, Smyth travelled to Australia to address the Victoria Branch of the BIWF at their annual conference.

What is the particular attraction of British-Israelism for Ulster Protestants? As Donald Akenson and others have demonstrated, the concept of national election, pickled in Reformed Protestant soteriology, provides an eschatological understanding of history that equips its devotees not only for periods of great imperial glory but also for periods of apparent hardship and marginalisation. Thus, peculiarly Protestant modes of nationalism appear to develop covenantal themes, based in part on the image of Israel as small, embattled, priestly nation. The latter theme provided the basis for a peculiarly Ulster-Protestant mode of British-Israelist belief. But, as Alan Campbell said, this particular and singular image of Ulster would provide British-Israelists with a new image of Britain-Israel as a whole.

British-Israelist responses to the War of Independence

A group of British-Israelists, including the Reverend James Connellan and W.C. Slator (associate secretary for the British Israel Association of Ireland), met in Albert Hall on Peter Street in Dublin on 11 April 1916 to discuss the significance of a variety of Bible passages. They finished the evening by singing the Doxology and the National Anthem.[67]

Two weeks later, on 24 April 1916, the Military Council of the Irish Republican Brotherhood – which included the leaders of the Irish Volunteers, Pádraig Pearse, and the Irish Citizen Army, James Connolly – staged a rising in the city of Dublin. The revolutionary forces dug trenches on St Stephen's Green and barricaded the surrounding area. They occupied significant sites of industry including Boland's Mill and the South Dublin Union. The leaders established a revolutionary headquarters at the General Post Office, on the steps of which they read out the Proclamation of the Irish Republic. The British Army positioned field artillery at Trinity College, from where they shelled the rebel positions. Four hundred people were killed. After a week, the rebels surrendered. In all, 3,500 people were arrested. Ninety were sentenced to death. Amongst these were James Connolly, Pádraig Pearse, Thomas MacDonagh, Tom Clarke and Joseph Plunkett. The brutal repression of the Easter Rising only led to an increase in popular support for the Nationalist movement. When, three years later, two police officers were shot dead by members of the Irish Republican Army, it triggered three years of bloody violence. British auxiliary forces – commonly known as the Black and Tans – were deployed to suppress seditionary activity, but their recklessness led to an intensification of the conflict. Cork city was burned to the ground and hundreds of civilians were killed without discrimination.[68]

Insofar as the nationalist movement was taken on its own terms by British-Israelists, it was identified as a sectarian movement, of ethnically Canaanite, Roman Catholics against the Protestant people of Israel. 'The fear of Ulster,' wrote David Leitch in 1917, 'centres on the religious question.'[69] In a 1917 edition of the *Quarterly Notes of the Protestant British-Israel League*, an oath sworn by Ribbonmen fifty years earlier was reproduced – in all of its gruesome, xenophobic excesses – under the heading 'A Sinn Fein Oath.' The oath threatened that Sinn Feiners would 'wade knee-deep in

Orangemen's blood' and would 'aid and assist when called upon to massacre Protestants.'[70]

As violence erupted, British-Israelist Loyalists tended to present the conflict as an ethnic cleansing of the Protestant minority in the South. For the most part, the Irish people were portrayed as the source of the problem. The cause of the ordinary Irish people's antagonism to England was explained – like so much in British-Israelist ideology – by genealogy. The Irish were the sons and daughters of Canaanites, brought over by Phoenician traders. This even explained the nomenclature used by activists for Irish independents: Fenian was a derivation of the word Phoenician. Given that Numbers 33 had promised that the Israelites would be punished for failing to exterminate the Canaanites and that the Canaanites would 'remain as pricks in Israel's eyes' for as long as this annihilation was deferred, it was therefore understandable that 'this terrible unrest in Ireland,' would continue. It was to be expected, furthermore, that 'Ireland [would be] condemned to play that role for eternity.'[71] One self-described Loyalist, writing in *The Banner of Israel* in June 1921, reported that 'every day we publish the news of the murder of a Protestant farmer in County Cork.' Cork was labouring 'under a reign of terror,' the report continued. Irish Protestants were presented as 'a loyal and well-disposed people'; the 'Sinn Feiners' as 'a murder gang,' and the nationalist cause, as 'a pretext . . . for shooting Protestants.' There would be no peace, it was believed, until the 'Sinn Feiners' were 'driven from Ireland as St. Patrick drove out the snakes.'[72] When the time came for the 'Canaanite' to be driven from the land, 'Sinn Fein' would 'find themselves ejected from the Island of Ireland by forces which they can neither see or control.'[73] These comments characterise Sinn Fein as the interloper, the snake, the cancer within the body politic. This is in keeping with a long-standing tenet of British-Israelism which characterised Ireland as an Israel nation corrupted by Canaanite influence.[74]

Whilst many did see the War of Independence as an attempt by the Irish Catholic population to overthrow Israel, many others were sceptical that the war was nothing more than an attempt by the children of Ireland to strike for her freedom. More often than not, the campaign was depicted by British-Israelists as a black operation conducted by Israel's more powerful adversaries. *The Banner of Israel* characterised the rising as an ill-disguised German plot. 'The Sinn Fein revolt,' Vincent Cox wrote, 'was financed and instigated by our bitter, crafty and unscrupulous enemy.'[75] The identity of Israel's antagonist was almost interchangeable. Whilst Cox saw Sinn Fein as a German conspiracy, other's blamed the new Bolshevik threat. 'The Sinn Feiners of Ireland,' one anonymous author claimed, 'are in full cooperation with the Bolsheviks of Russia.' On the other hand, the author was equally convinced that 'this conspiracy against British influence and power appears to be engineered and financed by Jews.' He was apparently baffled by the possibility that 'certain evil-minded Jews are plotting for the overthrow of that same beneficent power.'[76]

As always, however, British-Israelists saw the cephalopodous influence of Babylon in these events. In 1917, *The Prophetic News and Israel's Watchman* warned that 'the hand of Rome can be seen behind the recent rebellion in Ireland.' The Easter rising was understood by the author to be part of a worldwide plot by the Vatican to 'extirpate' Protestantism. Irish Republicanism was portrayed as nothing more than a front for this movement: the Sinn Fein Rebellion was a 'Popish Plot' and the 'Sinn Feiners' themselves were 'in the hands of the Popish priests.'[77] The power of the Catholic Church as a political force in Ireland was described as clandestine, dissembling and malign. Protestants were warned that the Church 'maintained a spy system' and that 'the Romanist girl in the Protestant home in the capacity of a servant, conveys to the priest the inner secrets of the family.'[78] 'There can be no settlement of the Irish question until the interests of Protestants are safeguarded and the priests robbed of all political and social power,' one author warned.[79] The 'hatred of English,' amongst ordinary Irish people was 'based solely on the fact that England is Protestant.' This hatred of English Protestantism was inculcated in Irish children in 'priest-dominated National Schools.'[80] John Alfred Kensit's *Rome Behind Sinn Fein* was met with favourable reviews in the pages of *The Banner of Israel*. 'This book is without doubt the most convincing history of a great Papal plot,' one reviewer wrote: 'in it, the author proves conclusively that the Sinn Fein movement is only another of Rome's intrigues to gain control of Britain for the Pope.'[81] Kensit described the Catholic Church as 'a sucker on the whole country' of Ireland. Romanism, furthermore, was 'a gigantic political machine,' whose members' 'own allegiance only to the headquarters in Rome.' Only in one corner of the country was the hegemony of Rome resisted. In Protestant Ulster, 'loyalty is as much a passion . . . as disloyalty is with the Catholics of the other Provinces.'[82] This belief has lasted throughout the entire history of the British-Israel movement in Ireland. In 1985, an article in *The Link* explained that Ulster Protestants instinctively treated Catholics with 'suspicion, distrust and intolerance' because 'the Protestant is subconsciously aware that he is facing, not so much a member of another Christian denomination, but the representative of a powerful, international, political organization.'[83]

As late as June 1921, the editors of *The Banner of Israel* continued to crow that 'there will never be a Republican government in this country or in Ireland.'[84] They were mistaken. Within months, it became clear that the only appetite that existed amongst those negotiating an end to the conflict was for Ireland to be independent in some form. British-Israelists turned their ire on De Valera. He was endangering the ordinary people of Ireland they argued. Firstly, in accordance with Genesis 12, the Irish as cursers of Israel Britain would themselves be cursed. Secondly, since Britain was ordained by God to be safe from harm, Ireland's only choice was to 'march forward hand in hand with the company of nations . . . or to drag herself down to extinction.'[85]

For some, the upheaval in Ireland was explained with reference to British infidelity. Augusta Cook, leader of the Protestant British-Israel League, gave a lecture in Southport on 14 December 1920, in which she suggested that the decision by Balfour to request an audience with the Pope and the continued maintenance of a British envoy to the Vatican were sufficient explanation for Britain's reversals in Eire.[86] But most British-Israelists would maintain that the blame for the conflict lay at the doors of a cabal of diabolical conspirators against Israel. The war in Ireland – seen by many as a David and Goliath conflict, in which Britain represented the latter – was considered by British-Israelists to represent the inverse. Britain, according to Israelists, was the underdog, a small nation confronting a shadowy, international foe. Whether this was the Germans, the Bolsheviks or the papacy was immaterial. This struggle was to be embodied in the Protestant people of Ulster.

British-Israelist responses to partition

By 1921, it was widely agreed that the situation in Ireland was not tolerable. The British government anxiously sought to establish home rule without inflaming tensions within the Unionist community. The Ulster Volunteer Force was armed and declared itself ready to resist the imposition of Irish government. The Long Committee was convened to find an answer, and it came to the conclusion that partition of Ireland into two territories – Northern Ireland and Southern Ireland – was the only feasible solution. This resolution formed the basis of the Anglo-Irish Treaty of 1921, the signing of which – by Lloyd George, Michael Collins and Arthur Griffith – marked the end of the War of Independence and the beginning of the Irish Civil War.

With the dawn of the Irish Free State, at Christmas in 1921, the editors of *The Banner of Israel* reiterated their commitment of solidarity with the Unionist community. They expressed sanguinity about the loss of the South of Ireland ('the Lord is on His Throne and the safety of the Empire is secure'), whilst acknowledging that the treaty provided only 'a regrettable solution.' Some suggested that the loss was in fact a fulfilment of prophecy, specifically Zechariah 14, in which the prophet predicts that 'in the day of the Lord . . . there shall be no more the Canaanite in the house of the Lord of hosts.' Others contented themselves with the retention of the province of Ulster and with the assurance that Loyalists would remain true to the Empire regardless of the constitutional claims of the new Republic. 'Ulster and the Loyalists of Ireland are one with us,' wrote the editor, 'and it is unthinkable that they would ever bend the knee to Sinn Fein.'[87]

As the years progressed, it became increasingly clear that the loss of Ireland was not to be the last of Britain's territorial haemorrhages. Burma, Egypt, Palestine and India all followed. The sense that the Empire – and with it Britain's prestige – was 'disintegrating' afflicted even the most ardent British-Israelists.[88] But they were not to be faint-hearted. The ways of God are not the ways of man. Britain, it seemed, was not to be chosen as a great imperial power, but rather as a sanctified, isolated, beleaguered and embattled remnant. This was the time for Britain-Israel to 'enter her chambers.'[89] As for Ireland, the decision by her people to 'deliberately become aliens themselves from the Commonwealth of Israel' – in accordance with the 1949 Republic of Ireland Act – was an act of infidelity for which she would be forced to pay.[90]

A new political settlement was established in Ulster with a new political elite creating the conditions for the creation of the Orange State. Amongst these was John Leech KC. Leech was most famous in Ireland as the architect of the gerrymandered local government boundaries in 1922. This would serve to shut Catholics in Northern Ireland out of the democratic process for three generations.[91] In his judicial capacity, Leech was considered 'the Father of the North West Bar and of the Northern Circuit of Ireland.' But he combined these duties with a position on the Court of the Diocesan Synod and with the Presidency of the Irish Church Union. As such, Leech's influence stretched across the province. Leech was also an officer of the BIWF and was, given that he was responsible for converting George Jeffrey's to the doctrine, one of the most influential people in the history of the movement. At Christmas in 1927 he spoke to an audience in Belfast and expressed the view that 'the work of awakening the British people to a knowledge of their racial identity and of the wonderful promises to them,' was his foremost responsibility.[92]

Partition created the context for a new conception of the Protestant people of Ireland. British-Israelist literature had described the Protestant people as an Israelite minority immersed in a non-Israel majority. With the establishment of the Stormont government, Northern Ireland could now be characterised as a small, embattled and Godly statelet.

British-Israel and Orangeism

The mythology of the Orange Order has much in common, thematically, with the mythology of British-Israelism. Orangeism recalls heroic, providential victories, brought about by divine intervention. Like all 'covenantal cultures,' it survives because of its connection with a deeply mythologised past.[93] As Akenson notes, the covenanting tradition is mediated through the process of asserting the difference between the chosen Protestant people and Catholics. As such, the ritualised reminders of this demographic discrepancy was the key mode of remembrance of God's covenant with Ulster.[94] Whilst these rituals may be triumphalist in appearance, as Akenson writes, Orangeism is essentially concerned with the impression of the Protestant people 'as a persecuted minority.'[95]

British-Israelists were fond of the mythology of Orangeism. In 1972, the Covenant People's Fellowship organised a series of rallies in the province. As part of this project, the editors of *Brith* included a feature article in their magazine which recalled the triumph of King Billy in the Jacobite

War. 'It was a terrific battle,' they informed their readers, noting that 'William excelled himself and put all he had into gaining the victory, and ensuring for himself everlasting fame and renown amongst the Protestants of Ireland.'[96] In an edition of the SPBI's youth magazine, *Toren*, Helene van Woelderen told young readers that the 'province of Orange was always a spiritual bulwark against Roman Catholicism.' The province was 'on the side of the Cathars,' who were 'mostly murdered by the Inquisition.' 'So you see,' wrote van Woelderen, 'the Protestant Orange Order . . . is not so far removed spiritually from the ancient city of Orange in France.'[97]

The feeling, for many Orangemen, was mutual. Orange ritual carries within it a number of British-Israelist themes. New Orangemen, for example, are sometimes sworn into the order using the following formulation:

What art thou? One of the elect. Of what house? The house of Israel.[98]

The affinity with the people Israel – both Biblical and modern – which can be found in loyalist culture in general as well as in Orangeism in particular centres around a notion of Israel as an embattled minority. 'The common bond between Israel and Ulster,' an official document of the Orange Lodge reads, 'lies in their desire to maintain their own identity.' Kaufman has referred to the Orange Order's 'Old Testament siege mentality.'[99]

Amongst the members of the Orange leadership who held British-Israelist beliefs was John Bryans.[100] Like many Orange Lodge leaders, Bryans was a preacher – the 'top preacher at the North Belfast mission' – who preached on a weekly basis throughout the 1950s from the steps of the Belfast Customs House. He earned the nickname 'Hellfire Jack' as a result of his zeal.[101] Bryans led negotiations with the state during the 1970s regarding the policing of Orange parades.[102] Alongside John Bryans as a prominent Orangeman and British-Israelist was Jack Wintersgill. Wintersgill was a chaplain of the Loyal Orange Order and was also a BIWF Commissioner for the North West.[103]

In the 1970s, the doctrines of British-Israelism and the iconography of Orangeism were combined in the writings and activities of William McGrath. McGrath was a Loyalist activist in the mid-twentieth century who was prominent in the Orange Order before being expelled from the organisation because of accusations of child abuse. McGrath was notable for his vitriolic anti-Catholicism, even within Loyalist circles. He established an organisation, known as Tara, with Clifford Smyth. Although Tara had ties with the UVF, its ideology was distinctive from the ideology of mainstream Loyalism in its foregrounding of British-Israelism. McGrath organised a militia, using his ties with other Loyalist paramilitaries, and continued to exert influence within the Loyalist community until his arrest in 1981 on charges of child abuse relating to the

Kincora Boy's Home scandal.[104] In a manifesto which was released by Tara in 1974, God's covenant with the people of Israel is evoked. 'Ulster is God's anvil,' the text reads, 'on which is being forged the future not only of Ireland but of all British people. . . . Hammer away ye hostile bands, your hammers break. God's anvil stands!'[105]

The connection between the Loyal Orders and the various British-Israel groups has continued to the present day. In 2009, Reverend Richard Harvey wrote an article for publication in *The Covenant Nations*. An Orangeman and member of LOL 844 (based in Sheffield) from the late 1970s, Harvey was grand chaplain of the Grand Orange Lodge of England from the early 2000s. In 2009, Harvey wrote that 'the British-Israel-World Federation and the Loyal Orange Institution of England as Bible-believing Protestants who love our Queen and country and share many values in common.' Fundamental to these shared values was a commitment to the claim that 'the British Family of nations are a special people, called of God to a role in the world which no other nation can fulfil.'[106]

British-Israelist responses to the Troubles

The 1960s saw the emergence of a campaign for voting and civil rights in Northern Ireland to be extended to the Catholic minority. This was met with fierce backlash from Loyalist militants who responded to Civil Rights marches with violent attacks on Catholic-owned businesses and property in Belfast and Derry. When, on 30 January 1972, thirteen unarmed NICRA marchers were shot dead by the British Army in Derry, hostility towards the British presence in Northern Ireland and to the Loyalist community increased dramatically within Nationalist quarters. Distrust and tension increased on both sides of the sectarian divide. New paramilitary groups – the Provisional IRA, the INLA, the UVF and the UDA – were established and armed. Entrenched hostilities and tit-for-tat violence continued for twenty-five years. Fifty thousand people were directly affected by violence during this period, and 1,840 civilians were killed.[107]

At the outset of the Troubles, members of the SPBI called on their leader, C.S. McKelvey, to explain the prophetic significance of these events. McKelvey responded with an article in *Brith*. McKelvey saw the conflict in Ulster as evidence that 'Satan is working hard to tear the Anglo Saxon world apart.' Ireland was just the latest in a long series of battles that Israel would do with Satan, following the upheaval in South Africa and Rhodesia. 'Canada seems to be next on his list,' McKelvey wrote, 'and then New Zealand and Australia.' Despite this, McKelvey was certain that Satan's plan 'would not work.' 'This is all part of Jacob's trouble,' McKelvey assured his readers, 'but we are told that he will be saved out of it.' In the near future, Israel could look forward to a day of victory, 'the fall of the Roman Church,' and a period of 'glorious unity with the Lord.'[108]

Amongst the first commentators to write at length on the Troubles from a British-Israelist perspective was Cleeland Bean. Bean was an educator, chairman of the Belfast Branch of the Workers Education Association and an ecologist.[109] He wrote a long piece, entitled 'Britain's Gibraltar in the North,' in a 1974 edition of *The National Message*. Bean was at pains to stress the image of Ulster as an embattled Protestant enclave, threatened with immersion in a global Roman Catholic empire. The 'Anglo-Scots of Ulster,' he wrote, 'form a distinctive community, and have done for centuries.'[110]

Some reporting of the Troubles in British-Israelist publications during this period came from anonymous sources. One such, entitled a 'Heart Cry from Ulster' captures the millenarian tenor of many of these texts:

> Lecturers have been telling us that, in the very last days before the Lord's return, the Kingdom would be under attack from within and without. These attacks have now been going on for over three years without being recognised as such. As yet they have been confined to the Ulster part of the Kingdom. . . . All these things are aimed at severing us from the Crown, to be submerged in the Irish Republic.[111]

Throughout the Troubles, British-Israelists on the mainland made repeated declarations of affinity with Ulster Protestants. In February 1975, an edition of *Songs of Praise* was broadcast from Ballymena. 'We hope our Ulster kinsmen may feel encouraged to know,' wrote the editors of *The National Message*, 'that the sturdy manner in which they continue to maintain their trust in God brings uplift to compatriots in Britain's homes.'[112] In the meantime, British-Israelists reiterated their claim that the non-Canaanite Irish were ethnically predisposed to Protestantism. This, for Reginald Cox, was the providential crux at the heart of the Irish conflict. 'As the only Israel country which has remained in the shackles of the Catholic Church,' he wrote in an edition of *The Link* in 1985, 'Ireland's reformation would . . . bring about an immediate solution to the so-called Irish Problem.' Nevertheless, British-Israelists were reminded that 'there can be no rapport between Protestants and Catholics until the political influence of the Catholic Church ceases.'[113] British-Israelists pleaded with Irish citizens to 'obey the Lord's injunction aimed at those [Israelites] long held captive by Rome: Come out of her.'[114]

Clifford Smyth's writing on the subject suggested a concerted effort by the Catholic Church, the European Union and the government of the Republic of Ireland to disenfranchise Northern Protestants. In his 1972 pamphlet, 'The Axis Against Ulster,' Smyth describes the European Union as a Roman Catholic project, designed to facilitate papal hegemony. Evidence for this could be found in Edward Heath's termination of Stormont rule in 1972. Smyth suggested that the 'Roman Catholic countries of the E.E.C.' were 'putting great pressure on Heath over Ireland.' Heath, according to Smyth, 'had bartered Stormont as part of his E.E.C. dowry.' All of this led him to the conclusion that 'Common Market membership [was] a lever towards

Irish unification.' In 1972, Smyth predicted a military invasion of the UK by the army of Eire. He claimed that 'compromised by his E.E.C. vision . . . Heath will, in such day and hour, welcome with bitter words and inaction, Eire's *fait accompli*.'[115] In a later text, Smyth pointed to what he saw as the 'prophetic significance' of the 'abuse and persecution of Ulster Protestants.' The leadership of Sinn Fein, he wrote, was committed to the 'ethnic cleansing' of Protestants from Ireland. The intention of the mainstream, nationalist parties, Smyth claimed, was to isolate the Protestant minority, to leave them 'on their own, without political friends or allies.' This association of Godliness and isolation is a perennial of Protestant homiletics and identity from Foxe's *Actes and Monuments* to the sermons of Ian Paisley.[116] Smyth adopts a prophetic mood in his writing, at one point imploring his reader: 'Pray that God will raise up prophets to speak to the dry bones of Ulster Protestantism! To tell a despised and rejected people that God really loves them.' Referring specifically to a Catholic boycott of Protestant businesses in Castlederg in 1996, Smyth suggested that this was in partial fulfilment of Revelation 13, in which it is prophesied that, under the reign of the Beast, 'no man might buy or sell, save he that had the mark, or the name of the beast.' Smyth took this to refer to a situation in Ulster in which only Catholics would be permitted to trade.[117] Similar sentiments were expressed in response to calls to ban handguns in the aftermath of the Dunblane massacre. 'Tell the Protestant farmers on the Ulster/Eire border to give up their guns,' wrote one British-Israelist, 'and ethnic cleansing rampages through their homesteads.' The Ulster Protestant was both an Israelite and a member of the 'front-line oppressed.' As such he was 'covered by Exodus 22:2.'[118]

British-Israelists, during this period, argued that Republican violence was part of a wider Soviet attempt to destabilise the United Kingdom. In the aftermath of the Le Mon bombing in 1978, Lieutenant Michael Hart suggested that the situation in Ulster was 'impossible.' The main culprits, he suggested, were the IRA, the Soviet Union and the Irish government, a 'nefarious brotherhood of iniquity.'[119] One of the most strident critics of the British government and its handling of the Irish crisis was General Sir Walter Walker: former NATO Commander in Chief of the Allied Forces in Northern Europe and a founding member of the paramilitary organisation Civil Assistance. He gave an interview to *The National Message* in August 1974, in which he placed great emphasis on the connection between the IRA and international communism. Walker suggested that the building of a Soviet Embassy in Dublin was designed to provide a 'back door' for the KGB to arm IRA militants. He said that the British public should be 'constantly reminded that the IRA is a Marxist party and that both wings of the IRA have had contact and help from revolutionaries in Libya, Cuba, Algeria and Palestine.' The aim of the IRA as Walker saw it was 'to subvert Ireland and convulse Britain.'[120] Gladys Taylor agreed. Writing in 1974, she suggested that 'communism has many strange bedfellows' and that it would 'use any disturbing influence that comes to hand, such as the I.R.A.'[121]

To most, the Catholic Church and the Soviet Union may seem like strange bedfellows indeed. In fact, these allies were not as incompatible to British-Israelists as they may have been to non-British-Israelists. It was a common-place of British-Israelist eschatology during this period that the Soviet Union and the Vatican represented two sides of the same coin. Both would play a role in the impending onslaught against Palestine, which would bring about the consummation of the prophecies of Revelation 16. They would be the kings that would gather together in 'that place known in Hebrew as Armageddon.' In keeping with the exegesis of John Nelson Darby, Walter Milner and Hal Lindsay, most British-Israelists believed that Russia represented the apocalyptic topos of Gog and Magog. The Church – of course – was seen as the embodiment of Babylon.[122] This is what the British-Israelist and Member of Parliament Robert Bradford meant, when he declared, at a conference in 1974, that:

> The problems of Northern Ireland are the result of three things: The Roman Catholic Church, International Marxism and Ecumenism. As a British Israelite I believe that scripture can be interpreted and understood very clearly in the light of current events.[123]

Despite the massed forces of the Catholic Church, the Republic of Ireland and the Soviet Union, British-Israelists remained confident that Loyal Ulster would remain faithful. 'These are Protestants in the true sense of the word,' wrote BIWF president Matthew Browning, 'and they are Israel. Loyal Ulster will not be moved. This truth . . . was the lesson of the siege of Londonderry.'[124] Nevertheless, the lot of God's people was expected to be one of hardship. At a BIWF rally in Newtownabbey in 1990, Tom Price preached on the subject of 'the Furnace of Affliction.' For models of fidelity, he preached, Ulster Protestants should look to their ancestors: Shedrach, Meshach and Abednego.[125]

British-Israelist responses to Anglo-Irish cooperation

On 15 November 1985, Margaret Thatcher signed the Anglo-Irish agreement. It was to signal a sustained period of Anglo-Irish cooperation. The terms of the agreement dictated that the Irish government take an advisory role in the governance of the province, established the principle that a majority consensus would need to be secured if reunification was to take place in the future, and laid out plans for a possible devolved government. Response in the Loyalist community was ferocious. The 'Ulster Says No' campaign was led by Reverend Ian Paisley. On 17 November, a week before he led a march on Belfast City Hall, Paisley led a public prayer against the deal and against the premiership of Margaret Thatcher at the Martyrs' Memorial Hall in Ormeau. For British-Israelists, Paisley's intervention was characterised as an 'Elijah prayer': a 'prayer against the leadership of

Britain-Israel.' Michael Clark praised the Loyalists of Ulster for standing against the tides of integration and assimilation.[126] Clifford Smyth, enraged by the prospect of 'collaboration' with Eire, called for a resumption of direct rule from Westminster.[127]

On 10 April 1998, representatives of the Irish and British governments, along with representatives of the major political parties of Northern Ireland, signed an agreement which signalled the end of violence in the province. The Belfast Agreement proposed a period of reconciliation designed to facilitate the cessation of hostilities between different factions and offered a road-map for shared governance of the province. When the Belfast Agreement was put to a referendum, several organisations in the province campaigned against its ratification. These included both dissident republican and dissident loyalist minority parties.

British-Israelists were critical of the Good Friday agreement which they perceived, primarily, to have exonerated terrorists. General Sir Walter Walker wrote a letter to the *Sunday Telegraph* that was published on 21 August 1998. Walker was excoriating in his criticism of politicians who had applied the 'velvet glove' instead of the armed fist. No 'murderers now in prison' should be released, he argued, without significant concessions from the IRA.[128] In November, the Kingdom Foundation published an edition of *Wake Up* in which the supplement (titled *The New Covenant Times*) was entirely given over to an article written by Roger Hutchison. Hutchison was – at the time – an assembly member, representing the UK Unionist Party. In his article he professed a belief that George Soros had sought to affect the result of the referendum by making large contributions to the 'Yes' campaign. Hutchison claimed that the attempted 'domestication of terrorists' was a harbinger of the end of democracy in the UK.[129] This was a period in which the British-Israelist movement had pivoted in a number of its eschatological claims. No longer did Russia take centre stage in the expected eschatological denouement. Instead, British-Israelists saw the chimerical figure of 'the Globalist' as the enemy of Israel. Soros, therefore, was identified as the latest in a long line of diabolical agents, plotting the persecution of Israel in Ulster.[130]

When the people of Ulster did vote to surrender the authenticity of their identity, in ratifying the Good Friday agreement, British-Israelists predicted providential reprisals. Shortly following the ratification of the Good Friday Agreement, a group of dissident republicans detonated a bomb in a crowded shopping centre in Omagh. Without adequate prior warning, the shopping centre was not evacuated. The loss of civilian lives numbered twenty-eight. For some British-Israelists, the attack at Omagh was a sign of providential judgement on Britain for helping to facilitate the Good Friday Agreement. 'The Watchman,' in his column in *Wake Up* magazine, noted that the Good Friday Agreement would lead to the end of a meaningful border on the island of Ireland. He cited a passage from Deuteronomy 32 which states that national borders and boundaries have been appointed by the

Lord God. When Jeshurun abandoned God's Law, Deuteronomy states, 'the sword without and the terror within destroyed the young and the old, the infants and the gray-haired.'[131] This same punishment was being meted out to Britain, 'the Watchman' suggested, for ignoring the boundaries that God had ordained for his people:

> It has been an immense folly for the separate racial and cultural identity of the Ulster people not to have been properly understood and defended by the British Government. . . . Every nation has its own border and in respect of the people of God in Ulster we should refer to the law of the Lord.[132]

Conclusion

British-Israelism is a Protestant tendency which is often associated with imperialism. The presumption at the heart of this analysis is that British imperialism preceded British-Israelism. The Irish experience demonstrates that this is only half true. British-Israelism made headway in Ireland because it appealed to long-held convictions and sensibilities at the centre of Loyalist identity. These sensibilities were the legacy of a distinctly British mode of Reformed Protestantism, characterised by Biblicism, predestinarianism and a strong sense of the connection between Godliness and martyrdom.

Ulster Protestantism became a powerful symbol of British Israel in the twentieth century for two reasons. Firstly, in the portrayal of the Loyalist community as a Godly remnant, beset on all sides by the forces of Babylon, British-Israelists saw the image of Israel. Ulster Protestants were the leaven of the movement, the salt of the earth, in whose trials the true image of British Israel was revealed to all (including the British-Israelists themselves). This, perhaps, was what Alan Campbell meant when he spoke of Ulster Protestants showing the British their origins. It was also what William McGrath meant when he described Ulster as the anvil upon which God's people would be forged.

If the people of Britain-Israel were revealed, most explicitly, in their experiences in Ulster, then the forces of Babylon were revealed most clearly there also. The British-Israelist accounts of the history of Ireland provide a perfect example of the malleability of British-Israelist prophecy. The British in Ireland were defined in antithesis to the Irish in Ireland. The Irish in Ireland were defined in antithesis to the British in Ireland. If Britain was Israel, then the trials of Britain must be blamed on the eternal antagonists of Israel: Babylon. Here again, the interaction between the label and the labelled is far from clear-cut. Those entities in Ireland – whether the EU, the Catholic Church, Sinn Fein or Soros – which were perceived as antagonists were identified with the topos of Babylon. The topos of Babylon altered and developed to accommodate these new elements.

Moreover, the experience of the Irish in the story of British Israel demonstrates the malleability of the topos of Israel. British-Israelists are first and foremost concerned to maintain and police the boundaries between peoples, categories, nations. All of these elements are themselves, of course, constructed. When the process of maintaining those boundaries becomes too problematic, the boundaries themselves are allowed to change. The Irish, once thought of as an Israel people, are redefined as an Assyrian people. The boundaries change, the territory shrinks, the membranes become less porous, the authenticity is maintained.

In the 1920s, Britain lost her territories in the South of Ireland, but gained some territory in the land of Palestine. Ronald Storrs expressed his vision for the new mandate in Palestine:

> Enough [Jews] could return, if not to form The Jewish State . . . at least to prove that the enterprise was one that blessed him that gave, as well as him that took by forming for England a little loyal Jewish Ulster in a sea of potentially hostile Arabism.[133]

If the foundation of Northern Ireland had helped to show the British a vision of their origins, the foundation of the state of Israel would disrupt this vision.

Notes

1 Sheridan Gilley, 'English Attitudes to the Irish in England,' in Colin Holmes (ed.), *Immigrants and Minorities in British Society* (London: Routledge, 1978), 98–100.

2 Paz, *Popular Anti-Catholicism*, 50–51, 79–80; Lewis Perry Curtis, *Anglo-Saxons and Celts: A Study of Anti-Irish Prejudice in Victorian England* (New York: New York University Press, 1968); Lewis Perry Curtis, *Apes and Angels: The Irishman in Victorian Caricature* (Newton Abbot: David and Charles, 1971).

3 *Brith*, no. 6 (March 1946), 8.

4 Grimaldi, *The Queen's Royal Descent from King David the Psalmist*, 1–5; Walter Milner, *The Royal House of Britain* (London: Covenant Publishing, 1909); Allen, *Judah's Sceptre and Joseph's Birthright*, 250.

5 *Brith*, no. 321 (October 1972), 15.

6 *Brith*, no. 4 (January 1946), 3–4.

7 F.R.A. Glover, *England, the Remnant of Judah* (London: Rivington, 1861).

8 Jeremiah 43: 6.

9 *The Illustrated Police News*, no. 973 (7 October 1882), 3.

10 *Leaflets for the Last Days*, no. 10 (January 1897), 2.

11 *The Belfast Newsletter*, no. 26,232 (31 August 1899), 6.

12 *Shields Daily Gazette*, no. 14,746 (23 October 1903), 2.

13 Mairead Carew, *Tara and the Ark of the Covenant* (Dublin: Royal Academy, 2003).

14 Walter Milner, *Tara Vindicata* (London: Banks and Son, 1903), 1–20 [20].

15 *The Banner of Israel*, vol. 41, no. 2,119 (1 August 1917), 167.

16 *The Banner of Israel*, vol. 41, no. 2,139 (26 December 1917), 436.

17 *The Banner of Israel*, vol. 41, no. 2,137 (12 December 1917), 421.
18 Hine, *Fourty-Seven Identifications of the Anglo-Saxons with the Lost Tribes of Israel*, 96.
19 *The Banner of Israel*, vol. 45, no. 2,284 (6 October 1920), 345.
20 *The Banner of Israel*, vol. 44, no. 2,286 (20 October 1920), 364.
21 *The Banner of Israel*, vol. 43, no. 2,216 (18 June 1919), 221.
22 *The Banner of Israel*, vol. 45, no. 2,284 (6 October 1920), 345.
23 Gresty, *Satan Fights for Muscovy*, 34.
24 *The Link*, vol. 4, no. 6 (June 1985), 124.
25 *Crown and Commonwealth*, vol. 2, no. 4 (Winter 2002), 19.
26 *The National Message*, vol. 55, no. 1,634 (January 1976), 18–19.
27 *The National Message*, vol. 50, no. 1,577 (April 1971), 108.
28 *The Link*, vol. 4, no. 6 (June 1985), 124.
29 *The Banner of Israel*, vol. 41, no. 2,093 (7 February 1917), 66.
30 *The Banner of Israel*, vol. 43, no. 2,243 (24 December 1919), 447; *Lancashire Evening Post*, no. 10,429 (25 November 1919), 2.
31 *The London Daily News*, no. 20, 450 (26 September 1911), 4.
32 *Belfast Telegraph* (1 March 1932), 7.
33 *Larne Times* (20 February 1937), 5.
34 *Belfast Telegraph* (1 May 1931), 11.
35 *Northern Whig*, no. 38,196 (2 February 1931), 9.
36 *Northern Whig*, no. 38,198 (4 February 1931), 1.
37 *Salt Lake Telegram* (9 September 1950), 6; War Office 374/12458.
38 *Grosse Pointe News*, vol. 15, no. 45 (11 November 1954), 7.
39 *Brith*, no. 358 (February 1976), 32.
40 James McConell, *The Good, the Bad and Jesus Christ* (Magherafelt: Maurice Wylie, 2016), 15.
41 *Belfast Telegraph* (25 August 1950), 2.
42 *Londonderry Sentinel* (23 March 1957), 2.
43 *Belfast Telegraph* (27 October 1958), 7.
44 Bradford, *A Sword Bathed in Heaven*, 74.
45 *The National Message*, vol. 56, no. 1,655 (September 1977), 286.
46 *The National Message*, 53, no. 1,618 (September 1974), 283; *The National Message*, vol. lvii, no. 1,659 (February 1978), 40.
47 *Covenant Voice* (August 1989), 27.
48 *Covenant Voice* (March 1989), 28.
49 'The Covenant People's Fellowship Annual Report for 1990,' British Library, P881/444, 12.
50 *BIWF Quarterly*, vol. 2, no. 1 (April 1989), 15.
51 *Bible Truth*, no. 204 (April 2000), 24.
52 *Sunday Life* (25 February 2001), 10.
53 *The Covenant Voice*, vol. 40, no. 12 (December 1984), 30.
54 Ulster Folk and Transport Museum Archives, Recordings R86–224.
55 'Nelson McCausland (Born 1951),' in *Who's Who* (Oxford: Oxford University Press, 2018).
56 *BIWF Quarterly*, vol. 4, no. 1 (January 1991), 10.
57 'British Israel World Federation Annual Accounts and Reports for 1990,' British Library, ZC.9.a.2499, 12.
58 *Crown and Commonwealth*, vol. 1, Special Edition (2001), 7.
59 *The BIWF Newsletter* (January 2009), 8.
60 *Life at the BIWF*, no. 16 (April 2012), 3.
61 The Charity Commission, Registered Data for the financial year ending 31st March 2017, British Israel World Federation.

62 *Life at the BIWF*, 12 (January 2019), 2.
63 British Library, *British Israel World Federation Annual Accounts and Reports* (1990), 12.
64 *BIWF Quarterly*, vol. 4, no. 2 (April–June, 1991), 10.
65 *Wake Up!*, vol. 12, no. 4 (July 1998), 81.
66 *Life at the BIWF*, no. 7 (April 2017), 1.
67 *The Banner of Israel*, vol. 40, no. 2,053 (3 May 1916), 187.
68 Michael Hopkinson, *The Irish War of Independence* (London: Gill, 2004), 80–83.
69 *Quarterly Notes of the Protestant British Israel League*, vol. 6, no. 4 (October 1916), 135.
70 *Quarterly Notes of the Protestant British-Israel League*, vol. 7, no. 3 (July 1917), 110.
71 *The Banner of Israel*, vol. 44, no. 2,252 (25 February 1920), 67.
72 *The Banner of Israel*, vol. 45, no. 2,320 (15 June 1921), 213.
73 *The National Message*, vol. 1, no. 1 (7 January 1922), 11.
74 *The Link*, vol. 4, no. 6 (May 1985), 122, 135.
75 *The Banner of Israel*, vol. 40, no. 2,060 (21 June 1916), 256.
76 *The Banner of Israel*, vol. 45, no. 2,298 (1 December 1920), 409.
77 *The Prophetic News and Israel's Watchman*, no. 12 (December 1917), 191.
78 *Quarterly Notes of the Protestant British-Israel League*, vol. 6, no. 4 (October 1916), 133.
79 *The Prophetic News and Israel's Watchman*, no. 12 (December 1917), 191.
80 *The Banner of Israel*, vol. 45, no. 2,298 (1 December 1920), 409.
81 *The Banner of Israel*, vol. 45, no. 2,318 (1 June 1921), 192.
82 J.A. Kensit, *Rome Behind Sinn Fein* (London: Protestant Truth Society, 1921 [3rd edition]), 7–8, 52.
83 *The Link*, vol. 4, no. 6 (May 1985), 122.
84 *The Banner of Israel*, vol. 45, no. 2,320 (15 June 1921), 212.
85 *The Banner of Israel*, vol. 45, no. 2,339 (26 October 1921), 378.
86 *The Banner of Israel*, vol. 45, no. 2,300 (26 January 1921), 34.
87 *The Banner of Israel*, vol. 45, no. 2,348 (25 December 1921), 488.
88 *Brith*, no. 39 (February 1949), 15.
89 *Brith*, no. 13 (October 1946), 7.
90 *Brith*, no. 43 (July 1949), 1.
91 Tim Pat Coogan, *Ireland in the Twentieth Century* (London: Arrow, 2003), 305; David Harkness, *Northern Ireland Since 1920* (Dublin: Helicon, 1983), 28.
92 *Western Daily Press*, vol. 139, no. 23,378 (17 December 1927), 11.
93 Akenson, *God's Peoples*, 140.
94 Akenson, *God's Peoples*, 201.
95 Akenson, *God's Peoples*, 140.
96 *Brith*, no. 318 (July 1972), 17.
97 *Toren*, vol. 2, no. 1 (January 1965), 8.
98 Paul Malcolmson, *Inside the Loyal Black Institution* (Londonderry: Evangelical Truth, 2009), 239.
99 Eric Kauffman, *The Orange Order* (Oxford: Oxford University Press, 2007), 302, 54.
100 Buckley, 'We're Trying to Find Our Identity,' 191.
101 Harbinson, *The Dust Has Never Settled*, 21.
102 *The Guardian* (8 July 1970), 1.
103 *The National Message*, vol. 43, no. 1,491 (February 1964), 39.
104 Northern Ireland Historical Institutional Abuse Inquiry, vol. 9, module 15, chapter 29, pp. 8–12; Martin Dillon, *God and the Gun* (London: Routledge, 1999), 235.

105 Chris Moore, *The Kincora Scandal* (Dublin: Marino, 1996), 240.

106 *Covenant Nations*, vol. 2, no. 7 (2009), 11.

107 Tim Pat Coogan, *The Troubles* (London: Palgrave Macmillan, 2002).

108 *Brith*, no. 299 (November 1970), 24.

109 Cleeland Bean, 'Adult Education as a Unifying Influence,' in *Education and Training*, 19, no. 6 (January 1977): 169–170.

110 *The National Message*, vol. 53, no. 1,612 (March 1974), 88.

111 *The National Message*, vol. 51, no. 1,586 (January 1972), 20.

112 *The National Message*, vol. 54, no. 1,623 (February 1975), 49.

113 *The Link*, vol. 4, no. 6 (May 1985), 122, 135.

114 *BIWF Quarterly*, vol. 3, no. 1 (January 1990), 22.

115 Clifford Smyth, *Axis Against Ulster* (Belfast: Smyth, 1972), 9, 11.

116 Discussion of the role of Foxe's great work in the development of the 'elect nation' narrative in Protestant Britain is ongoing [see for example William Haller, *Foxe's Book of Martyrs and the Elect Nation* (London: Jonathan Cape, 1963); William Lamont, *Godly Rule* (London: Palgrave Macmillan, 1969); Viggo Olsen, *John Foxe and the Elizabethan Church* (Berkeley: University of California Press, 1973); Patrick Collinson, 'John Foxe and National Consciousness,' in Christoper Highley (ed.), *John Foxe and His World* (Farnham: Ashgate, 2002), 10; Katherine Firth, *The Apocalyptic Tradition in Reformation Britain, 1530–1645* (Oxford: Oxford University Press, 1979), 108; Richard W. Cogley, 'The Fall of the Ottoman Empire and the Restoration of Israel in the "Judeocentric" Strand of Puritan Millenarianism,' in *Church History*, 72, no. 2 (2003): 304–332; Richard Bauckham, *Tudor Apocalypse* (Appleford: Sutton Courtenay, 1978), 70–88.

117 Clifford Smyth, *Boycott: An Examination of the Abuse and Persecution of Ulster Protestants* (Belfast: Inheritance, 1997).

118 *BIWF Quarterly*, vol. 10, no. 1 (January 1997), 21.

119 *The National Message*, vol. 57, no. 1,661 (April 1978), 113.

120 *The National Message*, vol. 53, no. 1,617 (August 1974), 229.

121 *The National Message*, vol. 53, no. 1,617 (August 1974), 239.

122 Henry Grattan Guinness, *Light for the Last Days* (London: Hodder, 1888), 222–225; *Brith*, no. 35 (October 1948), 16; *Toren*, no. 6 (October 1964), 15.

123 Bradford, *A Sword Bathed in Heaven*, 106.

124 *BIWF Quarterly*, vol. 3, no. 3 (July 1990), 9.

125 *BIWF Quarterly*, vol. 3, no. 2 (April 1990), 17; *BIWF Quarterly*, vol. 3, no. 1 (January 1990), 4.

126 *Wake Up*, vol. 12, no. 4 (July 1998), 83.

127 *The Link*, vol. 4, no. 6 (May 1985), 128.

128 *The Daily Telegraph*, no, 44,533 (21 August 1998), 27.

129 'New Covenant Times,' supplement to *Wake Up*, vol. 12, no. 6 (November 1998), 1.

130 *Wake Up*, vol. 12, no. 3 (June 1998), 54; *Wake Up*, vol. 9, no. 11 (October 1993), 251.

131 Deuteronomy 32: 25.

132 *Wake Up*, vol. 12, no. 4 (July 1998), 84.

133 Ronald Storrs, *Orientations* (London: Nicholson, 1937), 404.

6 British-Israelism and the state of Israel

On 11 December 1917, General Allenby led the Egyptian Expeditionary Force of the British Army into Jerusalem. The victory was met with euphoria from many quarters. Lloyd George acknowledged as much in his telegram to Allenby:

> The war Cabinet wishes to congratulate you on the capture of Jerusalem, which is an event of historic and world-wide significance and has given the greatest pleasure to the British and other Allied people.[1]

Many – within evangelical circles in particular – saw providential and even eschatological significance in the victory over the Ottoman army.[2] For British-Israelists living in 1917, this event was especially notable. It appeared to represent a consummation of the beliefs at the very heart of their movement. Here, at last, the Holy City was passing back into the control of Israel, nearly two thousand years after the destruction of the Second Temple. Surely, this represented a precursor to the events described in John's Apocalypse.[3] In a letter written to *The Banner* in 1918, one B.H. Norton of Wincanton expressed relief that – now that the armies of Israel were returning to their native soil – new weapons of war, such as the submarine, would be powerless to defeat them.[4]

But the millennium was not inaugurated by Allenby's triumph. What followed was a series of reversals for British interests in Palestine, concurrent with the gradual disintegration of the Empire more broadly. An almost irrefutable repudiation of British-Israelist expectations came to pass in 1948, as Israel-Britain withdrew from Palestine, leaving the door open to the establishment of an independent Jewish state. How British-Israelists dealt with successive failures of prophecy relating to Palestine and how they incorporated (and continue to incorporate) the modern state of Israel into their eschatological narratives is the subject of this chapter.

Andrew Crome's account of the history of Christian Zionism, based in part on Bauman's theoretical claims, rests on three key points. First, he contends that the Jewish people long represented – for the British – an irreducible other. Second, this otherness was the result not of xenophobia but rather of proteophobia. Third, the restoration of the Jews would represent for British Protestants an opportunity to perform a task which would identify them as a providentially appointed people. As such, the perpetuation of the Jews as an authentic people was not a threat to, but in fact was crucial to, the image of Britain as a chosen nation. For this reason, the chosenness narratives of the Hebrew Bible and the chosenness narratives of British nationalism do not – according to Crome – necessitate a 'clash of competing chosen peoples.'[5] As we shall see, the second of these points is crucial to our understanding of British-Israelist responses to the foundation and continued existence of the state of Israel. The continued existence of the Jewish people as a discrete polity serves to bolster British-Israelist conviction, since it provides evidence that God works through nations. At the same time, British Israel requires the radical ambivalence and, by extension, the perceived imperfection of the Jewish people to remain in tact, the better to contrast with the wholeness and perfection of Britain-Israel. As such, Britain-Israelism can never – to use Bauman's terms – 'interact with Jews on their own terms.'[6] Insofar as Israel is allowed to perform her role in providential history and the Jewish people perform *their* role, then British-Israelist allosemitism takes on a philo-Semitic complexion. When – conversely – the roles allotted to these different groups become complicated or disrupted by events, then the allosemitic attitude of the British-Israelists takes on a fundamentally anti-Semitic hue.

In 1922, Burry Pullen-Burry wrote of his travels in Palestine. Pullen-Burry was a British-Israelist, a medical doctor and an occultist who was an early member of the Hermetic Order of the Golden Dawn. In Palestine, he encountered examples of both the idealised Israelite culture described in the Biblical texts and the European Jewish culture of the *aliyot* which he so despised. Seeing this apparent mixture of the divine and the profane in the faces of the ordinary people of Palestine, Pullen-Burry despaired. He wrote:

> To turn the somewhat repulsive looking, curly locked, mid-European, ghetto-bred Jews into anything approaching the level of their great forefathers . . . would be a sheer miracle.[7]

This proteophobic attitude, this 'repulsion' at the seemingly uncanny combination of 'Judah' and 'Jewry' would characterise British-Israelist attitudes to the new state of Israel for generations to come.

British-Israelist Zionism

Writing in 1916, Thomas Plant attested to the existence of enthusiasm for Zionism amongst the ranks of the British-Israel movement. The subject of Judah's restoration 'never fails to arouse the interest of the audience,' he wrote. Even the 'most confirmed British-Israelites' were 'aware of several of the specific references to the future settlement of the Jews in Palestine.'[8]

As the First World War progressed, the likelihood of a Jewish home became less and less remote. Whilst readers of the *Prophetic News and Israel's Watchmen* magazine were aware that a variety of options was being mooted for the location of Jewish settlement, it was agreed that 'Palestine is at once a likelier and a preferable locality.' One British-Israelist celebrated the renewal of Jewish culture in Palestine, the fact that 'one hundred thousand' Jews were now living in the territory and that 'the ancient tongue is spoken once more.'[9] A 'Miss Chadwick' wrote excitedly of the things she had heard at Reverend Schor's lecture on Palestine in 1917. 'The Turks,' she reported, 'are emigrating to America.' Thus 'God is providing homes for His people the Jews.'[10] Most expected that the Jews did not have ambition for an independent state but simply protection from the persecution that they experienced in other nations. So it was that Ralph Darlington could write in 1917 that 'the Jews desire not an independent kingdom. . . [their] one desire is to live under British protection.' 'The Jew,' after all, 'for generations, has looked to Britain as his protector.'[11]

Scepticism existed regarding the Jewish Zionist movement, however. The Zionist movement was beginning to move from the fringes of Jewish culture to the centre. Theodor Herzl's *Judenstaat* had been translated into dozens of languages and the World Zionist Organisation was entering its second decade. At the same time, alternative modes of Zionism were being proposed in the writings of Zionist luminaries like Ahad Ha'am, Nahum Sokolow and Chaim Weizmann. In 1917, the editors of *Israel's Watchman* warned against setting too much store in the ambitions of the Jewish Zionist movement:

> Disappointment always awaits those who look to events and expect much from them. We have spoken repeatedly in these pages on the great movement of Zionism. We have cautioned again and again our readers against looking upon Zionism as the restoration of the Jews to their land as promised in the word of God.[12]

As with all great historical developments, British-Israelists believed that the advent of Jewish nationhood in the modern world would be brought about not through human action but rather through divine intervention. When these developments did eventually unfold, therefore, it was important for British-Israelists to identify the signs of providence which accompanied them.

British-Israelist responses to the battle of Jerusalem

The editors of *The Banner of Israel* – principle organ of the British-Israelist movement during the early twentieth century – expressed enthusiasm about General Allenby's successes. In the 9 February 1918 issue, it included in its folds a commemorative, glossy photograph of the eastern walls of Jerusalem. An article in the same edition, written by one Henry Marchant, claimed that in the different brigades gathered on that occasion, there were representatives of all the twelve tribes of Israel.[13] J.G. Taylor's editorial was equal celebratory in tone. 'The deliverance of Jerusalem from Gentile tyranny,' he wrote, 'forms a landmark in God's purposes.'[14] An anonymous correspondent to the journal of the Protestant British-Israel League, meanwhile, suggested that Jerusalem – rather than London – should become the seat of the Imperial Council of the British Empire. This would have profound eschatological implications. Augusta Cook, founder of the league, went even further in her response to this suggestion:

> We of the British Empire will, in the present war, probably get possession of Palestine . . . But finally the idea is that it will be London – Capital City of the Empire – that will be transferred, with throne court and all else to Jerusalem and the British Empire will change into the Kingdom of United Israel.[15]

The capture of Jerusalem – accompanied as it was, within a few months, by widespread military successes for the allied forces – was a tonic for those who may have started to doubt the validity of British-Israelism. In January, *The Banner* included an article which claimed that 'all but those blinded by prejudice' would now have to concede that 'the safety of this island, the stability of the monarchy and the continued prosperity of the Empire,' depended upon 'whether we are Israel or not.' Henry G. Locke wrote, in the same edition, that 'God has never swerved in his affection for his elect race.'[16]

Public curiosity about Palestine was widespread. Lowell Thomas' travelogue, entitled *With Allenby in Palestine*, was shown at the Royal Philharmonic Hall.[17] Allenby's mythos was associated with that of T.E. Lawrence and Thomas quickly decided to combine his documentary footage of the latter with that of the former to create a longer film. This version proved even more popular with queues for tickets 'wrapped around the venue.'[18] The British occupation of Jerusalem triggered a surge of eschatological expectation within Evangelical circles more widely. Albert Benjamin Simpson, originator of the Four-Fold Gospel tradition, heard the news of Allenby's victory whilst on a lecture tour, 'hurried to his hotel room and, falling to his knees beside his bedside, burst into tears of joy, because of the culmination of his lifelong hope.'[19]

British-Israelists were quick to point out that certain prophetic claims were *only* intelligible if the British-Israel doctrine was true. In particular, British-Israelists identified Jeremiah 3 and Ezekiel 37 as newly consummated Biblical prophecies.[20] Jeremiah 3 suggested that the rulers of Israel would return from exile in the 'northern lands.' Meanwhile, Ezekiel 37 suggested that the stock of Ephraim would be *joined* with the stock of Judah in the land of Israel at the appointed time. Several British-Israelist commentators drew attention to the correlation between the prognostications of

Dr Henry Grattan-Guinness and the events of 1917. In his 1888 work *Light for the Last Days*, Grattan-Guinness predicted that 1917 would see the end of the age of the Gentiles and of the 2,520 years long Gentile occupation of Jerusalem. Grattan-Guinness claimed that the dawn of Islam could be dated to 622, 1,295 years before the year 1917. Given that Islam was 'the power which for more than twelve centuries had trodden down Jerusalem,' the end of this prophetically significant period was also expected by Grattan-Guinness to mark the end of the period of the occupation of Jerusalem by Muslims. He concluded that 'the year 1917 is therefore doubly indicated as a final crisis date, in which the seven times run out.'[21]

Some claimed that Allenby himself was compelled and emboldened by this suggestion. In his 1939 memoir, General Sir Henry de Beauvoir De Lisle recalled a conversation with Allenby in advance of the latter's deployment in Palestine:

> In June 1917 I was on leave for ten days in London and saw in *The Times* that Allenby had been selected as Commander in Egypt. Knowing he was at the Grosvenor my wife and I went there to congratulate him.
>
> 'No cause for congratulation,' said Allenby. 'Had to give up a jolly fine army to take over a rotten show. Archie Murray is a good man and he couldn't succeed. I don't see how I can.'
>
> 'My dear Allenby,' I replied. 'Nothing can prevent you from being in Jerusalem by the 31st of December.'

De Lisle would go on to claim that he advised Allenby to walk rather than riding into Jerusalem, which advice, De Lisle claimed, Allenby followed.[22]

The Battle of Jerusalem would also mark a high point in British-Israelist relations with the Jewish community. In 1918, Henry Marchant reported the story of a rabbi in Brighton who 'fell on his knees, thanked God and wept for joy,' when he heard that the British had taken Jerusalem.[23] Such exemplars were used by British-Israelists as evidence of a rapprochement between Israel and Judah resulting from Allenby's success:

> These kindly feelings now existing between the Jewish and the British races show that our heavenly Father has begun His good work of uniting the two sticks.[24]

The battle would continue to hold a prominent place in the eschatological schema of successive generations of British-Israelist adherents and students. 'The time of the Gentiles began to end in 1917,' C.S. McKelvey wrote in an editorial to the second issue of *Brith* in 1945. 'Jerusalem ceased to be trodden down,' he maintained, 'when British forces drove out the Turks who had oppressed the city for centuries.'[25] Francis Thomas, in 1989, pointed out a number of providential signs which accompanied the event. Just as Isaiah had predicted that the power of the Lord would pass over Jerusalem 'like birds' and shield it from harm, Allenby had called for the 14th Squadron of the Royal Flying Corps to fly over the city. 'The Turkish soldiers took fright and ran,' wrote Thomas.[26] In 1974, Gladys Taylor repeated the claim that 'Grattan-Guinness uncovered the astronomical clues pointing to 1917' and that the year 1917 remained significant as the year which marked the *beginning* of 'the final period of Gentile power.'[27] Later that year, Gilbert Saddler reiterated Grattan-Guinness' calculations.[28] R.D. Porter, writing in 1983, predicted that 1987 – coming as it did seventy years after the end of Ottoman control of Jerusalem, would mark the *final* ending of the time of the Gentiles and the return of 'true Israel' to Jerusalem.[29] On 26 March 1988, the third Viscount Allenby and his wife Lady Sara were given a commemorative picture at a ceremony promoted by the Board of Management of the BIWF, to mark the 70th anniversary of the battle.[30] Lady Sara Allenby remains a trustee of the BIWF to this day, following the death of her husband in 2014.

British-Israelist responses to the Balfour declaration

There was, however, a fly in the ointment. The capture of Jerusalem was shortly preceded by the Balfour declaration. In November 1917, with the foretaste of victory in Palestine, the then foreign secretary Arthur Balfour wrote what Chaim Weizmann called 'an expression of sympathy and support' for the Zionist project. Balfour's statement, in full, read:

> His Majesty's Government views with favour the establishment in Palestine of a national home for the Jewish people, and will use their best endeavours to facilitate the achievement of this object, it being clearly understood that nothing shall be done which may prejudice the civil and religious rights of existing non-Jewish communities in Palestine, or the rights and political status enjoyed by Jews in any other country.[31]

Large sections of the British public agreed. Three hundred thousand copies of a pamphlet entitled 'Great Britain, Palestine and the Jews,' which explained 'Jewry's Celebration of its National Charter' were distributed by the Ministry of Information across the UK.[32] Winston Churchill asked: 'where else would the Jews settle but in the land of Palestine?' It would be 'good for the Jews and good for the British,' he suggested.[33] In April 1920, the prime ministers of Britain, France and Italy met at San Remo and agreed the terms on which the British mandate in Palestine would be established.

Response to the Balfour declaration from the British-Israelist community was mixed. They looked on with pleasure at 'the great excitement and enthusiasm' that greeted the ratification of international support for the aims of the Balfour declaration at San Remo.[34] They were aware of the 'clamorous call on the part of the Zionists,' for Britain's help in their project. The Jewish people were 'voicing their gratitude for the declaration,' they believed.

It was not – however – the restoration of the Jews to Palestine that pleased British-Israelists, but rather the fact that the restoration of the Jews heralded the future restoration of all Israel. The 'great leaders of Judah' – it seemed clear – would 'unconsciously . . . throw open wide the door' to the House of Israel.[35] Many saw the role which Britain appeared to be playing in the restoration of the Jews as yet greater evidence of the providential role which 'true Israel' would play in the final days. *The Banner* editorial of 9 January 1918 expressed this sentiment with the claim that: 'if Israel [Britain] is to restore the Jews (their brethren) it will conclusively establish her identity.'[36] This position was shared by the editors of *The Southern Star*, a British-Israelist newspaper published on behalf of the British-Israel National Union. The first edition of the newspaper was published in January 1919 and it carried an editorial which proposed an acid test for the legitimacy of the British-Israelist claim. 'If we are *not* Israel,' it predicted, 'we shall have to give up Jerusalem again.' The author reasoned that it was 'only Israel which is to win back the land and revive Jerusalem so that the Jews may return and prosper.'[37]

Nonetheless, the British-Israelist contention that Jews constituted only a minority of Israel led some to treat the promise of the Balfour declaration with caution. 'The Jews in Israel are as a penny to a shilling,' they complained, and as such it was only the 'clemency and kindness,' of British-Israel that would allow the Jews to settle 'in the dear old land of their fathers.'[38] Daniel Whitelaw, also writing for *The Banner*, agreed. Having read the declaration, he reminded his readers that 'whatever claim the Jew has to that land' it was shared with 'the other tribes.'[39] Many, at the time, believed that the Balfour declaration was nothing more than sentimentalism. Most Jewish people had no desire to return to Palestine, they predicted, since: 'England is the land flowing with milk and honey,' and 'residence in Palestine would be exile.' At the same time, they warned that attempts by the Jews of Eastern Europe to escape persecution by migrating to Palestine would lead to chaos, given that such a development would not have divine mandate:

> This repatriation will not be the God-appointed Restoration of Scripture. . . . The Jewish return now contemplated is man-ordained and is only revealed to us in Scripture as an accomplished event which meets with disaster.[40]

As the years went on, many British-Israelists would look back at the Balfour declaration as a touchstone for British infidelity and as an example of the inefficacy and incompetence which they saw as characterising the post-imperial era.[41] Thirty years after Balfour, British-Israelists lamented what they saw as the seeds of the downfall of the British presence in Palestine. The hope that the *aliyot* were a fulfilment of the prophecy that the Jews would return to the promised land had been 'proved once and again' to be 'a fallacy.'[42] 'If we had known His Word,' wrote another, 'we would have made no agreement with Jewry concerning the land.'[43] Zionism, they came to believe, was 'the bane of the world.'[44] All of this had resulted from the Balfour declaration. 'That one mistake has brought its wake dozens of mistakes ever since,' lamented C.S. McKelvey, writing in 1949.[45]

British-Israelist responses to the British Mandate in Palestine

The British Mandate in Palestine was initiated in the aftermath of the San Remo conference in 1920. At the outset, many British-Israelists were excited by the idea of the Jewish people being restored to Palestine. Primarily, these sentiments were aligned with the belief that, in Palestine, Jewry would become more easily recognisable as a nation. Perhaps the restoration of Jewry would serve to bolster the authenticity of the Jewish people. In addition, British-Israelists were supportive of the Zionist case, conditional on the understanding that Palestine was to be British, 'not a Jewish dominion.'[46]

In this regard, the desires of British-Israelists coalesced with the desires of many within the Jewish community. In 1919, *The Banner of Israel* reprinted an article which had originally appeared in January of that year in the *New York Tribune*. The article was written by Rabbi Professor Moses Gaster, Hakham of the Sephardi community in Great Britain. In this article, Gaster claimed that 'the centuries which my people have spent among their Gentile neighbours' had 'created a great confusion in the minds of many Jews,' in that many Jews 'had dispensed with any idea of a return to the Holy Land.' Gaster believed that these deracinated Jews were 'living a double life as Jews and non-Jews,' but that – with the restoration – they would become 'Jews within and without.'[47] In this sense, British-Israelists (and some Jews) looked forward to a new era of Jewish authenticity in the restoration of the Jewish home.

For many British-Israelists, enthusiasm about the British presence in Palestine dissipated almost as abruptly as it had begun. In October 1920, the Protestant British-Israel League published, in its quarterly magazine, an account of the distrust in which the indigenous population of Palestine (Jewish, Christian and Muslim) held the newly arrived Zionists. The author expressed the view that 'millions of Jews in Russia alone (many of them, of course, Bolsheviks) are ready to come over.'[48] In 1923, it was agreed that Britain would adopt an administrative role on behalf of the League of Nations with the object of facilitating the establishment of a 'Jewish home' in Palestine. Already in the early 1920s, the British had a sense that both the Arab and Jewish populations were ungovernable. The 'Winston's Own' regiment – an auxiliary counter-insurgency unit – was deployed in 1921 to counter-act the developing disturbances, but over the coming decades the situation would become gradually more – rather than less – febrile.[49]

In 1926, the editors of *Covenant Race* expressed the view that the problems that were besetting the Palestinian mandate originated in British incompetence and infidelity:

> All the trouble has come about through our own folly, by our persistent and stupid mistake in taking the Jews to be the whole of Israel and in so blinding us to the fact of the existence among ourselves of the other tribes, the House of Israel. If only our eyes were opened to see that in the British and Americans are to be found the one time 'lost ten tribes,' the solution of the problem would come to us as life from the dead. But we stupidly refuse to see that we can be any part of Israel, God's peculiar people.[50]

There were some dissenting voices. Major General Hadfield (then president of the BIWF) continued to promote the claim that Britain's identity as Israel was affirmed by her role in the restoration of the Jews. 'If the British be not Israel,' he asked, 'is it mere coincidence that Britain is given a mandate over Palestine and is repatriating the Jews'?[51] In 1929, the *British Israel Pilot* magazine remained steadfast. 'Peace is not yet reigning in the land, neither is unrest removed from its borders,' wrote one correspondent, 'but conscious of its sacred calling and inheritance, [Israel] is marching ever to victory and peace.' An editors note added, parenthetically: 'Why should Great Britain be in Palestine if we are not God's continuing serving people?'[52] Long into the 1930s, British-Israelists continued to claim that the existence of the British mandate was the primary evidence for the 'covenant belief.' Claude Coffin, writing in 1936, stressed that British-Israelists had 'irrefutable proof of our British Israel contention,' since 'the City of the Great King is again in the possession of the nucleus of God's Kingdom on Earth.'[53]

Nonetheless, the notion that the British Mandate represented a foreshadowing of the Kingdom of God on Earth was waning in salience with every passing year. Discomfort about the emergence of Zionism as a political force in Palestine also visited the British-Israelists during this period. Chaim Weizmann, with the announcement of the mandate, had formed the Zionist Commission with the intention of facilitating the establishment of the Jewish home. Jabotinsky was appointed to the Zionist Executive, but resigned in protest at Weizmann's perceived lack of radicalism. Jabotinsky would go on to lead the Zionist opposition to British presence in Palestine.[54]

At the start of the period of the British mandate, there was hope in some quarters that the Zionist movement would find common cause with British Israel. In February 1918, Vincent Cox reported to the readers of *The Banner of Israel* that a meeting had been held in Belfast, chaired by Sir William Whitla – ostensibly to discuss and express condemnation of the Petliura pogroms – at which Yitzhak Herzog had expressed his belief that the British Empire's successes correlated with those of the Jews. At the time of this meeting, Herzog's wife Sara was pregnant with Chaim Herzog, future president of the state of Israel.[55] The editors of *Prophetic News* saw the British Empire as providing the best route to a Jewish Palestine:

> Only the Jews with their passionate love for Zion can put to the maximum use the soil and the other natural resources of Palestine and convert it into a rich and densely populated country. To that end not only the Jews actually settled in Palestine, but all good Jews throughout the world will bring their material, intellectual and spiritual treasures to bear. Palestine under the British flag is to be a Jewish Palestine.[56]

Many believed it possible that the British Mandate could facilitate the precipitation of the divinely mandated restoration of the Jews. In a cruel irony, one British-Israelist commentator predicted – in 1918 – that the period of the Gentiles should be dated as lasting 2,520 years from the destruction of the first Temple. That period would elapse in 1933, at which point 'the suffering of the Jews would be complete.'[57]

In many circles, nonetheless, anxiety prevailed about the possible problems that would arise from the 'premature' return of the Jewish people to the Holy Land. The Reverend C.H. Gil, Secretary of the London Jews Society (a Recordite, conversionist-philo-Semitic organisation), wrote of his fears that Jewish immigrants would seek to establish a 'Jewish culture' in Palestine, an eventuality which was to be 'feared by Christianity.'[58] In 1925, the *British Israel Star and Circle* promised that 'there will never be a Jewish government in Palestine apart from Britain. The land belongs to Britain.'[59] This was to prove a failed prophecy.

A further claim was made by British-Israelists to mitigate the possible association of Judeocentrist millenarian belief with the rise of political Zionism. Political Zionists, they emphasised, tended to be recruited from the ranks of 'atheistic Jewry.' The advocates of a Jewish state were 'atheistic Zionist Jews' who could be imagined as saying: 'I as a Jew, do not care at all for the Jewish religion. All I want is that we Jews have a national home in Palestine.'[60] British-Israelists believe that ethnicity and faith are two strands of a single helix. Israel is identified both by her fidelity and her genealogy. The belief that political Zionism was typically an atheistic doctrine entailed – therefore – that its adherents were not *of* Israel proper. Writing in 1974, Gladys Taylor bemoaned the fact – as she saw it – that 'people seem inclined to regard those followers of Judaism who are furthest removed, racially, from the Hebrew stock as the Chosen People.' In support of this claim, she noted that 'it is the non-Israelite element which most loudly claims the name and land of Israel and its outlook.'[61]

In the years that followed the Second World War, it became steadily more apparent that the expectations of the British-Israelists and those of the political Zionists were mutually exclusive. On 11 July 1947, a ship left Sete near Montpellier bound nominally for Istanbul. The ship was a packet steamer, named *The President Warfield*. It was built in 1927 to ferry passengers from

Norfolk to Baltimore. In 1946, however, it was bought by the Haganah for the purpose of transporting Jews from mainland Europe to Palestine. It was renamed *Exodus*. The ship was boarded by British troops, twenty nautical miles north of Haifa. After disembarking in Haifa, the refugees were re-embarked on three deportation vessels and were shipped back to France, from whence they had come. Eventually the refouled refugees were housed in refugee camps in Schleswig-Holstein. The *Exodus* debacle drew significant opprobrium from the international community towards the British administration in Palestine. A Yugoslav delegate to the United Nations Special Commission on Palestine called it 'the best possible evidence we have for allowing Jews into Palestine.'[62] The Zionist policy of unauthorised sailings would prove to be amongst its most effective strategies.[63]

Many British-Israelists took an opposing view. *The National Message* was scornful of those who had 'lamented the forced return of the illegal Jewish immigrants to Europe for the inferred reason that Palestine is the land of the Jews.' 'It is difficult to conceive of a more profound error,' the author suggested.[64] The *Exodus* mission was also described as an 'illegal immigration plot' in the pages of *Brith*.[65] Whilst British-Israelists accepted the reality of the Holocaust and commiserated with the Jews for the hardships that they had endured, they also often suggested that the Holocaust was a providential event, visited on the Jews as a punishment for their infidelity. Furthermore, they suggested that the Zionist solution would not ameliorate the condition of European Jews:

> We are aware of the suffering that has been the lot of Jewry. But this has not been due to the fact that they do not have a National Home, but because of their rejection of the Saviour Jesus Christ.[66]

Nonetheless, the push for Israeli sovereignty intensified. The mid-1940s saw the development of militant Zionist groups who grew to see British presence in Palestine as inimical to their ambitions. The most prominent of these were Irgun and Lehi. The assassination of Walter Guinness in 1944 and the bombing of the King David Hotel was a source of alarm for all those involved in the British administration in Palestine.

British-Israelists responded to these activities with disbelief. These groups were labouring under a condition of 'fanatical madness,' wrote one. 'In blind anger,' it seemed, the Zionist movement was 'turning against the one people whom it could turn to for help.'[67] 'The Jews are making a great mistake,' wrote another, 'and are heaping up trouble for themselves by turning against Britain.'[68] Zionist militants were never to be forgiven by British-Israelists. In 1970, Charles McKelvey recalled that 'the Zionist movement showed its hatred of Britain in sedition, anarchy, violence and murder.'[69] In the aftermath of the assassination of Count Folke Bernadotte, *The National Message* suggested that 'the violence of the seed of Esau-Edom is reflected in the activities of the Stern Gang and other Jewish terrorist organisations.'[70]

'Is it possible,' asked one author in 1978, 'that the evil line of the Edomite descendants of Heth are today represented by the atheistic line of Jewish Marxists?'[71] Regardless of their true identity, it was widely acknowledged amongst British-Israelists that 'most of the Jews who have subsequently crowded into the country in recent years are manifestly not of Judahite stock.'[72]

Despite the outrage expressed by British-Israelists, the British administration in Palestine appeared to be more and more amenable to the wishes of the Zionist elements in Palestine as the post-war years wore on. High Commissioner Alan Cunningham resisted calls from Field Marshal Montgomery to wage war against the Zionist insurgents and the Foreign Office continued to turn a blind eye to the activities of clandestine fundraising organisations which were operating in Britain and which were connected with the Haganah.[73] When Cyril Marriot learned of the Haifa assault on 20 April 1948, he cautioned that British troops avoid confrontation with the Haganah.[74]

Despite the signs of Britain's weakening control on the region throughout the 1940s, some British-Israelists steadfastly refused to countenance the possibility of the establishment of a Jewish state in Palestine. *The Times* published an editorial in September 1947, expressing the view that Britain should withdraw from Palestine. *The National Message* retorted violently, calling the international support for the Zionist cause an 'appalling display of human folly' since it was apparently predicated on a conflation of Israel with Jewry.[75]

British-Israelist responses to the foundation of Israel

On 29 November 1947, the United Nations passed Resolution 181 (II), requiring that Britain terminate the Mandate in 1948. Britain complied and declared an intention to withdraw all military personnel from Palestine on 1 August. Thirty-one years after Allenby's triumph, the British were forced to concede that their governance of Palestine had been a failure.

The disappointment of the Palestinian Mandate project was blamed by many British-Israelists on British strategic ineptitude. 'Instead of standing fast in our cause,' wrote one correspondent to *The National Message*, 'we have weakly fumbled from one position to another and have now asserted our intention of abandoning our homeland.'[76] The editors of *Brith* also saw the Palestine debacle as evidence of Britain's ever-diminishing prestige on the world stage. 'Completely beaten by the problem of Palestine,' they wrote, 'Britain passes it over to UNO after meekly accepting insults and revilings.' 'The world is sneering at Britain,' they added, 'as she humbly asks to be relieved of the mandate.'[77] Whilst British-Israelists believed that Britain-Israel had been *appointed* a task by God, this did not preclude the possibility that Britain could fail to accomplish this task.

Insult was added to injury – for British-Israelists – in the decision taken by the fledgling Jewish state to adopt the name 'Israel.' This decision was met with instant condemnation from Israelist quarters. Harold Stough – then secretary of the BIWF – wrote to *The Scotsman* in February 1948 to express his dismay. 'A great responsibility rests on the Jewish people to prove that they are descendants of Judah,' he wrote:

> And if they are successful in this . . . the extent of their claim would be limited to one twelfth portion of the land. . . . There is no justification for their confiscation of the name Israel – a name restricted in use to the whole of the 12 tribed kingdom.[78]

In an article entitled 'Ersatz Israel,' R.G. Simpson made several contentions about the illegitimacy of the claim that the Jews had a right to the land of Palestine. The Jewish nation was 'apostate,' 'not of Judah but of Esau-Edom,' he wrote.[79] At a meeting of the Bath branch of the BIWF in March 1949, T.A. Price explained that the federation 'deplores the use of the term Israel in connection with the new Jewish state.'[80] This sentiment was echoed throughout the British-Israelist community. 'There seems to be some consternation,' read the editorial of *Brith* in July 1948 'that [the Jewish state] has taken upon itself the name of God's chosen people. They are not Israel. . . . They are not even Jews, although there is a good proportion of Jewry amongst them.' A consensus existed amongst most British-Israelist organisations that the 'Republic of Israel' was 'a denial of God's kingship.'[81] As the years wore on and the state of Israel attained the recognition of the international community, British-Israelist pronouncements on her legitimacy became more shrill. 'The challenge of the new state of Israel is a challenge to all British Israelites,' wrote P.T. Egerton. 'The world is being deceived. We are the people who can reveal the deception to Anglo-Saxondom. We need an aggressive policy.'[82] In later years, some British-Israelists adopted a nomenclature which would make clear the distinction between Israel (as they saw it) and the Jewish state. Whilst Britain was referred to as Israel, the Jewish state was referred to as 'Israeli' or 'the State of Israeli.'[83]

Many voices within the British-Israelist milieu saw the loss of Palestine as a providential indication of God's displeasure with Britain. Britain's deference to the United Nations was an act of unforgivable infidelity, comparable with the Egyptian alliance of Isaiah 31. McKelvey wrote that 'we cannot possibly hold Palestine under these conditions, because our birthright is in jeopardy.' For this reason, he was: 'not surprised to see that the UNO is going to take over Palestine.' In fact, the act of taking responsibility for the Mandate in Palestine was *itself* portrayed as an act of hubris and of disobedience for which Britain-Israel was being punished. R.G. Simpson, writing in 1948, answered those who claimed that 'the Lord used British arms to deliver Jerusalem' by pointing out that 'our nation does not yet perform His Will as do the armed forces of the crown.'[84]

But for several British-Israelist commentators, the apparently premature abeyance of Israel-Britain's presence in Palestine was in fact a consummation – rather than a disconfirmation – of prophecy. Jeremiah 25 records the prediction that 'the nations' would have to drink from a cup of wrath, before the land was restored to Israel. In the meantime, the 'city that bears the Lord's name,' would be desolated. Zechariah 12 reiterates the association of Jerusalem with 'the cup of trembling' that would 'send the nations reeling' in the period before the restoration. Writing in 1947, with this in mind, McKelvey claimed that the people of Britain-Israel should rejoice – rather than being disappointed – if the Lord should take the cup away from them and deliver it to other nations.[85] R.G. Simpson noted, furthermore, that 'it was not from the Lord that Britain took the cup. She accepted that of the League of Nations and mercifully has been spared to hand it back.'[86] Whereas only a generation earlier, the victory in Jerusalem and the subsequent occupation of Jerusalem had been described as almost unassailable evidence of God's preference for Britain-Israel, occupation of Jerusalem was now described as a terrible curse and a burden to be avoided. McKelvey actively counselled, the following April, that Britain should 'get out and keep out until the Lord calls us to return after His coming.'[87] This apparent volte-face was made only weeks before the termination of the British mandate, at midnight 14 May 1948.

Predictions of doom for the new state emanated from all quarters of the British-Israelist milieu. A week before the state of Israel's independence was declared, *The National Message* news section reported that 'the Jewish Agency . . . with rashness that they may soon regret . . . will establish an independent Jewish State.'[88] For the readers of *Brith*, the establishment of the state of Israel was a divinely mandated event intended to bring about the ultimate eschatological battle between the forces of Israel and her final antagonist, the Soviet Union. 'Jewry,' in other words, was 'the bait to bring all nations again to Israel to battle.'[89]

Britain's withdrawal was similarly accommodated within the British-Israelist prophetic schema, such that any expected disappointment was nullified. Not only was Britain being exempted from the burden of the 'cup of trembling' but the manner in which the 'cup of trembling' was being passed over to the other nations was also providential. Isaiah 52 predicted that Israel would not 'go out by flight.' As McKelvey showed, this prediction corresponded precisely with Britain's experience. 'The fact that we will be giving up the mandate on 15 May and bringing our troops out by 1 August,' he wrote, 'is the fulfilment of this passage, for it is proof that we are not coming out with haste.'[90]

Within eight years, some British-Israelists had become so convinced that Jerusalem represented the 'cup of trembling' that they were prepared to make the claim that Britain should refuse to take back Jerusalem even should the opportunity arise to do so. 'All efforts by Jewry or the UNO to involve us in Palestine will fail,' one wrote, 'and all nations will hold that cup, therefore we must be separated from all nations. Palestine will see us no more until we return with our Lord Jesus as king.'[91] In retrospect, as British-Israelists writing in the 1970s agreed, 'Britain drank of that Cup of Trembling . . . until in 1948 she could drink no more and came out.'[92] This belief corresponded with a broader prophetic claim (prominent in the period immediately following the war), that British Israel would retreat into a position of isolation, thereby sacrificing her global influence. Some commentators believed that this retreat corresponded to the death of the Two Witnesses prophesied in Revelation 11. If so, they claimed, Britain should rejoice 'for it is written that death unto the world means that we will be alive unto our God.'[93] Meanwhile, Israel-Britain would 'enter her chambers' in preparation for the period of safe seclusion.[94] This was only evident, it seemed, to the most attentive students of prophecy. Writing in *Brith* in 1951, McKelvey claimed that 'unknowingly we are developing the very character of an Israel people. . . . The Bible says that Israel, just before the day of her crisis will become a doormat to the nations, and that is a true summing up of Britain today.'[95] Britain, readers were assured in 1947, would 'come out of the UNO.'[96] This was seen as 'the next phase of Britain's withdrawal into her chambers.'[97]

A direct corollary of this – newly necessary – prophetic commitment was the claim that 'Israeli' as the occupants of the land of Palestine could no longer be seen as fulfilling the role expected by previous generations of British-Israelists. More immediately this was because Jewry had accepted the cup of suffering at the point at which God had removed the cup of suffering from his servant people. Secondly this was because, in accepting the full status of nationhood, the Jewish people were seen as abandoning an aspect of their singularity: their statelessness. The foundation of Israel, in other words, came to be seen as irrefutable evidence that the majority of Jewry was not Judah. Here anti-Semitic proteophobia found a new setting in British-Israelist thought. The uncanny nature of 'the empirical Jew' occupying the space allotted for the 'conceptual' or (more specifically) the 'eschatological Jew' was clearly troubling for British-Israelists. It represented a form of idolatry: the most acute form of the uncanny.[98] British-Israelists reformulated their eschatological expectations. The Jewish people were now expected to be the victims, rather than the beneficiaries, of the eschatological denouement.

The disappointment mixed with disorientation which British-Israelists felt in response to the foundation of the state of Israel lasted down the generations. They mocked those Christians who subscribed to eschatological Zionism. 'We read about others who see the End Times of Revelation imminent,' wrote Matthew Browning, at the start of the twenty-first century, 'and they are right to be on alert; but they are grossly mistaken if the imagine these End Times unfurling a Jewish state of Israel.'[99] The history of the state of Israel in the decades which followed her foundation seemed, for British-Israelists, to only confirm this view.

British-Israelist responses to the Arab-Israeli conflict

The 1960s saw a surge in violence between the fledgling state of Israel and her Arab neighbours. This period also saw the alignment of the former with the United States and the latter with the Soviet Union in the broader geo-political context of the Cold War. This development served to demonstrate for British-Israelists that the various flashpoints of Arab-Israeli aggression were a foretaste of a coming conflict between Russia (which British-Israelists understood to be the prophesied army of Gog and Magog) and Israel. It was in this light that all conflict in the Middle East was perceived by British-Israelists and – as such – they found themselves drawn to supporting the state of Israel whilst expressing submission to the will of God in the unfolding of this eschatological drama.

The view that the Jewish people's premature annexation of Palestine was a recipe for disaster was commonplace in British-Israelist circles. For most British-Israelist commentators, the Arab-Israeli conflict was evidence of the illegitimacy of the state of Israel. The 'cup of trembling' prophecy was seen as being fulfilled in the conflict between Israel and her neighbours. Nevertheless, if this was to be the last battle, God would eventually rescue Israel. In September 1965, *Toren* reported that the 'teams are lining up' for the invasion of the Holy Land. Russia was 'pushing towards Palestine,' whilst a 'pan-Arab army' was expected to join them in an invasionary force. These 'teams' would be the antagonists in an imminent eschatological struggle, the author believed.[100]

1968 saw the Israeli army deliver a crushing victory over the Egyptian forces in the Six-Day War. This was read by many Jews and Evangelicals in a providential light.[101] British-Israelists expected that this defeat was but a deferral of Israel's fate. 'They will soon have the whole of their neighbor states ranged against them and straining to join with their Russian masters in fanatical crusade,' wrote one.[102] Because of Israel's apparent antagonism with the Soviet-sponsored Arab states in the region, it became imperative for British-Israelists to explain this antagonism in ethnic terms. It seemed evident that – by siding with Gog-Russia – the Palestinians were acting as enemies of God's people. It was troubling to British-Israelists, therefore, that the Arabs were commonly understood to be of Semitic heritage. This fact drew many to the conclusion that the 'Palestinian Arabs are not of true Arab stock.' An alternative genealogy was developed for them. The 'Palestinian Arabs' were likely to be 'the people of Moab who lived on the other side of Jordan.'[103] As such, their claims to the land of Israel were considered, by British-Israelists in the late 1960s, to be illegitimate.

Tensions exploded into violence once again in the early 1970s with the Yom Kippur War. 'The dream' of the 'persecuted and oppressed Jews' of having a 'new national home' was – according to C.S. McKelvey – 'becoming a nightmare.'[104] Whilst British-Israelists expected Israelis to suffer at the hands of a divinely appointed adversary, this did not entail any sympathy for the Palestinian cause. Support for the Palestinians was ascribed to 'misplaced sympathy.' They continued to call into question the authenticity of the Arabs as a Semitic people. The Arabs were 'not one single race.' On the contrary, they were 'a group of different races with one culture based on the religion of Mohammedanism.'[105]

By the end of the 1970s, some strides were being made towards a settlement between the two sides and the basis was laid for the Camp David accords. But at the same time, violence continued. With the rise of the Likud party, the policy of settlement-building (a point of contention in the Arab-Israeli dispute for decades to come) was initiated. In 1977, *Brith* reported on the Arab-Israeli peace negotiations. British-Israelists were unsurprised by the intransigence of both parties. These conflicts were determined not by politics, after all, but by providence.[106]

In September 1978, in the aftermath of the South-Lebanon War, H. Hartland Schooling wrote that

> the small community of Jewish folk who have sought sanctuary in the ancient land of Israel . . . have provided the world with an unsolvable problem *vis a vis* the Arabs. Some of the Israelis are Judaists. They are at present sitting tight on a powder keg.[107]

In April 1978, John Shenton expressed regret about the trajectory that the state of Israel had taken:

> Until recent years, many Christians would have hailed the presence of a section of Jewry in Palestine as the long-promised hope of Israel. This claim lost its attraction by reason of the fact that it has now been established that world Jewry contains only a tiny fraction of the present day descendants of God's chosen people.[108]

All of this promised doom for the fledgling state. The editors of *Wake Up* identified the Parable of the Talents – in which the master asks for 'those who would not be ruled by me,' to be killed – as a foreshadowing of a future destruction of the Jews.[109] Meanwhile, the editors of *The National Message* saw the ongoing antagonism between the Arabs and Israelis, coupled with the Soviet sponsorship of the former, as an irrefutable sign that Zechariah's vision was coming to fulfilment. 'Jewry in Palestine' would soon face 'a war for its survival against impossible odds.' Although it was clear that 'Jewry in Palestine contains a large proportion who . . . are descended from non-Israelitish ancestors,' it was nonetheless also clear that 'the peoples confederated against the Israelis are infidel.' As such, British-Israelists should expect that 'the Holy City will be partly overrun,' but that 'Divine Power will intervene, to force back and destroy the invading armies as a prelude to the establishment of Christ's Kingdom on earth.'[110] In other words, the

Arab-Israeli conflict would end in the defeat of the Israelis, but nevertheless, through divine intervention, it would precipitate the advent of the millennium. In this, God would use Gog and Magog for the purpose of eradicating the Edomite elements of Jewry, purifying Judah in advance of the joining of the two sticks.

Neither of these things happened. The terrible violence in the Middle East had been given meaning by British-Israelist exegesis. But with the failure of the Arab nations to resist Israeli expansion, and finally with the defeat of Gog-Russia in 1989, these systems of meaning began to fail. In the 1980s and 1990s, British-Israelism became increasingly entangled with what Michael Barkun has called 'conspiracy culture.'[111] Many conspiratorialist British-Israelists were shifting their focus away from the Soviet Union and towards another global antagonist: the globalists and federalists and Bilderbergers. They identified the foundation and maintenance of the state of Israel as a project of these forces. Pointing to the role played by Alger Hiss and other prominent Jewish figures in the foundation of the United Nations, McKilliam wrote that 'the UN is a Jewish ideal.' McKilliam saw the foundation of the state of Israel as a strategy of the 'world government,' which had established its 'seat' in Jerusalem.[112]

A gulf was beginning to emerge. More and more British-Israelists became unequivocally anti-Zionist. This stands in stark contrast with the phenomenon of Evangelical Christian Zionism which flourished during this period. Andrew Crome has drawn attention to the flexibility of 'providential Christian Zionism . . . as a tool for national identity construction.' The centrality of Zionism to the process of national identity construction, in the Anglosphere, does not necessarily imply that the latter is facilitated solely by unwavering support for all Zionist projects. As enthusiasm for the state of Israel increased in the American context, it saw a decline in the British context. But Crome is quick to note that this does not imply a conceptual unmooring of Britain's fortunes from those of the Jewish people. 'That some Christian Zionists have been quick to incorporate Britain's failure into their own providential readings of the Middle East,' he writes, 'suggests the adaptability of restorationist thought.' Perhaps, in her decline, Britain was being punished 'for her betrayal of the Jewish people' during the 1930s and 1940s. The loss of empire, the loss of faith, the loss of the mandate in Palestine and even the loss of Churchill as a leader 'can be understood in these terms.'[113]

A different but in many ways analogous dynamic is evident in the writings of British-Israelists. Whereas Christian Zionists anticipated the providentially appointed restoration of the Jews and the flourishing of a Jewish state in Palestine and explained the apparent impediments to the consummation of this on the sins of the world (particularly the Anglosphere), British-Israelists explained these setbacks by retroactively adapting their eschatological claims. It was clear now that the Jews were not the chosen people: they were a minority of Israel, they were an admixture of Israel and Edomite elements, they remained in a state of estrangement from God. Thus British-Israelists in the late twentieth century were able to reverse the claims made by their predecessors in the early twentieth century. In doing so they were able to indulge in anti-Semitic attacks on the validity of the state of Israel. The state had been founded because of the agitation of 'the Jewish lobby.' Those 'Bible Belt believers' who continued to support the claims of the Israelis were 'dupes.'[114] British-Israelists feared that this attachment to the myth that the Jewish people constituted Israel had dire geo-political consequences. The equation of 'Israel' and 'the Jewish mini-state' was a fundamental error at the heart of President Reagan's worldview, they argued, and 'the foreign policy of the United States is orientated by this dangerous misconception.'[115]

And, finally, British-Israelists moved towards a position of supporting the claims of Palestinians over the claims of Israelis. This radical shift was, in part, facilitated by the declining threat of the Soviet Union in the Middle East and a profound realignment of British-Israelist claims about the role of 'Gog and Magog' in the coming Last Battle. Palestinians were no longer portrayed as the drones of the Soviet Empire, but rather as the victims of a global Edomite conspiracy. 'Today Palestine is under occupation by Zionist Jews,' British-Israelists claimed, who were conducting 'a genocidal repression calculated to terrorize the inhabitants and precipitate an Arab exodus.'[116]

By the mid-1990s, some quarters within the British-Israelist community actively supported those agents who sought to rein in perceived Israeli hegemony in the Middle East. In 1991, *BIWF Quarterly* published an article which expressed support for Saddam Hussein on the basis that Iraq's acquisition of a nuclear arsenal would act as a deterrent to the militarism of the Israeli state. The invasion of Kuwait, wrote the author, 'is only the latest of many attempts to break the stronghold of the international power elite.' Meanwhile, the author claimed that 'Zionist ambitions for the Greater Israel,' were being defended by 'pro-Zionist propagandists throughout the world.'[117] In 1992, British-Israelists claimed that the 'Israeli state has secretly built up nuclear powers to match those of the USA.'[118]

Whereas in previous decades, British-Israelists were at pains to explain that the Arabs in Palestine were not truly Semites, in the late twentieth century, they revised this claim. Meanwhile the claim that the majority of Israelis were 'Ashkenazi Jewish people from Europe and Russia who are descended from the Khazars' was reinforced. As such, the foundation of the Jewish state was characterised as a fraud perpetrated on the Arab people and, indeed, on the global community, with terrible humanitarian consequences. It could have been avoided, if only 'a true understanding of identity had been known, both of the Jewish folk and of Celto-Saxondom.'[119]

In 1990, Noel Hunt asserted that the Jewish people had less right over the land of Israel than the Arabs and that the establishment of the state of Israel had seen the 'dispossession of Semites' by 'the Ashkenazi' who had 'arrogated to the new state the name "Israel" to which they have no racial or historical claim.' The adoption of 'the name of Israel for the Ashkenazi Zionist state' was described by Hunt as a 'satanic strategy of deception.'[120] Writing in 1998, Michael A. Clark repeated the contention that Israel had a greater affinity with the Arabs than with the Jews. 'The British got on well with the Arabs,' he wrote, 'because of the bond of family affinity.' The Arabs, and in particular the Hashmites, were descendants of Abraham just like the British. 'If DNA testing were to be carried out,' Clark assured his reader, 'confirmation of these relationships would be undoubtedly forthcoming.' Moreover, he contended that the Arab-Israeli conflict was predicated on a reasonable form of Arabic Judeophobia. 'The Arabs,' he wrote, 'have a deep, instinctive sense that the Jews in Palestine do not represent the greater Israel . . . that they do not descend from Jacob-Israel, but from Esau and non-Hebraic origins.' In particular, Clark was scornful of European Ashkenazi Jews. 'They are Jewish by religion and not by race,' he wrote, 'which means that between them it is the Palestinian Arab who has the far better claim to occupy Palestine.'[121]

If Arabs were Semites, a new understanding of geo-politics was required. 'It is interesting,' Noel Hunt wrote, 'that none of the talking heads, has yet seen fit to tell us that by opposing Saddam . . . we are . . . being anti-Semitic.'[122] In 2001, Stephen E. Jones conceded that Christians should condemn the World Trade Centre bombers, but only with the following caveat:

> Terrorist attacks worked well for the Zionist Jews in 1948 and some Arab countries decided to do the same later. The Zionists being experts on terrorism understand that this could be their worst nightmare. . . . Today we are being told that we should declare war on terrorists. That would be fine if we did not distinguish between Jewish and Arab terrorists.[123]

In the later twentieth century, in short, it became apparent to British-Israelists that the Jewish people could not easily be accommodated in their eschatological schemata. Whilst the 1970s saw the possibility of a cuppelling of Jewry, a winnowing away of the Edomite elements in advance of the restoration of all-Israel, the apparent success of Israeli militarism dispensed with this notion, creating a failure of prophecy. With the establishment of a powerful, Jewish state in the middle east, which seemingly was not threatened with destruction at the hands of a divinely appointed foe, the authenticity of the Jewish people seemed lost. This loss of authenticity, the normalisation of the Jewish people which the foundation of the state of Israel represented, threatened to allow the Jew 'to melt into the crowd.'

Conclusion

The decline of the empire is usually identified by historians as the harbinger of the decline of the British-Israelist movement. British-Israelism, successive

scholars have claimed, was nothing more than a fig leaf for British imperialist triumphalism, 'jingoism with a biblical sanction.' This claim was
problematised in the scholarship of John Wilson. Wilson demonstrated that
British-Israelism increased in popularity precisely during the period of imperial decline. Writing in 1968, Wilson reported that British-Israelism was
'flourishing' and was 'attracting members who have not experienced a truly
imperial Britain.' In 1968, after all, 'Britain's international circumstances
[were] not such that recruits [were] likely to be swept to the movement on a
tide of emotional imperialism.'[124]

Paul Mendes-Flohr's essay on 'Zionism's ambivalence towards Israel's
election,' bears the title 'In Pursuit of Normalcy.' It could be that the decline
of British-Israelism corresponded not with the decline of the empire but
rather with the relative normalisation of the status of 'the Jew' in Western
culture. With the rise of secularism in Europe, the rise of Reform and irreli-
gious Judaism, and with the founding of the Jewish homeland in Palestine,
the Jews could no longer be so easily identifiable with the topos of 'radical
ambivalence.' The contradictions which the Jew appeared to stand for – a
nation without a home, a religion abandoned by its God, a people both
blessed and cursed – no longer retained their salience. If it was the salience of
the category of 'the Jew' that provided the necessarily ballast to the covenantal and missional nationalistic claims of British-Israelism, then it is intuitive
that the failure of the former would correspond to the failure of the latter.

Juan Tebes has noted the perennial topos of Edom in ancient Jewish sacred
texts. Edom is identified, by Jewish authors, as a sibling people. At the same
time, Edom is identified with all that Israel is not. This trope is mirrored in
many aspects of Christian writing about the Jewish people, nowhere more
so than in the writings of British-Israelists. British-Israelism relied on two
things: the difference between Britain-Israel and the Jews and the similarity between British-Israel and the Jews. In a leaflet, issued by the BIWF in
1951, Claud Coffin suggested that 'while Jewry came into being within the
framework of Israel, at no time have Israel and Jewry been incorporated.'[125]
A close connection exists between autosemitism and allosemitism in British-
Israelist theory, as (I suspect) it does in the Christian Zionist milieu more
broadly. Allosemitism is an essential component of these movements. The
ambivalent, un-whole, contradictory nature of 'the Jew' is reinforced in
order to create the point of comparison for the whole, stable, and coherent
Christian counterpart. Moreover, the reification of 'the Jews' as an entitative, recognisable and authentic group undergirds the essential claim that
God works through nations and peoples – continuously and not only in the
Biblical past. This attitude is no better expressed than in an article written by
C.F. Parker in *The National Message* in 1948. 'For both Jews and Britons,'
he wrote, 'isolation from the world around has helped to produce a unique
mentality.'[126] The antithesis, ever-threatening in the modern world, of this
'unique mentality' was – what John Shenton called – 'the mass man': with

'one world government, one monetary system, one citizenship.'[127] Thirdly, the existence of the Jewish people as the not-yet-redeemed, leaves the door open for the missional nationalism espoused by British-Israelists and Christian Zionists alike. But proximity – conceptually – to Jews is also essential, in order for the particular millenarian group to *highlight* these distinctions. One British-Israelist went as far as to claim that the people of Israel were as one: the Jewish people formed the body, whilst Britain-Israel formed the soul.[128] This was a point that Bauman made in his essay. Bauman reaches the conclusion that order and ambivalence are mutually interdependent. Without 'the Jew' – the ambivalence for which that name stands – British-Israelism could not live.

Notes

1 *The Times*, no. 41,658 (11 December 1917), 6.
2 *Watching and Waiting*, vol. 1, no. 2 (May, 1919), 11; *Watching and Waiting*, vol. 1, no. 10 (January, 1920), 108; *Watching and Waiting*, vol. 1, no. 19 (October, 1920), 213; *Alliance Weekly* (8 November 1919), 99.
3 Revelation 3:12; Revelation 21:2.
4 *Banner of Israel*, vol. 42, no. 2,142 (16 January 1918), 42.
5 Crome, *Christian Zionism and English National Identity*, 24.
6 Crome, *Christian Zionism and English National Identity*, 20.
7 Burry Pullen-Burry, *Letters from Palestine* (London: Judaic Publishing Company, 1922), 45.
8 *The Banner of Israel*, vol. 40, no. 2,036 (5 January 1916), 21.
9 *The Prophetic News and Israel's Watchman*, no. 10 (October 1917), 160.
10 *The Prophetic News and Israel's Watchman*, no. 1 (January 1917), 18.
11 *The Prophetic News and Israel's Watchman*, no. 8 (August 1917), 128.
12 *The Prophetic News and Israel's Watchman*, no. 11 (November 1917), 176.
13 *Brith*, no. 23 (October 1947), 13.
14 *The Banner of Israel*, vol. 42, no. 2,140 (2 January 1918), 5.
15 *Quarterly Notes of the Protestant British-Israel League*, vol. 7, no. 2 (April 1917), 55.
16 *The Banner of Israel*, vol. 42, no. 2,158 (14 September 1918), 222.
17 *The Daily Telegraph*, no. 21,230 (9 May 1923), 9.
18 Justin Fantauzzo, 'A Tribute to the British Empire: Lowell Thomas with Allenby and Lawrence in Arabia,' in Michael Walsh (ed.), *The Great War and the British Empire* (London: Routledge, 2017), 204.
19 *Alliance Weekly* (8 November 1919), 99.
20 *The Banner of Israel*, vol. 42, no. 2,142 (16 January 1918), 21, 37.
21 Grattan Guinness, *Light for the Last Days*, 222–225.
22 De Lisle, *Reminiscences of Sport and War*, 226–231.
23 *The Banner of Israel*, vol. 42, no. 2,171 (March 1919), 289.
24 *The Banner of Israel*, vol. 42, no. 2,142 (16 January 1918), 35.
25 *Brith*, no. 2 (October 1945), 7.
26 *Covenant Voice*, vol. 38, no. 4 (April 1983), 27.
27 *The National Message*, vol. 53, no. 1,614 (May 1974), 84, 132.
28 *The National Message*, vol. 53, no. 1,617 (August 1974), 276.
29 *Covenant Voice*, vol. 38, no. 4 (April 1983), 28.
30 *Wake Up*, vol. 7, no. 3 (May 1988), 69.
31 *The Telegraph*, no. 19,525 (9 November 1917), 7.

32 James Renton, *The Zionist Masquerade: The Birth of the Anglo-Zionist Alliance* (Basingstoke: Palgrave Macmillan, 2007), 82.
33 National Archives, Colonial Office, 935/1/1.
34 *The Banner of Israel*, vol. 44, no. 2,256 (24 March 1920), 97.
35 *The Banner of Israel*, vol. 44, no. 2,269 (23 June 1920), 215.
36 *The Banner of Israel*, vol. 42, no. 2,142 (16 January 1918), 50.
37 *The Southern Star*, no. 1 (January 1919), 3–4.
38 *The Banner of Israel*, vol. 42, no. 2,145 (19 March 1918), 63.
39 *The Banner of Israel*, vol. 42, no. 2,141 (9 January 1918), 17.
40 *The Banner of Israel*, vol. 41, no. 2,134 (21 November 1917), 402.
41 *The National Message*, vol. 27, no. 1,189 (14 February 1948), 61; *The National Message*, vol. 43, no. 1,499 (October 1964), 312.
42 *Brith*, no. 353 (June 1975), 17.
43 *Brith*, no. 23 (October 1947), 6–7.
44 *Brith*, no. 362 (June 1976), 8.
45 *Brith*, no. 40 (March 1949), 1.
46 British Israel World Federation, *A Paper Submitted for the Attention of the Anglo-American Joint Commission on Palestine* (London: Covenant Publishing, 1947), 7.
47 *The Banner of Israel*, vol. 42, no. 2,149 (6 March 1918), 97.
48 *Protestant British Israel League Quarterly Notes*, vol. 10, no. 4 (October 1920), 131.
49 Michael J. Cohen, *Britain's Moment in Palestine* (Abingdon: Routledge, 2014), 213; Douglas Duff, *Bailing with a Teaspoon* (London: Jonathan Long, 1953); 'Police Report of Sir Charles Wickham,' National Archives, CO 537/2269; 'General Situation in Palestine,' National Archives, FO 371/23229.
50 *The Covenant Race*, no. 1 (April 1926), 2.
51 *British Israel Star and Circle*, no. 40 (April 1925), 59.
52 *The New British Israel Pilot*, no. 3 (1 September 1929), 37.
53 *The National Message*, vol. 15, no. 901 (25 April 1936), 44.
54 Colin Shindler, *The History of Modern Israel* (Cambridge: Cambridge University Press, 2013), 28–30, 130–131.
55 *The Banner of Israel*, vol. 42, no. 2,140 (2 January 1918), 6; William Rubinstein and Hilary Rubinstein, *Philosemitism: Admiration and Support in the English-Speaking World for Jews, 1840–1939* (Basingstoke: Palgrave Macmillan, 1999), 80.
56 *Prophetic News and Israel's Watchman*, no. 5 (May 1917), 80.
57 *The Banner of Israel*, vol. 42, no. 2,142 (16 January 1918), 35.
58 *The Banner of Israel*, vol. 42, no. 2,144 (30 January 1918), 59.
59 *The British Israel Star and Circle*, no. 37 (January 1925), 5.
60 *Brith*, no. 40 (March 1949), 6.
61 *The National Message*, vol. 53, no. 1,612 (March 1974), 9.
62 Aviva Halamish, *The Exodus Affair* (Syracuse: Syracuse University Press, 1998), 144.
63 Arieh Kochavi, 'Britain and Illegal Immigration to Palestine from France Following World War II,' in *Holocaust and Genocide*, no. 6 (1991): 383–395.
64 *The National Message*, vol. 26, no. 1,179 (27 September 1947), 290.
65 *Brith*, no. 23 (October 1947), 6.
66 *The National Message*, vol. 27, no. 1,189 (14 February 1948), 61.
67 *Brith*, no. 23 (October 1947), 6.
68 *Brith*, no. 20 (July 1947), 4.
69 *Brith*, no. 299 (November 1970), 6.
70 *The National Message*, vol. 27, no. 1207 (23 October 1948), 340.
71 *Wake Up*, vol. 2, no. 9 (September 1978), 194.
72 *Brith*, no. 355 (November 1975), 27.

73 'Arab Reactions Following Concessions to the Jews,' National Archives, CO 537/2296; 'Situation in Palestine,' National Archives, FO 371/68501.
74 'Haifa Incident,' National Archives, CO 537/3860.
75 *The National Message*, vol. 26, no. 1,179 (27 September 1947), 290.
76 *The National Message*, vol. 26, no. 1,181 (25 October 1947), 325.
77 *Brith*, no. 17 (February 1947), 4, 13.
78 *The Scotsman*, no. 32,647 (16 January 1948), 4.
79 *The National Message*, vol. 27, no. 1,197 (5 June 1948), 177.
80 *Citizen*, no. 265 (10 March 1949), 5.
81 *Brith*, no. 32 (July 1948), 1–2.
82 *Brith*, no. 41 (April 1949), 19.
83 *Brith*, no. 141 (January 1958), 7; *Brith*, no. 301 (January 1971), 23.
84 *The National Message*, vol. 27, no. 1,196 (22 May 1948), 174.
85 *Brith*, no. 17 (February 1947), 13.
86 *The National Message*, vol. 27, no. 1,196 (22 May 1948), 174.
87 *Brith*, no. 30 (May 1948), 4.
88 *The National Message*, vol. 27, no. 1,195 (8 May 1948), 146.
89 *Brith*, no. 260 (September 1967), 10.
90 *Brith*, no. 31 (June 1948), 3.
91 *Brith*, no. 127 (August 1956), 1–8.
92 *Brith*, no. 299 (November 1970), 7.
93 *Brith*, no. 17 (February 1947), 16; Brith, no. 29 (April 1948), 2.
94 *Brith*, no. 13 (October 1946), 7.
95 *Brith*, no. 63 (February 1951), 5.
96 *Brith*, no. 24 (November 1947), 15.
97 *Brith*, no. 257 (June 1967), 7; *Brith*, no. 258 (July 1967), 23–25.
98 Leora Batnitzky, *Idolatry and Representation: The Philosophy of Franz Rosenzweig Reconsidered* (Princeton, NJ: Princeton University Press, 2000), 81–105.
99 *Crown and Commonwealth*, vol. 2, no. 4 (Winter 2002), 17.
100 *Toren*, no. 6 (October 1964), 15.
101 Hal Lindsay, *The Late Great Planet Earth* (Grand Rapids: Zondervan, 1970), 167–168.
102 *The National Message*, vol. 47, no. 1,540 (March 1968), 75.
103 *Brith*, no. 293 (May 1970), 27.
104 *Brith*, no. 336 (January 1974), 23.
105 *Brith*, no. 337 (February 1974), 17.
106 *Brith*, no. 381 (February 1978), 7.
107 *Wake Up*, vol. 2, no. 9 (September 1978), 202.
108 *Wake Up*, vol. 2, no. 4 (April 1978), 83.
109 *Wake Up*, vol. 7, no. 3 (May 1988), 108.
110 *The National Message*, vol. 53, no. 1,619 (October 1974), 304.
111 Barkun, *A Culture of Conspiracy*, 26.
112 McKilliam, *The Annihilation of Man*, 73, 77.
113 Crome, *Christian Zionism and English National Identity*, 273–274.
114 *Bible Truth*, no. 222 (March 2003), 16.
115 *Wake Up*, vol. 6, no. 7 (September 1987), 156.
116 *Wake Up*, vol. 7, no. 8 (March 1989), 173.
117 *BIWF Quarterly*, vol. 4, no. 1 (January 1991), 21–23.
118 *Wake Up*, vol. 9, no. 7 (March 1992), 42.
119 *Wake Up*, vol. 8, no. 5 (November 1990), 101.
120 *Wake Up*, vol. 8, no. 4 (August 1990), 91.
121 *Wake Up*, vol. 12, no. 3 (June 1998), 57–58.

122 *Wake Up*, vol. 8, no. 4 (August 1990), 96.
123 *Crown and Commonwealth*, vol. 1, Special Edition (2001), 17.
124 Wilson, 'British Israelism,' 48, 55.
125 Claud Coffin, *British-Israelism* (London: Covenant Publishing, 1951), 1.
126 *The National Message*, vol. 27, no. 1,186 (3 January 1948), 9.
127 *Wake Up*, vol. 2, no. 4 (April 1978), 80.
128 *British Israel Star and Circle*, no. 37 (January 1925), 5.

7 British-Israelism and Russia

Much of the history of the twentieth century was dominated by an ideological struggle between capitalism and communism. The key actors in this struggle were the United States and the Soviet Union. Particularly during the later years of the Cold War, in America, the latter was seen as the embodiment of anti-Christian values. As Ronald Reagan had it, the Soviet Union was the 'evil empire,' a place of 'totalitarian darkness' whose people did not have 'the joy of knowing God.' Some in evangelical circles took this vision of Soviet communism more literally. Billy Graham believed that communism was 'masterminded by Satan.' Successive Soviet leaders were identified as possible anti-Christs.[1] In 1988, Robert Faird wrote a book-length investigation entitled *Gorbachev: Has the Real Anti-Christ Come?* Faird sought to prove that the name 'Gorbachev' could be numerologically converted into the number 666.[2]

Many, however, saw in the Soviet Union a different prophetic figure. The prophet Ezekiel described how the armies of Gog and Magog would attack the newly restored Israel, only to be finally defeated by divine intervention. The identification of Gog and Magog with 'the North' caused many premillenialists to contend, in the nineteenth and twentieth centuries, that Russia was the fulfilment of this long-awaited foe. This contention can be found in the writings of the dispensationalist founder of the Plymouth Brethren, John Nelson Darby.[3] However, in the late twentieth century, with Soviet Russia seen as the most powerful menace to Christianity, this belief gathered momentum. In 1970, Hal Lindsay's *The Late Great Planet Earth* was published. Lindsay predicted that Russia – 'a country founded on atheism' – would invade the state of Israel. His book sold over fifteen million copies.[4]

This eschatological reading of the Cold War was shared by the majority of British-Israelists throughout this period. British-Israelists were told by their leaders that the armies of Russia would invade Israel in the last days. In the mainstream fundamentalist context, the merging of 'superpatriotism' – of the kind espoused by Faird, Graham and others – with premillenialism has provided a conundrum to scholars. How, as Robert Fuller asks, could one pledge 'sole loyalty to the coming Kingdom of God,' whilst embracing 'the American way.' This is clearly less problematic for British-Israelists.

The British-Israelist eschatology, like the Judeocentric eschatology, does not describe the end of days as a time for the annihilation of human difference, but rather as a consummation, a glorification of these differences.[5] Few of the prophetic claims held dear by British-Israelists have been undeniably disconfirmed. Most prophetic expectations are either suspended or postponed or euphemised in some way. In the twentieth century, though, British-Israelists made claims about the identity of Russia – or more accurately the Soviet Union – in the drama of the apocalypse. This focus on Russia's role in the impending *eschaton* became more and more central to British-Israelist writings over the course of the twentieth century, leading to a significant failure of prophecy when – in 1989 – the Berlin Wall fell and the USSR spun into a cycle of rapid and irreversible decline. How British-Israelists addressed the rise of the Soviet Union and its fall is the subject of this chapter.

Cognitive dissonance theory

> Suppose an individual believes something with his whole heart; suppose further that he has a commitment to this belief and that he has taken irrevocable actions because of it; finally, suppose that he is presented with evidence, unequivocal and undeniable evidence that his belief is wrong: what will happen?

This was the question posed by Leon Festinger in 1956 at the start of his investigation into the phenomenon of cognitive dissonance. His response to the question was counter-intuitive. Such an individual would – Festinger contended – 'emerge, not only unshaken, but more convinced of the truth of his beliefs than ever before.' In fact, this individual may 'show a new fervor about convincing and converting other people to his view.'[6] Festinger made this claim on the basis of observations that he had made of the behaviours of the followers of Marian Keech following the failure of the events that she predicted to materialise.

A number of Festinger's peers in the field of social psychology have taken issue with the methodological soundness of his research. Others have conducted research which drew conclusions that refute or refine Festinger's hypothesis. Recently, sociologically oriented scholars have taken issue with the etic nature of Festinger's research. Pollman asserts that the notion of a 'failed prophecy' is a negotiated term, one which is predicated on a socially constructed reality which resists straightforward falsification. Working on this principal, Joseph Zygmunt produced an historical account of the experience of 'disappointment,' in the Jehovah's Witnesses community. He noted three distinctive responses to the apparently empirical failure of prophecy. The first is to reject the validity of the prophecy. The second is to blame the failure of the prophecy on external forces. The third is to deny that the failure has occurred.[7]

The findings of Zygmunt, in particular, informed George Melton's thesis: that 'prophecies do not fail.' Melton wrote that the attitude of 'denial,' which Zygmunt had identified, was 'not just another option,' but was in fact, 'the common mode of adaptation of millennial groups following the failure of a prophecy.' Whilst denial is the most common strategy, it carries with it the challenge of 'adaptation' to the criteria of a new empirical reality. Melton identifies two key strategies for denial of prophecy failure. The first, the 'cultural mode' is the spiritualisation of the prophecy. The second, the 'social mode,' is the reaffirmation of the prophecy. The retroactive 'spiritualisation' of a prophecy is a relatively common occurrence in prophetic, millenialist groups. As Melton puts it:

> The believer does not react to the non-occurrence of the event by admitting failure. To do so would call into question the total experience of the group. Instead the believer begins a process of reinterpretation. The believer begins to see not that the prophecy was incorrect but that the group merely misunderstood it in a material, earthly, manner. Its truth came at a spiritual level, invisible except to the eye of faith. Thus from the original, prophesied event, the believers create an invisible, 'spiritual,' and, more importantly unfalsifiable event.

The potential for such a dynamic to generate its own self-perpetuating 'Emperors-new-clothes,' narrative is evident. Another, complimentary, method of denying the failure of prophecy its efficacy is to annex the experience of failure as a method of reaffirming the coherence of a group. In such instances, the disappointed devotees of the prophecy, fearful of the threat of exposure and disintegration which prophecy failure poses for religious cults or groups, actively assert their sense of communality and thereby find a renewed zeal for the broader experience of shared faith and community membership:

> Some action must be taken to repair the social fabric torn in the prophecy's failure. At such moments groups tend to turn inward, as much as their environment will allow them, and engage in processes of group building.[8]

Diana Tumminia, in her study of the Unarius Academy of Science, corroborated Melton's hypothesis. Tumminia's *When Prophecy Never Fails* argues that, for the truly persuaded devotee, prophecy can never be sensibly talked about as 'failed':

> What appears to be seemingly irrefutable evidence of irreconcilable contradiction to outsiders, like Festinger, can instead be evidence of the truth of prophecy to insiders.[9]

Tumminia's study showed that the tardiness of flying saucers did little to dent the enthusiasm of the Unarians. Each 'disappointment,' was attributed to memories of past lives, misinterpreted as prophetic anticipations of the future.

Simon Dein's study of the Lubavitcher community in Stamford Hill led him to similar conclusions. He recorded several different responses by Lubavitcher Hasidim to the death of Rebbe Menachem Schneerson. Some believed that the death of Schneerson itself heralded a new messianic era. Some looked forward to his resurrection. Some lamented that the Moshiach was not able to reveal himself because of the faithlessness of the world. These attitudes all constitute different strategies of adaptation, seeking to maintain status quo and to reinforce the unfalsifiability of the prophecy.[10]

In part, the following will be an attempt to add to this literature, suggesting the possible factors which allowed British-Israelists to respond to the failure of their prophetic expectations in the way that they did. In general, British-Israelists conformed to the pattern described by Dein, Tumminia and Melton. Far from being discouraged by the disconfirmation of prophecy, British-Israelists compensated by replacing an earthly foe – in the Soviet Union – with an even more vast, formidable foe: the all-powerful figure of the Babylonian system.

Antipathy to pre-revolutionary Russia

British-Israelist antipathy towards Russia did not begin with the rise of the Soviet Union. Even before the revolutions of 1917, British-Israelists professed the belief that Russia was a foe of Israel. Russia and Britain had competed periodically during the period of the late nineteenth century as part of the 'Great Game,' before ultimately forming an alliance which would last for the majority of the First World War.[11] However, partly as a cultural legacy of the Crimean War, jingoistic Russophobia was typical in late-nineteenth-century Britain. In popular literature, Russians were typically portrayed as 'war-loving,' 'barbaric,' 'savage and cruel,' 'bent on invading the civilised world.'[12] This belief fed into the portrayal of Russia as a global menace in the pre-revolutionary, British-Israelist sources. In 1911, with war a likely possibility, the editors of *The British-Israel Ecclesia* predicted that 'when the time is ripple . . . Russia will strike the blow which will set the world at war and bring on the great day of God Almighty.'[13]

During this period, Russia was also heartily criticised by British-Israelists for its treatment of the Jewish people. Russia had 'tyrranised over Poles and Jews,' Augusta Cook told the Sixth Annual Convention of the Protestant British Israel League. Her people would survive 'only for further and more awful judgement.'[14] This theme was revisited again and again in British-Israelist reporting on the events of the First World War. In *The Prophetic News and Israel's Watchman*, in April 1917, reports were published of anti-Semitic violence on the Romanian front. The Romanians and Russians 'burned and slew and looted the Jewish population,' readers were told. These peoples had 'long been distinguished by their cruelty and oppression of the Jews.' This writer believed that God would punish – and indeed *was* punishing – Russia for her treatment of Judah. 'Romania's turn to learn that the God of Israel reigneth in the kingdom of men has come at last,' the author wrote. 'In the great invasion of Poland and Russia by the Teutonic powers, God began judgement on Russia for her awful treatment of the Jews in the past forty years.'[15]

Part of the reason that British-Israelists presented Russia in this light was based on British-Israelist beliefs concerning the origins of the Russian people. Many British-Israelists during this period espoused the belief that the Russian people were the descendants of the Assyrians. During the last years of the First World War, the claim that Russia and Germany were ethnically related – both having their origins in Assyria became more widespread. Germany and Russia were 'Babylonian Assyrians,' who were 'brothers in crime and mischief,' wrote one.[16] Some took a slightly modified view: that all Russians were not Assyrian but that Assyria *ruled* Russia. This had especial significance for Britain since 'Assyria, after Babylon, is Israel's last enemy.'[17] Others bought into the notion that Russia was the fulfilment of the prophecies concerning Gog and Magog, in the thirty-eighth and thirty-ninth chapters of Ezekiel. Here, they would read some details of Gog and Magog's invasion of Israel. In these texts, the prophet describes how the Lord God would implant the desire to invade a neighbouring land in the minds of the leaders of Gog and Magog. This land would be populated by a people who had come from amongst the many nations. They would be a peaceful people, an unsuspecting people, who lived without walls, without gates or bars. Gog and Magog would 'come from the far north,' with 'many nations' and 'a mighty army.' They would advance against Israel 'like a cloud that covers the land.' But in that day, the Lord God would come to the aid of Israel against Gog and Magog:

> with plague and bloodshed; I will pour down torrents of rain, hailstones and burning sulfur on him and on his troops and on the many nations with him. And so I will show my greatness and my holiness, and I will make myself known in the sight of many nations. Then they will know that I am the Lord.

A succession of premillenialist writers of the nineteenth century had identified Russia with Gog. In 1855, John Cumming wrote that Russia had 'a dread mission, to cleave her way to the plains of Palestine.'[18] Twelve years later, Henry Cowles identified Russia's expansionism as a prequel to the end times. A few years before the Revolution, Arno Gaebelein believed that Russia was 'practically within striking distance' of Palestine.[19] British-Israelists embraced this idea. Herbert Aldersmith warned that Britain could expect an army of forty million Russians to invade Israel before the coming of

Christ.[20] With the victory of the Russian revolutionaries – who 'repudiated Christianity and espoused atheism' – this identification 'took on a new lease of life.'[21]

British-Israelist responses to the Russian revolution

'The paroxysm is over,' wrote the *Telegraph* special correspondent from Petrodgrad on 20 March 1917, adding that it was 'bewhildering to see the red flag flying everywhere.'[22] The speed of the events that took place in 1917 took British-Israelists by surprise just as much as it did the rest of the population. 'The Czar of the Russians is in exile and revolutionaries hold the reins of government,' reported F.E. Marsh in December of that year, exclaiming: 'What rapid changes we have seen!'[23] As with many great events, British-Israelists saw the upheavals that took place in Russia in the summer of 1917 as evidence that the day of judgment was at hand. 'The last Plague of God is now upon the world,' wrote the editors of the *Quarterly Notes of the Protestant British Israel League*, describing the Russian revolution as 'an earthquake.'[24]

Very soon, British-Israelists adopted an attitude of hostility towards the new regime in Russia. By 1920, the Bolshevik government was identified as a 'sinister power.' Many believed that the events of the revolution were serving to affirm the belief that Russia was the embodiment of Gog and Magog. In 1919, Florence Nuttall of Cheltenham wrote to *The Banner of Israel*. The events of the preceding years, she believed, had resulted in 'a continent stretching from the Baltic to the Pacific being given up to the Evil One and his hosts.' 'Hell has been let loose,' she wrote. Her conclusion was that Russia was preparing to take on a significant role in the story of the end of the days. 'It does not take an Israelite,' she wrote, 'to foresee Gog and Magog in the Northern hordes.'[25]

A similar view was extolled by H.D. Carver in an article published in *The Banner of Israel* in March 1920. Carver declared that 'the Bible gives us a fairly clear idea as to what people or nations are to form the armies of Antichrist' and noted that 'Bolshevist propaganda is being successfully spread.'[26] The first secretary of the BIWF, Herbert Garrison – speaking at an event in Devon in 1931 – described the Soviet administration as 'devilish.'[27]

Most expressions of anxiety expressed by British-Israelists related to the possible threat of Bolshevism on British shores that might be exacerbated by the success of the Bolshevik party in Russia. 'We may confidently assert that Bolshevism wants to make a little headway in our Isles,' wrote one commentator. Whilst it was expected that the Lord would prevent this, confidence was to be tempered with humility: 'but for the knowledge of our identity we might well tremble for the future of our country.' Whilst Britain's immunity to Bolshevism may have been safeguarded by her chosen status – and specifically by the fact that 'the British throne, being David's, can never be overthrown' – the same could not be said for some of the imperial territories.

'[Bolsheviks] are disseminating their propaganda in every country where our flag flies,' the same article read, particularly citing Ireland, Egypt and India as vulnerable areas.[28]

The characterisation of Bolshevism as an international and a clandestine conspiracy shared some characteristics with the characterisation made by some British-Israelists of the role of 'international Jewry.' This family resemblance was further supported by the fact that the leading figures of the revolution were perceived to be Jewish. The Bolshevists, the Jews, and in particular the Bolshevist Jews were all considered to be part of a 'sinister power' which 'regard[ed] our nation with the bitterest animosity.'[29] 'Is there any doubt that some of the most zealous Bolshevists are Jews?' asked H.D. Carver in 1920. 'And are not both Russia and Germany full of Jews of like feelings?'[30] The claim that the Russian revolution was the result of an international Jewish conspiracy gathered traction in British-Israelist circles as the twentieth century progressed. John Morey portrayed 'Jewish Bolshevism' as the sole cause of the revolution.[31] William Finlayson postulated that Marxism was simply an excrescence of rabbinic Judaism. It was, indeed, one of 'many manifestations of phariseeism in more recent history.' The contention that 'communism . . . was a manifestation of Talmudism' was easily proven by the fact that 'Marx, who was a Jew, is universally acknowledged to have been the father of modern communism. His *Das Kapital* is its bible.' The success of Marxist thought was also explained by Marx's lineage since Finlayson considered it to be the wont of the 'Talmudic Jew to insinuate himself into every sphere and to change it to suit the anti-Christian purpose.' A network of Jewish Marxists had perpetuated Marx's thought. 'The prominent participation of a number of Jews in the establishment of the USSR,' Finlayson claimed, 'is a matter of historical record.' He cited the examples of 'Trotsky, Zinoviev, Kamenev and Serdlov,' clarifying that 'these Jews made a show of dissociating themselves from their racial kinsmen by virulent agitation against the Jewish bourgeoisie and Jewish tradition generally.'[32] The proclivity of Jews for Marxism was also explained in genealogical terms, with some suggesting that Jewish Marxists represented the 'Edomite,' rather than the Judah element within Jewry.[33] The anti-Semitic activist K.R. McKilliam shared this perspective and his views were given a forum in *BIWF Quarterly* in the late 1980s. McKilliam claimed that Marx – 'the son and grandson of Khazar Jew rabbis' – was 'commissioned by the Twelve Just Men of the Illuminati to compile the Communist Manifesto based on the Talmud and the writings of Weishaupt.'[34] The belief that Bolshevism was a Jewish conspiracy also helped to form British-Israelists' interpretation of the phenomenon of secular Zionism. Responding to the foundation of 'a hundred Jewish communal settlements' in Palestine, in 1939, A.J. Ferris informed his reader that the kibbutzim were 'anti-British' and 'pro-Russian' and were 'led by the Russian Jew Jabotinsky.'[35] Ferris' titles sometimes sold into the tens of thousands, and one of his pamphlets was reviewed in 1942 by George Orwell in the pages of the *New Statesman*.[36]

Other conspiracy theories abounded, within British-Israelist circles, concerning the origins of the Bolshevik movement. One widely disseminated theory brought together Adam Weishaupt, the Order of the Illuminati, the Jesuits and Marx himself as key protagonists. In an article written in 1976, W.F. Finlayson traced the lineage of Soviet-style communism to the writings of Weishaupt. Weishaupt was a 'Bavarian, educated by the Jesuits.' He had founded 'a secret organization from which had evolved the main instrument of World Revolution.' This organisation was 'an abomination which was a diabolical blend of Jesuitism and what we now know as communism.' It promoted the Jesuit doctrine that 'the end justifies the means,' which itself provided the basis for revolutionary Marxist thought.[37] Once again, British-Israelist eschatology posited a global conspiracy of individuals seeking to eradicate national authenticity, who would only be defeated by Israel – which stood, ultimately, *for* sovereignty and authenticity.

All of this positioned British-Israelists awkwardly when Britain became part of the alliance to defeat Nazism in the Second World War. British statesmen were being 'pressed to combine with Soviet Russia for the restraint of aggression.' British-Israelists were enjoined to recall that the land of Gog was 'destined to be the chief antagonist in the final drama which is to be enacted upon the mountains of Israel in the Holy Land.'[38] These anxieties were greatly increased when it began to appear that the role of Russia in defeating the Nazis might be decisive. Most British-Israelists described the Nazis as a diabolical force.[39] The role of Russia as the Nazis' chief antagonist was deeply disruptive to the British-Israelists Manichean worldview. Some had gone so far as to insinuate that Russia, 'rather than Israel,' was destined to be 'God's battle-axe' in the fight against the diabolical forces of Germany. This claim was strenuously refuted by the editors of *The National Message*, who 'steadfastly maintained that the Anglo-Saxon peoples are to be identified as the modern descendants of the Israel peoples.'[40]

The Cold War and the apocalypse in British-Israelist writing

In November 1943, General Jan Smuts gave a speech to the Empire Parliamentary Association. He expressed the view that Britain, America and Russia should form a troika in leading the new United Nations Organisation. In the most part, this was intended as a strategy for restraining the imperialist ambitions of Stalin's Russia. Smuts issued a stern warning about the threat from the East:

> Russia is the new colossus in Europe – the new colossus that bestrides this continent. When we consider all that has happened to Russia within the last twenty-five years, and we see Russia's inexplicable and phenomenal rise, we can only call it one of the great phenomena in history.[41]

Smuts' speech was commended to the readers of *The National Message* but with some caveats. After all, for British-Israelists, Soviet Russia's ascent was far from 'inexplicable.' In the spring of 1944, W.B. Grant cautioned against the kind of pessimism that Smuts expressed. British-Israelists must recall, he wrote, that 'only one confederation is destined to become the final great world power.'[42]

In 1931, *The Homeland Pilot* included an editorial which predicted that Russia would 'conquer the world' by 1934. This would lay the groundwork for the Last Battle in which Russia will be 'cleared out of the way.' Britain would 'assist in doing this.'[43] All of this was in keeping with Ezekiel 38 and 39. In the middle of the twentieth century, these passages came to be known within Evangelical circles as 'the Russian chapters' of Ezekiel. This was the title of a book by Walter Milner, published by Covenant in 1933. Milner believed that the ethnic Mongolians, who had 'poured over Russia' at various points in her history, were identical with the Biblically prophesied people of Magog.[44] The belief that Russia could be identified with Gog and Magog was reinforced by the fact that the names given to the allies of Gog and Magog – Rosh, Mesheck and Tubal – sounded similar to Russian place names. It was clear to some that 'the Rosh mentioned in Ezekiel may reasonably be equated with the modern name Russia.'[45] Most British-Israelists agreed that 'these are old names for Russia, Moscow and Tobolsky.'[46] It was also deemed likely that the 'many other nations in train' mentioned in Ezekiel 28 referred to the client nations of the Soviet Union.[47]

During the post-war period, the belief that Russia would be the long-expected invader of the Holy Land, whose ultimate defeat would mark the beginning of the millennial reign of Christ on Earth, gathered impetus amongst British-Israelists. No longer did British-Israelists feel constrained in criticising 'Gog and Magog' by the fact of Britain's alliance with the Soviets. The pressing question for editors of *The National Message* in the mid-1940s was 'How will Russia use her power?' It was becoming clear that a large number of 'countries and races' were coming 'so completely within the sphere of Russia's influence that they will be absorbed in that great confederacy known as the Soviet Union.'[48]

The aftermath of the Second World War, and the subsequent expansion of the Russian sphere of influence in Eastern Europe, served further to convince British-Israelists of Russia's identity. The 'sponsoring' of Eastern Bloc countries was seen as a fulfilment of the prophecy of Ezekiel 38:7 in which the Lord instructed Gog and Magog to 'get ready; be prepared, you and all the hordes gathered about you, and take command of them.'[49]

These events were also understood to be a fulfilment of Isaiah 19. In this text, the prophet speaks of Egypt being ruled over by a cruel king, being humbled and riven with civil strife in preparation for a day in which she will be cowed before Judah. In the late 1940s, the Soviet Union argued for Egypt's case against British military presence in Egypt.[50] For British-Israelists, the 'cruel king' of Isaiah's prophecy was understood to represent the Soviet Union, taking advantage of nationalist unrest in Egypt to foment socialist revolution.[51]

The expansion of the Soviet Union was also seen as a consummation of prophecies in the eleventh chapter of Daniel. In this chapter, the prophet predicts the coming of a 'King from the North,' who would wage war against his neighbours. He would 'storm . . . with chariots and cavalry and a great fleet of ships.' He would 'invade many countries and sweep through them like a flood.' But ultimately, in his attempts to take the 'holy mountain,' the King of the North would be thwarted. Divine providence would lead to the downfall of Gog and Magog:

> This intervention will be so devastating and catastrophic that it is hard to see at this stage the terrible consequences. . . . There will be the greatest earthquake of all time [Joel 2] which will split the mount of Olives making a valley from east to west. . . . At this time the greatest event of God's intervention will take place. The Lord will return physically, visibly and will appear on the mount of Olives to commence His reign on earth as supreme Monarch over all the earth.[52]

Alongside Biblical sources, British-Israelists turned to apocryphal literature to support their claims. McKelvey believed that the ascendancy of the Soviet Union had been predicted in the second book of Esdras. The three-headed eagle of 2 Esdras 11 was taken to represent the three heads of the Babylonian system: Fascism, Nazism and communism. As Esdras predicted, one head – that of communism – had grown stronger than the others. This head would be 'far more dangerous in the future,' and 'the evil which we have seen during the past few years' would be 'insignificant compared with the evil yet to be.'[53]

The belief that Russia would eventually succumb to the divinely inspired desire to invade the Holy Land informed British-Israelist arguments about Britain's foreign policy in many areas. In 1946, for example, with Britain's grasp on power in Egypt weakening, British-Israelists advised that Britain should surrender control to the nationalists, since it was clear that if 'Britain stays in Egypt she will have to defend Egypt when Russia comes down.' This, they believed, would 'not only mean a major war with Russia but a great Russian Victory.'[54]

Many British-Israelists expected that the Jewish population of Russia would play a crucial role in Russia's imminent invasion of Palestine. There was 'no doubt,' wrote A.J. Ferris in 1939, that 'many Jews will be in Russia's army or come down as colonists ready to occupy the land.' Nevertheless, this was a cause for hope rather than for despair. It was anticipated that the Jewish elements in Russia's invasionary force would recognise the eschatological significance of the battle, during the event, and would experience a 'change of heart.' When they saw 'the awful destruction meted out on the invading armies,' they would 'recognise it as the hand of God' and would 'realise that they will have made a mistake.'[55]

The anti-clericalism of the Soviet Union seemed to reinforce the claim that communism was diabolical conspiracy. For some, this was sufficient to prove that Russia was under the control of the Beast. The form of this influence, according to C.W. Green, could be found 'in men and nations who take no account of God into their thoughts, words or works.' This was – of course – the case with Russia. They 'acknowledge no God.' Nor did they 'acknowledge any responsibility to God as a judge, arbiter or a rewarder of the good.'[56] In all of this, it appeared that Soviet Russia had supplanted the Catholic Church in the eschatological schemata of British-Israelism. Indeed, some believed that Russia would *literally* supplant the Catholic Church.

This new understanding that Russia was the principle antagonist of Israel-Britain fed into a Manichean understanding of geo-politics during the early years of the Cold War. For some this situation mirrored the parable of the sheep and the goats with the 'sheep on the right, the goats on the left,' a world 'split into two camps of nations.'[57] The world, McKelvey wrote, 'is divided into two camps and at last the die is cast.' The choice before the world was stark: 'Russia or Anglo-Saxondom? Communism or Freedom?' McKelvey presented the Soviets as a diabolical and deeply destructive presence in the world. They were the chief disseminators of 'a delusion based upon a lie closely associated with the Man of Sin, who reaches the height of power and control and continues to deceive and enslave the Gentile world.' They would accept as success only a situation in which they had 'full and complete control over all nations.' In the coming years they would 'turn upon the Anglo-Saxon world with all the hatred of Hell.' And yet – despite his warnings – McKelvey was certain that the nations of the world would fall, one by one, to the forces of the Man of Sin:

> We believe the Gentile nations will form a Gentile block which the leaders of Moscow will dominate and that whoever obtains supreme command in Moscow will be the Man of Sin.

The last battle, he expected, would arise in 1953 and would be precipitated by a war between Russia and the United States.[58] Some British-Israelists presented the Cold War as a struggle between Russia and Britain, to a greater degree than would be reasonably born out of the facts. In a letter to the *Eastbourne Gazette*, in 1959, an anonymous British-Israelist suggested that Russia's 'ultimate programme is to destroy the British Empire.'[59]

Throughout the decades of the Cold War, British-Israelist publications stoked anxiety and paranoia about the threat posed by Soviet Russia. In L. Buxton Gresty's *Satan Fights for Muscovy*, the author described the 1950s as 'the age of fear.' He described communism as 'a nightmare which is thrusting feelers westwards in a resolve to dominate the souls of men.'

It was 'a vision of worldwide enslavement so terrifying that the man in the street closes his eyes to the spectre which flaunts itself from the Kremlin's walls.'[60]

Much of this anxiety centred on the possibility of a nuclear holocaust. The development of the nuclear stand-off between the US and Russia during the mid-twentieth century stimulated many apocalyptic, prophetic movements.[61] British-Israelism was no different. In *The Covenant Message*, in 1960, Felix Lutz reported that 'more and more the conviction seems pressed upon one that the End-of-the-Age Tribulation will be caused by the action of Atomic, Hydrogen and Cobalt bombs.' But whilst British-Israelists expected nuclear weaponry to form one aspect of the coming tribulation, they did not believe that 'escaping to some island in the Pacific' or to 'less densely populated areas of the globe' would be either necessary or wise. 'All that is asked for,' Lutz wrote, 'is a willingness to be rescued, an inquiry of the Lord to do it for us. He will do all that is necessary.'[62] In this, Lutz echoed the sentiment expressed in Isaiah 31. Israel was not to rely on the resources of man, but solely on the almighty.[63] Indeed, many saw the imminent nuclear apocalypse as a necessary stage in the foundation of the Kingdom of God on Earth. Only at the point at which there was to be a true, existential threat to the human species – they believed – would the Lord God intervene in world affairs. This belief was founded on a text from Job 34, in which it is made clear that God does not desire for 'all flesh' to perish.[64] 'The Lord will intervene to stop a form of destruction lest, as He said, all flesh shall perish,' wrote the Reverend G.H. Nicholson in *The National Message* in 1962, and given that 'we cannot conceive of any form of destruction, apart from nuclear warfare, which could bring this about,' it seemed reasonable to assume that this statement referred to an eschatologically necessary nuclear conflict.[65]

The Cold War played out on the cultural as well as the military battlefield. Some believed that Britain had less to fear from nuclear warheads than she did from Russia's more insidious weapons. Amongst these, the editors of *The Ambassador* magazine considered 'Rock and Roll music' to be of foremost concern. It was a given, wrote the editors, that this music was 'primitive, savage, even suggestive.' Their contention, however, was that – beyond its savagery – rock and roll was also 'a diabolical secret weapon . . . relying on music and hypnotism . . . used by our enemy to produce menticide.' It was of course the Soviets who had developed this weapon. After all, it 'took the twisted Communist mind to use these experiments to tamper with the minds of the youth.'[66]

Throughout this period, though, British-Israelists were assured that none of Russia's actions could realistically be resisted, nor could the coming conflict be averted. Everything that the Soviet Union did was to be understood – ultimately – as the working out of a providential plan. Russia's leaders, British-Israelists believed, were 'simply being led to do the things commanded by the Lord.' The preparations that Russia was making, for 'the coming conflict' were 'at the express command of the Lord God.'[67] Again, the providentialism at the heart of British-Israelist account of the

Cold War informed their attitude to the West's strategic policies. In 1968, in the pages of *The National Message*, Buxton Gresty cautioned that the US should withdraw from Vietnam. The US policy of 'containing communism' was 'doomed to failure.' Instead of fighting communism, British-Israelists believed that the West, 'swallowing our sorrow,' must 'draw comfort from our conviction that our latter day Israel has of necessity to pass through this humbling phase . . . in order that the non-Israel nations be brought to Armageddon.'[68]

Indeed, British-Israelists appeared to view Soviet Russia as a potential instrument of justice in the hands of God. There are biblical precedents for this claim. In 2 Kings 18 the Lord God uses the armies of Assyria to chastise the Northern Kingdom for her infidelity. In Jeremiah 25, the prophet insinuates that God used Nebechudnezzar as a servant, in punishing Judah. Equally, in British-Israelist literature, we find reference to prophecies which suggest that the diabolical power of Russia would be turned against God's enemies in the Gentile world. British-Israelists pointed to the success of Communist parties across Europe in the 1960s as a sign that God was using communism as a weapon against the Papacy. As 'the nations that once were the continental Holy Roman Empire' began to 'throw in their lot with Russia,' the power of the 'Roman Church' would gradually be eroded. Eventually, as a result of this progress, British-Israelists expected that 'the Roman Church will cease to exist.'[69] Others saw a more violent end for the Church of Babylon at the hands of Gog and Magog. Writing in 1972, Francis Thomas expected that 'Papal Rome' would be 'destroyed by the ten horns when the scarlet coloured beast rages and the full might of communism is unleashed.' After the final defeat of Babylon, communism would reign 'until the Lord's return.'[70] In the 1970s, British-Israelists also expected that 'the Common Market will collapse' when 'Communist Russia takes over.' The armies of Russia 'will have to be careful when [they] are moving down into Palestine, not to leave armies in these nations.'[71] The success of Gog and Magog would lead to the failure of Babylon. The 'judgement of Russia' would not come until after 'Babylon's collapse,' when 'Russia will eventually take control of ten countries which have been dominated for centuries by Rome.'[72]

During the later decades of the Cold War, an increasing proportion of column inches were devoted – in British-Israelist journals – to the question of Soviet expansion into the Global South. More frequently, during this period, contributions were made by American commentators. One such was J.A.B. Haggart. Haggart was a Methodist preacher based in California. During the late 1970s and early 1980s he contributed to a number of British-Israelist publications including *The Message*. Haggart noted that the Russian state was reliant on an oil supply which was at a breaking point. This – he believed – would prove to be the trigger for the Russian expansion into the Middle East. 'They have the motivation which will cause them to seize the oil countries,' he wrote, 'and God, through Ezekiel, says that they will!'[73] Any measures taken to pacify or reach détente with the Soviet Union were also met with scorn with British-Israelists. Attempts being made to 'secure world peace' were based only in fear: the fear that Britain was 'no longer able to stand alone.'[74] British-Israelists continued to maintain that 'communism [was] conquering the world.'[75] The signs seemed to suggest, they wrote, that 'the great Soviet treachery is approaching.' They warned their readers not to trust that an arms deal could be struck which would benefit the 'Christian Israel nations.' War was imminent. The time for supporting 'the false Peace Movement' was over. The West was called upon to 'remain awake to this fact.'[76]

Principal amongst those British-Israelists who agitated against détente with Russia was General Sir Walter Walker. Walker had been commander-in-chief of allied forces in Northern Europe. In his latter years, he became a prominent voice in the anti-Communist movement. He founded the Civil Assistance organisation in 1974 with the express intention of violently disrupting trade union activity in Britain. Walker's activities in the late 1970s caused some disturbance in Whitehall, and for some time his activities were closely monitored.[77] A decade later, he was appointed a patron of the Western Goals Institute, an affiliate of the World Anti-Communist League. Western Goals maintained close ties with the Conservative Party during this period, and many of its employees were also members of the Monday Club. In his work with the BIWF, Walker's main contribution was to write opinion pieces for *The National Message* and *Wake Up* magazine on the subject of the Russian threat. In 1988, unaware that the end of the conflict was imminent, Walker wrote the following:

> There is growing evidence that Russia is preparing actively for war. The Soviets believe that a world war could be waged for a period of time with conventional weapons only. Great importance is attached by them to the initial phase of a war because to a large degree it would determine the course of all subsequent actions.[78]

Even in June of 1989, British-Israelists continued to promote the thesis that the 'Communist system' was 'growing in dominance over the nations of the EEC.'[79] All of this was clearly in keeping with the prophetic claims that British-Israelists had maintained for over half a century by this point. The Russian chapters had promised that 'in Satan's final attempt to conquer and destroy Israel, the atheistic USSR and her confederate nations would play a leading role,' and as such this was expected to happen regardless of the contingencies of the Soviet economy.[80] 'Soviet Russia,' the 'great Gog confederation of Ezekiel 38' was perceived to be as hell-bent on 'plunging the world into chaos' and 'frustrating the establishment of the Kingdom of God with skill and diabolical cunning' and fomenting 'conspiracy against the Christian Israel nations' in 1988 as it was in 1928.[81]

And yet there was some misgivings. James Haggart had expected that 1980 would be the year Russia would be drawn towards the Holy Land. When this failed to materialise, Haggart wrote of his deeply held conviction that 'the delay cannot last much longer':

> God's word says that certain things are going to happen. Now, today, we can see the pieces of the puzzle falling into place and the completed picture begins to emerge![82]

Emerge it did not.

British-Israelists and the fall of the Berlin Wall

'It is undoubtedly true to say,' Francis Thomas wrote, as the 1980s became the 1990s, 'that our minds are filled with consternation.' This consternation was caused by the fall of the Berlin Wall in December of 1989 and by the succession of political calamities that had befallen the Soviet Union in the weeks that had followed. 'Governments have resigned and presidents and general secretaries have relinquished their offices; quite powerful men have become weak,' he wrote. The tenor of this text is remarkable. Thomas confesses that he is unsure whether to be pleased, 'affrighted,' 'dismayed,' or 'fearful.' He was pleased that 'communism [was] discredited.' He was fearful, he claimed 'in the sense that we wondered what was likely to happen next.' None of these events could have been expected by British-Israelists. As Thomas freely admitted: 'never in our wildest expectations did we think that such a time was so near.'[83] The same 'mixed emotions' were expressed by Alan Campbell in the same journal two months later:

> We have witnessed the strangest events, which will prove to be memorable. Since last October/November the peoples of Eastern Europe have danced, sung – and wept – and doubtless many in the West uttered a sincere Thank You to the Lord of hosts for these events.[84]

For many decades British-Israelists had been taught that the *eschaton* would be precipitated by a Russian invasion of the Holy Land. This would prove to be the consummation of the prophecies of Ezekiel 38 and 39. But in 1990, British-Israelists were forced to confront the distinct likelihood that this prophecy would not be fulfilled and that – in fact – it had been disconfirmed.

Thomas was relatively sanguine in his response to this failure. 'Back to the drawing board brothers,' he wrote. 'Let us proceed with diligence as we seek to compare Scripture with Scripture as European events move apace.'[85] Others were less so. Some claimed that the increased rate of chaos was itself sufficient to point to the imminence of the end times. One correspondent expressed this view in a January edition of *Wake Up* magazine:

> The continuing cascade of changes in Eastern Europe increasingly confirms the great significance of the Scriptural chronological pattern linked to the period at the end of last year.[86]

Some refused to believe that the Soviet Union was really in a state of rapid and terminal decline, choosing instead to ask 'what is really happening behind the scenes in the Soviet Union?' One response was to claim that, whilst British-Israelists had long expected that the power of Babylon-Rome would be destroyed by Gog-Russia, in actuality the reverse was taking place. This was the position adopted by the future president of the BIWF, Michael Clark. 'Christians must wake up,' he warned, to the reality of 'a new Vatican Kremlin axis.' He expected that the coming decades would see a realisation of 'the universalist religious design of Pope John Paul.'[87] Many saw the fall of communism as the precursor to an 'enlarging of the territory of Europe,' which was 'the Pope's dream.'[88] This claim was bolstered by the fact that on 1 December 1989, Gorbachev was granted a papal audience. 'This development is surely of great prophetic importance,' British-Israelist attendees at the Annual General Meeting in 1989 were told.[89]

Others saw the fall of the Soviet Union as a victory for the Babylonian European Union. In September 1990, the *Covenant Voice* editorial warned that a united Europe was inevitable. Meanwhile, it was precisely what the Vatican had always intended. 'Only the Pope has real plans for Europe,' wrote the editors: 'a Europe united, including Russia.'[90] Others saw the newly emancipated European countries as the hosts of a virus that would infect Europe with the tendencies proper to Gog and Magog. 'The USSR and its satellites line up in neo-Socialism just in time for the new European Order of Federalism,' wrote one such in the following year.[91]

Still others saw the fall of Gog-Russia as a prelude to the rise of a new global antagonist. From this point, British-Israelists turned their attentions away from Russia (and even away from the Catholic Church) and towards the spectral figure of 'the Globalists': 'the Warburgs, Rothschilds, Schiffs, Lehmans, Melchiors, Hambros and Mayers.'[92] The 'One worlders,' they began to see, were seeking to bring about a 'convergence with Eurasia' and events in Eastern Europe were interpreted as a manifestation of this strategy. 'We are witness to the workings of a very powerful force in international politics,' Michael Clark wrote in the winter of 1990.[93] At the Annual General Meeting of the BIWF, in the same year, Matthew Browning spoke about the great changes that had taken place in the previous calendar year. In his speech, Browning refused to relinquish the claim that 'communism is an Age end demonic force.' Far from having disappeared from the stage of the eschatological drama, the force of Gog had 'converged with apostasy in

Europe and the world.' As such, the nations were entering into a 'time of the greatest deception.'[94]

British-Israelists and Putinism

With the fall of communism, Russia entered a new era. After a brief interlude during the premiership of Boris Yeltsin, Vladimir Putin came to power and has maintained his grip on power up to the present day.

For some British-Israelists, the rise of Putin as a powerful leader in Russia has brought the comparison between Gog and Russia new relevance. Putin is recognised by many as representing a continuity between modern Russia and her Soviet past. Putin rose to power through the ranks of the KGB, only retreating from the Soviet intelligence community in 1991. At the High Leigh Conference of the Covenant People's Fellowship in 2017, Cora Birch reiterated the claim that Russia was Gog and Magog, predicting that they would 'lead an anti-Western, anti-American alliance, including certain Islamic, Asian and Communistic nations, against Britain and America.'[95]

For others, however, Putin's rise has led to an increasing, rather than lessening, enthusiasm amongst British-Israelists for Russia. In 2002, in the pages of *Crown and Commonwealth*, Barrie Williams played down possible associations between Gog and Russia with the somewhat gnomic claim that 'prophecy will be fulfilled in God's way in God's good time.' At the same time, he pointed to the similarities between Putin and the rulers of Russia during the country's most sustained period of prosperity in the eighteenth century. 'Putin seems to follow in their footsteps,' Williams wrote, 'and how much he has achieved in two years.'[96]

In 2013, British-Israelist leaders expressed even more admiration for President Putin. In an editorial in *The Covenant Nations* magazine, Ernest Gage informed readers that Vladimir Putin had 'shifted to a more conservative stance since he returned as president last year.' Putin's intention was understood to be 'to strengthen a new national identity on conservative traditional values such as the Orthodox Church.' Gage praised Putin for 'making a stand against homosexuality and protecting children in their education on this issue.' He recognised that Putin had 'admonish[ed] the West as to its moral declension,' whilst the West had responded with anger. 'Is it possible that Russia could yet perform an important role in revealing the Kingdom truth?' Gage asked.[97]

Some went further, asking whether Russia could – in light of more recent events – be identified as an Israel nation. The task of proving this claim was taken up by the Danish Israelist Mikkel Kragh. Kragh noted the uptick in participation in Christian worship in Russia following the fall of communism. He proposed that the martial ethic of the Cossacks and their apparently providential ability to resist invasion by successive forces were sufficient sources of evidence to demonstrate that Russia could – indeed – be populated with descendants of the tribe of Gad.[98]

Conclusion

The ease with which many British-Israelists were able to adapt to the dramatic failure of prophecy that took place in 1989 is striking. British-Israelists, almost immediately, turned their attentions to other perceived foes of Israel. Some turned to the Catholic Church, fearing that the delicate balance of power that had thwarted Catholic hegemony in Europe during the twentieth century had been disrupted by the fall of the Soviet Union. Others turned to a new and more chimerical foe: the 'Globalist,' exemplified in the mid-1990s and up to the present day in the person of George Soros.

All of this appears, in part, to confirm what Zygmunt and Tumminia and Dein predicted: prophecy simply does not fail. Perhaps this observation is even more reliable, though, in traditions, like British-Israelism, whose adherents see history in a profoundly providential way. For British-Israelists, the prophecies of the Hebrew Bible are alive in the present. But this is not to say that the prophetic topoi of Babylon, Gog, Magog, Israel and Assyria are static. In each iteration of British-Israel prophecy, these topoi become attached to and, necessarily, affected by another (this time contemporary) topos. The world, for British-Israelists, is divided along stark lines, between Israel nations and anti-Israel nations. The identification of the Soviet Union as an anti-Israel nation served to bolster the salience of this prophecy, such that the failure of the Soviet Union represented nothing more than the dying of one bulb in an entire constellation, easily replaced.

This is, however, only part of the story. Zygmunt Bauman's analysis suggests that the fundamental concern which governs Christian attitudes toward 'the Jew' is the maintenance of boundaries. The separation of 'the Jew,' the othering of 'the Jew,' is manifest in the attitude of allosemitism. Allosemitism is a form of proteophobia rather than heterophobia. 'The Jew' is identified, not simply as the 'other' but as the object of radical ambivalence. As we have seen, intolerance of ambiguous entities or categories is a defining characteristic of the British-Israelist mindset. It is a characteristic which is inherited from the Protestant reformers and ultimately from the authors of the Levitical legal codes. British-Israelists are primarily concerned with the separation of people, things and time into authentic, salient categories. Insofar as a thing, time or people represents a 'mixed' category, it is stigmatised by British-Israelists. Insofar as a thing, time or people represents an authentic category, it is celebrated by British-Israelists. In all of this, nevertheless, the object of creating salient categories – between the sacred and the common, to use Klawans' nomenclature – remains foremost. We see precisely this tendency played out in the interaction between British-Israelists and the prophetic topos of Russia. Russia, in the era of Soviet rule, represented a mixed, inauthentic category, which mirrored the Biblical topoi of Babylon and Magog: a people who sought to amalgamate, homogenise and de-authenticate others, thereby amalgamating, homogenising, de-authenticating and losing itself. As such, Russia was identified as separate from Britain-Israel as a foe. In later times, Russia became identifiable with an authentic category: it was a newly nationally conscious state, with a new, nationally conscious leader. As such it remained possible for British-Israelists to separate Israel from Russia, but this time in a philo-Russian, rather than an anti-Russian mode. The prophecy, in other words, remained sound. The separation of peoples remained in place. The shift from positive to negative was easily accomplished, because it was always of secondary concern.

Again, this account highlights the superficiality of the claim that British-Israelist accounts of ethnicity precede British-Israelist accounts of the relationship between nations. When the boundaries between Israel nations and anti-Israel nations become too difficult to police, they are altered and adapted, better to facilitate their own maintenance. Russia was once Gog and Magog. Now, with the rise of Vladimir Putin, some British-Israelists have discovered that Russia is Israel after all.

Notes

1 Robert Fuller, *Naming the Anti-Christ: The History of an American Obsession* (Oxford: Oxford University Press, 1995), 150–160.
2 Robert Faird, *Gorbachev! Has the Real Antichrist Come?* (Tulsa: Victory House, 1988).
3 John Nelson Darby, *Lectures on the Second Coming* (London: Paternoster, 1868), 183–184.
4 Lindsay, *The Late Great Planet Earth*, 65.
5 Sutcliffe and Karp, 'Introduction,' 3.
6 Leon Festinger, *When Prophecy Fails* (London: Pinter and Martin, 2008 [1956]), 3.
7 Joseph Zygmunt, 'Prophetic Failure and Chiliastic Identity: The Case of the Jehovah's Witnesses,' in *American Journal of Sociology*, vol. 75, no. 6 (May 1970): 926–948.
8 J. Gordon Melton, 'Spiritualization and Reaffirmation: What Really Happens When Prophecy Fails,' in *American Studies*, 26 (Fall 1985): 17–29.
9 Diana Tumminia, 'How Prophecy Never Fails: Interpretive Reason in a Flying Saucer Group,' in *Sociology of Religion*, 59 (1998): 165.
10 Simon Dein, *Lubavitcher Messianism: What Really Happens When Prophecy Fails?* (London: Continuum, 2011).
11 Evgeny Sergeev, *The Great Game, 1856–1907* (Baltimore: Johns Hopkins University Press, 2013).
12 Carol Peaker, 'We Are Not Barbarians: Literatureand the Russian Émigré Press in England, 1890–1905,' in *Interdisciplinary Studies in the Long Nineteenth Century*, 3 (2006).
13 *The British-Israel Ecclesia*, vol. 5, no. 45 (August 1911), 75.
14 *Quarterly Notes of the Protestant British Israel League*, vol. 7, no. 1 (January 1917), 7.
15 *The Prophetic News and Israel's Watchman*, no. 4 (April 1917), 64.
16 *The Banner of Israel*, vol. 43, no. 2,207 (16 April 1919), 139.
17 *The Banner of Israel*, vol. 43, no. 2,193 (8 January 1919), 19.

18 John Cumming, *The End* (London, 1855), 66.
19 Arno Gaebelein, *Hath God Cast Away His People* (London: Gospel, 1905), 234.
20 *The Banner of Israel*, vol. 40, no. 2,069 (23 August 1916), 336.
21 Paul Boyer, *When Time Shall Be No More* (Cambridge: Belknap, 2009), 156.
22 *The Telegraph*, no. 19,325 (20 March 1917), 7.
23 *The Prophetic News and Israel's Watchman*, no. 12 (December 1917), 185.
24 *Quarterly Notes of the Protestant British Israel League*, vol. 7, no. 3 (July 1917), 97.
25 *The Banner of Israel*, vol. 43, no. 2,243 (24 December 1919), 447.
26 *The Banner of Israel*, vol. 44, no. 2,256 (26 March 1920), 99.
27 *Exeter and Pymouth Gazette*, vol. 159, no. 26,528 (30 June 1931), 7.
28 *The Banner of Israel*, vol. 44, no. 2,253 (3 March 1920), 70.
29 *The Banner of Israel*, vol. 44, no. 2,253 (3 March 1920), 71.
30 *The Banner of Israel*, vol. 44, no. 2,256 (26 March 1920), 99.
31 *Middlesex County Times*, vol. 63, no. 4,072 (6 March 1926), 6.
32 *Wake Up*, vol. 8, no. 4 (August 1990), 87.
33 *Wake Up*, vol. 2, no. 9 (September 1978), 194.
34 *BIWF Quarterly*, vol. 2, no. 4 (October 1989), 7.
35 A.J. Ferris, *When Russia Invades Palestine* (London: Clarendon Press, 1939), 10.
36 *New Statesman* (9 January 1943), 18.
37 *The National Message*, vol. 55, no. 1,636 (March 1976), 74.
38 *Norfolk and Suffolk Journal and Diss Express*, no. 3,885 (21 April 1939), 2.
39 *The National Message*, vol. 24, no. 1,130 (24 October 1945), 199.
40 *The National Message*, vol. 22, no. 1,072 (4 August 1943), 128.
41 'Speech to Private Meeting of the United Kingdom Branch of the Empire Parliamentary Association, Houses of Parliament, London, 1943.' In J. van der Poel (ed.), *Selections from the Smuts Papers*, vol. 6 (Cambridge: Cambridge University Press, 1973), 461.
42 *The National Message*, vol. 33, no. 1,087 (1 March 1944), 34.
43 *The Homeland Pilot*, no. 25 (July 1931), 102.
44 Walter Milner, *The Russian Chapters of Ezekiel* (London: Covenant Publishing, 1933), 14.
45 *The National Message*, vol. 50, no. 1,578 (May 1971), 151.
46 *Brith*, no. 292 (April 1970), 108.
47 *The National Message*, vol. 24, no. 1,120 (6 June 1944), 106.
48 *The National Message*, vol. 22, no. 1,074 (1 September 1943), 141.
49 *Brith*, no. 5 (February 1946), 2.
50 *The Telegraph*, no. 28,755 (21 August 1947), 6; Talal Nizameddin, *Russia and the Middle East* (London: Hurst, 1999), 18.
51 *Brith*, no. 13 (October 1946), 7.
52 *Brith*, no. 348 (January 1975), 28–31.
53 *Brith*, no. 17 (April 1947), 7.
54 *Brith*, no. 13 (October 1946), 7.
55 Ferris, *When Russia Invades Palestine*, 10.
56 *The National Message*, vol. 45, no. 1,523 (October 1966), 308.
57 Gresty, *Christ or the Kremlin*, 7–8.
58 *Brith*, no. 27 (February 1948), 1.
59 *Eastbourne Gazette*, no. 5,199 (14 January 1959), 7.
60 Gresty, *Satan Fights for Muscovy*, 1.
61 Michael Barkun, 'Millenarianism in the Modern World,' in *Theory and Society*, 1, no. 2 (1974): 117–146; Kenneth Berrien, 'Shelter Owners, Dissonance and the Arms Race,' in *Social Problems*, vol. 11, no. 1 (1963): 87–91.
62 *The Covenant Message*, vol. 29, no. 2 (February 1960), 62.
63 Gordon Wong, 'Isaiah's Opposition to Egypt in Isaiah 31,' in *Vetus Testamentum*, 46, no. 3 (July 1996): 392–401.

64 Job 34: 15–17.
65 *The National Message*, vol. 41, no. 1,472 (July 1962), 201.
66 *The Ambassador* (April 1966), 9.
67 *Brith*, no. 298 (October 1970), 21.
68 *The National Message*, vol. 47, no. 1,548 (November 1968), 362.
69 *The National Message*, vol. 45, no. 1,523 (October 1966), 308.
70 *Brith*, no. 322 (November 1972), 24.
71 *Brith*, no. 321 (October 1972), 4.
72 *Brith*, no. 380 (February, 1978), 23.
73 *The Message*, vol. 1, no. 4 (October 1981), 24–25.
74 *Brith*, no. 332 (September 1973), 11.
75 *The Message*, vol. 1, no. 3 (September 1981), 7.
76 *The Link*, vol. 4, no. 4 (January 1985), 93.
77 'Biography of Walter Walker: Discussion of Contentious Material,' National Archives, DEFE 24/648.
78 *Wake Up*, vol. 7, no. 2 (March 1988), 31.
79 *Wake Up*, vol. 7, no. 9 (June 1989), 197.
80 *Wake Up*, vol. 7, no. 6 (November 1988), 139.
81 *Wake Up*, vol. 7, no. 1 (January 1988), 21.
82 *The Message*, vol. 1, no. 4 (October 1981), 24–25.
83 *Covenant Voice* (January 1990), 5–7.
84 *Covenant Voice* (March 1990), 5.
85 *Covenant Voice* (January 1990), 5–7.
86 *Wake Up*, vol. 8, no. 1 (January 1990), 5.
87 *Wake Up*, vol. 8, no. 8 (September 1991), 177.
88 *Covenant Voice* (June 1990), 6.
89 'British Israel World Federation Annual Accounts and Reports for 1989,' British Library, ZC.9.a.2499, 13.
90 *Covenant Voice* (September 1990), 6.
91 *Wake Up*, vol. 8, no. 9 (November 1991), 197.
92 'New Covenant Times Supplement,' in *Wake Up*, vol. 12, no. 2 (March 1998), 1.
93 *Wake Up*, vol. 8, no. 5 (November 1990), 109.
94 'British Israel World Federation Annual Accounts and Reports for 1990,' British Library, ZC.9.a.2499, 13.
95 *Covenant Viewpoint* (Autumn 2017), 2–3.
96 *Crown and Commonwealth*, vol. 2, no. 3 (Autumn 2002), 9.
97 *Covenant Nations*, vol. 2, no. 12 (2013), 5.
98 *Covenant Nations*, vol. 2, no. 12 (2013), 8.

8   British-Israelism and the European Union

On 10 June 1978, Australian diplomat Vic Garland flew to Brussels to reason with the European Commission about their policy of subsidising European lamb production. The following week, *The Economist* reported their meeting, noting that 'the Australians feel they have nothing left to lose and have started an argument with the Commission over who is the more protectionist.'[1]

These events were recorded somewhat differently, at the start of July, by a contributor to *Wake Up*, the monthly periodical of the BIWF. Reflecting on the commission's rebuttal of Mr. Garland, the writer opined:

> It is more evident than ever that the Common Market is emerging as an instrument to break up and destroy the unity of the English speaking world which constitute modern Israel, who – twenty centuries ago – escaped the Satanic ascendancy of Babylon.[2]

Throughout the twentieth century, the thousands-strong British-Israelist community of the United Kingdom threw their weight behind the campaign to prevent and subsequently to annul Britain's membership of the European Union. Throughout this period, prominent public figures – MPs, MLAs, television personalities and peers – wedded British-Israelist conviction with Eurosceptic zeal. What follows is a discussion of the points of commonality between these two political, cultural and religious traditions.

As we have seen, there are some limitations to the claim that the topos of Israel represented, for Israelists, providentially mandated imperialism or even racial superiority. The concept of chosenness – both in its Biblical and British-Israelist settings – is more associated with separation, with the strengthening of boundaries between God's people and the nations, and with the maintenance of authenticity, than with power, prestige or status. It is in this light that British-Israelist attitudes to the European Union should be read. It is only in this context that some British attitudes to the European Union can be understood. The following sections trace British-Israelist responses to the sequence of events which mark the history of Britain's involvement with the European project from the Treaty of Rome up until the 2016 referendum.

British-Israelism and Europe

The first great schism-causing controversy, within British-Israelist circles, hinged on the question of whether mainland Europeans (and most importantly Germans) could be part of Israel. The very earliest British-Israelists believed that Britons and Germans both constituted the nations of Israel. By the end of the nineteenth century, however, this position became politically untenable. 'Anti-Teutonists' like Edward Hine promoted the idea that many mainland Europeans were of Canaanite or Assyrian rather than Israelitish stock. This position became mainstream during the period when Germany and Britain reached the nadir of their relations at the start of the twentieth century. During the First World War, a consensus grew – fuelled by the editorials printed in *The Banner of Israel* – around the claim that Germany was certainly *not* Israel and, more specifically that Germany was in fact Assyria. In 1918, Ernest Jordan wrote that

> the Germans in many respects, are very like what the Assyrians were.... We have Assyrian cruelty and German cruelty. Since the opening of this fearful war, the Germans have been revealed to us as a remarkably cruel and ruthless people.[3]

'The Assyrians are generally accepted as the Teutonic people of Europe,' wrote another in the following year.[4]

Menno Spiering has proposed a cultural account of the 'essentialised Euroscepticism' evident in many quarters of British life. Many British people, Spiering argues, consider themselves to be fundamentally un-European. Spiering traces the cultural roots of Euroscepticism to the Protestant reformation, when the image of Britain as a 'proud and independent Island race' and the image of Europe as 'Catholic, corrupt and collective,' first emerged. Spiering notes that cultural Eurosceptics often invoke 'islandness' both as a distinguishing aspect of British character and as an explanation of Britain's distinctiveness from Europe. Spiering dates the origins of 'islandness' to the end of the Hundred Years' War.[5] Grob-Fitzgibbon agrees that Britain has long 'revelled in its island nature,' despite being easily accessible from mainland Europe.[6] Islandness was not simply a matter of geographical location, after all. In his analysis of cultural Euroscepticism, Ben Wellings has dubbed Britain 'the Scotland of Europe': 'vocally different,' 'proud of its difference,' and secessionist in temperament.[7]

The presentation of Britain as an island nation is central to British-Israelist mythology. Firstly, several prophecies upon which British-Israelists rested their claims of Israelitish descent centred around the notion of Britain as an island nation. 'The British live in islands (or dwell alone) as Israel were to,' Douglas Parker reminded his readers in 1922.[8] This claim was based upon Numbers 23, and Balaam's vision of the people 'who live apart,' and on the promise, in Jeremiah 31, that Israel would be sent to 'the far off isles.' 'Islandness' goes hand-in-hand with 'living apart.' It denotes separation, fortification and the maintenance of authenticity. 'At the Dover crossing we are a little over twenty miles from the French coast,' Patience Strong wrote, 'but they remain foreign and we remain Islanders proud of our separateness.'[9] As a corollary to this, British-Israelists have long objected to and campaigned against any efforts to eliminate the natural boundaries between Britain and Europe. The first British-Israelist campaign against the Channel tunnel was launched in 1916.[10] When the tunnel was first approved, in 1964, British-Israelists were scornful of those who, 'unaware of Israel's destined separateness,' had celebrated the announcement.[11] 'It was Almighty God . . . that set His reformed servant people apart in the Appointed Isles of the sea,' wrote one British-Israelist in 1988, but 'it is the One World enthusiasts who seek to defy this act of providence and link the Kingdom Isles with the EEC Babylon.'[12]

British-Israel and alliances

In the reign of King Hezekiah, a treaty was forged between Nubian Egypt and Judah. Sennacherrib of Assyria had moved to punish the Kingdom of Judah for her rebellion against his rule and Hezekiah turned to Memphis for support. In the twenty-ninth and thirty-first chapters of Isaiah, this decision is condemned by the prophet. 'Woe to those who rely on Egypt,' says the prophet, 'woe to those who rely on her horses, on her multitudes of chariots, on the strength of her horsemen.'[13]

There have been various interpretations of this text. Some have noted that the prophet condemns the leadership of Judah for failing to consult the oracle before making strategic decisions. Others have noted the perennial association of Egypt with slavery. Gordon Wong, in his analysis, notes that this passage appears to counsel not against the wisdom of the decision but rather to condemn the lack of faith in God which this decision denotes. For in making a pact with Egypt, Judah demonstrates a lack of conviction that God will protect His people in their hour of need. Secondly, it appears to demonstrate hubris: the leadership of Judah appears to have forgotten – in forging this alliance – that God's will will be done, regardless of the might of men.[14]

This warning against reliance on foreign powers, and the association of alliances with infidelity, is a perennial theme of British-Israelist literature. Often these condemnations of treaties and alliances represented a warning against human hubris. For example, in the aftermath of the First World War, when the nations of the world sought to build an omnilateral treaty organisation, the British-Israelists condemned it as a work of Satan. Satan was trying, they believed, 'to subtly' draw mankind into his plan 'in the temptation which he offers to the pride of men to secure for themselves, in their own way, blessings which are to be bestowed by God and to be administered by His chosen people.'[15] The League of Nations promised peace, but only God could offer true peace. As such, the League of Nations was a 'man-made millennium.'[16]

Isaiah warned, should Israel rely on Egypt, that Israel would be humiliated. The same promise was made by British-Israelists against Britain's entering into multi-national treaties in the twentieth century. These 'man-made millenia' were doomed to 'go down to posterity as an example of man's presumption and disregard of God's will and intentions.' Britain, if she fell in line with such plans would share in that humiliation.[17]

The answer for Britain, especially in her times of acute need, was not to rely on other nations or on man-made plans for world peace. Rather it was to turn fully to God, to rely fully on God. This was the attitude which informed British-Israelist responses to the European project. Britain could expect to be humiliated, like Judah, because she had 'consistently and wilfully rebelled against the laws of God,' but more importantly because she had 'failed to turn to Him with all our hearts.' 'All that is asked for,' as Felix Lutz wrote, 'is a willingness to be rescued, an inquiry of the Lord to do it for us. He will do all that is necessary.'[18]

Underpinning all of this – the prophetic claims of Isaiah and of the British-Israelists – is the assertion of Britain-Israel's singularity and her authenticity: two characteristics which could be fatally compromised by her entering into an international treaty. At the start of the century, Britain was 'in a state of distinction from other nations, peculiar and unique, dominant and supremely blessed, helpful and indispensable to the happiness of the world.' This position could only be maintained if she should 'preserve [her] divinely appointed splendid isolation.'[19] God had told Israel that He had 'separated us from other people' and that 'we were to remain separate.' He had 'warned us of the results of disregarding His instructions.' As such, British-Israelists cautioned that, if 'the nation is pushed into the market, disaster is certainly ahead.'[20]

British-Israelist responses to the Treaty of Rome

Britain was originally excluded from the European project. In 1958, the Treaty of Rome brought about the creation of the European Economic Community. It was signed by delegates from Belgium, France, Italy, Luxembourg, the Netherlands and West Germany. The intention of the Treaty of Rome was to steadily reduce and eventually disband all obstacles to trade between the European nations and to facilitate a degree of economic interdependency between the powers that had recently been at war with one another.

At this point, British-Israelists were already vocally opposed to Britain's membership of other international bodies. In the aftermath of the Second

World War, British-Israelists were assured that the best course of action for Britain was to maintain an attitude of isolationism. 'We must get rid of our foreign investments,' wrote one, in 1948.[21] In December 1957, the then editor of *Brith* – A.E.H. Parrot – wrote that the proposition of such agreements constituted a call 'to give up our rights as a sovereign state and tie ourselves up with other nations.' The editors of *Brith* called such attempts to surrender sovereignty 'the greatest sin that Israel can commit.'[22] British-Israelists were confident, as the 1960s progressed, that there was no appetite for Britain's integration into the European community and that 'a majority of the people would almost certainly recoil from [the treaty] if they but realised the truth.'[23] Britain had 'voted for governments opposed to this course' and, as such, the argument was settled.[24]

The Treaty of Rome, however, was considered especially objectionable because of the implicit association of Rome with the papacy. In the years leading up to the signing of the treaty, many of the organs of the British-Israelist community in England published editorials accentuating the distinctiveness of the providence that belonged to Britain compared to that which belonged to the continental European nations. Often, this distinction was made by accentuating the Protestant character of Britain, compared with the Catholic character of continental Europe. For example, the editorial column of *Brith* featured the following comments in October 1948:

> Roman Catholic Gentile Europe is steeped in idolatry and worships idols and wealth and power and materialism in every form. God is calling modern Israel out, lest the judgments of God fall on her too. Prophecy reveals a people distinguished from Gentile Europe. It is a people whose national religion is based upon the Bible – Protestant, and only the Anglo-Saxon nations can claim this Israel mark. It was Revelation 18:4 which inspired the Reformers and they clearly and fearlessly identified Babylon with the Church of Rome, but the Sixteenth Century Protestant Reformation was not a complete fulfilment of Revelation 18:4, it was anticipatory of fulfilment to take place when Babylonish Europe is destroyed under the Seven Vials.[25]

When, therefore, the treaty was ratified, creating an umbilical connection between the European project and the city of Rome, this confirmed what British-Israelists already suspected. They warned that 'the Roman Empire is destined to be revived.' As 'staunch' Protestants, they stood ready to 'stoutly maintain' Britain's Protestant heritage and to assert that 'we must not join with Roman Catholic Europe.'[26] 'We are disobeying the commands of God,' wrote Winifred Matthews in 1968, 'we are not sending forth the Glory of God to others, because we do not have it ourselves. Instead, we are seeking alliances with Rome – ecclesiastically and politically.'[27]

Many British-Israelists believed that the Catholic Church had been behind all kinds of attempts, over many centuries, to erode the entitativity and authenticity of nation-states. The Pope had asserted his authority over and above that of territorial monarchs. The Jesuits, they believed, had fomented revolutionary sentiment in France in order to precipitate a global embrace of enlightenment values. The Treaty of Rome, therefore, was but the latest and most undisguised of these attempts. As Commander Donald Macmillan – president of the BIWF – put it in a letter to Prime Minister Harold Macmillan:

> The long suffering people [of Europe] will not forget that the Paris Commune, and its child the Marxist Revolution in Russia, are respectively the monster progeny of those caricatures of the Christian Gospel imposed upon them for centuries by the Roman Church.[28]

The radical association of Catholicism with the European project – seemingly demonstrated by the fact of the existence of the Treaty of Rome – continued to be a thematic presence in the writings of British-Israelist Eurosceptics for decades to come. In 1969, the editorial of *Brith* advised its readers that 'the Common Market is not only evil, but it is doomed to failure.'[29]

In 1972, Clifford Smyth portrayed the European project as a papal conspiracy whose sole aim was to dismantle the United Kingdom.[30] With the passing of the Maastricht Treaty in 1992, British-Israelist writers suggested that 'the design of the EC from its inception was an idea in the mind of the Vatican to re-catholicise Europe.'[31] According to the pseudo-scientific racial theories espoused by British-Israelists, the affinity of continental Europeans for Catholicism had a genealogical explanation. The 'confederacy of powers' which formed the 'Babylonish Roman' system were believed to be 'partly Esau orientated in racial descent.'[32]

In 1973, C.S. McKelvey interpreted the relationship between Britain and Europe in light of Daniel 2. This chapter recounts the dream of Nebuchadnezzar. The King dreams of a giant statue with feet of clay and iron. McKelvey believed that the statue represented the Church of Rome, whilst three of the ten toes of the statue represented the EEC countries. The Roman Church had taken over the Roman Empire and had 'carried it into the present day' with the construction of the Common Market.[33] The *topoi* of Rome and Babylon are intimately linked in Protestant, millenarian tradition. With Britain's entrance into the European Union, many British-Israelists came to see parallels between the European Union and Israel's oldest enemy.

British-Israelist responses to Britain's membership in the European Union

In 1964, *The National Message* was already promoting the work of the Anti-Common Market League. This organisation met at Pont Street in London and was led by three Conservative Party politicians: Michael Shay, John Paul and Viscount Hinchingbrooke.[34] In 1966, John Paul penned a number of articles which were published in *The National Message*.[35] The association of Euroscepticism and British-Israelism had already begun. On 24 May 1971, at Caxton Hall in Westminster, the BIWF promoted a public meeting 'on the effects of Britain joining the Common Market.' It was organised jointly by the Protestant Truth Society and the Lord's Day Observance Society. The speakers included the long-standing general secretary of the Lord's Day Observance Society, Harold Legerton, Mr P.H. Rand – senior Wycliffe preacher at the Protestant Truth Society – and Dr Basil Atkinson, the keeper of the manuscripts at the University of Cambridge Library.[36]

Despite the best efforts of the BIWF, events were already in motion to move Britain into a closer union with her continental neighbours. The early 1970s marked a period in which Britain's full membership of the European Communities was codified. In January 1972, a treaty of accession was signed, leading to the admission of Denmark, the UK and Ireland into the EEC. Following the general election of 1974, an electoral mandate was sought for continuing membership. A referendum was called the following year and the result demonstrated a sizeable majority of public support for Britain's membership.

The suggestion that Britain, having sacrificed her worldly prestige, would now compromise its authenticity and its separateness from 'the nations' was a frightful prospect for British-Israelists. In the early 1970s, British-Israelist publications made many declarations, predicting the doom that would befall Britain should she choose to join the EEC. The EEC was identified with the 'covenant of death' described in Isaiah 28. When this passage was read as the first lesson of morning prayer on the very morning that the British House of Commons voted in favour of a decision to accede to the Treaty of Rome (on 29 October 1971), this was understood by British-Israelists to be a sign, and a 'powerful warning.'[37] In this chapter, the prophet envisions a covenant signed by the 'rulers of the people' with 'the realm of the dead.' Blenkinsopp explains that this terminology is used here to describe a twofold blasphemy: the treaty signed by the rulers of Judea with the Egyptians in anticipation of the Assyrian invasion and the 'parody of Sinai' which was involved in the ceremonial covenant made with the Canaanite God Motu.[38] In these dual acts, Israel is marked as an adulterer, seeking other sources of protection from the Assyrian foe. The treaty of accession to the EEC, British-Israelists claimed, was such a 'covenant of death.'[39] This prophetic claim had practical ramifications. *The National Message* published a range of stories promising doom and hardship if Britain should vote for continued membership. 'Rabies,' Lieutenant-Commander Michael Hart predicted, 'would become endemic amongst the foxes and bats and the natural fauna.' 'If we lose,' he continued, 'this is the Anglo-Saxon twilight for Britain.'[40] Michael Bennett, who would later become president of the British-Israel Bible Truth Foundation, claimed that any attempt to join the Common Market would constitute 'a large step down the path towards self-destruction.'[41] C.S. McKelvey wrote that membership of the EEC would lead to the decimation of Britain's 'farms, orchards and fisheries.'[42] As such, the campaign to pursue this self-destructive path was described as diabolical. 'Satan is attempting to make us one of the European nations,' claimed the editors of *Brith*. 'The Devil is hard at work making us the slaves of Europe.'[43] *The National Message* provided all of its readers with an 'Anti-Common Market Petition Form.' Emblazoned across the bottom of the petition form were the words: 'Come out of her my people that ye be not partakers in her sin.'[44]

At every stage in the process, British-Israelists continued to predict that God would not allow His people to become 'lost' in 'the nations.' 'This is the year,' wrote one commentator, 'when Britain will come to herself. We will no longer want to join Europe. . . . We will make a new start with God.'[45] They were scornful of those in the political elite who had adopted European membership as their project and – in doing so – who had set their face against divine fiat. Their efforts were doomed, British-Israelists predicted, and 'everything they touched [would] turn to ashes.'[46]

The BIWF's most high-profile campaigner in the fight to prevent Britain entering the EEC was Ross McWhirter. McWhirter was – at this point – a recognisable television personality. At the 54th Annual Congress of the BIWF, held in Sheffield on 29 September 1973, McWhirter delivered an address entitled 'Deceived in her Grants.' In this address – later published in *The National Message* – McWhirter made a series of claims concerning the role of the EEC in relation to British national sovereignty. Britain, he claimed, had a particular talent for flourishing in the conditions of adversity. Financial gain or even international prestige were not a fair price for sovereignty or authenticity. 'This,' he said, 'is why the British Israel belief is a true statement.'[47] The following year saw victory for pro-Europeans in Britain. The British people decided to remain in the European community. British-Israelists continued to discredit the result. 'The people who voted Yes,' wrote Michael Clark, 'were blinded by a propaganda blitz.'[48] Nonetheless, the referendum of 1975 was decisive and would appear to settle the matter of Britain's membership for a number of decades.

British-Israelist Euroscepticism

The democratic mandate for Britain's membership of the European Community did not prevent British-Israelists from continuing to campaign against European membership. In 1976, Reginald Cox threatened that God's 'instructions in this crucial matter remain as they have existed for more than thirty centuries: Come out – or take the consequences.'[49]

Britain's membership was seen by many as an indication both of her diminishing role in the world and – by extension – of her infidelity. 'We have become a third rate power,' wrote one: 'a small island.'[50] Now, though, British-Israelist prophetic claims were again recalibrated in order to demonstrate the correlation between Britain's role in the world and the role ascribed to Israel in the Hebrew Bible. The European Union was now characterised in British-Israelist literature as Babylon, the slaver of Israel. In 1972, Reginald Bradbury wrote that the 'Tory government are betraying the trust of the British Electorate by taking this formerly great nation into European bondage.'[51] In October 1973, *Brith* reported that 'we have gone into the ECM that is surrounded by three nations belonging to the Babylon image.' These countries had 'every right to be worried about the future,' claimed the editorial, 'for they are gentiles.'[52]

The authors of the prophecies of Daniel used the cultural and historical memory of Israel's tribulation in Babylon as a strategy for warning against the diffusion of Israel's singular character in the context of the Seleucid supremacy.[53] This tropological use of the figure of Babylon was revisited by the author of the book of Revelation.[54] It was revisited again by the Protestant Reformers of the seventeenth century in their critique of Roman Popery. In the Biblical texts, God instructs the people of Israel to avoid corruption by avoiding contact with Babylonish things and practices.[55] In much the same way, British-Israelists represent the EU as a force committed to the diffusion British singularity. As such, all things which were associated with the European Union now became identifiable with Babylon. Eschewing those things, therefore, became a marker of identity.

Fears were widespread that the Anglo-Saxon system of Common Law would be replaced by 'Roman' jurisprudence.[56] As early as 1961, Commander MacMillan promised that entering the EEC would destroy the system of Common Law and would 'draw us back to the rule of Roman concepts.'[57] Victor Walkley warned against 'the abandonment of . . . our Common Law for the One Nation concept that follows the Roman Law of Europe.'[58] For many Eurosceptics, British Common Law is a touchstone and a symbol of national sovereignty and distinctiveness. As Jeremy Black wrote, the Common Law tradition is perceived as:

> the cause of legal, intellectual and political divergence between England and the Continent, the separation of English, and thus eventually Anglo-American, traditions, theories and practices from their Continental counterparts.[59]

Many British-Israelists complimented this claim with the argument that British Common Law had its roots in the 'Shemitic law,' whereas 'Roman law' was Babylonian in origin.[60]

On 27 October 1970, Tony Benn MP told the House of Commons that he had been sent a pamphlet in the mid-1960s – entitled *The Battle for the Inch* – which he had 'treasured' for four years. In describing the pamphlet, he identified a Biblical argument against metrication based on Leviticus 19:35.[61] The pamphlet to which Benn referred was written by the prominent British-Israelist Hew B. Colquhoun.[62] British-Israelists expressed violent opposition to decimalisation. One editorial in the June 1978 edition of the magazine *Wake Up* referred to the 'chaos of anti-Christian measurement' and the 'atheistic metre.'[63] The metre was 'false' and based on a 'false premise.'[64] In the same year, *The National Message* responded to a story first published in the *Express* – which predicted that 'it will be possible to fine a draper £250 and send him to prison for selling four feet of curtain material,' – with the claim that 'the feet of clay are showing signs of faltering,' that the 'nations of modern Israel,' were being instructed to 'come out!'[65] Any number of 'European' innovations, from 'decimal currency' to 'the Europeanization of road signs' to 'the adoption of the breathalyser,' were described as examples of covert federalism.[66] BIWF President Michael Clark revisited and reiterated many of Colquhoun's arguments in a pamphlet of 2012 entitled *Britain's God-given Scientific Heritage Destroyed by Metrication Madness*. In this work, Clark claims that the metric system is a creature of the French Revolution. The same genesis is described for the European Union. As such, the introduction of metric measurements, Clark argues, is an attempt to ensnare the British in an 'atheistic' system.[67]

In the Babylonian context, the people of God were described as having an opportunity to exhibit their distinctiveness and, by extension, their commitment.[68] Apocalyptic writing, according to Anathea Portier-Young, became a powerful cultural tool for those seeking to retain positive distinctiveness and entitativity in the precarious context of the Seleucid supremacy.[69] British-Israelists lived in equally uncertain times. And whilst Britain's membership in the European Union had been anticipated as a mark of defeat, it unexpectedly presented Israelists with the opportunity to hone a new, minority identity: that of Euroscepticism. Britain was no longer a nation on its own, but – like Israel – it was now able to take on the especially entitative role of the colonised, even *enslaved* minority.

Despite the assurance of authenticity that could be attained in the attitude of Euroscepticism, British-Israelists were always enjoined to heed the words spoken by the 'voice from heaven' described in Revelation 18: 'Come out of her, my people, that ye be not partakers of her sins, and that ye receive not of her.' The threat remained that, should Israel tarry in Babylon for too long, she would become genealogically and providentially deracinated. This, according to some British-Israelists, had been the fate of some other Israel nations. Belgium, for instance, 'due to her involvement in the EEC,' had 'become lost.'[70] They looked forward to a date – prophesied in Hosea 2:5–7 – when the 'covenant of death' would be destroyed by the Lord and that 'EEC Babylon would drink from the sacred revels of Britain-Israel's heritage no more.'[71] As such, when the opportunity arose to depart from Babylon in 2016, it was considered by British-Israelists to be a moment of profound eschatological significance.

British-Israelist responses to the EU referendum of 2016

British-Israelists do not typically make economic arguments for Britain's withdrawal from the European Union. Prominent British-Israelist

Eurosceptics have conceded that withdrawal from the European Union would lead to deepening isolation and even impoverishment. So – in 1982 – Francis Thomas was able to predict that 'we may not be economically viable' in the event of leaving the European Union. Furthermore, he predicted that 'the number of the unemployed may be great.' Nonetheless, 'Europe will have to learn the lesson that Egypt learned: Israel belongs to God.' Once again, chosenness did not correlate with prestige in the British-Israelist prophetic system.[72]

Withdrawal from the European Union held great promise for British-Israelists not in the economic benefits that they could reap, but rather in the sense of Godly authenticity which political sovereignty promised. In 1982, James Robbie predicted that the EEC would be destroyed. When this event came to pass, he claimed, Britain would be gripped 'with an outpouring of patriotic sentiment.'[73] Similar claims were made by Robert Philips thirty years later when, on 21 May 2016, he addressed a rally in support of the Leave campaign:

> It was not until the remnant of Judah came out of Babylon, that God restored them as a people. They were filled with sadness, their harps were hung on the willow trees but Nehemiah tells us when they returned to Jerusalem, their harps were played again. A joy that will return to this land, especially to the House of God, as harps are taken down from the willow trees, and God brings us out of Euro-Babylon, to revive and restore our Christian heritage. This is a 'Battle for Britain'. This is not just a contest between two political campaigns and viewpoints. This is a BATTLE with the FORCES OF EVIL.[74]

Paul Boyd-Lee, a British-Israelist and sometime member of the Central Board of Finance of the Church of England, claimed that a primary motivation for many Christians who eventually chose to vote to leave the EU was an awareness of the continuities that existed, linking Biblical Babylon with the institutions of the European Union.[75]

For Michael Clark, the numerological significance of the dates of Britain's expected exit from the EU was evidence of a providential mandate for leaving. The number 1,260 has important connotations for all Christian millenarians. It represents the number of days invoked in Revelation 11 and 12 to describe the period of time during which the Gentiles will 'trample Jerusalem,' during which the 'two witnesses' will prophesy and during which 'the woman' will reside in the wilderness. Typically, historicists have suggested that the prophecies relating to 1,260 days actually refer to 1,260 years. Usually, the period of 1,260 years is taken to represent the period of the ascendancy of the papacy, from the demise of the Ostrogothic power in the fifth century until the rise of the secular revolutions in the eighteenth. In Michael Clark's system, however, the period is taken to represent the lifespan of a particular doctrine: replacement theology. Clark dates the origins of this doctrine to 758. Since that point, he argues, the diminution of *racial* Israel's prophetic role has been largely proportional to the ascent of the belief that *spiritual* Israel (that is the Church) has superseded racial Israel. The nadir of this humiliation for Israel, he writes, came 'with the attempt to create a European superpower based on the Treaty of Rome in 1957.' This event represented a move by 'spiritual Israel' – the Roman Catholic Church – to finally eradicate the sovereignty of national Israel. 'The recovery of Sovereignty by the United Kingdom from the European Union,' Clark writes, 'is the necessary precursor to the return of Jesus Christ as King of kings to take up the Throne of David.'[76]

But British-Israelists did not confine themselves to commenting on events leading up to the referendum. On the contrary, they picketed, campaigned and held rallies in support of the Leave campaign. Indeed, some ties existed in the period leading up to the referendum between fringe elements of the United Kingdom Independence Party and British-Israelist institutions. In the April 2016 edition of *Bible Truth* – principal organ of the British Israel Bible Truth Foundation – the editors cited and commended the work of a group called 'Christian Soldiers for UKIP.' The latter organised fringe events at the UKIP party conference in 2014 and 2015.[77]

In the aftermath of the 2016 referendum on Britain's membership of the European Union, the BIWF released a pamphlet entitled *A Day to Rejoice*. In it, Michael Clark referred to the act of 'national adultery' that had been committed upon Britain's entry into the European Union. As a result of the referendum victory, he wrote, Britain was 'now returning to her first husband.' In this, Clark draws heavily upon imagery derived from the book of Hosea. The prophet warns Israel against the sin of national adultery, comparing the infidelity of his own wife – Gomer – with the infidelity of Israel to Yahweh. Israel is accused of infidelity because of her worship of other Gods, but the prophet also makes reference to attempts by Israel to secure support and help from rival powers – Egypt and Assyria – rather than depending on the Lord.[78]

God, it is claimed, demonstrated his favour for the Leave campaign in the course of the referendum process. Shortly after the referendum, Boyd-Lee claimed that dramatic meteorological events which took place in the days around the referendum were indicators of the providential significance of the result. In particular, he claimed that the adverse weather conditions around London 'in the early hours on Referendum day' were an indication of God's displeasure with the capital: 'one of the few areas where a majority voted to remain with the European Union.'[79]

Conclusion

Writing in the mid-1980s, the bestselling poet and ardent British-Israelist Patience Strong expressed her view of the relationship between Britain and the continent:

> Willing to be friends, and allies if need be, but remaining British, apart, with our own language, our own history and our own Church. Come

out from among them my people, and be ye separate. Thus speaks the Bible out of its ancient authority.[80]

In 1982, a British-Israelist writer described the role of the British-Israelists in modern life. He acknowledged that British-Israelists' claim of national election was sometimes challenged by the evidence. Furthermore, he acknowledged that both British and non-British readers of British-Israelist literature were likely to reject it. On this basis, he proposed a new motto for the British-Israelist community: 'no-one likes us. We don't care!'[81] One axiomatic definition of British-Israelism describes it as a form of 'jingoism with a Biblical sanction.'[82] The tradition of reading British-Israelism in this way stems partly from a teleological perspective, based on observation of American, Christian-Identitarian Israelism, and partly from a belief (exemplified by Anthony Smith) that English typological identification with Biblical Israel was an extreme manifestation of supersessionism.[83] In recent times, Andrew Crome and others have expressed doubt about the usefulness of this paradigm. One of Crome's most important contributions has been to point out the very significant difference between ethnic supremacy and ethnic chosenness. For most of those who suggested that England had a particular providential role in the history of God's people, that role did not denote grandeur, prestige or wealth. Often it denoted struggle and marginalisation. As one writer put it, in 1992, the role of the chosen nation was simple: 'to remain separated unto God in national, local and personal life.'[84]

In April 2019, then Foreign Secretary Boris Johnson urged Prime Minister Teresa May to channel the spirit of the Israelites escaping from slavery in Egypt. The template for this form of nationalism is available as a tool for assuaging anxieties relating to perceived minority or marginal status in the pages of the Hebrew Bible. It was to the slaves of Egypt, rather than to the Kings of Israel, that the British turned in the twentieth century, when they sought a model of authentic nationhood.[85]

Notes

1 *The Economist*, vol. 267, no. 7,033 (17 June 1978), 63.
2 *Wake Up*, vol. 2, no. 6 (June 1978), 135.
3 *The Banner of Israel*, vol. 42, no. 2,152 (27 March 1918), 120.
4 *The Banner of Israel*, vol. 43, no. 2,207 (16 April 1919), 139.
5 Menno Spiering, *A Cultural History of British Euroscepticism* (Basingstoke: Palgrave Macmillan, 2014), 44, 47.
6 Grob-Fitzgibbon, *Continental Drift*, 7.
7 Ben Wellings, 'Beyond Awkwardness: England, the European Union and the End of Integration,' in Karine Tournier-Sol (ed.), *The UK Challenges to Europeanization* (London: Springer, 2015), 33–51.
8 Parker, *Why Great Britain Will Never Be Destroyed*, 2.
9 Strong, *Someone Had to Say It*, 56.
10 *The Banner of Israel*, vol. 40, no. 2,066 (2 August 1916), 323.
11 *The National Message*, vol. 43, no. 1,492 (March 1964), 70.

12 *Wake Up*, vol. 7, no. 2 (March 1988), 29.

13 Isaiah 31:1–9.

14 Wong, 'Isaiah's Opposition to Egypt in Isaiah 31,' 392–401.

15 *The Banner of Israel*, vol. 43, no. 2,203 (19 March 1919), 103.

16 *The Banner of Israel*, vol. 43, no. 2,206 (9 April 1919), 129.

17 *The Banner of Israel*, vol. 43, no. 2,222 (30 July 1919), 264.

18 *The Covenant Message*, vol. 29, no. 2 (February 1960), 62.

19 *The Banner of Israel*, vol. 43, no. 2,222 (30 July 1919), 264.

20 *The National Message*, vol. 41, no. 1,474 (September 1962), 262.

21 *Brith*, no. 30 (May 1948), 5.

22 *Brith*, no. 143 (December 1957), 7.

23 *The National Message*, vol. 47, no. 1,538 (January 1968), 19.

24 *The National Message*, vol. 47, no. 1,541 (April 1968), 116.

25 *Brith*, no. 35 (October 1948), 16.

26 *The National Message*, vol. 41, no. 1,470 (May 1962), 147.

27 *The National Message*, vol. 47, no. 1,538 (January 1968), 30.

28 *The National Message*, vol. 41, no. 1,475 (October 1962), 291.

29 *Brith*, no. 286 (October 1969), 4.

30 Smyth, *Axis Against Ulster*, 9, 11.

31 *Wake Up*, vol. 9, no. 9 (May 1993), 203.

32 *Wake Up*, vol. 12, no. 4 (July 1998), 84.

33 *Brith*, no. 326 (March 1973), 3–5.

34 *The National Message*, vol. 43, no. 1,490 (January 1964), 19.

35 *The National Message*, vol. 45, no. 1,523 (October 1966), 311.

36 *The National Message*, vol. 50, no. 1,578 (May 1971), 159.

37 *Crown and Commonwealth*, vol. 4, no. 4 (Winter 2004), 79.

38 Joseph Blenkinsopp, 'Judah's Covenant with Death (Isaiah 28, 14–22),' in *Vetus Testamentum*, 50, no. 4 (January 2000): 465–483.

39 *New Covenant Times*, no. 23 (May 1992), 1; *The Kingdom Voice*, vol. 33, no. 8 (August 1972), 2.

40 *The National Message*, vol. 54, no. 1,624 (March 1975), 73.

41 *Bible Impact*, no. 9 (December 1972), 4.

42 *Brith*, no. 305 (May 1971), 9.

43 *Brith*, no. 324 (January 1973), 10–11; *Brith*, no. 335 (December 1973), 11.

44 *The National Message*, vol. 50, no. 1,577 (April 1971), 127.

45 *Brith*, no. 301 (January 1971), 3.

46 *The National Message*, vol. 53, no. 1619 (October 1974), 299.

47 McWhirter, *Ross Was Right*, 1; *The National Message*, vol. 53, no. 1,611 (February 1974), 38.

48 *Wake Up*, vol. 8, no. 7 (July 1991), 150.

49 *The National Message*, vol. 55, no. 1,642 (September 1976), 262.

50 *Brith*, no. 301 (January 1971), 3.

51 *The Kingdom Voice*, vol. 33, no. 12 (December 1972), 1.

52 *Brith*, no. 333 (October 1973), 5.

53 Rainer Albertz, *A History of Israelite Religion in the Old Testament Period, Volume 2* (Louisville: Westminster John Knox, 1994), 564; Anathea Portier-Young, *Apocalypse Against Empire* (Cambridge: Eerdmans, 2014), 115.

54 Revelation 17–18.

55 Isaiah 52: 11.

56 *The Kingdom Voice*, vol. 33, no. 6 (June 1972), 3.

57 *The National Message*, vol. 40, no. 1,462 (September 1961), 266.

58 *Wake Up*, vol. 12, no. 4 (July 1998), 77.

59 Jeremy Black, *Convergence or Divergence: Britain and the Continent* (London: Palgrave Macmillan, 1994), 117.

60 *The National Message*, vol. 35, no. 1395 (February 1956).
61 Hansard, *House of Commons Debate*, vol. 805, coll. 76–168 (27 October 1970).
62 *BIWF Quartlery*, vol. 2, no. 1 (January 1989), 7.
63 *Wake Up*, vol. 2, no. 6 (June 1978), 135.
64 *The National Message*, vol. 47, no. 1,540 (March 1968), 90.
65 *The National Message*, vol. 57, no. 1,661 (April 1978), 113.
66 *The National Message*, vol. 47, no. 1,552 (March 1969), 92.
67 Michael Clark, *Britain's God-Given Scientific Heritage Destroyed by Metrica-tion Madness* (Bishop Auckland: Covenant Publishing, 2012), 1.
68 Albertz, *A History of Israelite Religion*, 564.
69 Warren Carter, 'James C. Scott and New Testament Studies,' in Richard Hors-ley (ed.), *Hidden Transcripts and the Arts of Resistance: Applying the Work of James C. Scott to Jesus and Paul* (Atlanta: SBL, 2004), 81–94; Portier-Young, *Apocalypse Against Empire*, 115.
70 *Wake Up*, vol. 9, no. 8 (March 1993), 174.
71 *Wake Up*, vol. 6, no. 3 (November 1989), 266–268.
72 *Covenant Voice*, vol. 37, no. 10 (October 1982), 14.
73 *Covenant Voice*, vol. 37, no. 10 (October 1982), 28.
74 *Bible Truth*, no. 283 (September 2016), 7.
75 *Bible Truth*, no. 283 (September 2016), 12, 15–16.
76 Michael Clark, 'The Kingdom in our Midst,' 20 February 2018. www.britishisrael.co.uk/print_art.php?id=119.
77 *Bible Truth*, no. 264 (October 2011), 36.
78 Michael Clark, 'Britain and the Almighty in Covenant Bond,' 16 January 2018. www.associationcovenantpeople.org/2018/01/britain-almighty-covenant-bond/; Hosea 5: 13, 7:11.
79 *Bible Truth*, no. 283 (September 2016), 12.
80 Strong, *Someone Had to Say It*, 56.
81 *The Message*, vol. 1, no. 9 (March–April 1982), 3.
82 Reisenauer, 'That We May Do Israel's Work,' 104.
83 Smith, *Myths and Memories of the Nation*, 214.
84 *Wake Up*, vol. 9, no. 2 (March 1992), 31.
85 *Brith*, no. 7 (March 1946), 9.

Conclusion

On 5 January 1977, a Prayer and Prophecy Convention was held at the Alliance Hall in St James' Park. Prayers were said for 'the Queen and the Royal Family, the Israel Commonwealth, for Northern Ireland, for South Africa and for Rhodesia.'[1]

It is telling, perhaps, that the British-Israelists of 1977 believed that there was such strong affinity between themselves, the Queen and these three polities. In one sense, this event could be understood as an iteration of 'Die-Hardism': delusional imperialists, labouring in denial of the demise of the Empire.[2] The Empire, we might say, was the consummation of British-Israelist prophecy. By attending this vigil, the British-Israelists who gathered in St James' Park were exhibiting nothing more than their own disavowal of reality.

Alternatively, we might see this group of people as exhibiting profound feelings of affinity with the Protestants of Ulster and the white South Africans. Both of these groups were identified by Donald Akenson as 'covenanting peoples.' Their sense of being chosen by God provided them with a contextual framework within which to interpret their successes and failures. It prevented them from seeing or being troubled by the contingency of history, genealogy and ethnicity. This sensibility was shared by the Protestants of Britain for much of the four hundred years that divided the Protestant Reformation from the Prayer and Prophecy Convention of 1977. It was held also by the Protestants who gathered at that convention. As such, it remained, imprisoned in amber, in the British-Israel movement.

This sensibility was a bequest of the Protestant Reformation. It was the unintended consequence of two Protestant ideas: predestinarian soteriology and Biblicism. The latter provided Protestants with a vision of a chosen people who were identified and set apart by God both in their triumphs and in their afflictions. It provided an image of God, as desirous of maintaining strict boundaries and categories. The former provided an image of humanity, cleft in two. On the right, was the Godly remnant. On the left the mass of the reprobate.

In the history of Western culture, some have argued, feelings of connection to the nation supplanted feelings of connection to the divine. David Bell argued that secular religion was a product of the retreat of God from

Enlightenment society and the rise of Deism.[3] In this respect, his research compliments that of Elie Kedourie. Kedourie argues that autonomy, rather than religious heteronomy, is a theme which has its source in the Enlightenment, in the writings of Kant, which runs through the French revolutionary principle that 'the principle of sovereignty resides . . . in the nation,' through the 'addresses' of Fichte and which emerges in the secular nationalist movements of the nineteenth century. Kedourie acknowledges that nationalism can *use* religion. In Egypt and India and in contemporary Russia, we find holy and unholy alliances forged between ethnonationalists and religious leaders.[4] Perhaps we could argue that this is precisely what British-Israelists were doing in the nineteenth and twentieth centuries. That certainly appears to be the assumption at the heart of Kidd, Barkun and Reisenhauer's analyses. Even Anthony Smith countenances the possibility that nationalists may have 'sought, more or less consciously, to harmonise the two [biblical religion and nationalism] to fit nationalism into a biblical mould.' It is worth, nevertheless, considering the alternative.

Anthony Smith proposes that nationalism is a form of religion. At the very least, this can be interpreted as referring to a Durkheimian model of religion, wherein beliefs and ritual practices serve as an adhesive, forming and affirming the entitativity of the community. From this system, Smith scrupulously excludes religion. 'Religious nationalisms,' he observes, are more likely to exemplify 'nationalisms using religion.'[5] In the case of British-Israelism, I do not believe that this applies. British-Israelism is first and foremost a religious tradition, and it is one which explicitly avows its inheritance from the Biblicist traditions of the Protestant reformers and from the Biblical religion with which the Protestant Reformers had such affinity. It is also a form of nationalism, whose adherents express their nationalism in religious terms. To reduce British-Israelism to a form of 'nationalism using religion' is to promote British-Israelist attachment to the nation above their attachment to the authenticity and separation of *nations*. I believe that the former is a product of the latter, rather than the other way around.

Religion, though, is not a catch-all term here. Many scholars have noted the apparent affinity of Anglophone Protestantism for covenantal style nationalism, based on the Biblical topos of Israel. In the example of British-Israelism, we find a much thicker account of the meaning of Israel to British Protestants. Israel does not simply stand for the notion of a 'chosen people.' As Crome points out, if this was the case then the likelihood would be that a doppelganger effect would emerge in the interaction between British Protestants and Jews. This is not the case. For all the complications in the relationship between British Protestants and Jews, there has never been a widespread call amongst the former for the annihilation of the latter. Instead, as we have seen, British-Israelists appear to have inherited, from the covenantal account of the relationship between God and Israel, a dedication to the task of separation: the separation of objects, people and time.

British-Israelism, as we have seen, does not exactly essentialise ethnicity. British-Israelists continually engage in the construction of ethnicity, in an ongoing process. At certain times Afrikaners, the Irish, the Russians, the Jews, the Germans and others have been considered Israel nations. At other times Afrikaners, the Irish, the Russians, the Jews, the Germans and others have been considered antagonists to the Israel nations. This does not, counter-intuitively, suggest that the maintenance of boundaries between categories of races was not of concern for British-Israelists. It remains their pre-eminent concern. However, it is the process of separating, rather than the state of separation, that concerns them. The process of maintaining a distinctive, singular and authentic ethne served (and serves), for British-Israelists, Christian Zionists, Reformed Protestants, the Biblical Hebrews and innumerable other groups in the history of the Judeo-Christian tradition, to affirm the providential nature of history and the presence of God in the world. The existence of distinctive, singular and authentic ethnes relies on – or can be perpetuated and protected by – a number of different epiphenomena. It can be protected by the celebration of rites and rituals by the in-group which distinguish the in-group from the out-group. It can be protected by the heterophobic stigmatisation of out-group characteristics. It can equally be protected by the celebration of out-group characteristics (as in the philo-Semitic mode of allosemitism). It can be protected by the promulgation of a stigmatised form of knowledge, available only to the providentially appointed elect group and scorned by the providentially appointed reprobate groups. In most instances the existence of the ethne precedes the process of safeguarding the authenticity of the ethne. Because the maintenance of authentic *ethnes* (plural) is the ultimate goal, however, at other times, the latter can coincide with or even precede the former. The covenant with Abraham simultaneously constructed and protected the covenanted people. The covenant with Moses simultaneously constructed and protected the covenanted people. In the British-Israel tradition, the chosenness of the Israel nations does not only guarantee the authenticity or the separateness of the Israel nations (although it does), it also *affects* and indeed *determines* the parameters of the chosen people. This separateness is not defined by *essential* differences but rather by constructed differences. And these constructed differences rely, in no small measure, on the proximity of the differentiated group. This is as true of the relationship between Israel and Jewry, in British-Israelist literature, as it was of the relationship between Esau-Edom and Jacob-Israel in the Biblical literature. Kaufmann is correct to say that 'difference energises rather than detracts from nationalism.'[6] This, however, does not necessarily entail that difference needs to be sought out. Difference can also be constructed. This is the bequest of the Biblical narratives, when combined with Protestant soteriology, which was left to the British-Israelists who stood in St James Park on Wednesday 5 January 1977.

This bequest provided British-Israelists with the resources required to navigate the vicissitudes of the twentieth century. The nineteenth had seen imperial glory and the start of the British-Israel movement. If British-Israelists believed that God had promised imperial glory for Israel, then that prophecy was disconfirmed by the events of the twentieth. And yet the British-Israel movement continued to grow and flourish, attracting members and adherents who had never experienced imperial Britain. The twentieth century brought with it yet more failures of prophecy. The expected victories of Gog over Jewry never materialised. Ireland abandoned the commonwealth of Israel but was not destroyed. Britain was not punished for her perfidious decision to enter the EEC, and the Pope did not wrest control of global politics. But British-Israelists continued to maintain their beliefs. The ageing nature of the British-Israelist community is evidence of its inability to convince new adherents but is also evidence of the tenacity of British-Israelists to their doctrines. As we have seen, particularly in the case of British-Israelist attitudes to the Soviet Union, in part this is because British-Israelists have a profoundly providential view of history. The world, for British-Israelists, is a tightly intertwined helix of prophecy and lived experience. Each prophetic topos stands not only for a political entity but also for a set of tropes and concepts. These tropes and concepts are in turn moulded in relationship with the entities to which they become attached. The concept of Babylon, in British-Israelist thought, is deeply affected by its interaction with the British-Israelist Reformed Protestant conception of the Catholic Church. Babylon stands for global power, for cosmopolitanism, for inauthenticity. As such, Babylon stands for all that Israel is not. It is the projection of Israel: the antithesis of all that Israel should be, by which, apophatically Israel is defined. This Manichean understanding of the relationship between the chosen people and their adversary informs British-Israelist readings of politics, culture and history. They see Babylon everywhere: from the state of Israel to the World Council of Churches to the Trade Union Congress. Such is their sense of the pervasiveness of Babylonian power, they are able to easily find substitutes when one apocalyptic adversary falls away and a new apocalyptic adversary comes to the fore. Tradition, as Edward Shils writes, 'is the past in the present, but it as much in the present as any recent innovation.'[7] This ability to reform and reconstitute the in-group in response to changes in the out-group mirrors precisely the prevailing modes of national identity formation as described in the work of Tim Edensor. 'National identity,' according to Edensor, is a complex matrix 'within which some branches wither, are renewed, transplanted or emerge.' All the while, though, these 'ongoing processes . . . feed back into each other, consolidating the naturalness of modes of understanding and enacting national identity.' This makes the task of analysing national identity based solely on its epiphenomena very difficult. 'Those who attempt to fix the meanings of nationalism,' Edensor continues, 'cannot incorporate the matrix.'[8]

Most of the people of British Israel do not know that they are of British Israel. This truth is as old as the doctrine itself and even older if we take the writings of Richard Brothers into account. British-Israelists launched publicity campaigns throughout the twentieth century with the aim of alerting the people of Britain to their unknown heritage. Part of the point of this book has been to suggest that, just as British Israel is not aware that it is British Israel, many British-Israelists are not aware that they are British-Israelists. When Boris Johnson summoned up the spirit of Exodus in his description of Britain's relationship with the European Union, he spoke to the children of the children of people who were steeped in the images and literature that British-Israelists remain steeped in today. We are living in an era when populist politicians speak before vast crowds of the importance of maintaining authenticity, separation of peoples, the singularity of national cultures whilst at the same time evoking the image of faceless, rootless, Global elites, desirous of the erasure of these same cultures. To claim that a thousand years of immersion in Biblical prophecy, in the antagonism of Israel and Babylon, in the mythology of the Protestant martyrs, in the Manichean division between the elect and the damned has nothing to do with this is, I believe, provincial.

It is easy to associate populist nationalism of the sort espoused by Johnson, Thatcher, Powell and others with the covenantal tropes of British, Protestant culture. As David Edgerton has shown, however, the notion that transformational change is facilitated by the emergence of a newly authentic, newly coherent, newly entitative 'nation,' beguiled the left as much as the right in the middle decades of the twentieth century. Nationalist language suffused the economic and social reforms introduced by Labour and Conservative administrations in the decades following the war. Whereas many other socialist movements adopted the language of internationalism during this period, the Left in Britain was ideologically committed to the concept of the nation.[9] Covenantalism is not a political ideology or a product of partisan rhetoric. It is a facet of our culture.

In 1967, the sociologist David Martin described the sense, amongst some British evangelicals, that Britain remained the centre of the Christian world. The extreme end of this spectrum, he observed, was occupied by the British-Israelists. The milder end of the spectrum was occupied by those 'who hint that the recent withdrawal of divine support is due to national apostasy and neglect of the Bible.' There was also a secularised form of this belief, Martin suggested, which could be found amongst those who expressed the belief that Britain held 'the burden of bearing white civilisation.' This attitude could be found, he wrote, in the pages of the *Daily Express*.[10] Perhaps there is another, covenantal rather than missional, element to this secularised belief. Perhaps it lies in the belief that the British, for the good of the world, must remain separate from the nations around them.[11]

Notes

1 *Brith*, no. 368 (December 1976), 16.
2 Gerald Studdert-Kennedy, 'The Christian Imperialism of the Die-Hard Defenders of the Raj, 1926–35,' in *The Journal of Imperial and Commonwealth History*, 18, no. 3 (1990): 342–362.

3 David Bell, *The Cult of the Nation in France* (Cambridge: Harvard University Press, 2001).
4 Gilles Kepel, *The Revenge of God* (Cambridge: Cambridge University Press, 1990); Peter van der Veer, *Religious Nationalism: Hindus and Muslims in India* (Berkeley: University of California Press, 1994).
5 Smith, 'Nation and Covenant,' 218.
6 Eric Kaufmann, 'Complexity and Nationalism,' in *Nations and Nationalism*, 23, no. 1 (2017): 21.
7 Shils, *Tradition*, 12.
8 Tim Edensor, *National Identity, Popular Culture and Everyday Life* (London: Bloomsbury, 2002), vii.
9 Edgerton, *The Rise and Fall of the British Nation*, 243–244.
10 David Martin, *The Religious and the Secular: Studies in Secularization* (New York: Schocken, 1969), 121.
11 Ezra 9:1.

Select bibliography

Primary sources

Newspapers and magazines

The Ambassador

- April 1966
- May 1966
- June 1966
- July 1966.

The BANNER of Israel

- Volume 40, number 2,036 (5 January 1916).
- Volume 40, number 2,053 (3 May 1916).
- Volume 40, number 2,057 (31 May 1916).
- Volume 40, number 2,060 (21 June 1916).
- Volume 40, number 2,063 (12 July 1916).
- Volume 40, number 2,064 (12 July 1916).
- Volume 40, number 2,065 (26 July 1916).
- Volume 40, number 2,066 (2 August 1916).
- Volume 40, number 2,069 (23 August 1916).
- Volume 40, number 2,075 (4 October 1916).
- Volume 41, number 2,088 (3 January 1917).
- Volume 41, number 2,093 (7 February 1917).
- Volume 41, number 2,094 (14 February 1917).
- Volume 41, number 2,119 (1 August 1917).
- Volume 41, number 2,134 (21 November 1917).
- Volume 41, number 2,137 (12 December 1917).
- Volume 41, number 2,139 (26 December 1917).
- Volume 42, number 2,140 (2 January 1918).
- Volume 42, number 2,141 (9 January 1918).
- Volume 42, number 2,144 (30 January 1918).

- Volume 42, number 2,146 (13 February 1918).
- Volume 42, number 2,149 (6 March 1918).
- Volume 42, number 2,152 (27 March 1918).
- Volume 42, number 2,159 (15 May 1918).
- Volume 42, number 2,179 (9 October 1918).
- Volume 43, number 2,193 (8 January 1919).
- Volume 43, number 2,203 (19 March 1919).
- Volume 43, number 2,205 (1 April 1919).
- Volume 43, number 2,206 (9 April 1919).
- Volume 43, number 2,207 (16 April 1919).
- Volume 43, number 2,210 (7 May 1919).
- Volume 43, number 2,212 (21 May 1919).
- Volume 43, number 2,213 (28 May 1919).
- Volume 43, number 2,216 (18 June 1919).
- Volume 43, number 2,218 (2 July 1919).
- Volume 43, number 2,222 (30 July 1919).
- Volume 43, number 2,243 (24 December 1919).
- Volume 44, number 2,245 (7 January 1920).
- Volume 44, number 2,252 (25 February 1920).
- Volume 44, number 2,253 (3 March 1920).
- Volume 44, number 2,256 (26 March 1920).
- Volume 44, number 2,254 (10 March 1920).
- Volume 44, number 2,267 (9 June 1920).
- Volume 44, number 2,286 (20 October 1920).
- Volume 44, number 2,287 (27 October 1920).
- Volume 45, number 2,298 (12 January 1921).
- Volume 45, number 2,299 (19 January 1921).
- Volume 45, number 2,318 (15 June 1921).
- Volume 45, number 2,320 (15 June 1921).
- Volume 45, number 2,348 (25 December 1921).

Bible Impact

- Number 6 (January 1972).
- Number 7 (March 1972).
- Number 8 (June 1972).
- Number 9 (December 1972).

Bible Truth

- Number 204 (April 2000).
- Number 206 (July 2000).
- Number 207 (September 2000).
- Number 209 (January 2001).
- Number 222 (March 2003).

- Number 231 (September 2004).
- Number 236 (July 2005).
- Number 241 (May 2006).
- Number 242 (July 2006).
- Number 254 (April 2009).
- Number 264 (October 2011).
- Number 279 (July 2015).
- Number 283 (September 2016).
- Number 288 (October 2017).

Brith

- Number 1 (September 1945).
- Number 2 (October 1945).
- Number 3 (November 1945).
- Number 4 (December 1945).
- Number 10 (July 1946).
- Number 12 (September 1946).
- Number 13 (October 1946).
- Number 16 (January 1947).
- Number 17 (February 1947).
- Number 20 (July 1947).
- Number 23 (October 1947).
- Number 24 (November 1947).
- Number 30 (May 1948).
- Number 32 (July 1948).
- Number 35 (October 1948).
- Number 38 (December 1948).
- Number 39 (February 1949).
- Number 40 (March 1949).
- Number 41 (April 1949).
- Number 43 (July 1949).
- Number 51 (February 1950).
- Number 63 (February 1951).
- Number 67 (June 1951).
- Number 77 (May 1952).
- Number 127 (August 1956).
- Number 141 (January 1958).
- Number 160 (May 1959).
- Number 183 (April 1961).
- Number 233 (June 1965).
- Number 257 (June 1967).
- Number 292 (April 1970).
- Number 293 (May 1970).
- Number 299 (November 1970).

- Number 318 (July 1972).
- Number 319 (August 1972).
- Number 321 (October 1972).
- Number 322 (November 1972).
- Number 325 (February 1973).
- Number 326 (March 1973).
- Number 328 (May 1973).
- Number 335 (December 1973).
- Number 336 (January 1974).
- Number 348 (January 1975).
- Number 349 (February 1975).
- Number 350 (March 1975).
- Number 351 (April 1975).
- Number 353 (June 1975).
- Number 354 (July 1975).
- Number 355 (November 1975).
- Number 358 (February 1976).
- Number 362 (June 1976).
- Number 365 (September 1976).
- Number 366 (October 1976).
- Number 368 (December 1976).
- Number 370 (March 1977).
- Number 379 (December 1977).
- Number 380 (January 1978).
- Number 381 (February 1978).
- Number 407 (April 1980).
- Number 408 (May 1980).
- Number 410 (July 1980).
- Number 413 (October 1980).
- Number 414 (November 1980).

The British-Israel World Federation Quarterly

- Volume 2, number 4 (October 1989).
- Volume 3, number 1 (January 1990).
- Volume 3, number 2 (April 1990).
- Volume 3, number 3 (July 1990).
- Volume 4, number 1 (January 1991).
- Volume 4, number 2 (April-June 1991).
- Volume 10, number 1 (January 1997).

The British-Israel Herald

- Volume 5, number 48 (January 1928).
- Volume 5, number 52 (April 1928).

- Volume 5, number 53 (May 1928).
- Volume 5, number 54 (June 1928).

The British-Israel Pilot

- Number 87 (7 April 1929).
- Number 91 (15 July 1929).

British Israel Star and Circle

- Number 37 (January 1925).
- Number 39 (March 1925).
- Number 40 (April 1925).
- Number 41 (May 1925).

Covenant Message

- Volume 29, number 1 (January 1960).
- Volume 29, number 2 (February 1960).
- Volume 29, number 3 (March 1960).
- Volume 29, number 4 (April 1960).
- Volume 29, number 5 (May 1960).
- Volume 29, number 6 (June 1960).

Covenant Nations

- Volume 1, number 1 (November 2007).
- Volume 2, number 7 (November 2009).
- Volume 2, number 12 (December 2013).
- Volume 3, number 4 (April 2014).

Covenant Voice

- Volume 37, number 5 (May 1982).
- Volume 37, number 10 (October 1982).
- Volume 37, number 11 (November 1982).
- Volume 38, number 4 (April 1982).
- January 1989.
- September 1989.
- January 1990.
- March 1990
- February 1991.
- April 1992.
- December 1992.

Crown and Commonwealth

- Volume 1, number 1 (Spring 2001).
- Volume 1, number 2 (Summer 2001).
- Volume 1, number 3 (Autumn 2001).
- Volume 1, number 4 (Winter 2001).
- Volume 2, number 1 (Spring 2002).
- Volume 2, number 2 (Summer 2002).
- Volume 2, number 3 (Autumn 2002).
- Volume 2, number 4 (Winter 2002).
- Volume 4, number 1 (Spring 2004).
- Volume 4, number 4 (Winter 2004).

The Homeland Pilot

- Number 20 (March 1931).
- Number 21 (April 1931).
- Number 23 (May 1931).
- Number 25 (July 1931).

The Link

- Volume 4, number 4 (January/February 1985).
- Volume 4, number 5 (April 1985).
- Volume 4, number 6 (May/June 1985).

The National Message

- Volume 1, number 5 (4 February 1922).
- Volume 15, number 901 (25 April 1936).
- Volume 22, number 1,072 (18 August 1943).
- Volume 22, number 1,074 (1 September 1943).
- Volume 23, number 1,087 (1 March 1944).
- Volume 24, number 1,120 (6 June 1944).
- Volume 24, number 1,130 (24 October 1945).
- Volume 25, number 1,156 (23 October 1946).
- Volume 26, number 1,179 (27 September 1947).
- Volume 26, number 1,181 (25 October 1947).
- Volume 27, number 1,186 (3 January 1948).
- Volume 27, number 1,187 (17 January 1948).
- Volume 27, number 1,189 (14 February 1948).
- Volume 27, number 1,195 (8 May 1948).
- Volume 27, number 1,196 (22 May 1948).
- Volume 27, number 1,197 (5 June 1948).
- Volume 27, number 1,198 (5 June 1948).

- Volume 27, number 1,199 (3 July 1948).
- Volume 27, number 1,207 (23 October 1948).
- Volume 31, number 1,291 (26 January 1952).
- Volume 31, number 1,294 (23 February 1952).
- Volume 31, number 1,299 (3 May 1952).
- Volume 31, number 1,303 (28 June 1952).
- Volume 35, number 1,395 (February 1957).
- Volume 35, number 1,398 (April 1957).
- Volume 41, number 1,467 (February 1962).
- Volume 41, number 1,472 (July 1962).
- Volume 41, number 1,475 (October 1962).
- Volume 43, number 1,491 (February 1964).
- Volume 43, number 1,494 (May 1964).
- Volume 43, number 1,495 (June 1964).
- Volume 43, number 1,496 (July 1964).
- Volume 43, number 1,497 (August 1964).
- Volume 43, number 1,502 (January 1965).
- Volume 45, number 1,514 (January 1966).
- Volume 45, number 1,523 (October 1966).
- Volume 47, number 1,538 (January 1968).
- Volume 47, number 1,540 (March 1968).
- Volume 47, number 1,541 (April 1968).
- Volume 47, number 1,542 (May 1968).
- Volume 47, number 1,543 (June 1968).
- Volume 47, number 1,547 (October 1968).
- Volume 47, number 1,548 (November 1968).
- Volume 49, number 1,562 (January 1970).
- Volume 49, number 1,564 (March 1970).
- Volume 49, number 1,566 (May 1970).
- Volume 49, number 1,568 (July 1970).
- Volume 50, number 1,576 (March 1971).
- Volume 50, number 1,580 (July 1971).
- Volume 50, number 1,581 (August 1971).
- Volume 50, number 1,583 (October 1971).
- Volume 50, number 1,585 (December 1971).
- Volume 51, number 1,586 (January 1972).
- Volume 53, number 1,611 (February 1974).
- Volume 53, number 1,612 (March 1974).
- Volume 53, number 1,614 (May 1974).
- Volume 53, number 1,617 (August 1974).
- Volume 53, number 1,618 (September 1974).
- Volume 53, number 1,619 (October 1974).
- Volume 53, number 1,620 (November 1974).
- Volume 54, number 1,623 (February 1975).
- Volume 54, number 1,624 (March 1975).

- Volume 55, number 1,634 (January 1976).
- Volume 55, number 1,635 (February 1976).
- Volume 55, number 1,636 (March 1976).
- Volume 55, number 1,637 (April 1976).
- Volume 55, number 1,639 (June 1976).
- Volume 55, number 1,643 (October 1976).
- Volume 55, number 1,644 (November 1976).
- Volume 55, number 1,645 (December 1976).
- Volume 56, number 1,649 (April 1977).
- Volume 56, number 1,650 (May 1977).
- Volume 57, number 1,658 (January 1978).
- Volume 57, number 1,659 (February 1978).
- Volume 57, number 1,661 (April 1978).
- Volume 57, number 1,662 (May 1978).
- Volume 57, number 1,663 (June 1978).
- Volume 59, number 1,682 (January 1980).
- Volume 59, number 1,683 (February 1980).
- Volume 59, number 1,684 (March 1980).
- Volume 59, number 1,685 (April 1980).
- Volume 59, number 1,686 (May 1980).

News of the New World

- Volume 1, number 1 (January 1966).
- Volume 1, number 3 (February 1966).
- Volume 1, number 5 (April 1966).

The Quarterly Notes of the Protestant British Israel League

- Volume 6, number 2 (August 1916).
- Volume 6, number 3 (September 1916).
- Volume 6, number 4 (October 1916).
- Volume 7, number 1 (January 1917).
- Volume 7, number 2 (April 1917).
- Volume 7, number 3 (July 1917).

Toren

- Volume 2, number 1 (January 1965).
- Volume 2, number 3 (March 1965).
- Volume 2, number 5 (September 1965).
- Volume 3, number 1 (January 1966).
- Volume 3, number 2 (March 1966).
- Volume 6, number 1 (April 1969).

Wake Up

- Volume 2, number 4 (April 1978).
- Volume 2, number 7 (July 1978).
- Volume 2, number 9 (September 1978).
- Volume 5, number 4 (March 1981).
- Volume 7, number 2 (March 1988).
- Volume 7, number 3 (May 1988).
- Volume 7, number 10 (August 1989).
- Volume 8, number 2 (March 1990).
- Volume 8, number 4 (August 1990).
- Volume 8, number 6 (January 1991).
- Volume 8, number 7 (July 1991).
- Volume 8, number 8 (September 1991).
- Volume 8, number 9 (November 1991).
- Volume 12, number 2 (March 1998).
- Volume 12, number 4 (July 1998).

Books

Abraham, Dorothy. *What Is British Israel?* (London: Covenant Publishing, 1954).

Allen, John. *Judah's Sceptre and Jacob's Birthright* (Boston: Beauchamp, 1917).

Armstrong, Herbert. *The United States and British Commonwealth in Prophecy* (Pasadena: Ambassador, 1967).

Aronson, Theo. *Princess Alice, Duchess of Athlone* (London: Cassel, 1981).

Bassin, Elieser. *The Lost Ten Tribes* (London, 1884).

Bentham, Joseph. *The Saints Societie* (London, 1636).

Bradford, Norah. *A Sword Bathed in Heaven* (Basingstoke: Pickering, 1984).

Brightman, Thomas. *A Revelation of the Apocalypse* (London, 1611).

Brightman, Thomas. *A Commentary on the Canticles* (London, 1644).

British Israel World Federation. *A Paper Submitted for the Attention of the Anglo-American Joint Commission on Palestine* (London: Covenant Publishing, 1947).

Burgess, Thomas. *Tracts on the Origin and Independence of the Ancient British Church* (London: Rivington, 1815).

Buxton Gresty, L. *Satan Fights for Muscovy* (London: Covenant Publishing, 1952).

Buxton Gresty, L. *Christ or the Kremlin* (London: Covenant Publishing, 1976).

Clark, Michael. *Britain's God-Given Scientific Heritage Destroyed by Metrication Madness* (Bishop Auckland: Covenant Publishing, 2012).

Cooksley, Vivien. *The Biblical Food Laws* (Bishop Auckland: Covenant Publishing, 2017).

Crawford, Alexander. *Progression by Antagonism* (London: Murray, 1846).

Crawford, Alexander. *Creed of Japhet* (Beccles: William Clowes, 1891).

Cumming, John. *The End* (London, 1855).

Darby, John. *Lectures on the Second Coming* (London: Paternoster, 1868).

de Lisle, Henry. *Reminiscences of Sport and War* (London: Eyre and Spottiswoode, 1939).

Debrett's Peerage and Baronetage (London: Debrett, 2011).

Denison, Stephen. *A New Creature* (London, 1619).

Dod, Robert. *The Peerage, Baronetage and Knightage of Great Britain and Ireland* (London, 1862).

Duff, Douglas. *Bailing with a Teaspoon* (London: Jonathan Long, 1953).

Faird, Robert. *Gorbachev! Has the Real Antichrist Come?* (Tulsa: Victory House, 1988).

Falconer, John. *A Briefe Refutation of John Traske's Judaical and Novel Fancyes* (St. Omer, 1618).

Ferris, A.J. *God's Education of the Anglo-Saxon-Israel Race* (London: Marshall, 1934).

Ferris, A.J. *When Russia Invades Palestine* (London: Clarendon Press, 1939).

Filmer, W.E. *A Synopsis of the Migration* (London: Covenant Publishing, 1966).

Finch, Henry. *The Worlds Great Restauration or the Calling of the Jews* (London, 1621).

Gaebelein, Arno. *Hath God Cast Away His People* (London: Gospel, 1905).

Glover, F.R.A. *England, the Remnant of Judah* (London: Rivington, 1861).

Grattan Guinness, Henry. *Light for the Last Days* (London: Hodder, 1888).

Grimaldi, A.B. *The Queen's Royal Descent from King David the Psalmist* (London: Banks, 1885).

H., A.R. *British Israel and the Herrenvolk* (London: British-Israel World Federation, 1942).

Hadfield, Charles. *British Israel, Fact Not Fiction* (Bishop Auckland: Covenant Publishing, 2015 [4th edition]).

Hanan, Denis. *British Israel Truth* (London: Covenant Publishing, 1932).

Heath, Alban. *The Faith of a British Israelite* (London: Covenant Publishing, 1937).

Hine, Edward. *Fourty-Seven Identifications of the Anglo-Saxons with the Lost Tribes of Israel* (New York: Huggins, 1879).

Koestler, Arthur. *The Thirteenth Tribe* (New York: Random House, 1976).

Leone, Jacopo and Victor Considerant. *The Jesuit Conspiracy* (London: Chapman, 1848).

Lindsay, Hal. *The Late Great Planet Earth* (Grand Rapids: Zondervan, 1970).

MacKenzie, Compton. *The North Wind of Love* (London: Chatto and Windus, 1944).

Margoliouth, Moses. *The History of the Jews in Great Britain* (London: Bentley, 1846).

McConell, James. *The Good, the Bad and Jesus Christ* (Magherafelt: Maurice Wylie, 2016).

McKilliam, Kenneth. *The Annihilation of Man* (Devon: Britons, 1972).

McKilliam, Kenneth and Mary Stanton. *Free Society* (London, 1972 [Handbill]).

McWhirter, Ross. *Ross Was Right: The Queen Betrayed* (Bishop Auckland: Covenant Publishing, 2014).

Milner, Walter. *Tara Vindicata* (London: Banks and Son, 1903).

Milner, Walter. *The Royal House of Britain* (London: Covenant Publishing, 1909).

Milner, Walter. *The Russian Chapters of Ezekiel* (London: Covenant Publishing, 1933).

Moore, George. *The Lost Tribes and the Saxons of the East and West* (London, 1861).

Norden, John. *A Mirror for the Multitude* (London, 1586).

O'Casey, Sean. *Oak Leaves and Lavender* (London: Palgrave Macmillan, 1946).

O'Hart, John. *Irish Pedigrees* (Dublin: Duffy, 1892).

Oldroyd, W.E. *The Case for British-Israel* (London: Marshall Brothers, 1922).

Palfrey Baldwin, Catherine. *And Men Wept* (New York: Our Publications, 1955).

Parker, Douglas. *Why Great Britain Will Never Be Destroyed But Will Stand Forever* (Sowerby Bridge: Edwards, 1922).

Parsons, Kirsten. *Revival in a Canteen* (Hove: Hove Shirley, 1942).

Piazzi Smyth, Charles. *Our Inheritance in the Great Pyramid* (London: Isbister, 1874).

Radnor, Helen Countess Dowager. *From a Great Grandmother's Armchair* (London: Marshall, 1927).

The Roadbuilder. *The Destiny of Britain and America* (London: Covenant Publishing, 1921).

Rosling Howett, Thomas. *Anglo-Israel* (Philadelphia: Spangler and Davis, 1892).

Ross, Kenneth. *Dangerous Delusions* (Oxford: Mowbray, 1961).

Sayce, Archibald. *The Races of the Old Testament* (London: Religious Tract Society, 1891).

Smyth, Clifford. *Axis Against Ulster* (Belfast: Smyth, 1972).

Smyth, Clifford. *Boycott: An Examination of the Abuse and Persecution of Ulster Protestants* (Belfast: Inheritance, 1997).

Stanton, Mary. *Announcing the Resurrection of the Dead* (London, 1972).

Stennet, Edward. *The Royal Law Contended for* (London, 1666).

Thatcher, Margaret. *The Path to Power* (London: Harper Collins, 1995).

Thatcher, Margaret. *The Collected Speeches of Margaret Thatcher* (London: Harper Collins, 1997).

van Woelderen, Helene. *Strange Parallels* (Glastonbury: Real Israel Press, 1971).

Whitaker, Joseph. *An Almanack for the Year of Our Lord 1897* (London, 1898).

Williams Morgan, Richard. *St Paul in Britain* (London: Parker, 1861).

Wilson, John. *Our Israelitish Origin* (London: Nisbet, 1840).

Archival material

'Arab Reactions Following Concessions to the Jews,' National Archives, CO 537/2296.

'Biography of Walter Walker: Discussion of Contentious Material,' National Archives, DEFE 24/648.

'British Israel World Federation Annual Accounts and Reports for 1989,' British Library, ZC.9.a.2499.

'British Israel World Federation Annual Accounts and Reports for 1990,' British Library, ZC.9.a.2499.

'British Israel World Federation Annual Accounts and Reports for 1998,' British Library, ZC.9.a.2499.

'British Israel World Federation Annual Accounts and Reports for 1999–2000,' British Library, ZC.9.a.2499.

'Charles Ashton Maliciously Set Fire to 6 Buckingham Gate,' National Archives, MEPO 3/1257.

'Correspondence with the British-Israel World Federation Concerning Lectures and Meeting,' London Metropolitan Archives, ACC/3121/B/04/B022.

'Covenant People's Fellowship Annual Report for 1982,' British Library, P881/444.

'Covenant People's Fellowship Annual Report for 1990,' British Library, P881/444.

'Deed of Foundation of Trust,' Bedfordshire Archives, HO/D/6.
'General Situation in Palestine,' National Archives, FO 371/23229.
'Haifa Incident,' National Archives, CO 537/3860.
Hansard, House of Commons Debates, volume 805.
Hansard, House of Lords Debates, volume 231.
'Letter from Herbert Garrison to Sir Francis Dalton,' National Museums Liverpool, Maritime Archives, D/D/V/2/36.
'Letter from Lord Gisborough, United Protestant Council,' The Parliamentary Archives, BL 114/11/5.
'Letters from HRH Princess Alice of Athlone to Anthony Eden,' Cadbury Research Library, AP30/F.
'Metropolitan Anglo-Israel Association, Report for the Proceedings at the First Annual Meeting,' British Library, 4034.i.2.
'Naturalisation Certificate of Eliezer Bassin,' National Archives, HO 334/12/4226.
'Papers Relating to the General Administration and Funding of the Junior Constitutional Club,' Wiltshire and Swindon Historical Centre, 947/880.
'Police Report of Sir Charles Wickham,' National Archives, CO 537/2269.
'Situation in Palestine,' National Archives, FO 371/68501.

Secondary sources

Articles and chapters

Almond, Philip. 'Thomas Brightman and the Origins of Philo-Semitism: An Elizabethan Theologian and the Return of the Jews to Israel,' in *Reformation and Renaissance Review*, 9, no. 1 (2007): 3–25.
Barkun, Michael. 'Millenarianism in the Modern World,' in *Theory and Society*, 1, no. 2 (1974): 117–146.
Bauman, Zygmunt. 'Allosemitism: Premodern, Modern, Postmodern,' in Bryan Cheyette and Laura Marcus (eds.), *Modernity, Culture and 'The Jew'* (Cambridge: Polity, 1998), 143–156.
Berman, Joshua. 'Histories Twice Told: Deuteronomy 1–3 and the Hittite Treaty Prologue Tradition,' in *Journal of Biblical Literature*, 132, no. 2 (2013): 229–250.
Berrien, Kenneth. 'Shelter Owners, Dissonance and the Arms Race,' in *Social Problems*, 11, no. 1 (1963): 87–91.
Black, Gerry. 'The Right School in the Right Place: The History of the Stepney Jewish School, 1864–2013,' in *Jewish Historical Studies*, 45 (2013): 131–144.
Blenkinsopp, Joseph. 'Judah's Covenant with Death (Isaiah 28, 14–22),' in *Vetus Testamentum*, 50, no. 4 (January 2000): 465–483.
Bratt, James. 'Calvinism in North America,' in Martin Hirzel and Martin Sallman (eds.), *John Calvin's Impact on Church and Society, 1509–2009* (Cambridge: Eerdmans, 2009), 49–67.
Buckley, Anthony. ' "We're Trying to Find Our Identity": Uses of History Among Ulster Protestants,' in Elizabeth Tonkin, Maryon McDonald and Malcolm Chapman (eds.), *History and Ethnicity* (London: Routledge, 1989), 183–197.
Burke, Tony. 'Apocrypha and Forgeries,' in Tony Burke (ed.), *Fakes, Forgeries and Fictions: Ancient and Modern Christian Apocrypha* (Eugene: Cascade, 2015), 236–240.

Carter, Warren. 'James C. Scott and New Testament Studies,' in Richard Horsley (ed.), *Hidden Transcripts and the Arts of Resistance: Applying the Work of James C. Scott to Jesus and Paul* (Atlanta: SBL, 2004), 81–94.

Coakley, John. 'Religion and Nationalism,' in Daniele Conversi (ed.), *Ethnonationalism in the Contemporary World* (London: Routledge, 2002).

Collinson, Patrick. 'The Cohabitation of the Faithful with the Unfaithful,' in Ole Grell, Jonathan Israel and Nicholas Tyacke (eds.), *From Persecution to Toleration* (Oxford: Clarendon Press, 1991), 51–76.

Connor, Walker. 'The Politics of Ethnonationalism,' in *Journal of International Affairs*, 27, no. 1 (1973): 17.

Cowan, Douglas E. 'Theologizing Race: The Construction of Christian Identity,' in Craig Prentiss (ed.), *Religion and the Creation of Race and Ethnicity* (London: New York University Press, 2003), 112–124.

Crome, Andrew. ' "The Proper and Naturall Meaning of the Prophets": The Hermeneutic Roots of Judeo-Centric Eschatology,' in *Renaissance Studies*, 24, no. 5 (2010): 725–741.

Darby, Robert and John Cozijn. 'The British Royal Family's Circumcision Tradition: Genesis and Evolution of a Contemporary Legend,' in *Sage Open*, 3, no. 4 (October 2013): 1–10.

Dimbleby, J.B. 'The Lost Ten Tribes: Where Are They?' in *Past and Future*, 4 (June 1898): 120–130.

Fantauzzo, Justin. 'A Tribute to the British Empire: Lowell Thomas with Allenby and Lawrence in Arabia,' in Michael Walsh (ed.), *The Great War and the British Empire* (London: Routledge, 2017), 199–215.

George, Timothy. 'War and Peace in the Puritan Tradition,' in *Church History*, 53 (1984): 492–503.

Gilley, Sheridan. 'English Attitudes to the Irish in England,' in Colin Holmes (ed.), *Immigrants and Minorities in British Society* (London: Routledge, 1978), 98–100.

Guibbory, Achsah. 'The Reformation of Hebrew Scripture: Chosen People, Chosen Nations, and Exceptionalism,' in *Reformation*, 23, no. 1 (2018): 100–119.

Hill, Christopher. 'Till the Conversion of the Jews,' in Richard Henry Popkin (ed.), *Millenarianism and Messianism in English Literature and Thought 1650–1800* (Leiden: Brill, 1988), 12–36.

Hobsbawm, Eric. 'Inventing Traditions in 19th Century Europe,' in *Proceedings of the Past and Present Society Annual Conference 1977* (London: Past and Present, 1977), 1–25.

Hogg, Michael. 'Uncertainty-Identity Theory,' in *Advances in Experimental Social Psychology*, 39 (2007): 69–126.

Hogg, Michael. *Extremism and the Psychology of Uncertainty* (Sussex: Wiley-Blackwell, 2012).

Hogg, Michael. 'From Uncertainty to Extremism,' in *Current Directions in Psychological Science*, 23 (2014): 338–342.

Kay, William. 'George Jeffreys: Pentecostal and Contemporary Implications,' in *Religions*, 9, no. 2 (2018): 60–71.

Keith, Arthur. 'The Evolution of Human Races: Huxley Memorial Lecture,' in *Journal of the Royal Anthropological Institute*, 58 (1928): 306–321.

Kumar, Krishan. 'Britain, England and Europe: Cultures in Contraflow,' in *European Journal of Social Theory*, 6, no. 1 (February 2003): 5–23.

Lake, Peter. 'Anti-Puritanism: The Structure of a Prejudice,' in Kenneth Fincham (ed.), *Religious Politics in Post-Reformation England* (Woodbridge: Boydell, 2006), 80–97.

Mach, Michael. 'Justin Martyr's *Dialogus cum Tryphone Iudaeo* and the Development of Christian Anti-Judaism,' in Guy Stroumsa and Ora Limor (eds.), *Contra Iudaeos: Ancient and Medieval Polemics Between Christians and Jews* (Tubingen: Mohr, 1996), 27–85.

McFarland, Michael and Glenn Gottfried. 'The Chosen Ones: A Mythic Analysis of the Theological and Political Self-Justification of Christian Identity,' in *Journal for the Study of Religion*, 15, no. 1 (2002): 125–145.

Melton, J. Gordon. 'Spiritualization and Reaffirmation: What Really Happens When Prophecy Fails,' in *American Studies*, 26 (Fall 1985): 17–29.

Morrill, John. 'The Religious Context of the English Civil War,' in *Transactions of the Royal Historical Society*, 34 (1984): 155–178.

Oliver, Eric and Thomas J. Wood. 'Conspiracy Theories and the Paranoid Style(s) of Mass Opinion,' in *American Journal of Political Science*, 58, no. 4 (2014): 952–966.

Peaker, Carol. 'We Are Not Barbarians: Literature and the Russian Émigré Press in England, 1890–1905,' in *Interdisciplinary Studies in the Long Nineteenth Century*, 3 (2006).

Pierard, Richard. 'The Contribution of British-Israelism to Anti-Semitism,' in Hubert G. Lock and Marcia Sachs Littell (eds.), *Holocaust and Church Struggle: Religion, Power, and the Politics of Resistance* (Lanham: University Press of America, 1996), 45–68.

Reisenauer, Eric. ' "That We May Do Israel's Work": Racial Election in British Imperial Thought,' in *Proceedings of the South Carolina Historical Association 1999* (1999): 97–112.

Reisenauer, Eric. ' "The Battle of the Standards": Great Pyramid Metrology and British Identity, 1859–1890,' in *The Historian*, 65, no. 4 (Summer 2003): 931–978.

Reisenauer, Eric. ' "The Merchants of Tarshish, with All the Young Lions Thereof": The British Empire, Scripture Prophecy, and the War of Armageddon, 1914–1918,' in *Journal of the Bible and Its Reception*, 4, no. 2 (2017): 287–318.

Smith, Anthony. 'Nation and Covenant: The Contribution of Ancient Israel to Modern Nationalism,' in *Proceedings of the British Academy*, 151 (2007): 237.

Trevor-Roper, Hugh. 'The Highland Tradition of Scotland,' in Eric Hobsbawm (ed.), *The Invention of Tradition* (Cambridge: Cambridge University Press, 1983), 13–41.

Tumminia, Diana. 'How Prophecy Never Fails: Interpretive Reason in a Flying Saucer Group,' in *Sociology of Religion*, 59 (1998): 157–170.

Walsham, Alexandra. 'The Happiness of Suffering,' in Michael Braddick and Joanna Innes (eds.), *Suffering and Happiness in England 1550–1850* (Oxford: Oxford University Press, 2017), 45–64.

Weiss, Daniel H. 'Impurity Without Repression: Julia Kristeva and the Biblical Possibilities of a Non-Eliminationist Construction of Religious Purity,' in Robbie Duschinsky, Simone Schnall and Daniel H. Weiss (eds.), *Purity and Danger Now: New Perspectives* (London: Routledge, 2016).

Wellings, Ben. 'Beyond Awkwardness: England, the European Union and the End of Integration,' in Karine Tournier-Sol (ed.), *The UK Challenges to Europeanization* (London: Springer, 2015), 33–51.

Westermann, Edward. 'The Royal Air Force and the Bombing of Auschwitz,' in David Cesarini and Sarah Kavanagh (eds.), *Holocaust: Responses to the Persecution and the Mass Murder of the Jews* (Abingdon: Routledge, 2004), 195–210.

Wilson, John. 'British Israelism,' in *Sociological Review*, no. 16 (1968): 41–57.

Wilson, John. 'British Israelism: A Revitalization Movement,' in *Archives de Sociologie des Religions*, 13, no. 26 (January 1968): 73–80.

Wilson, John. 'The Relation Between Ideology and Organization in a Small Religious Group: The British Israelites,' in *Review of Religious Research*, 10, no. 1 (1968): 50–51.

Zygmunt, Joseph. 'Prophetic Failure and Chiliastic Identity: The Case of the Jehovah's Witnesses,' in *American Journal of Sociology*, 75, no. 6 (May 1970): 926–948.

Books

Adorno, Theodor, Else Frenkel-Brunswik, Daniel J. Levinson, and R. Nevitt Sanford. *The Authoritarian Personality: Part Two* (New York: Wiley, 1950).

Akenson, Donald. *God's Peoples* (Ithaca: Cornell University Press, 1992).

Albertz, Rainer. *A History of Israelite Religion in the Old Testament Period*, vol. 2 (Louisville: Westminster John Knox, 1994).

Amit, Yaira. *Hidden Polemics in the Biblical Narrative* (Leiden: Brill, 2000).

Anderson, Benedict. *Imagined Communities* (London: Verso, 2003 [1986]).

Barkan, Elazar. *The Retreat of Scientific Racism* (Cambridge: Cambridge University Press, 1992).

Barkun, Michael. *Religion and the Racist Right* (Chapel Hill: University of North Carolina Press, 1997).

Barkun, Michael. *A Culture of Conspiracy* (Berkeley: University of California Press, 2003).

Barrett, David V. *The Fragmentation of a Sect: Schism in the Worldwide Church of God* (Oxford: Oxford University Press, 2013).

Batnitzky, Leora. *Idolatry and Representation: The Philosophy of Franz Rosenzweig Reconsidered* (Princeton, NJ: Princeton University Press, 2000).

Bauman, Zygmunt. *Modernity and the Holocaust* (Cambridge: Polity, 1989).

Behrman, Cynthia. 'The Mythology of British Imperialism, 1890–1914' (Doctoral Thesis: University of Boston, 1965).

Benite, Zvi Ben-Dor. *The Ten Lost Tribes: A World History* (Oxford: Oxford University Press, 2009).

Benstock, Bernard. *Sean O'Casey* (Cranbury, NJ: Associated University Press, 1970).

Black, Jeremy. *Convergence or Divergence: Britain and the Continent* (London: Palgrave Macmillan, 1994).

Boyarin, Daniel. *Borderlines: The Partition of Judaeo-Christianity* (Philadelphia: University of Pennsylvania Press, 2004).

Boyer, Paul. *When Time Shall Be No More* (Cambridge: Belknap, 2009).

Breuilly, John. *Nationalism and the State* (Manchester: Manchester University Press, 1993).

Cambers, Andrew. *Godly Reading: Print, Manuscript and Puritanism in England, 1580–1720* (Cambridge: Cambridge University Press, 2011).

Carew, Mairead. *Tara and the Ark of the Covenant* (Dublin: Royal Academy, 2003).

Cohen, Michael J. *Britain's Moment in Palestine* (Abingdon: Routledge, 2014).

Colley, Linda. *Britons* (New Haven and London: Yale University Press, 1992).

Connor, Walker. *Ethnonationalism* (Princeton, NJ: Princeton University Press, 1994).

Coogan, Tim Pat. *Ireland in the Twentieth Century* (London: Arrow, 2003).

Corthorn, Paul. *Enoch Powell* (Oxford: Oxford University Press, 2019).

Crome, Andrew. *Christian Zionism and English National Identity* (London: Palgrave Macmillan, 2018).

Davidiy, Yair. *The Khazars: Tribe 13* (Jerusalem: Russel-Davis, 1993).

Davidiy, Yair. *Ephraim: The Gentile Children of Israel* (Jerusalem: Russel-Davis, 1995).

Davidiy, Yair. *Germany and Edom* (Jerusalem: Russel-Davis, 2015).

Dein, Simon. *Lubavitcher Messianism: What Really Happens When Prophecy Fails?* (London: Continuum, 2011).

Desmond, Ray. *Kew: The History of the Royal Botanic Gardens* (London: Harvill, 1995).

Douglas, Mary. *Purity and Danger* (London: Routledge, 2003 [1966]).

Dudley Edwards, Ruth. *The Faithful Tribe* (London: Harper Collins, 1999).

Edgerton, David. *The Rise and Fall of the British Nation* (London: Penguin, 2018).

Endelman, Todd. *The Jews of Britain: 1656–2000* (London: University of California Press, 2002).

Farrell, Michael. *Northern Ireland: The Orange State* (London: Pluto, 1980).

Festinger, Leon. *When Prophecy Fails* (London: Pinter and Martin, 2008 [1956]).

Fredriksen, Paula. *Augustine and the Jews* (New Haven: Yale University Press, 2008).

Fuller, Robert. *Naming the Anti-Christ: The History of an American Obsession* (Oxford: Oxford University Press, 1995).

Gager, John. *The Origins of Anti-Semitism* (New York: Oxford University Press, 1983).

Gellner, Ernest. *Nations and Nationalism* (Cornell: Cornell University Press, 1983).

Grob-Fitzgibbon, Benjamin. *Continental Drift* (Cambridge: Cambridge University Press, 2016).

Halamish, Aviva. *The Exodus Affair* (Syracuse: Syracuse University Press, 1998).

Harkness, David. *Northern Ireland Since 1920* (Dublin: Helicon, 1983).

Hopkinson, Michael. *The Irish War of Independence* (London: Gill, 2004).

Idel, Moshe. *Messianic Mystics* (New Haven: Yale University Press, 1998).

Kauffman, Eric. *The Orange Order* (Oxford: Oxford University Press, 2007).

Kedourie, Elie. *Nationalism* (London: Wiley, 1993).

Kidd, Colin. *The Forging of Races* (Cambridge: Cambridge University Press, 2006).

Klawans, Jonathan. *Impurity and Sin* (Oxford: Oxford University Press, 2000).

Klawans, Jonathan. *Purity, Sacrifice and the Temple* (Oxford: Oxford University Press, 2006).

Kochavi, Arieh. 'Britain and Illegal Immigration to Palestine from France Following World War II,' in *Holocaust and Genocide*, no. 6 (1991): 383–395.

Kraemer, David. *Jewish Eating and Identity Through the Ages* (London: Routledge, 2007).

Kumar, Krishan. *The Idea of Englishness* (Abingdon: Routledge, 2016).

Lockley, Philip. *Visionary Religion and Radicalism in Early Industrial England from Southcott to Socialism* (Oxford: Oxford University Press, 2013).

Luomanen, Petri. *Recovering Jewish-Christian Sects and Gospels* (Leiden: Brill, 2012).

Madden, Deborah. *The Paddington Prophet* (Manchester: Manchester University Press, 2010).

Malcolmson, Paul. *Inside the Loyal Black Institution* (Londonderry: Evangelical Truth, 2009).

Marks, Lara. 'Irish and Jewish Women's Experience of Childbirth and Infant Care in East London 1870–1939: The Responses of Host Society and Immigrant Communities to Medical Welfare Needs' (DPhil Thesis: Wolfson College, Oxford, 1990).

Martin, David. *A Sociology of English Religion* (London: SCM, 1967).

Moore, Chris. *The Kincora Scandal* (Dublin: Marino, 1996).

Nairn, Tom. *The Break Up of Britain: Crisis and Neo-Nationalism* (London: Verso, 1977).

Nizameddin, Talal. *Russia and the Middle East* (London: Hurst, 1999).

Parfitt, Tudor. *The Lost Tribes of Israel* (London: Phoenix, 2003).

Paz, Denis. *Popular Anti-Catholicism in Mid-Victorian England* (Stanford: Stanford University Press, 1992).

Pearson, Joanne. *Wicca and the Christian Heritage: Ritual, Sex and Magic* (Abingdon: Routledge, 2007).

Perry Curtis, Lewis. *Anglo-Saxons and Celts: A Study of Anti-Irish Prejudice in Victorian England* (New York: New York University Press, 1968).

Perry Curtis, Lewis. *Apes and Angels: The Irishman in Victorian Caricature* (Newton Abbot: David and Charles, 1971).

Portier-Young, Anathea. *Apocalypse Against Empire* (Cambridge: Eerdmans, 2014).

Pugh, Martin. *Hurrah for the Blackshirts: Fascists and Fascism in Britain Between the Wars* (London: Pimlico, 2006).

Quarles, Chester. *Christian Identity: The Aryan American Bloodline Religion* (Jefferson: McFarland, 2003).

Renton, James. *The Zionist Masquerade: The Birth of the Anglo-Zionist Alliance* (Basingstoke: Palgrave Macmillan, 2007).

Rubinstein, William and Hilary Rubinstein. *Philosemitism: Admiration and Support in the English-Speaking World for Jews, 1840–1939* (Basingstoke: Palgrave Macmillan, 1999).

Ruether, Rosemary. *Faith and Fratricide* (Eugene: Wipf, 1995).

Scott, Jonathan. *England's Troubles* (Cambridge: Cambridge University Press, 2000).

Sergeev, Evgeny. *The Great Game, 1856–1907* (Baltimore: Johns Hopkins University Press, 2013).

Sheffy, Yigal. *British Military Intelligence in the Palestine Campaign* (Abingdon: Routledge, 1998).

Shils, Edward. *Tradition* (Chicago: University of Chicago Press, 1981).

Shindler, Colin. *The History of Modern Israel* (Cambridge: Cambridge University Press, 2013).

Smith, Anthony D. *Myths and Memories of the Nation* (Oxford: Oxford University Press, 1999).

Smith, Anthony D. *Chosen Peoples* (Oxford: Oxford University Press, 2002).

Smith, Anthony D. *The Cultural Foundations of Nations* (Oxford: Blackwell, 2008).

Spiering, Menno. *The Cultural History of British Euroscepticism* (Basingstoke: Palgrave Macmillan, 2014).

Spraggon, Julie. 'Puritan Iconoclasm in England, 1640–1660' (PhD Thesis: University of London, 2000).

Sutcliffe, Adam and Jonathan Karp. 'Introduction,' in Adam Sutcliffe and Jonathan Karp (eds.), *Philosemitism in History* (Cambridge: Cambridge University Press, 2011).

Suzman, Mark. *Ethnic Nationalism and State Power* (Basingstoke: Palgrave Macmillan, 1999).

Uscinski, Joseph and Joseph M. Parent. *American Conspiracy Theories* (Oxford: Oxford University Press, 2014).

Vallance, Edward. *Revolutionary England and the National Covenant* (Woodbridge: Boydell, 2005).

van der Poel, Jean. *Selections from the Smuts Papers*, vol. 6 (Cambridge: Cambridge University Press, 1973).

Walsham, Alexander. *Providence in Early Modern England* (Oxford: Oxford University Press, 1999).

Walsham, Alexandra. *Charitable Hatred: Tolerance and Intolerance in England, 1500–1700* (Manchester: Manchester University Press, 2006).

Wellings, Ben. *English Nationalism and Euroscepticism: Losing the Peace* (Bern: Peter Lang, 2012).

Wilson, Bryan R. *Sects and Society: A Sociological Study of the Elim Tabernacle* (Los Angeles: University of California Press, 1961).

Index

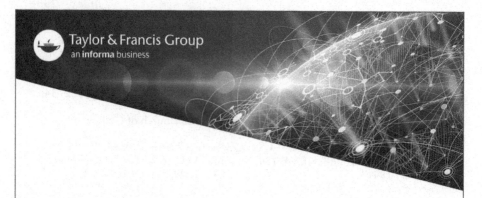